A GUIDE FOR THE PLAINTIFFS' LAWYER

WINNING MEDICAL NEGLIGENCE CASES

ATLA PRESS

WILLIAM TRINE AND PAUL LUVERA

Published by
ATLA Press
1050 31st Street, NW
Washington, DC 20007

Cover Design by
Greenfield/Belser, Ltd.

Library of Congress Catalog Number 93-2351
ISBN 0-941916-53-7

Printed in the United States of America

ACKNOWLEDGMENTS

I have discovered that writing a book is like running a marathon—easy to start, hard to finish, and accomplished only with the help of others along the way. I am grateful to Shirley Lara, my dedicated assistant, who has worked on this book from the beginning while at the same time orchestrating my professional career. My sincere thanks also go to the ATLA Press staff, whose support and hard work made this book possible, in particular, Cathy Kruvant, April Gustafson, Laura Rucker, Kathleen Murray, and Lou Leto—and to Jack Marshall and Arnett Holloway, who developed this project and encouraged my participation.

Deep appreciation must also be expressed to my law partners and staff, who have been supportive and loyal for many years, particularly Conard Metcalf and Betty Flagg.

Further, I would like to acknowledge my early mentors Norm Kripke and Charles Williams as well as my dear friends Joe Cotchett, George Shadoan, Dean Robb, Ralph Nader, Joan Claybrook, and Ted Warshafsky, who have all inspired me in recent years.

Finally, and most importantly, I dedicate this book to my wife, Jeni, who has made everything, including this book, possible.

Bill Trine, Boulder, Colorado

Working on this book with Bill Trine has made me understand why he is such an exceptional advocate. He has been tenacious in his efforts to complete this book, and his contributions are invaluable. Bill deserves the credit for making this project a reality.

I acknowledge my debt to the many trial champions whose writings and guidance have educated me over the years; their counsel has been an inspiration. I hope this book may be a modest repayment.

I want to express special appreciation to my wife, Lita Barnett-Luvera, an accomplished trial lawyer, for her understanding and encouragement throughout this project. Her suggestions and advice made a difficult task much easier.

Paul Luvera, Mount Vernon, Washington

CONTENTS

INTRODUCTION

Medical negligence litigation is difficult and complex. The defendant is often a hardworking and respected physician who has been negligent on a particular occasion, causing injury and damages to the plaintiff. The doctor's conduct is seldom grossly negligent or reckless, and juries will often excuse simple negligence out of sympathy.

The defendant always has more than enough expert witnesses willing to testify on his behalf, no matter how egregious the conduct, but the medical profession's conspiracy of silence and noncooperation hampers the plaintiff in seeking similar assistance and expertise. It is not surprising, therefore, that only a small percent of legitimate claims are pursued, that plaintiffs lose the majority of medical negligence lawsuits, and that only about 50 percent of the claims made that are resolved out of court result in a payment.[1]

The complexity and expense of medical negligence litigation has greatly increased in the last decade for a number of reasons. The practice of medicine has become far more complicated and sophisticated, with a resulting increase in the number of specialties and subspecialties. The insurance industry, along with the medical profession, has blamed the rising cost of health care and medical malpractice insurance premiums on the increasing number of cases being filed.

Politicians have jumped on the bandwagon, enacting regressive and unwarranted legislation in nearly every state and making it harder for victims of medical negligence to recover for their injuries. A massive publicity campaign by the insurance industry and the medical profession, designed to influence politicians, potential jurors, and the judiciary, has met with some success. As a result, it has become more difficult to select a fair jury, and judges have often been inclined to favor the defense.

---

1 Paul Marcotte, *Medical Verdicts Tightrope*, A.B.A. J., June 1989, at 29.

Also, the Reagan/Bush/Quayle regime made an unprecedented attack on the civil justice system, demanding "tort reform," which had an additional impact on medical negligence litigation. Although the pendulum may now be starting to swing back, handling a medical negligence case remains one of the most challenging tasks of a trial lawyer. To be successful, you must be an experienced, skilled expert in this subspecialty of civil litigation.

To achieve success, you must very carefully screen your potential cases and accept only the meritorious ones. You need to conduct thorough informal and formal discovery and cautiously select expert witnesses. You must analyze and plan the order of discovery and identify all problems and weaknesses in both your case and the defendant's position. As emphasized throughout this book, thoughtful preparation is the key to success; thoroughly plan your trial strategy, and work long and hard hours in trial preparation and in trial.

Those who have achieved success and have long fought the battles of medical negligence cases have carried the torch of hope for a better life to many victims who would not otherwise have been compensated. The dedicated work of those lawyers has also had the salutary effect of monitoring the medical profession at a time when it was not being adequately policed by its own membership or by regulatory and disciplinary authorities. The trial lawyers' work has helped the public too, as their successful settlements and courtroom victories have had the dual effect of weeding out bad doctors and encouraging better medical practice.

This book includes the combined experience and wisdom of two of those trial lawyers. We hope it proves useful for all those interested in medical negligence litigation. Although trial lawyers have faced an increasing number of obstacles in this area of litigation, the rewards of overcoming the challenges and helping needy victims are many. We enthusiastically urge the younger generation of trial lawyers to carry the torch forward in this field.

CHAPTER ONE

GATHERING FACTS AND MATERIALS

FINDING MEDICAL NEGLIGENCE CASES

Medical negligence cases come into an attorney's office through various means and for various reasons. Clients often contact attorneys about medical negligence claims after reading, seeing, or hearing something that makes them believe they have a claim. Clients consulting attorneys about routine legal matters, such as divorces and wills, may inadvertently indicate that they have a medical negligence claim. Clients with workers' compensation claims or general personal injury claims, for example, often have medical negligence claims as well. If clients are not aware of their medical negligence claims, their claims may go unrecognized. Be alert for and recognize indications that a client has a medical negligence claim.

If you wish to establish a medical negligence practice, you should pursue activities that may lead to referrals. These activities include attending medical negligence seminars, advising other attorneys of your interest and qualification in medical negligence cases, and giving lectures on medical negligence. If you lack the expertise to handle a medical negligence case generally, or to handle a specific case, you should associate with a qualified attorney. This association also may create future referrals. Subject to ethical restrictions, you may advertise your medical negligence practice; a system for carefully screening cases should accompany any advertising. For example, a well-trained paralegal, preferably a nurse, should obtain enough information from a prospective client to determine whether the facts of the client's case warrant a preliminary investigation. The rejection of any case, whether before or after a preliminary investigation, should be confirmed in writing with appropriate advice on any applicable statute of limitations or notice-of-claim requirement. A referral for a second opinion also should be made when appropriate.

In handling medical negligence cases, you must first be able to recognize a claim, and then you must be qualified to assert it. Successful management of medical negligence cases will create referrals based on reputation.

When a new client asks questions about the processing of a case, you should provide written information about your office and its operation. This gives the client confidence in your ability to handle the claim and provides useful information.[1]

Give your client clear advice about the statute of limitations and any notice of claim that must be filed as a prerequisite to suit. If a claim involves a federal tort, for example, explain the statute relating to federal torts. If the initial contact between you and your client is made by telephone, and you agree to further investigate the potential claim, always send a letter confirming the call and reminding the client about the statute of limitations.[2] However, when electing not to investigate the potential claim (for example, because of a conflict of interest), some lawyers send a letter confirming the case rejection and reminding the caller of applicable statutes of limitation or notice of claim provisions. Others do not, believing that rendering legal advice based on limited facts is not appropriate. Rendering legal advice may also establish an attorney-client relationship with corresponding duties to provide proper advice, which the lawyer may not be prepared to do on the limited facts obtained in a telephone call.

When you do agree to investigate the matter further, you and your client should have a written fee agreement. In some states, the code of professional responsibility requires a written agreement in contingent fee cases.[3] The client should receive a copy of this written agreement. In addition, the client should sign and receive a copy of waivers allowing you access to medical records.[4]

Because processing medical negligence cases is expensive, many attorneys require a deposit, even in the initial evaluation period, to defray the cost of evaluating the claim. Physicians charge to review cases even if the cases don't have merit. Hospitals and doctors, as

---

1 See Appendix A.1 for an example of a brochure.

2 See Appendix A.2 for an example of a confirmation letter.

3 See Appendix A.3 for an example of a fee agreement.

4 See Appendix A.4 for an example of a waiver.

well as other records custodians, will charge for copying the records. Unless you are prepared to fund these costs yourself, collect a deposit.

REFERRING THE CASE

Preparing and trying a medical negligence case requires experience. Recognize your limits. One way to get experience is to refer a case to an experienced attorney but remain on the case for its educational value. In most states, the Code of Professional Responsibility permits clients to authorize attorneys to divide fees based on their work.

You have a professional duty to your clients, the defendants in your cases, the community, and the justice system. Medical negligence cases are time-consuming, expensive, and traumatic for everyone involved. They should not be brought lightly. You have an obligation to evaluate cases before bringing them and to be qualified to process them. Be practical; remember that you may face legal negligence claims if you accept cases you are not qualified to handle. Health-care providers may countersue you if you bring a frivolous lawsuit.

COLLECTING THE FACTS

A thorough client interview is important. Because clients frequently lack either understanding or knowledge of their cases, they may not have the facts essential for you to evaluate them. Your client is, nevertheless, the first and primary source of information about the potential claim. Gather information from the client identifying physicians, dates of treatment, and other important facts. Consider using a client questionnaire as an initial interview form, and ask more detailed follow-up questions to obtain a full and complete history and to ensure that you do not overlook important areas of inquiry necessary to evaluate the potential claim.[5] Having the client provide the information requested in the client questionnaire reduces the amount of time you and your staff spend screening potential cases, and the information provided gives you a format for more detailed questioning during the first client interview.

Because your client's credibility frequently is an issue in medical negligence cases, evaluate your client. Some clients are neurotic; some may be frauds. In some cases, the client's personality may make it difficult, if not impossible, to win the case regardless of its

---

[5] See Appendix A.5 for an example of a client questionnaire.

merits. Note your reaction to the client at the initial interview. A jury probably would have the same reaction later.

COLLECTING THE MEDICAL RECORDS

Order all medical records. This is one of the most important initial steps in evaluating a claim. Most people who seek legal representation for a medical negligence claim do so because they are dissatisfied with the medical care they received, but they often do not understand why the doctor made a misdiagnosis or why the treatment was unsuccessful. Health-care providers frequently give no explanation or an unsatisfactory explanation for a bad result. Reviewing all the medical records often is the only way to find out what happened and to determine whether medical negligence occurred. You will therefore need all medical records regarding the incident, including those of treating physicians, clinics, and hospitals.

Past Medical Records

You should also collect all the client's other medical records before deciding whether to take the case. These include past medical records that may appear irrelevant. Often these records contain information regarding preexisting conditions that you will need in order to decide whether to accept a case.

There are clues contained in past medical records that may either suggest that medical negligence did occur or show that there was no negligence. Some important things to look for include the following:

- A doctor may have negligently overlooked past medical records showing a preexisting condition that contraindicated the procedures the doctor used and made the procedures unsuccessful.
- Past records occasionally show that the client's complaints of a bad medical result can be attributed to a preexisting medical condition, not the present care.
- A doctor's awareness of preexisting conditions contained in past records may help explain the doctor's diagnosis and why the doctor appropriately substituted a riskier form of treatment for the preferred treatment.
- The doctor may have relied on erroneous information contained in past medical records, causing a misdiagnosis.
- Past medical records may contain unfavorable information about the client, such as a history of alcohol and drug abuse, that would make the case less attractive for settlement purposes or would mitigate damages if revealed to a jury.

Requests for Hospital Records

Some hospitals customarily notify any treating physician when an attorney requests hospital records, which will alert the physician that the patient has consulted an attorney. The hospital frequently will not forward the records to you until the physician has had an opportunity to review them. This gives the doctor an opportunity to alter records or make late self-serving entries. Examine the records carefully to determine whether the doctor has altered them.

Inform the client that your request for hospital records could interfere with any ongoing medical care the client is receiving from the doctor against whom you may file a claim. This gives the client an opportunity to either arrange for other medical care before you request the records, or to delay requesting the records until treatment is complete.

You may obtain records directly from the hospital,[6] or you may hire a service to obtain them. Acquire relevant records from all health-care providers who are potential defendants. Use a form letter to collect additional medical records from the physicians who have treated the client but are not potential defendants in the case.[7]

When you receive the records, always check them immediately to see that they are complete. Legible and complete medical records are essential to your evaluation of a medical negligence case. Be sure the records include all laboratory and nursing notes and all hospital and clinic records, not only for the incident that is the focus of the claim but for all the patient's past treatment. Separate the records into categories, such as emergency room treatment, outpatient treatment, and surgical treatment. Separate other material, such as fetal monitor tapes and X rays, into categories as well.

Incomplete or Altered Records

Records are commonly incomplete or altered. If you suspect alteration, consider having the original records reviewed by handwriting or other specialists. These specialists, who advertise their services in professional journals and the telephone book, can check records in various ways to determine whether they have been altered. Handwriting experts, for example, can compare the handwriting of the individual who purportedly made the record with the handwriting

---

[6] See Appendix A.6 for a sample letter requesting records.

[7] See Appendix A.7 for a sample form letter.

in the record itself. Laboratory equipment can be used to compare the ages of inks in a record. Experts can compare the typewriting in records for differences and similarities.

Experts who are health-care providers often question whether a medical record has been altered if the content of the record is not consistent with their professional experience. For example, a nurse may question whether a record has been altered if an entry is not consistent with normal nursing practice. An expert who is a physician may find a detail in an operative record that is inconsistent with normal operative records.

Always examine the original record because copies of hospital records do not show the color or type of ink used. Frequently health-care providers make records using different colors of ink, either because the hospital requires it or because different pens were used on different occasions. The color of ink used may be a clue to who made an entry or when an entry was made. For example, hospitals sometimes require that a different color of ink be used by each shift when nurses make entries in patient records. The wrong color of ink may indicate that an entry was not made at the time indicated in the records, but was entered at a later time or date.

ORGANIZING THE CASE MATERIALS

It is important to organize the case materials for easy reference as a part of the preliminary investigation and for later use if you decide to take the case. If new materials are obtained through formal discovery, they should be added to the previously organized materials.

Many attorneys organize hospital records in three-ring binders using dividers. You may label the dividers by subjects such as admitting history, operative notes, or X rays. Number all pages as you organize them for easy reference. You may divide clinic records similarly, in their own binders. Then index all records with reference to the page-numbering system you have used.[8] Create a chronology for significant entries. This can be a simple chronology[9] or a more detailed report prepared by trained people[10] If a portion of the records should be summarized separately for easy reference when

---

[8] See Appendix A.8 for an example of an index.

[9] See Appendix A.9 for an example of a summary of general hospital records.

[10] See Appendix A.10 for an example of a detailed report.

taking depositions, have your trained personnel prepare such a summary.[11] If you use medical research, you should organize it in notebooks by both subject and author.

Prepare a glossary of medical terms you will need to know. List common abbreviations and shorthand used in the medical records and in other aspects of the case. Note areas of inquiry for discovery.

Summarize records of the patient's vital signs, symptoms, medical history, diagnostic testing, and other similar data.[12] Connect significant entries to medical literature, using margin notes in the record and yellow highlighting with corresponding margin notes in the literature. The literature may be copied and taped to the back of the opposite page of the record for easy reference.

In negligent treatment cases, create both a detailed description of the inappropriate treatment, explaining why it was inappropriate, and a detailed description of the proper treatment, supported by medical literature.

Many attorneys employ an assistant either in-house or for specific cases to organize and review medical information. Some attorneys employ nurses, who make particularly helpful and qualified assistants, or other health-care professionals to do this work. In almost every state you may hire nurses (and sometimes physicians) by the case to review and organize the record, to identify the significant entries, and to create chronologies.

Meet with your assistant or consulting health-care professional after the facts and records have been prepared and are ready to be sent to an expert witness for evaluation. At the meeting, make a list of questions or issues that you and your consultant or assistant have raised and prepare an outline of the key facts of the case. Organize these key materials in another three-ring notebook to use throughout the case.

At this point, you will be ready to begin a thorough medical, legal, and financial evaluation of the case. Remember, however, that no matter how competent and thorough you and your assistant or consultant have been in organizing and assessing the case's facts and records, further review of the case may suggest changes in previously developed issues and theories.

---

11 See Appendix A.11 for an example of a summary of pulmonary care records.

12 See Appendix A.10 for an example of a detailed report.

CHAPTER TWO

EVALUATING THE CASE

Because medical negligence cases are costly to litigate in terms of both time and money, it is crucial that you make a complete and accurate evaluation of each case you consider. Your evaluation should be divided into three parts: medical, legal, and financial. Generally, all three evaluations should be conducted simultaneously because many of the factors to be considered are interrelated. However, you can sometimes reject a potential case based solely on one of the three evaluations without thoroughly conducting all three. For example, a legal evaluation may reveal that the claim is clearly barred by a statute of limitations and that it is unnecessary to conduct a thorough medical or financial evaluation before rejecting the case. Similarly, you might reject a case based solely on a financial evaluation showing that the cost of litigation would exceed the maximum recoverable damages. Nevertheless, you must carefully consider all three before accepting a case.

MAKING A MEDICAL EVALUATION

Once you have collected the medical records, you should identify their significant sections. Consider having an experienced, trained nurse complete the first evaluation. Nurses are less expensive than physicians—they can spend more time than physicians for the same cost—and they are often more practical than physicians in their approach to reviewing records. A nurse can suggest areas of special concern or inquiry and can provide insight in evaluating the merits of the claim as well as the areas, including specialty areas of medicine, that ought to be investigated further.

The next evaluation should be made by a physician. A general practitioner can do this first review; a general practitioner may provide a broader perspective on the case than a specialist would. If the case involves a specialized area, however, you will need a specialist's review.

A case may need to be reviewed by different medical specialists before you can decide whether it has merit. In obstetrical cases you may need to have a specialist in brain pathology review the record because the defense may question the cause of the obstetrical injury. The defense may argue, for example, that a baby's brain injury existed before the labor and delivery and was not caused by the defendant. An expert in obstetrics may have to review the records to determine whether the care provided by the person delivering the child was appropriate. Nursing experts may be required to evaluate the conduct and care of the nurses involved.

Attorneys often construct a pyramid of specialists to consult with, starting with the least technical. For example, you might start with an obstetrical nurse and, if the nurse's report is favorable, continue on to a general practitioner, and then on to a specialist, until representatives from all relevant specialty fields have had a chance to review the records to determine the merit of the claim.

Finding experts is the most difficult part of the medical evaluation process and the most important. Look for experts who are well qualified and conservative so that you get an accurate and unbiased assessment of the claim. You can find experts through several sources, including medical schools, the ATLA Exchange, attorneys who have handled similar cases, professional organizations, and physician friends. One way to find a reviewer is to read medical books and articles relevant to the case, then ask an author you have read to review the records of the case.

The civil rules in some states and federal jurisdictions may require that you identify your consulting experts. In these jurisdictions, you must identify your consulting experts even if your opponent is not entitled to have the experts' opinions. In some cases expert witnesses may condition their involvement in a case on your guarantee of confidentiality. You should be aware of this potential conflict between the requirements of the civil rules and the conditions of your consulting expert. If your expert insists on a guarantee of confidentiality and you cannot give it, do not use the expert.

Under the civil rules, the opinions of the consulting experts are not discoverable except under exceptional circumstances. For this reason you should treat all expert witnesses initially as consulting experts. After you decide whether to accept the case and which theory of liability to assert, you can make a decision about whether to characterize these witnesses as testifying experts.

Any experts you use will need a copy of the medical records. Do not give busy experts large volumes of material that will confuse and discourage them, but be sure that they have the essential information. In almost all jurisdictions that follow the federal rules of discovery, courts require that the experts to be called at trial divulge the information provided to them about the case. While some courts limit the discovery to information the expert used to reach an opinion, other courts require that all information and materials given to the expert be made available to the opponent. Evaluate the information you give to your experts in light of this possibility. Assume that you will have to give your opponent all the information you give your expert. Courts in some jurisdictions require that experts write a report and supply it to the opponent. In those jurisdictions, some attorneys get written affidavits from the experts regarding their findings and opinions. This practice provides a report if one is required and solidifies the expert's opinion.

Medical research is important in a medical negligence case. Review standard textbooks and articles dealing with the procedure or subject current at the time of the incident. If informed consent is an issue, carefully review the medical literature on known and inherent risks of the medical procedure involved. Summarize the key points of the medical research. Organize the research so that both you and your experts can use it.

MAKING A LEGAL EVALUATION

An early evaluation of the claim to assess its legal viability is critical. A statute of limitations, a failure to file a notice of claim, or governmental or charitable immunity may already bar the claim. Furthermore, laws that place caps on damages, eliminate joint liability, allow the defense to designate nonparties at fault, and require that noneconomic damages be reduced to present value can sometimes combine to make an otherwise viable claim economically prohibitive. A preliminary legal evaluation of the potential claims often results in a decision to reject a case before substantial time and expense are devoted to an exhaustive investigation of the facts. If you do not reject the case after your initial legal evaluation, you should do another legal evaluation after completing your factual investigation.

In addition, laws that expose the client to liability for defense costs, restrict contingent fees, and severely limit the use of expert testimony can have a chilling effect on your pursuit of a meritorious claim. Carefully consider the following items in deciding whether the claim is viable.

Determining Duties Owed

A Physician's Standard of Care

The duty of care owed by a physician to a patient is generally expressed in terms of reasonable care exercised by other physicians under the same circumstances. This common law obligation is sometimes expressed as follows:

A physician has a duty to exercise the degree of skill and care expected of a reasonably prudent physician acting in the same or similar circumstances at the time of the care or treatment in question. The failure to do so is negligence.

The obligation owed at common law will also depend on the defendant's medical training. For example, a specialist will be held to the standard of care of a specialist in the same field.

However, in light of tort reform statutes that have redefined the common law test of negligence, it is important that you review the legal standard used in the jurisdiction in which you will file your action. Also review the test of negligence, which will vary from jurisdiction to jurisdiction.

In evaluating the liability issues in the case, both you and any expert you consult must use the correct standard of care in determining whether a physician's conduct constitutes negligence. Establish whether the jurisdiction where the action will be filed follows a "locality rule": is the standard limited to the community where the tort happened or does a nationally recognized standard apply? Most states have abandoned the test that limits the standard to the specific community.

A Hospital's Standard of Care

A hospital has a common law duty to provide the services and exercise the care expected of a reasonably careful and prudent hospital acting under the same or similar circumstances. The difference between the standard for a physician and the standard for a hospital is the concept of agency: as a legal entity the hospital can act only through its officers or employees. Hence as part of your investigation and analysis, you must determine who is an officer or employee of the hospital.

Further, if a hospital nurse or other hospital health-care provider may be personally responsible for an act of negligence, the standard that applies to that person for individual liability will differ from the standard that applies to a hospital sued for the negligence of its officers or employees.

When you investigate a case against a hospital, be sure to research the hospital's internal rules or policies. In some jurisdictions, a violation of these rules or policies may be evidence of negligence.

Many hospitals are accredited by the joint commission on accreditation of hospitals (JCAH), a hospital accreditation board, and are subject to JCAH's policy requirements involving every aspect of hospital patient care. A violation of these policy requirements might also be evidence of negligence.

Most jurisdictions recognize "corporate negligence" when a hospital allows unqualified physicians to practice. The evaluation of the standard of care or negligence in this kind of claim will vary from one state to another. In considering such a claim it is important to determine the legal test that will be applied to the claim.

Weighing Alternate Causes of Action

Constitutional Issues

With the advent of new and restrictive legislation regarding medical negligence claims, you may need to raise constitutional issues that your jurisdiction has not yet resolved. Carefully evaluate these constitutional issues before raising them. Advise your client of the potential for an appeal to a higher court and a retrial if you prevail in the lower court. Similarly, advise your client that legislation may raise new issues that are still unresolved at the appellate level; let him know that he may face an appeal following trial.

Informed Consent

Generally, a health-care provider has a duty to inform a patient of all material facts regarding the patient's health, including risks and alternatives that a reasonably prudent patient would need to know before making an informed decision about whether to consent to or reject a proposed course of treatment. A material fact is generally said to be one to which a reasonably prudent patient under the circumstances would attach significance in making a decision. If the facts of your case warrant it, consider claiming that your client's injury resulted from the defendant's failure to properly inform your client.

The legal test of informed consent differs from jurisdiction to jurisdiction and has been changed by statute in many states as part of the tort reform movement. Be careful to verify the standard for the state in which you file.

There are three reasons the plaintiff seldom prevails on a claim of lack of informed consent. First, the defendant-doctor invariably testifies that she properly advised the patient of the risks of the procedure and the alternative treatment available. If there is no written record of this advice, the doctor will testify that it is her custom and practice to inform patients of those risks. Informed consent thus becomes a credibility issue, and the jury most often resolves that issue in favor of the doctor. Second, it is difficult to show that the patient would not have consented to the procedure had he been advised properly. Third, the patient sometimes is aware of the procedure's risks from sources of information other than the doctor, and thus cannot show that he relied on the doctor to provide him with the information on which he based his consent.

In evaluating a potential claim based on the failure to obtain an informed consent, you must determine whether this failure was a legal cause of any injury or damages. To do so, you must know whether the court will apply an objective test or a subjective test. That is, will the court use the objective test and instruct the jury that it can only find for the plaintiff if a reasonable person under the same circumstances would not have consented to the procedure, had that person been properly informed? Or will the court use the subjective test and instruct the jury that to find for the plaintiff it must find that the plaintiff would not have consented to the procedure if he had been properly advised of the risks associated with that procedure and the alternative treatment available?

If the court uses a subjective test, it will often permit the plaintiff to testify that he would not have consented to the procedure if he had been informed of its risks. If the court uses an objective test, it will usually exclude such testimony by the plaintiff. If the plaintiff is permitted to testify that he would not have consented to the procedure had he been informed of the risks that led to the bad result, the jury will reject that testimony if it is not believable. For example, if there was no alternative treatment available and the plaintiff's condition was intolerable, a jury will probably conclude that despite the plaintiff's testimony to the contrary, he would have consented to treatment even if he had been advised of the risks.

Res Ipsa Loquitur

Do not overlook the doctrine of presumptive negligence, res ipsa loquitur, when evaluating potential theories. The common law recognized that the burden of proof was altered in a situation in which the agency or instrumentality causing injury was under the control of a defendant and the injury would not have occurred if the defendant had used ordinary care. In that situation, in the absence of a satisfactory explanation, one could infer, but was not required to infer, that the defendant was negligent.

The doctrine of res ipsa loquitur has been applied in medical negligence cases. However, there is controversy about whether the doctrine applies in such cases and, if so, whether it is a question of law or fact. If it is a jury issue, there is further controversy over whether the doctrine creates a rebuttable or irrebuttable presumption of negligence and, if rebuttable, the quantum of proof necessary to rebut the presumption.

Consumer Protection Acts

Some states have consumer protection statutes that apply to hospitals, physicians, and health-care providers. These statutes may provide a plaintiff with the right to sue for an unfair or deceptive trade practice or act that affects the public as well as injures the plaintiff. The benefit of such statutes is that they often provide for attorney fees or economic sanctions that apply to medical negligence cases.

Tort of Outrage

Some states recognize the tort of outrage. Liability may arise when a person causes severe emotional distress to another through intentional or reckless conduct that is so outrageous or extreme that it exceeds the bounds of decency and cannot be tolerated in a civilized society.

When the outrageous conduct of a health-care provider is directed toward a patient but occurs in the presence of the patient's family and causes the family members to suffer severe emotional distress, these family members may have a claim against the health-care provider.

If this theory is available in your jurisdiction, you ought to consider it in evaluating the case and claims to be made.

Other Possible Defendants

Your legal evaluation is not complete until you consider naming any party that may have been responsible for the plaintiff's injuries.

Often in a case where a drug has caused the plaintiff's injury, to cover all avenues of liability you must name the pharmaceutical company as a defendant and assert a claim of products liability. Remember, however, that the law governing products liability differs from that governing medical negligence, and many jurisdictions have amended their products liability statute as a part of tort reform efforts.

Consider manufacturers of other products, such as surgical equipment, as potential defendants in cases that involve both physician treatment and a failed product. If a patient is injured because an instrument breaks or malfunctions during surgery, you may have reason to file two claims: one against the physician for poor technique and one against the manufacturer for product failure.

In some cases, a medical negligence claim may overlap with common law negligence claims against others who are not health-care providers. For example, a plaintiff may have a claim of negligence arising from an automobile accident as well as a medical negligence claim arising from later medical treatment at the hospital. Check to see if your medical negligence clients might also have claims against others who caused the injuries that resulted in the need for medical care.

Other Legal Claims

In evaluating the legal aspects of a case, do not overlook the possibility of claims not usually associated with health-care negligence, such as assault and battery in cases of surgery on the wrong body part, outrageous conduct in cases of doctors performing surgery while intoxicated, breach of contract in cases of patient abandonment, and negligent misrepresentation in cases involving a misrepresentation of material facts.[1]

Considering Proximate Cause

Your analysis of the case must involve proximate cause. Proximate cause requires a connection between the claimed negligence and the injury. The definition of proximate cause is important and varies among jurisdictions.

Assuming you can show that a defendant is negligent, if that negligence did not cause additional injury or damages, the defendant will not be liable. This is a basic defense used by attorneys in medical negligence claims who might assert, for example, that even if the defendant had discovered and treated the plaintiff's cancer six months earlier, the plaintiff still would have died.

Causation is a basic element of proof you must satisfy, and no evaluation of a medical negligence case is complete until you have established causation. Normally you will need expert medical testimony

---

1 An example of negligent misrepresentation is when a physician falsely claims to have successfully performed many of the surgical procedures recommended to a patient.

to establish causation. Furthermore, the testimony must meet the burden-of-proof test of medical probability. While some jurisdictions recognize a claim for reducing a person's chance of living a full life or a claim for increasing the chance of an early death, all jurisdictions require some proof that the "loss of a chance" was caused by the defendant's negligence.

Evaluating Damages

Caps on Damages

Some states have enacted legislation placing caps on the amount of damages that can be recovered. These laws have sometimes been successfully challenged on constitutional grounds. Familiarize yourself with the legislation in your jurisdiction and its effect on the legal and economic evaluation of your case. Know whether your court may apply the damages laws of another state, particularly if the plaintiff is a nonresident who was in your jurisdiction temporarily for the medical treatment that resulted in injury or death.

Punitive Damages

Not all states allow punitive damages. Furthermore, tort reform statutes in states that permit punitive damages often have altered the common law or previous statutory right of recovery. It is important to check the current status to see if punitive damages are allowed and, if so, to see what legal test will be applied in order to claim them.

Don't assert a claim for punitive damages simply because state law allows the claim and there may be some evidence to support it. First consider the advantages and disadvantages of asserting the claim and determine which outweigh the other. Jurors often react negatively to such a claim, but if the defendant's conduct has been especially reprehensible, your punitive damages claim might add substantially to your client's eventual recovery.

Some jurisdictions permit the defendant's financial worth and income to be introduced as evidence when punitive damages are claimed; others do not. Medical liability insurance policies generally do not provide coverage for punitive damages, and the defendant may be judgment-proof. Further, a claim of punitive damages might interfere with settlement if the defendant-physician perceives the claim as a gross exaggeration of the negligent conduct and if he believes that a settlement constitutes an admission that he acted maliciously or with willful and wanton conduct. An angry physician often will not permit the insurance carrier to settle and will insist on a trial to vindicate his honor and reputation.

Consulting Expert Witnesses

Expert Witness Statutes

Legislation may restrict your use of expert witnesses and thus may be a factor in the legal evaluation of your case. Some jurisdictions have recently passed legislation to regulate the plaintiff's use of expert witnesses in medical negligence cases. Local statutes may prohibit you from using a retired physician, a physician who has never performed the precise procedure involved, a physician who does not practice in the same field or subspecialty practiced by the defendant, or a physician who does not spend a prescribed percentage of time performing the type of procedures involved in the litigation.

Certificate of Review

On filing a lawsuit, you may be required by statute to file a certificate with the court certifying that you have consulted an expert witness in the same or similar field of practice as the defendant and that you have been informed by that expert that your case has merit. If you are contacted by a client shortly before his claim will be barred by a statute of limitations, you may not have time to obtain all medical records, have them reviewed by expert witnesses, and comply with a certificate of review statute. If that is the case, check whether the statute permits you to file the certificate within a prescribed time after filing the lawsuit. If not, you may have to reject the case without investigating it further.

A certificate may not be needed, however, if establishing your claim does not require expert witness testimony. Check the law in your jurisdiction to determine when expert testimony is necessary. Most jurisdictions do not require expert testimony if the negligent conduct is within the common knowledge of lay people and can be understood without expert testimony or if the tort or claim involved—such as breach of contract, assault and battery, or negligent misrepresentation—does not require expert testimony.

Judging Possible Bars to Claim

Statute of Limitations

A statute of limitations or a statute of repose may bar one or more of the potential claims in any case. Familiarize yourself with the statutes involved, the tolling provisions, and any exceptions recognized by statute or case law. A statute of limitations generally does not begin to run until the plaintiff discovers, or reasonably could have discovered, an injury and the medical cause of that injury. However, the time limit for filing actions varies according to jurisdiction and type of claim. A federal tort claim must be filed within two years of a negligent act. In some states, the time limit for filing an action involving an instrument or object left in the body after surgery is different from the time limit for filing actions involving other types of injury. Actions involving children may have a statute of limitations different from that for adults.

In some instances, statutes of limitation may provide a narrow exception where the person did not discover the negligent act until well after the act's occurrence.

In a case in which your client is a parent who is suing for an injury to a child at birth, you will often face statute of limitations problems. For example, a child's claim may be recognized, but the parent's consortium claim may be barred by the statute. These types of issues frequently involve factual disputes. Consequently, the evaluation of the case requires a full investigation and analysis of the facts.

Apply the law to the facts of your case to determine whether the defense will argue that the statute of limitations has run and whether the court may grant summary judgment on that issue as a matter of law.

In addition to recognizing the usual tolling provisions, such as minority, incompetency, and fraudulent concealment, some jurisdictions recognize the continuing care and treatment doctrine, which tolls a statute of limitations, or perhaps a statute of repose, until the treatment is terminated.

If your claim involves a federal tort, you must know the notice requirement, the statute of limitations and potential tolling provisions, and the restriction on contingent fees.

Governmental or Charitable Immunity

Often public hospitals or not-for-profit charitable organizations are immune from suit, or if they are not totally immune from suit, they are protected by statutory caps on damages. Sometimes this immunity extends to the teaching members of the hospital staff, the residents, and the interns. Generally, you must file a notice of claim before bringing suit.

Case-Specific Legislation

Some states have enacted legislation regarding specific types of medical procedures. For example, at the date of this writing, intrauterine fetal asphyxia cases resulting in brain-damaged babies are subject to special procedures and limited damages in two states.[2] Similar legislation has been proposed in other states. In some states, blood banks are not strictly liable; negligence or willful and wanton conduct must be established. In some jurisdictions, doctors providing free clinic care are protected from suits based on negligence, and some states have good samaritan statutes that protect health-care workers who respond to emergencies from suits based on negligence.

Defenses

For every claim you plan to assert, you should analyze the available defenses. In states that bar recovery in cases of contributory negligence, you must analyze the plaintiff's negligence. In those states where comparative negligence is recognized, your analysis must include the question of the degree to which the plaintiff contributed to his own injury. In many states, such as Colorado, a finding of 50 percent or more comparative negligence results in a judgment for the defense. Even if a finding of comparative negligence only reduces damages, the reduction, in combination with other damages-reducing factors previously discussed, could make the case economically prohibitive.

In addition, you should evaluate assumption of risk as a potential defense if the jurisdiction in which the case is to be filed recognizes this defense. You must discover whether assumption of risk in your jurisdiction bars recovery or simply limits it.

Under the doctrine of mitigation of damages, a defendant is not responsible for damages the plaintiff could have avoided by exercising reasonable care. Some defense attorneys use this doctrine to assert that the plaintiff should have taken affirmative action to mitigate the damages. For example, the defendant-doctor may claim that the plaintiff should have obtained treatment to reduce the injury.

The defendant may assert that intervening conduct on the part of some other person or entity contributed to or caused the plaintiff's injury. You must analyze the conduct of all possible defendants, not only to assess their individual liability and whether they should be

---

[2] Both Florida and Virginia have passed so-called "bad baby" bills that greatly restrict the damages children born with cerebral palsy can recover. FLA. STAT. ANN. § 766.301 to .316 (West Supp. 1993) and VA. CODE ANN. § 38.2–5000 to –5021 (1990).

sued, but also to anticipate the defense that an intervening cause or the liability of a person or entity you failed to sue invalidates your claim.

Even in jurisdictions that permit suits against state or municipal entities, the defense may claim that the activities in question fall within an unwaived discretionary area of immunity. Also, in suits against the federal government, remember that many of its activities are protected under an immunity doctrine.

Claim Requirements

If your claim involves any governmental agency or entity, you must look carefully in applicable statutes for notice of claim requirements. Most jurisdictions require that before you file a lawsuit against certain government agencies or the state or federal government, you first file a written claim with the agency or government involved.

Statutes that require submitting a written claim prior to filing suit will contain specific requirements as to what must be included in the claim. In some jurisdictions, strict compliance with the contents of the claim must be observed, or the claim is invalid.

In addition, these statutes often contain their own statutes of limitation for filing the written claim, as well as waiting periods that specify the number of days you must wait to file suit after filing your claim with the agency. Be sure to carefully review your jurisdiction's statutes regarding claim requirements before accepting a case against a governmental entity.

Binding Arbitration

In some jurisdictions a physician has a statutory right to refuse to provide treatment unless the patient first signs a binding arbitration agreement. The agreement provides that if the patient is injured through the negligence of the physician, the patient waives the right to bring suit against the physician, and any claim is subject to binding arbitration. When confronted with such an agreement, make certain that its provisions do not unduly favor the physician, thus making the recovery of adequate damages unlikely. In many instances, the client may welcome binding arbitration, particularly when the damages do not warrant the expense of litigation. If the arbitration agreement is unfair or arbitration is undesirable, determine whether the agreement is subject to attack because it is an adhesion contract or because it is against public policy.

Screening Panels

Some jurisdictions require that a screening panel hear the plaintiff's claim before a lawsuit can be brought. The screening panel's membership and procedures and the effect of the panel's decision on subsequent litigation vary from jurisdiction to jurisdiction. The panel is generally composed of doctors, lawyers, hospital administrators, nurses, lay people, or some combination of the above. Research to determine whether the law permits the panel's findings or decision to be revealed to a jury in subsequent litigation, or whether, as is the law in some jurisdictions, the panel's findings are confidential and cannot be revealed. If the panel finds that negligence caused the injury, the panel is sometimes obligated to provide the plaintiff with expert witnesses.

MAKING A FINANCIAL EVALUATION

In addition to weighing the medical and legal merits of your case, you should evaluate its financial merits. Medical negligence cases are notoriously expensive. In major cases, it is not uncommon for an attorney to advance $50,000 to $100,000 in costs by the end of trial. Occasionally a medical negligence claim is brought in combination with a products liability claim, for example in the case of a medical device that failed, and bringing the additional claim substantially increases the cost of litigation. Even in cases of simple medical negligence, the cost of medical experts, depositions, and discovery may be prohibitive. Unfortunately, attorneys must decline to process many otherwise worthy cases because the cases lack financial merit.

The court system in your jurisdiction may have a mandatory arbitration procedure that makes the case financially feasible. In some states, arbitration procedures save time and money by allowing a case to be arbitrated rather than tried in court. In other instances, the hospital or health-care provider may have an agreement with patients that gives patients the option of arbitrating the case.

If the law in your jurisdiction provides for mandatory screening procedures and panels before a lawsuit can be brought and the panel determines that a doctor was negligent, a settlement can sometimes be reached without your filing suit. This can be an economical way of recovering damages when litigation is not financially feasible. On the other hand, many lawyers complain that panel procedures most often unfairly favor the defense and that therefore panel decisions do not prevent disputes from having to be resolved by formal arbitration or litigation.

Considerations about the issue of jurisdiction are applicable to a financial evaluation as well as to a legal evaluation: Can you file the case in federal instead of state court? Are the verdicts in one jurisdiction higher than in another? Because plaintiffs lose the great majority of lawsuits brought to trial involving claims of medical negligence, it is important for you to evaluate your chances of winning the case, regardless of its merits, in the jurisdiction in which you plan to file it.[3]

You need to be aware that some jurisdictions now regulate and restrict contingent fees in medical negligence cases. The client's recovery, and hence your fees, may be further restricted by several liability, nonparty liability, caps on damages, and other special-interest legislation.

In some jurisdictions, the defendant-physician can make an offer of settlement and, if the verdict is for an amount less than the offer made, the plaintiff must pay all costs incurred by the physician subsequent to the date of the offer. In Colorado, for example, where a large percentage of medical negligence cases result in a verdict for the defense, it is a common practice for the physician to make a one-dollar offer of settlement after the lawsuit is filed. If the verdict is rendered for the doctor, the doctor can claim all the costs of litigation, including expert witness fees. If there are multiple defendants who do likewise, the costs can be substantial. Forewarn your client of this risk.

In a similar vein, tort reform advocates are urging legislative bodies to adopt the "English Rule," which would allow the prevailing party to recover attorney fees. You must be aware of the status of legislation that could affect your evaluation of a medical negligence case.

Comparing Costs to Possible Return

Before you decide to accept a case, you need to analyze its value. Your analysis should project the case's processing costs, from expert witness bills to deposition expenses and other major expenditures.

---

3 Although not a nationwide sampling, a comprehensive analysis of data from all reported medical negligence jury verdicts in 46 counties in 11 states for the period 1981–85 shows that plaintiffs won only 32.4 percent of the time. The failure rate varied from jurisdiction to jurisdiction and from county to county in each jurisdiction. The range of jury verdicts in medical negligence cases likewise varied considerably from jurisdiction to jurisdiction. See Daniels, *Tracing the Shadow of the Law: Jury Verdicts in Medical Malpractice Cases*, 40 DEF. L.J. 415, 423 (1991).

Compare the processing costs to the case's probable settlement or verdict value.

When you see how the case's costs compare to its value, you will be better able to decide whether it is economically feasible to accept the case. Neither you nor your client will benefit if the cost of processing the case exceeds the case's return. If your client is obligated by contract to reimburse you for all costs advanced, it is particularly important that the client know the potential financial risk if there is no recovery as compared to the potential benefit if the claim is successfully resolved.

After you estimate the case's value, you will be in a better position to decide whether to agree to attempt settlement without filing the case, or to agree to file the case if settlement negotiations are unsuccessful. You will also be better able to gauge how much money you should devote to preparing and trying the case. From the time you begin evaluating the case to the time the case is concluded by settlement or verdict, you must closely watch the ratio between costs advanced and potential return.

Evaluating Liability and Damages

Another aspect of your financial evaluation of a case involves weighing your chance of winning against the potential settlement or verdict value. A case with major damages and clear liability does not have the same settlement or verdict value as the same case with borderline liability. Evaluate liability, damages, and costs throughout the case, from your first assessment of the case through every stage of its processing.

If you conclude that the case is not economically feasible in spite of its merits, explain this to the client and suggest that the client consult another attorney. Another lawyer may be willing to handle a case for a smaller hourly return.

CONSIDERING THE PROS AND CONS OF YOUR CASE

After collecting information from the client, doctors, and hospitals, preparing the information, and evaluating the case medically, legally, and financially, you should carefully consider the pros and cons of accepting the case.

Cons

The following are examples of negative factors that might affect a medical negligence case:

Liability Issues

- The defendant may be highly qualified and widely respected. This may affect your ability to find medical experts willing to testify against the defendant. The high regard for the defendant in the community may also affect your ability to obtain a judgment or reasonable settlement if you do find medical experts willing to testify. Extraordinary efforts may be required to locate competent experts who are willing to testify, increasing your costs.
- The only negligence in your case may be incompletely informed consent or misrepresentation. These cases are difficult to win because they often test the competing credibility of the health-care provider and the plaintiff, and juries tend to favor the health-care provider. These cases also present the problem of proving that the client would not have agreed to the treatment if he had been informed of its risks.
- The defense may be able to raise affirmative defenses. For example, you may need to resolve factual issues concerning the statute of limitations or the plaintiff's failure to mitigate damages. If there is evidence to support affirmative defenses, carefully weigh the facts and the law and calculate the percentage chance of the defense prevailing on these issues. If there are genuine affirmative defense issues for the jury to resolve, the plaintiff should expect a compromise verdict of less than the reasonable value of the claim. Whenever a serious factual dispute causes debate among the jurors, resolving that dispute in the plaintiff's favor often requires a compromised verdict on damages. This occurs because jurors who favor the defense on affirmative defense issues often are conservative in calculating damages after they concede the liability issues.
- There may be serious causation issues, and causation may be difficult to prove. If so, as with affirmative defenses, you must evaluate the case carefully to determine whether the plaintiff may lose entirely or whether a dispute among jurors over causation could result in a reduced damages verdict even if the jury resolves the causation issues in the plaintiff's favor.
- The case may involve a unique medical subspecialty or procedure that makes locating expert witnesses nearly impossible. For example, there may be only a handful of surgeons in the United States who perform penile implants. It may happen that none of those surgeons are willing to review a potential case involving this procedure or to testify against another member of the group. This problem arises when a new medical procedure or device is used and a limited number of physicians have performed the procedure or are familiar with it. Members of this close-knit group usually will not testify against each other because they do not want adverse publicity about the procedure they

are promoting or because they have frequently met with each other to exchange information and have developed friendly relationships.

- Even if the plaintiff can locate an expert witness who becomes familiar with the procedure through research and study, the expert's qualifications may fall short of those required by the court, or a jury may decide that the expert is not qualified. In such cases, the defendant can produce several friendly members of the same subspecialty to testify for the defense.
- The locality rule may apply, requiring that the plaintiff's expert witness on liability be familiar with the standards of practice in the defendant's community or in similar communities. The locale rule is still recognized in many jurisdictions, particularly when the defendant is not board certified and is a general practitioner. When the negligent act occurs in a small community, it is nearly impossible to locate a doctor in that community willing to testify, and it becomes necessary to find an expert who is familiar with the standards of practice in that small community or in similar communities. Although this can be done, it is often difficult and adds to the expense of the litigation.
- The defendant may be practicing in a school of medicine or field of expertise—such as podiatry, osteopathy, neurosurgery, or obstetrics—that makes it difficult to locate expert witnesses willing to testify for the plaintiff. Health-care professionals in some specialty fields are more protective of one another and less inclined to assist the plaintiff who has a meritorious case. Those willing to testify may not have the desired qualifications. Accordingly, the plaintiff may be at a distinct disadvantage in the courtroom.

Medical Issues

- The bad result may not be obvious to a lay person or the medical issues may be complex. The more complex the medical issues, the more difficult it will be to persuade a jury that the doctor was negligent. For example, the jury may excuse a medical mistake made in a difficult and complex surgical procedure lasting many hours. On the other hand, the jury may not excuse a doctor's failure to recognize a broken bone on X rays when the fracture is obvious.
- The jury may perceive an elective procedure, such as cosmetic surgery, as frivolous. Jurors often believe that people undergoing these procedures are vain and assume the risk of a bad result.
- The plaintiff's condition may be terminal or so serious that jurors will excuse simple acts of negligence if they did not cause significant additional injury or damages. In short, jurors often find the "I saved his life" defense compelling enough to excuse negligence.

- Multiple physicians may have treated the plaintiff with multiple bad results. When this occurs, it is sometimes difficult to separate the injuries resulting from negligence from other injuries. Sometimes non-negligent conduct and negligent conduct combine to cause bad results.

  If all the physicians involved were negligent and must be sued, for example in states with several liability only, it may be difficult to persuade a jury that several physicians fell below the standards of practice. Jurors may view the lawsuit as frivolous and as a shotgun attack on everyone involved.

  In addition, a suit against multiple physicians in different specialties or fields of practice requires that the plaintiff find expert witnesses in each field of practice, a difficult and costly undertaking. Expert witnesses in different fields of practice often protect their field of practice and blame physicians in other fields of practice who contributed to the bad result. The experts may even be prohibited from testifying against physicians in other fields of practice.
- Physicians specializing in follow-up care may support the defendant-doctors. When this occurs, jurors may give the defense testimony greater weight, finding the plaintiff's experts less credible by comparison, and resolve the medical issues in favor of the defense.

Damages Issues

- Damages resulting from the injury may be minimal. The damages have to be large enough to justify the time and expense of asserting the claim. If the damages are obscure or difficult to demonstrate, the jury may not award damages sufficient to justify litigation. Even in jurisdictions in which binding arbitration is available, the damages may not justify the cost of arbitration.
- Enhanced risk may be the only damage and may not justify the time and expense of preparing and trying the case.
- Although the injuries may be serious and the damages substantial, legislation may limit the amount of damages recoverable. For example, the combination of caps on damages, reduction of noneconomic damages to present value, elimination of joint liability, designation of nonparties at fault, and disallowance of prejudgment interest can turn a substantial damages case into a minimal recovery case.

Financial Issues

- Avoid litigation in which the client's net recovery could be minimal. Often the client is required to reimburse insurance carriers, health-care providers, or others with a subrogated interest out of settlement or verdict proceeds. Medical negligence litigation is difficult, time-consuming, and "high risk," and it involves substantial costs that the plaintiff's counsel generally advances. The client generally must pay a 40-percent contingent fee. The fee, advanced costs, and subrogated claims all must be paid from settlement or verdict proceeds. If, in addition, tort reform legislation greatly reduces the verdict, the client may be left with little or no net recovery after undergoing the stress of lengthy litigation. A client may view the litigation as having benefited only the lawyers, expert witnesses, and subrogated claimants.

- Multiple defendants may be located in different jurisdictions. For example, medical negligence may occur in one state, with negligent follow-up care occurring in another state. If the jurisdictions involved have abolished joint liability, you must file suit in each jurisdiction to obtain a full recovery. It is often advisable to bring suit in both jurisdictions even when joint liability has not been abolished because the doctors in one jurisdiction may foist the blame on the doctors in another jurisdiction. Naming multiple defendants in different jurisdictions increases the time and expense required to litigate the claim. These costs diminish your client's net recovery from a settlement or verdict.
- The cost of litigating the claim may not warrant filing suit. For example, there may be multiple complex medical issues and multiple defendants and a plaintiff with moderate injuries. If the cost of the litigation could exceed $100,000, and the client's maximum recovery is $200,000, the litigation may not be advisable for economic reasons.
- A client may be unwilling to go to trial, but may want to litigate the claim for a settlement. This strategy may be dangerous, even if the client is willing to accept less than you recommend for settlement. The case may not settle for any number of reasons. If the client does not want to proceed, the case must then be dismissed at the client's request, after you and your client have expended substantial time and money. A physician sometimes is unwilling to consent to a settlement even though the liability insurance carrier and defense counsel recommend it. If the defendant has been sued successfully for negligence in the past, another settlement could trigger a licensing board review or jeopardize insurance coverage. The defendant may even refuse to settle out of stubbornness.

Pros

Positive factors affecting medical negligence cases include the following:

Liability Issues

- The mere recitation of facts may be enough for the average jury to find negligence. This is the case, for example, if the defendant failed to detect a tumor that is clearly visible to jurors on a CAT scan. Although you still need a medical expert, these cases often are difficult to defend because the jury assumes as a matter of common sense that the doctor must have been negligent. Jurors most often assume negligence in misdiagnosis cases as well. Jurors also suspect negligence when a plaintiff undergoes minor surgery and ends up with catastrophic injuries.

- There may have been misdiagnosis rather than negligent treatment. Jurors often understand misdiagnosis cases more easily than negligent treatment cases, and misdiagnosis cases generally are easier to prove than negligent treatment cases. Also, the defense is less likely to raise a causation issue in misdiagnosis cases.
- There may have been both misdiagnosis and negligent treatment. If you can establish both, the jury may view the doctor's conduct as gross misconduct rather than simple negligence, making a victory for the plaintiff more likely. Offensive or aggravated conduct can also increase the damages the jury assesses.
- The defendant may not be able to shift the blame to a nonparty. In jurisdictions that have abolished joint liability and permit the defense to designate nonparties at fault, it is important to determine whether the defendant may be able to shift part of the blame to a nonparty who is located in another jurisdiction who is otherwise unavailable, or who is immune to suit. When the defendant is unable to shift the blame to a nonparty, the plaintiff is more likely to receive full compensation.
- There may be only one defendant. Multiple defendants substantially increase the cost of litigation; often they make the litigation more complex and risky. Having only one defendant and a clean case enhances the plaintiff's chances of recovery. However, balance the benefits of having one defendant against the benefits of a case with multiple defendants. A case with multiple defendants who are clearly negligent carries with it the possibility that the jury will find that the defendants' conduct was aggravated. Also, if there are multiple defendants, chances are increased that there will be insurance or other financial resources available to compensate the plaintiff.
- The misconduct may be gross and therefore appealing to expert witnesses. In recent years, as the medical profession has united to pass legislation to defeat medical negligence claims, physicians have become reluctant to testify for plaintiffs unless a defendant's misconduct is aggravated or gross. Many doctors oppose the law permitting recovery for simple negligence; they believe that a doctor's conduct falling below the accepted standards of practice on one occasion should not subject the doctor to liability unless the misconduct is gross. Doctors who hold this view believe that the misconduct, though it fell below accepted standards of practice, was simply an "error in judg-

ment." Accordingly, when the defendant-doctor's misconduct is gross, the plaintiff is more likely to find competent expert witnesses willing to testify against the doctor.

- There may be no affirmative defenses. Obviously, the combination of strong evidence of medical negligence and no evidence supporting an affirmative defense enhances the plaintiff's chances of recovery.
- Causation may seem clear. The defense almost always raises a causation issue in medical negligence cases. When the defense does not raise causation, however, the plaintiff has an increased chance of full recovery. Causation is nearly always an issue because medical negligence most often occurs when a plaintiff seeks medical care for an existing disease, illness, or injury. To establish causation and damages, the plaintiff must show what his condition would have been if proper care and treatment had been rendered for the underlying medical condition. The defense invariably introduces evidence that the care and treatment would not have been as successful as the plaintiff claims; that if additional or different care and treatment had been provided, the underlying medical condition would not have been substantially improved; and that different treatment would not have cured the condition. Accordingly, the defendant's alleged negligence did not cause additional injury and damages. On occasion, the defendant cannot assert this type of causation defense, making the plaintiff's claim more viable.
- The defendant may have a poor reputation, have an undesirable bedside manner, or generally be an unattractive witness. These factors hurt the defendant's credibility and enhance the plaintiff's credibility by comparison. In this case, the jury is inclined to resolve the liability issues in the plaintiff's favor.
- The client's personality may appeal to the jury. A client's demeanor, personality, and credibility can be critically important, particularly when there is a factual dispute with the defendant over issues such as informed consent or admissions the doctor made to the plaintiff. Even when the plaintiff's credibility is not at issue, if the jury identifies with the plaintiff, the plaintiff will be more likely to prevail on liability and to obtain full compensation for damages.

Medical Issues

- There may be evidence that the patient was abandoned or treated casually when her condition demanded the best of medical care. Jurors are offended when it is apparent that a patient's condition warranted better care than was delivered. For example, the plaintiff may not have been admitted to the hospital, even though the condition for which she was treated in the emergency room was obviously deteriorating.

- There may be medical consensus on treatment and causation. On rare occasion, the medical community agrees that the wrong treatment was used, that it caused additional injury, and that there is no medical literature to support expert testimony to the contrary. In this scenario, the plaintiff has a strong case, and the jury will view expert witnesses who testify for the defense as lacking in credibility.
- Catastrophic injuries may have been unanticipated. For example, a plaintiff may undergo simple minor surgery and die under anesthesia or come out of the surgery with severe brain damage, paralysis, or some other catastrophic injury. In these cases, the jurors, most of whom have had minor surgery, will identify with the plaintiff and expect the defendant to compensate the plaintiff. As long as the plaintiff can show negligence, the catastrophic injury will help overcome any other trial problems.

Damages Issues

- The damages are substantial. Medical negligence litigation is most often economically feasible in cases in which there are substantial damages and a likelihood that the plaintiff will receive a satisfactory net recovery.
- The case may be inexpensive to litigate. If the case involves one defendant and one issue and is uncomplicated, the expenses associated with it may be small. Thus, the case may be feasible financially even if damages are not great.

CONCLUSION

The single most important step in the processing of a medical negligence case is the decision of whether to accept and pursue the case, and you must make the decision as soon as possible after the client approaches you. It is devastating to a client to have a case in an attorney's office for weeks, months, or even years, only to be advised that the case does not have merit and the attorney is withdrawing. It is financially disastrous for an attorney to invest time and money in a case only to find that the case is without merit. It is traumatic in every respect for the potential defendant to have the case pending for weeks or months only to be advised that the attorney has dropped the case because it does not have merit.

To make an intelligent decision about accepting a case, you must have the facts, including not only the client's version of the circumstances but all the relevant medical records.

Because the law in every jurisdiction requires that qualified medical experts be used to pursue most medical negligence claims and because an attorney may be accused of filing a frivolous claim, expert evaluation is a necessary and significant step in the evaluation process. It is not good enough for the attorney and the client to decide that there is a valid claim.

In evaluating whether to take a medical negligence case, you must combine a careful legal evaluation with an evaluation of all the other facts. Relate these evaluations to your financial evaluation. Weigh the negative factors against the positive factors, and thus base your decision of whether to take the case on the combined results of your medical, legal, and financial evaluations. If, after following this careful procedure, you decide to reject the case, confirm the rejection in writing and remind the client of the statute of limitations; when appropriate, recommend that the client solicit a second opinion. If on the other hand you decide to take the case, your next steps should be to enter into a fee agreement with the client (if you have not already done so) and to determine how to proceed in processing the case.

CHAPTER THREE

EARLY SETTLEMENT CONSIDERATIONS AND FILING THE LAWSUIT

Once you have accepted a medical negligence case, you will need to consider which approach you should take to resolve the conflict: settlement, arbitration, or filing.[1] Before filing a lawsuit you must first decide who to name as plaintiffs, who to sue, where to file, and when to file. In the absence of binding arbitration or a mandatory screening panel proceeding that results in settlement, you must then decide whether to attempt settlement before filing a lawsuit.

CHOOSING SETTLEMENT OR FILING

You must consider the applicable statute of limitations in deciding whether to file suit or to first attempt settlement. Remember that filing a lawsuit may affect the settlement posture of the case by either improving or reducing the chances of settlement. In making this decision, you should answer the following questions: Are the injuries fixed and well known, or is the client still under treatment and the prognosis doubtful? What are your chances of winning the case? If you believe your chances of winning are poor, an attempt at early settlement may be in your client's best interest. In fact, some attorneys accept medical negligence cases with the understanding that if they are not able to settle the case, the client will have to find another lawyer to pursue it.

---

1 See Chapter Two, "Evaluating the Case," for a discussion of arbitration and screening panels.

Examine the potential value of your case. In a case with major damages, it may be best to file as soon as possible and obtain an early trial date before attempting settlement. When the damages are substantial, it is difficult to negotiate an adequate settlement before filing suit. Further, if prejudgment interest is not allowed in your jurisdiction, it is in your client's best interest to file as soon as possible and obtain an early trial date rather than engage in drawn-out settlement negotiations, which may be unsuccessful, before filing suit. On the other hand, in a case with clear liability and major damages, an early attempt to settle may be appropriate.

FILING THE LAWSUIT: WHO TO NAME AS PLAINTIFFS

You must determine who has standing to bring the lawsuit and which persons have meritorious claims that can be filed. You must also pay attention to potential conflicts of interest.

Claims for a Person Other than the Injured Party

When you file a medical negligence case, you must address the question of who has a right to sue for injuries. Most jurisdictions now allow the spouse of a seriously injured person to file a claim for the damage to the relationship between them. Some jurisdictions allow children of an injured party to assert a claim for damages. A right of recovery is even allowed in some states to a third-party bystander who is in some way involved and emotionally damaged by what occurs.

Some jurisdictions require that both parents be notified when a lawsuit is filed for an injured child of divorced parents. Under such a requirement, even if you file a lawsuit on behalf of one parent, you must notify the other parent of the lawsuit to allow the other parent to join in the lawsuit. The failure to notify the other parent could result in your client assuming the risk of all litigation costs but having to share the proceeds of any settlement or verdict with the other parent.

Consider carefully whether you want to assert a claim on behalf of a spouse, child, or bystander because jurors may view such a claim negatively, resulting in an adverse effect on your overall case. Certainly if your primary plaintiff has been so seriously injured that a jury would understand how another member of the family, such as a spouse, has suffered, you should consider filing a loss of consortium claim. On the other hand, if you assert a loss of consortium claim and the jury believes that the claim is motivated by greed, this claim will contaminate the primary party's case.

Conflicts of Interest

Be aware of potential conflicts of interest when you represent more than one member of a family, and resolve any such conflicts early. For example, there may be a conflict between divorced parents who seek to be parties in the wrongful death of their child. Likewise, the future economic damages of a quadriplegic brain-damaged infant may be assessed either as damages that the parents will incur or as damages that the child will incur. Sometimes the damages overlap; for example, both the parents and the child may have standing to claim some of the same elements of damages. Sometimes this is not so. Familiarize yourself with the law in your jurisdiction relating to these issues.

FILING THE LAWSUIT: WHO TO SUE

In jurisdictions that have abolished joint liability, it is especially important that you name as defendants all health-care personnel who may be at fault; otherwise your client may not obtain a full recovery. Naming all the defendants may be a problem if several nurses and hospitals as well as practitioners of different specialties are involved because the cost of pursuing a case against numerous defendants of multiple specialties can be enormous when compared with the potential recovery. Thus your legal evaluation must overlap with your financial evaluation of a case.

Several liability can raise additional questions and problems. When medical negligence causes complications or additional injury in one state, the patient is often referred to a regional medical facility in another state for treatment. Additional negligence may then occur in the second state, causing further injuries. Because personal jurisdiction problems usually prevent physicians in different states from being joined in one lawsuit, consider filing a lawsuit in each jurisdiction. Failure to file in all jurisdictions in which injury occurred may result in an inadequate recovery if the jury assesses part of the blame to physicians who are not parties to the lawsuit.

In analyzing who to name as a defendant in your lawsuit, you should consider factors other than your client's right to sue a party. For example, remember that every physician or other defendant sued is likely to retain an attorney. The more attorneys retained by the defendants, the more expense and time you will spend on each motion and each deposition. The participation of multiple attorneys will also prolong and complicate the trial because every attorney has the right to participate in every aspect of the trial.

Furthermore, many states have adopted statutes that give defendants a right to sue any lawyer and party who bring a groundless or frivolous lawsuit against them. Some states also have statutes that allow defendants to be compensated by plaintiffs for reasonable attorney fees if the court grants the defendants summary judgment.

Some state statutes allow defendants to divert blame to a nonsued person or entity. These statutes often permit defendants to designate nonparties that are at fault but that the plaintiff was unable to sue because of unavailability or immunity. The designated nonparties are then listed on the jury verdict form, and the jury is permitted to assign a percentage of fault to nonsued entities, thus reducing the amount of recoverable damages assessed against named defendants. The nonparties have nothing to lose—the plaintiff collects nothing from nonsued entities found to be at fault. If they are called as witnesses, nonsued parties may protect the defendant by accepting responsibility for the plaintiff's damages or by accepting more than their fair share of the blame. And if they are not called as witnesses, the defense has an opportunity to place all or most of the blame on the nonparties who are not present to defend themselves. This can result in a defense verdict or reduce the recoverable damages to an extent that makes the case economically infeasible.

In another tricky situation, you may begin a case having the cooperation of a health-care provider whom you aren't suing, but that cooperation will end if you later sue the provider. Unfortunately, even if you don't want to sue the provider, the statute of limitations may force you to name additional defendants simply to protect the plaintiff's legal rights.

In a suit against a hospital, you must decide whether to name individual hospital employees or simply the hospital. You also need to analyze whether to name as defendants other health-care providers who may have provided treatment or had some other role in the case.

When assessing whether to name as defendants governmental agencies or the state or federal government, you should consider the claim filing requirements, statutes of limitation, and other legal requirements in your jurisdiction. Further consider that federal tort claims must be filed in federal court and are tried by a judge rather than a jury.

FILING THE LAWSUIT: WHERE TO FILE

State or Federal Court

In some cases you will have a choice between filing in state court or federal court—for example, where jurisdiction is based on diversity of citizenship and the amount in controversy is in excess of the minimum required under federal law.

When you are deciding who to name as defendants in the lawsuit, consider how the naming of each defendant will affect your choice of jurisdiction: naming certain parties as defendants may either enable or jeopardize the diversity of citizenship requirement for filing in federal court. Bear in mind that actions filed in state court may be subject by law to removal to federal court. Therefore, if you want to keep a case in state court, you should name as a defendant a resident of the state where the action is filed.

The decision of whether to file an action in state or federal court depends on issues too numerous to describe in detail here. One thing to consider, however, is whether the jury verdicts you expect in state court are larger than those you expect in federal court, or vice versa. You must also consider whether trying the case in federal court will give you additional rights of discovery. On the other hand, federal courts often operate under local rules that restrict discovery, require early disclosure of evidence, and severely limit the parties' right to participate in jury selection, while state rules may not have such requirements.

Choices of Venue within a State

Where you can select the venue within a state in which to file your action, you should analyze the advantages and disadvantages of each possible venue. Often jury awards are higher in one area than another. Local courts within one state may operate differently. Also consider the likelihood of the defendant's obtaining a change of venue to a state court that may be less favorable to the plaintiff, which may be permitted under state law. You might be able to file the case in a state court that will be unlikely to transfer the case to a less favorable state court if the defendant requests a transfer.

Choices of Venue between States

You may have a choice of states in which to file your action. To choose a venue wisely, you must analyze the relevant laws of those states, including statutes of limitation, rights of recovery of damages (including punitive damages), and standard-of-care requirements. Under "long arm" statutes, you can either file an action against an out-of-state defendant in the state in which the injury occurred or in the state in which the defendant resides. There are also other instances in which you have a choice as to which state to file in.

If you plan to file a lawsuit in a state other than the one in which you practice, you must comply with that state's rules governing out-of-state attorneys. Furthermore, when you act as an out-of-state attorney, it is essential that you consult local counsel to familiarize yourself with local rules or state law.

FILING THE LAWSUIT: WHEN TO FILE

Statute of Limitations Problems

You should consider numerous factors in deciding when to file suit, especially the statute of limitations. When the statute of limitations requires immediate filing, you will not have a choice of when to file. If you do have a choice and choose not to file the lawsuit immediately, you must establish a reminder system to ensure that you comply with the statute of limitations.

The Client's Age

The age of the client is another factor you should consider in deciding when to file a lawsuit. For example, on the basis of life expectancy, an elderly client's lawsuit may need to be filed immediately, whereas it may be better to delay a child's case. Because the nature and extent of an infant's injuries are sometimes not immediately apparent, it is sometimes better to delay litigation as long as possible under applicable statutes of limitation.

Nature of the Client's Injuries

The nature of the injuries involved is an important factor in deciding when to file a case. Where the injuries are fixed and known and the damages can therefore be evaluated, the case may be filed immediately. On the other hand, if the client is still in treatment and the prognosis is unknown, it may be preferable to wait until the full extent of the injuries is known before filing the lawsuit. If you have filed and obtained an early trial date and the nature and extent of the injuries are still unknown at time of trial, you may not be able to obtain a continuance of the trial date and as a result may receive an inadequate verdict based on inconclusive evidence regarding damages. You could be accused of negligence in handling the case if you hastily proceed to trial and additional injuries and damages later come to light.

Case Preparation

Another factor to consider in deciding when to file your lawsuit is your case preparation. If you do not have good expert testimony on all major points, it may be unwise to file the lawsuit because the defendant may be able to challenge the validity of the claims early in the proceedings through a motion for summary judgment. If the necessary documentation is not available, you may want to delay filing until you have the documentation. Generally speaking, it is advisable to fully prepare the case before filing the lawsuit. Once you file the lawsuit, the court may impose deadlines, and the defendant's right of discovery begins.

Trial Date Considerations

You must also evaluate how long it takes from the time of filing to the time of trial. In some jurisdictions there is a delay of years. You may need to file early just to get the case into the system and secure a trial date.

The Summons

After you have decided to file the lawsuit, make sure that your summons meets the wording requirements of the jurisdiction in which you file: both federal and state jurisdictions require strict compliance with statutory language in the wording of the summons. Federal courts may also require you to submit other forms with the summons. Furthermore, some jurisdictions require a specific person, such as a federal marshal, to serve the summons.

Because correctly serving the summons is essential to commencing the lawsuit, you should determine whom to serve with the papers. If the summons should be served to a corporation, obtain the name of the registered agent from the secretary of state's office or the state agency responsible for maintaining such records. Process servers may serve the wrong person or file incorrect affidavits if you give them incorrect information. Always verify that the service was made on the appropriate person in the manner required by law.

Reminder Systems Regarding a Response

All jurisdictions have a time limit for a defendant's response to a lawsuit. As soon as the service is made, you should mark on your calendar the date that the answer is due or use a fail-proof system to remind you of the due date. In most jurisdictions, the defendant's answer must be filed before you can request a trial date. In some instances, however, you may come to an agreement with the defense that they need not file an answer until you give them written notice to do so. You may use this approach if you want to delay the case to discuss a settlement.

PREPARING THE CASE AFTER FILING

Prepared Discovery Material

Since some jurisdictions have local rules regarding interrogatories and the extent of discovery, you must decide when you file the case what discovery requests you will make. After you file the suit, in most cases you can count on a prompt response from the defense. If possible, you should have your written interrogatories, requests for admissions, requests for production, and deposition requests ready from the time you file the suit.

Preparation of Client Information

The defendant will inevitably serve your client with interrogatories and may ask to depose your client. By the time you receive interrogatories from the defendant, you should have most of the information you will need to respond to them, including your client's initial questionnaire, in your client's file. Before filing a lawsuit, you should collect all information to which the defense is entitled, including wage-loss information.

Deadline Reminder Systems

Almost every court has local rules regarding deadlines and discovery cutoffs. To make sure that you comply with these deadlines, you must have a system in place at the time of filing that tracks the court's deadlines. Computer software is available for this purpose, or you can use a written reminder system and checklists.

File Organization

All case files, including all medical records, should be organized at filing. Having your files well organized will save you time in responding to discovery requests and preparing for depositions and will help you avoid mistakes and sanctions for failing to comply with discovery requests.

You should also organize your medical research so that you can furnish it to your expert witnesses and use it to respond to discovery requests.

Preparation of Experts

While experts may change their opinions based on material discovered after the case is filed, you should minimize these last-minute vacillations by preparing your expert witnesses thoroughly and providing them with all the information that is available to you when you file suit. Filing a lawsuit only to have it dismissed or to have summary judgment granted because you did not prepare your experts can be costly and time-consuming and may result in a charge of legal negligence.

CONCLUSION

Once you have selected a jurisdiction and venue for your case and filed a lawsuit, you should be ready to proceed with formal discovery.

CHAPTER FOUR

DISCOVERY IN A MEDICAL NEGLIGENCE CASE

Evaluation and discovery are the two most important aspects of any medical negligence case. Because the majority of medical negligence cases tried in court end in defense verdicts, you must evaluate potential cases carefully and accurately. Because most meritorious claims are settled based on information learned through discovery, discovery is a fundamental part of processing the case.

If discovery has not been conducted carefully, the case might be dismissed on summary judgment filed by the defendant. Furthermore, most lawyers prepare for trial by reviewing, summarizing, and relying on the discovery depositions and other materials. Because you will use discovery information to prepare for cross-examination of the defense experts or the defendants and to prove your case at trial, discovery is an essential step in winning your case. In some cases, you will need to offer the discovery materials by way of substantive proof.

Discovery should be complete enough to ensure that you have all the opinions of the expert witnesses, all the factual information, and all the defenses being asserted by the defendant. If you do not conduct such careful discovery, you run the risk of being surprised at trial by hearing witnesses' stories for the first time, having experts advance new theories, or learning other unexpected information.

Proper investigation of the case, on the other hand, saves you from legal negligence suits, mental distress, Rule 11 sanctions or countersuits by the physicians you sue, and lost out-of-pocket expenses. It also saves the client from trauma and the potential defendant from the unnecessary anguish caused by a frivolous lawsuit.

CONDUCTING DISCOVERY

The Federal Rules of Civil Procedure provide for several methods of discovery. These methods include (1) written interrogatories, (2) oral depositions, (3) requests for production, (4) requests for inspection, (5) requests for admissions, and (6) medical examinations. All of these discovery methods can be used in medical negligence cases.

Written Interrogatories (Fed. R. Civ. P. 33)

In most medical negligence cases, certain information must be collected early in discovery. Many attorneys obtain this information by using a standard set of written interrogatories that are useful in medical negligence cases.[1] Standard interrogatories are useful because you need certain general information in most medical negligence cases. Some jurisdictions, however, limit the number of interrogatories that may be asked; in those jurisdictions you must decide the relative importance of competing areas of inquiry.

Interrogatories should request background information. Use them to identify fact witnesses, experts to be called at trial, and information the defendant has regarding the plaintiff. Whether you ask questions concerning the issues of the case is a matter of judgment. You may want to ask these important questions in interrogatories, or you may decide to save them for the deposition. Some lawyers believe that you should save substantive questions for the deposition because the defendant's lawyers will answer the interrogatories, but the deponents themselves will answer deposition questions. Other lawyers believe that having the defendant state a position in writing before being deposed assists the deposing attorney in preparing for deposition. Your decision on when to pose these questions depends on your experience as well as your interrogatory goals.

Carefully review the interrogatory answers to make sure that you have a list of all witnesses who should be deposed. In some cases, the interrogatory answers will contain names of witnesses who should be deposed that are not found in the medical records. Review the interrogatory answers to determine whether they reveal additional materials that you may then want to obtain through a request for production. These might include photographs, clinic records, or other records.

---

1 See Appendix B.1 for sample interrogatories to individual doctors; see Appendix B.2 for sample interrogatories to a hospital.

The procedural rules generally obligate attorneys to supplement previous interrogatory answers. Nevertheless, most attorneys believe that it is a good practice to submit additional sets of interrogatories as the case progresses, specifically asking the opponent's attorney to supplement previous answers. This, in addition to the civil rules, puts the onus on the defense attorney to honestly and accurately supplement interrogatories.

At the same time, you should review your client's answers to interrogatories periodically to determine if they should be supplemented. This review satisfies your professional obligation to supplement answers and decreases the potential that the trial judge will rule that you may not use evidence or witnesses because you did not identify them in answers.

You should also consider whether to take your depositions before your written interrogatories. Some lawyers believe that you should take depositions before interrogatories, hoping that the defense will not be adequately prepared. Being served with detailed interrogatories before depositions forces the defense to focus on and discuss the facts and issues of the case, preparing the defendant to defend his position later during the deposition. When a deposition is taken before written interrogatories, defense counsel often finds it difficult to obtain time to prepare with a busy defendant. Defense counsel also finds it difficult to prepare because the plaintiff has not yet identified specific areas of inquiry. Attorneys who prefer to take depositions before written interrogatories believe that the opponent's attorneys screen, modify, and essentially prepare the opponent's answers to interrogatories. For that reason, they believe it is better to ask important questions in depositions instead of in interrogatories.[2]

Oral Depositions (Fed. R. Civ. P. 30–32)

First you must decide whom to depose. It is essential that you depose all persons involved in your client's care, including all nurses, pathologists, and anyone else who had contact with your client. You risk surprise at trial if you do not depose all those connected with your client's medical care. For instance, the defendant may blame someone you have not named as a party for your client's injuries after the statute of limitations has run. You should

---

2 For a more detailed discussion of the advantages and disadvantages of the use of written interrogatories either before or after depositions, see Chapter Six, "Interrogatories and Deposition of Defendant-Doctor."

depose all who might be responsible as a matter of form in every case.

Next you must decide the order in which you will take the depositions. Should the main defendant be the first deponent, or should you start with nurses, medical-records specialists, or other less significant deponents and work up to the key deponent?

Deciding whether to depose the main defendant depends on your goal in taking the deposition and the nature of your case. In some cases, depending on the issue involved, you should take the defendant's deposition immediately so that the defendant cannot change a position after hearing the testimony of experts. In other cases, it may be better to wait until you have deposed the defendant's experts and you know the defenses involved to take the defendant's deposition. In jurisdictions in which the deposition may be taken more than once, you may do both. For example, you may depose the main defendant immediately and again after you have deposed the experts.

Bring to the deposition a copy of all records in which the witness's name appears. If the witness made an entry in the chart, mark a copy of that particular page as an exhibit. Identify every page of the hospital record in which the witness made a record, and translate the writing. Consider using medical drawings as deposition exhibits or taking a video deposition and having a physician demonstrate what was done to your client. You may want to show the witness copies of authoritative medical books to see if the witness authenticates them as authoritative and agrees with them.

Chapter Five, "Preparing for Deposition," further discusses how to prepare for depositions.

Requests for Production (Fed. R. Civ. P. 34)

Requests for production are extremely important because the defendant frequently has documentary material you will need to evaluate the case, and your attempts to obtain this material through informal discovery before filing suit may be unsuccessful. For example, sometimes the defendant and other treating doctors possess the clinic records, and hospitals have records, X rays, and test results that can only be obtained through requests for production.

To assess the merits of your case, you will need to gather a lot of documentary evidence, including all hospital and medical records, doctors' telephone memoranda, and appointment books. The evidence you need will depend on the nature of the case and the information already obtained through informal discovery before the suit commenced. If some documents were not obtained through informal discovery, you must obtain them through formal discovery.

If your case involves a hospital, consider requesting the following:

- medical staff bylaws;
- medical staff rules and regulations;
- an organizational chart of administrative staff, nursing staff, and medical staff;
- an organizational chart of all hospital departments;
- an internal telephone directory;
- personnel files;
- credential files, including information regarding privileges;
- policies, procedures, rules, regulations, guidelines, standards, and written practices for various hospital departments;
- documentation regarding accreditation, licensing, and deficiencies, including surveys, inspections, deficiency reports, state inspection reports, and documents of the Joint Commission on Hospital Accreditation, the U.S. Department of Health and Human Services, Medicare, or any other health-care agency;
- diagnostics reports, such as X rays and fetal heart strips;
- documentation indicating the number of patients on the floor and the duration of their stays during your client's hospitalization;
- documentation on the procedures your client underwent, the operative logs, and the delivery and operating room logs;
- an index of training films;
- laboratory logs; and
- equipment records.

Requests for Inspection (Fed. R. Civ. P. 34)

Rule 34 grants the right to request entry on designated land or other property to inspect, measure, survey, photograph, test, or sample. This rule also allows you to request inspection of documents, writings, drawings, graphs, charts, photographs, or other data. For example, under this rule you may make a motion to inspect a physician's medical library, appointment book, or phone memo book. You may wish to obtain a court order under this rule that allows you to videotape hospital equipment, the surgical suite or delivery room, or simply to inspect the hospital with your expert witnesses.

Requests for Admissions (Fed. R. Civ. P. 36)

Under Rule 36, you may submit a written request to make admissions, such as admissions of fact and admissions concerning the genuineness of documents. Obtaining admissions of fact can be an important step in preparing a case. By having facts admitted as true, you can eliminate issues and enhance the position of your case. You can avoid the need to prove the authenticity of documents through requests to admit their genuineness. Furthermore, the civil rules contain sanctions for inappropriate responses to requests for admissions. These sanctions may include reasonable attorney fees and the exclusion of evidence.

In medical negligence cases, well-drafted requests for admissions of fact may frame the basic issues in the case and eliminate issues that are not supported by credible evidence. Generally, you should frame requests for admissions of fact after deposition testimony establishes the facts' accuracy and truthfulness. It is a good practice to submit, along with the request for admissions, interrogatories asking the reasons, facts, and evidence on which your opponent relied in refusing to admit any request. In this way, your opponent is faced first with the duty under the rules to be honest, second with the duty to respond honestly to requests for admissions, and third with the duty to explain any lapse in fulfilling these duties.

Medical Examinations (Fed. R. Civ. P. 35)

Under Rule 35, the defendant may have the plaintiff examined by a physician of the defendant's choosing. In some jurisdictions, your client has the right to have an attorney or medical representative present at the examination. Your client should have a medical representative present, if permitted. This representative may serve as a witness and will observe the amount of time spent by the opponent's examiner, the type of examination done, and what your client said to the examiner. These observations may prove important if the medical examiner's version of the examination differs from that of your client and the witness. If the court permits it, a videotaped, tape-recorded, or court-reported examination also will help prevent disputes.

To prevent disputes about the nature of the examination and what your client said about her medical history, you should prepare your client for the examination. Your client should recognize the importance of the examination, and as soon as it ends she should record everything she remembers about it.

ORGANIZING DISCOVERY MATERIALS

To make the most of your discovered materials, you must have a plan for organizing them. If you organize them well, they will be useful not just for the current case, but for future cases as well.

Discovery Notebook

Some attorneys create a three-ring notebook to keep discovery materials divided by subject. The subjects may include the following (though not necessarily in this order):

- a chronology;
- deposition outlines and questions;
- information concerning consulting experts;
- information concerning fact witnesses;
- clinic records of the care rendered in your case;
- hospital records of the care rendered in your case;
- other significant medical records that provide relevant medical history and information regarding preexisting conditions;
- summaries of all medical and hospital records;
- research of medical literature;
- deposition summaries;[3] and
- significant interrogatory answers.

Place the material you gather behind dividers by subject. For example, behind the divider for deposition outlines and questions, place questions from your consulting experts, questions from your medical research, questions from a review of similar cases, and your own questions. You might also keep a standard deposition outline behind this divider.[4] In addition, medical witnesses may use medical terms, and you should know their definitions. If the medical chart, records, or research contain medical terms, you should place the terms' definitions behind a subdivider for your reference during the deposition. Depending on the volume of the material and the intricacy of the case, you may want to use subdividers behind these general dividers.

---

3 Appendix B.3 is a sample outline of deposition testimony given by a defense expert rendering opinions on causation issues in an obstetrical negligence case.

4 Appendix B.4 is a sample of a deposition outline prepared before a deposition of defendant's expert witnesses in an obstetrical negligence case.

The chronology is an outline of significant facts that fixes the times and dates of the case's important events. You may organize the chronology and related material—a more detailed outline of the basic facts and a list of questions raised by the experts or yourself—behind subdividers.

Keep behind the "Consulting Experts" the notes you make concerning information you receive in meetings with your experts. Keep behind the "Fact Witnesses" divider deposition summaries and statements from fact witnesses. Place medical literature research behind the "Medical Literature Research" divide, along with an index and brief summary of each article in the notebook, and index it according to its origins. Place clinic and hospital records behind appropriate dividers with a summary of those records. If the records are too voluminous, include only the summary and significant pages of the records.

Take your notebook to depositions and expand it as the case develops. It is an abbreviated form of the entire case file.

Preserving Case Materials

Save for reuse all material you collect in each of your medical negligence cases. This material may prove helpful later in a variety of ways. First, your medical research may apply to future cases. Second, the same expert witness may appear in more than one of your cases, and their previous reports or depositions will be important if you meet them in future cases. Third, this material will shorten the time you need to prepare for similar cases in the future.

Save your three-ring discovery notebook, if you use one, as well as your deposition outlines, trial and medical research, and information concerning your experts and the defense experts. The same defendants and experts appear in many cases across the country. The exchange of information on these professional witnesses is a valuable aspect of the plaintiff's bar.

CONCLUSION

Thorough discovery allows you to assess the merits of the case. Reevaluate your case as each deposition is taken and as your opponent responds to each set of discovery requests. Contact your consulting experts and other experts again as you gather new information to keep them informed and to obtain their assistance in understanding and evaluating the new information received. Continually reassess the viability of your case as new information is received.

Discovery provides the information on which you will rely in deciding your approach to the case and its issues. Since most cases settle and are not tried, the information obtained through discovery often will determine whether you settle the case and the amount of the settlement.

CHAPTER FIVE

PREPARING FOR DEPOSITIONS

PREPARING YOURSELF FOR YOUR CLIENT'S AND WITNESSES' DEPOSITIONS

Before you prepare your client and other witnesses to be deposed, you must prepare yourself. Study the facts and information you have gained through investigation and other pretrial discovery. Review all your client's medical records and answers to interrogatories, any relevant medical literature, and information supplied by your consulting expert witnesses. Analyze what your client and other witnesses have told you to determine what they will say when deposed. Also look for any inconsistencies in information your client and other witnesses have given others. Determine whether your client's story and the witnesses' stories make sense and whether they are consistent with all the facts and testimony. Be prepared to discuss inconsistencies with your client and witnesses to either resolve them or explain them to the jury.

Based on your investigation and consultation with experts, you should have a theory of what the health-care defendants did, or failed to do, that damaged your client. You should also know how the defendant could have prevented your client's injury. In preparing for deposition, consider how each witness's testimony either supports your theory of the case or appears inconsistent with it. You should know what information each witness may be able to supply that strengthens your case. Your case should be supported by facts that a jury will believe and that will establish that the defendant's negligence caused your client's injury.

Know the law that applies to your case, including any affirmative defenses, and understand how the facts of your case relate to the law.

Use all available information to pinpoint the probable strengths and weaknesses in your witnesses' testimony. Consider your case's weaknesses, the problems you expect at trial, and the ways in which your witnesses' deposition responses may help overcome these problems. Know how to use your client's or expert's testimony best by assessing your case as though you were a juror. Prepare your client and witnesses so that jurors will understand and believe them.

PREPARING OPPOSING COUNSEL FOR YOUR CLIENT'S AND WITNESSES' DEPOSITIONS

Before the deposition, give your opposing counsel documents that may assist your witnesses in responding to questions, assist opposing counsel in eliciting testimony that supports your theory of the case, and possibly shorten the depositions. Provide resources such as an expert's resume, updated answers to interrogatories, copies of test results on which the expert will rely, medical reports and hospital records, and any exhibits that will help your witnesses give clear and concise statements during deposition. By supplying these documents ahead of time, you can prevent a claim of surprise by opposing counsel. If you don't produce the documents until the deposition, opposing counsel may request a postponement or a second deposition to explore the contents of documents that were not produced in advance.

On the other hand, there are some documents that should not be supplied to opposing counsel before deposition unless they are requested in formal discovery. One example is medical literature that your expert has reviewed and found to be consistent with her opinions. You may want to save that kind of literature for use in deposing the other side's expert witnesses or for cross-examination at trial.

Occasionally you can protect your client from trauma by discussing with opposing counsel how the deposition will be conducted. Sometimes counsel will agree not to inquire into certain irrelevant areas that would cause your client severe emotional trauma or even additional injury. Inform opposing counsel of any health problems suffered by your client that may be affected by the way in which the deposition is conducted; also disclose any limitations you will impose on the testimony of your expert witnesses. For example, you may want to inform counsel that your expert witness will give testimony only on the issue of causation and not on the issue of negligence or standards of practice, or that you will not permit counsel to inquire into irrelevant areas that will embarrass your client or invade his privacy.

PREPARING YOUR CLIENT FOR DEPOSITION

Your case can be damaged, sometimes irreparably, by a client who is not prepared to be deposed. Some clients need more help than others. You should help your client be a good witness by detecting problems in the client's responses that could damage his credibility or offend a jury.

Set aside adequate time to prepare your client to be deposed. Some clients require more time than others; complicated cases often require a full day of client preparation.

Before meeting to prepare for the deposition, ask your client to refresh his memory by reviewing interrogatory answers and any diaries or notes. Some attorneys prefer that the client review all medical records, paying particular attention to any of his statements that have been recorded in medical histories, nursing charts, and other hospital records. Other attorneys prefer that the client not review hospital and medical records before the deposition, fearing that this will make the client look like an advocate rather than an innocent victim giving factual testimony from memory. Attorneys who are reluctant to allow the client to review the records sometimes prefer to call the client's attention to specific facts in the records, so that the client will be able to explain those facts if questioned about them or to explain any inconsistencies or errors.

Give your client copies of all documents, interrogatories, pleadings, and medical reports that will help prepare him for defense questioning. Be careful not to give him documents for deposition preparation that are subject to work-product privilege and that you do not want the defense to gain through discovery. An example of this type of document is a confidential consultation report by a medical expert whom you do not intend to call as a witness at trial. Be careful that you and your client do not waive your work-product privilege.

In meeting with your client, explain what a deposition is and how it serves the following purposes:

- discovery of facts and evidence,
- impeachment,
- assistance to opposing counsel in jury selection, and
- settlement evaluation by opposing counsel.

Explain that opposing counsel will use the deposition to evaluate your client's credibility, demeanor, and appearance, as well as the impression your client will make on the jury. Advise the client on appropriate dress and behavior.

Let the client know that his role is to provide factual information based on his personal knowledge and observation, not on his reconstructions of events or facts. Help him distinguish between actual recollection of the events as they transpired and reconstruction or information learned since the event from others. Explain that he must not manufacture facts or information. Accuracy and truthfulness are necessary, even if he feels foolish. Warn him against giving inaccurate testimony out of intimidation, embarrassment, fear, or pride. Explain that he can ask for an occasional recess during the deposition to avoid becoming mentally exhausted. Also be sure that he knows not to look to others, including you, for help in answering questions.

Warn the client against being adversarial, angry, or sarcastic during the deposition. If a question can be answered in a general way, tell the client to summarize, permitting the opposing lawyer to lead into specifics. Explain when and how the client should qualify answers. Instruct him not to guess at the meaning of a question or to answer a question that contains an unfamiliar word without seeking clarification.

Explain the legal issues. Educate the client about the law that applies to the case so that the client understands the relevance and importance of pertinent facts. Explain that the case has some undisputed issues and some issues that are in dispute, and that you and he will focus on the disputed issues in preparing for deposition. Also, explain any motions in limine so that he understands why certain evidence will not be admitted at trial.

Discuss how you will handle problem areas, such as a failure to file income tax returns, a felony conviction, or a suicide attempt. If the client has previously made any inconsistent statements in police reports, medical history reports, other depositions or testimony, or statements to insurance adjusters, prepare him for questioning on the inconsistencies.

Warn the client about common or expected pitfalls. Review approaches defense counsel may use to secure concessions. Inform your client of the possible consequences of not conceding; let him know it is important to make concessions on certain matters, even if the case may be weakened as a result.

Alert the client to be aware of defense counsel's demeanor, personality, facial expressions, and body language. If not properly alerted and prepared, the client could be intimidated, misled, or charmed into making unnecessary concessions. For example, warn the client that defense counsel might try to influence his response by looking skeptical and disbelieving when asking a question like "You didn't really expect the doctor to go directly to the hospital, did you?" Likewise, inform the client that defense counsel might begin nodding his head yes or no while asking a leading question—"You knew that developing an infection was a risk of undergoing this surgery, didn't you?"—to suggest how the client should answer the question. The client should be careful not to make any unwarranted concessions simply because of defense counsel's tone of voice, facial expressions, and body language.

Your client should expect defense counsel to inquire into the general areas of education, health history, prior injuries, marital history, family history, employment history, circumstances surrounding the injury, and damages sustained.[1]

It is sometimes helpful to instruct your client in the following manner:

- Be totally honest, open, and polite. Do not treat opposing counsel as the "enemy."
- Let the lawyers, with their questions, lead into whatever areas are of interest to them, and respond to any questions fully and openly. Do not exaggerate symptoms or conditions. Likewise, do not underplay or minimize symptoms, injuries, or damages. In short, be accurate and truthful. This will establish credibility.
- Correct or clarify wrong or unclear answers.
- Listen carefully to each question. Do not anticipate questions and do not read false meanings into them. If you do not understand a question, ask to have it repeated, and then give a thoughtful answer. Do not rush an answer.
- Always tell the truth—even about matters that may be unfavorable or damaging to the case.

Do a dry run of the deposition with the client. Ask him to assume that you are opposing counsel, then ask questions that the defense counsel probably will ask. Pay particular attention to the critical areas in dispute. Make sure the client uses the techniques

---

1 Appendix C.1 is an outline of the areas of inquiry parents may be subject to during deposition in birth-injury cases.

you have explained, and interrupt whenever necessary to point out mistakes. The dry run should thoroughly cover the critical areas of the client's testimony.

Do the dry run of the deposition a day or two beforehand. The client will then have time to digest the instructions and other information you provide. He will also have time to study documents further, if necessary to refresh his recollection, and to prepare himself mentally for the deposition.

With thorough preparation, the client should feel relaxed and confident. He should know what to expect and how to testify. Fears should be alleviated and anxiety reduced.

PREPARING YOUR EXPERT FOR DEPOSITION

Although many experts are familiar with the deposition process, you should review the basics with your expert. Explain the legal criteria under which the court accepts an expert. Prepare the expert to respond to questions attacking her qualifications. Tell her to answer credibly and accurately. Stress that her credibility as an expert depends on her qualifications, the accuracy and thoroughness of her investigation and knowledge of the facts, the accuracy of the information on which her opinions are based (including hypothetical questions), the validity of her conclusions, and her appearance, demeanor, and attitude.

Emphasize that fairness and honesty are crucial. A good expert will concede what it is necessary to concede on cross-examination and will strongly support the points she has established and the opinions she has rendered. Tell the expert to respond directly to all questions and to qualify answers as necessary. Refusing to answer a question destroys an expert's credibility and allows the deposition to be used for impeachment. Warn the expert not to become angry or abusive, and advise her to cooperate fully if opposing counsel asks for an opinion based on assumed facts or variables, even those not supported by evidence and those requiring a modification of her opinion.

Tell the expert not to be concerned about questions based on hypotheticals that do not accurately describe the facts of the case because opposing counsel may not be permitted to ask these questions at trial. Explain that if opposing counsel relies on erroneous information or incorrect data in hypotheticals, a jury will discount the expert's opinions that are based on such hypotheticals. Accordingly, the expert should not debate with opposing counsel over the accuracy of information used in asking questions during the deposition. If the hypothetical is unintelligible or does not contain enough information, on the other hand, the expert should explain why she cannot answer it.

Since a portion or all of the expert's deposition may be read in court later, ask her to show respect for the court and for the jurors by speaking in lay language.

Experts' Opinions

Experts should never give opinions prematurely. Instruct an expert who has not yet arrived at an opinion to say that. Explain the distinctions between speculation and possibility, medical probability and medical certainty, and medical causation and legal causation. In medicine, physicians are accustomed to deferring opinions on the cause of a medical condition until the cause can be established with some degree of certainty. The expert must understand that legal causation is established by a preponderance of the evidence, meaning that the opinion can be based on 51 percent probability rather than on 75 percent or 90 percent. The expert should also understand that if there are a number of possible causes of the plaintiff's injuries, only one of which is medical negligence, the expert may express an opinion that negligence is the most probable cause if she has determined all other causes to be only possibilities.

Instruct your expert to qualify preliminary opinions that may change with additional information. Failing to qualify preliminary opinions can lead to inconsistent opinions if the expert later changes her opinion. The expert who gives conflicting or inconsistent opinions won't survive cross-examination with her credibility intact.

Advise your expert not to offer opinions in areas beyond her expertise. If she does so, opposing counsel may attack the foundation for the opinion as well as the expert's credibility. This attack will draw into question the expert's other opinions on matters that are within her expertise.

The expert should be prepared to support opinions with specific entries in the plaintiff's medical and hospital records, diagnostic test results, and medical literature. Failing to use records to support opinions can be disastrous, particularly if the opponent's expert witnesses use records to support their opinions. Before deposition, review with your expert witness any reports you have received or any information you have about the positions to be taken by the defendant's expert witnesses.

Familiarize your expert with all the facts, including those that are disputed, and prepare her to explain opinions when she is confronted with hypothetical fact situations. Instruct her not to volunteer opinions beyond the limited purpose for which she is giving testimony. The expert should be familiar with both the plaintiff's and the defendant's theories of the case; the facts that have been developed in discovery that support each theory; and the likelihood of a jury's rejecting an expert's opinion if the opinion is not based on the facts as the jury sees them. Be sure the expert knows which facts will probably be eliminated from jury consideration by motions in limine or evidentiary rulings during trial.

Standard of Care

Inform your expert of the law relevant to your case. Prepare her to respond to questions regarding negligence and the standard of care. Explain any law or rule that could significantly affect her testimony or what she is legally permitted to rely on in expressing an opinion. For example, explain the legal standard of care by which one physician is expected to measure the conduct of another, and then describe the circumstances under which one standard of care might be used instead of another, i.e., a national standard rather than a local one.

After you discuss this thoroughly with the expert, go over how the expert should respond if the defense counsel's questions during the deposition do not reflect the legal standard. Make sure the expert knows what to say if defense counsel asks any of the following questions:

- "How do you believe my client practiced bad medicine?"
- "Would you agree that it was appropriate for my client to render the diagnosis that he did?"
- "Are you saying that my client practiced bad medicine in rendering that diagnosis?"
- "Are you saying that my client is incompetent in having rendered that treatment?"
- "Are you saying that any physician in the United States who did what my client did would be negligent?"
- "Would you be surprised to learn that there are respected and competent physicians who would disagree with your opinion that my client was negligent?"

- "Why do you believe that my client is guilty of malpractice?"
- "I want to know specifically where you find fault in the treatment rendered by my client."

Warn your witness not to "bite" at such bait to render opinions that are not based on the legal standard of care. You can assist the witness by objecting to the form of the question and asking that the question be phrased in the legal standard. In the alternative, the expert should respond to questions using the legal standard. For example, the expert could respond to any of the above questions by stating, "I would expect a reasonably careful and prudent physician under the circumstances of this case to *[provide an explanation here]*. In my opinion, Dr. Smith's failure to do so falls below the generally accepted standards of practice."

Explain commonly used generic cross-examination, such as the following:

- "Doctor, do you believe that other competent and reasonable physicians might disagree with your opinions in this case?" (Response: "Not if those physicians are basing their opinions on the accepted standards of practice.")
- "Are you saying that no other physician in the United States would have made the diagnosis that the defendant-doctor made?" (Response: "No, I am saying that a reasonably careful and prudent physician would not make that diagnosis, and any doctor who would make it falls below the accepted standards of practice.")
- "In all fairness, doctor, would you concede that this was just a judgment call?" (Response: "Yes, but the defendant exercised negligent judgment in making that call. Everything we do in the practice of medicine requires the exercise of sound judgment, and when that judgment falls below the standards of practice, it is not an acceptable judgment call.")
- "Doctor, would you concede that you are not perfect and that you have made mistakes in the practice of medicine?" (Response: "Yes, we all make mistakes. Some are unavoidable and are acceptable, and others fall below the accepted standards of practice.")
- "Doctor, have you ever been negligent in caring for patients in you practice?" (Response: "I hope not, but if I were ever negligent and caused injury, then I would accept responsibility.")

Medical Literature

Prepare your expert for questions about medical literature. She may be asked if she is familiar with published studies or medical literature that expresses opinions contrary to those she has given. She may be asked to accept certain text as authoritative, or she may be asked if she relies on particular medical literature in her practice.

In response to such questions, the expert should use one or more of the following explanations: that medical literature does not deal with the question of whether a particular procedure falls below the accepted standards of practice; that medical literature sometimes contains opinions based on speculation and possibilities, as well as probabilities; that some epidemiological studies are more reliable than others; that some medical literature is more reliable than other medical literature; or that no medical literature is authoritative in the sense that everyone accepts it as the truth. Your expert must explain that she has relied only on literature that is generally accepted as reliable by her peers and that the literature is not based on speculation or possibilities but only generally accepted principles.

Caution the expert not to respond to questions based on medical literature that may be quoted out of context. She can state that she prefers not to answer the question without reading the chapter or text to determine the author's premise in making the quoted statement. If a quoted statement from medical literature does accurately describe the principle involved, on the other hand, the witness should concede that it does.

In your deposition preparation, guide your expert into the appropriate areas of inquiry by asking the following questions:

- Could this result have been avoided by the exercise of reasonable care?
- What would you or any reasonably careful and prudent physician do to avoid this result?
- What diagnostic tests or other resources were available to help the physician avoid this bad result?
- What signs and symptoms were suggestive of the proper diagnosis?

Out-of-Town Experts

Prepare your expert for likely problems. For example, defense counsel may argue that your out-of-town expert has insufficient knowledge of local standards of practice and is not qualified to testify as an expert in your case.

Through pretrial discovery, you can learn everything necessary to enable an out-of-town physician to know and understand the standards of practice in a community. During depositions of the defendant-doctors, ask about their medical training, their education, their experiences, relevant medical techniques with which they are familiar, their employment in other communities and hospitals, their staff privileges at hospitals in the community, the adequacy of their training or experience for properly treating the plaintiff's condition, and whether they believe local hospital facilities are equipped to perform the procedures in question. Provide this information to your expert witness before her deposition.

During depositions of defendants and other health-care personnel, obtain a detailed description of the local medical community, including a list of specialists available for consultation. You can conduct a study of the local medical community by interviewing physicians and hospital administrators, discovering the local hospital's latest accreditation study results, and obtaining other information necessary to enable an expert witness to testify regarding the local standards.

Get full information about the local community hospital from the hospital administrator, nurses, and other personnel. Collect lists of (1) all references and medical literature the defendant-doctors use in their practice, (2) continuing medical education programs and medical meetings the defendant-doctors customarily attend, and (3) the names of others in attendance at those meetings. Use this information to help your out-of-town expert become familiar enough with the local community's standard of practice to testify with authority.

In deposition, defendant-doctors will often concede that the technique they used is practiced regionally or nationally, that they are familiar with the minimum national standard followed by the medical profession, and that the minimum standard for the procedure in question does not vary between communities. Accordingly, there is no locality rule or community standard, only a regional or national standard used in the community in question, and the court will permit your out-of-town expert, who is familiar with the national standard, to testify.

Occasionally a physician's negligence is so gross that any physician, whether local or not, would recognize the error. One example of this would be a doctor's forgetting to order X rays to confirm or rule out a fracture. In a situation like this, you can establish that any physician should be permitted to testify with respect to the universal minimum standard of practice. The court should allow a physician who is not in the same field of practice as the defendant to testify.

Experts from Different Specialties

When the defendant is a board-certified specialist, most jurisdictions apply a national standard of practice, and a board-certified physician from any community can testify against another physician of the same specialty. Often, you can use an expert whose field of practice differs from that of the defendant-doctor if the expert is familiar with the standards of practice in the defendant's field. You can establish that your expert has this knowledge by showing that she exchanges referrals with specialists in the defendant's field and is familiar with the applicable standards of practice for consultation purposes. You can also cite your expert's participation in joint medical meetings, continuing medical education programs, study, and research.

An expert whose field of medicine differs from the defendant's is subject to cross-examination that might weaken the expert's opinions and damage her credibility. For example, the expert from a different field ordinarily will not have the experience that the defendant-doctor has in the procedure in question. The expert's opinions will be based on secondhand information from referral sources, consultants, medical literature, and medical meetings; she will not have the "hands-on" experience that the defendant-doctor possesses.

Other Preparation

Prepare the expert to deal with causation. Interrogate her on all possible causes of damages other than the claimed negligence, and prepare her to explain why she eliminated other possible causes. Make sure she can justify her opinion on causation.

Familiarize the expert with other testimony. If you have retained more than one expert, each should know the opinions of the others before deposition. Nothing is more devastating than having experts for the same party render conflicting opinions.

After carefully preparing your expert, you may want to do a dry run, depending on the nature and extent of the expert's experience in being deposed. At the very least, you should consider cross-examining your expert on the critical issues to make sure she understands the legal definition of negligence. The expert must understand the concept of negligence to be able to avoid traps set by defense counsel on issues regarding the basis for her opinions on negligence and causation and her qualifications for rendering those opinions.

You should prepare your expert several days or perhaps a week before the deposition; give her additional time before the deposition to further study the medical records, depositions of defendant-doctors, medical literature, and other documents she will rely on in testimony.

HELPING WITNESSES DURING DEPOSITIONS

Be ready to help your client and witnesses during their depositions. Correct the opposing counsel or the witness if necessary, for example, if both are operating under a false assumption. Generally, no one in a deposition wants to be misled due to a mistake. Ask opposing counsel to clarify ambiguous questions and to correct himself if he misstates your client's testimony.

Volunteering the use of demonstrative evidence, exhibits, photographs, or other documents may help your client respond accurately to questions. Object to the form of a misleading, compound, or otherwise unfair question, and state specific reasons for the objection, thereby alerting your client to the factors that make the question improper.

Help the expert when necessary by clarifying confusing questions and helping her understand the nature of the inquiries. If opposing counsel seeks opinions that go beyond the scope of your expert's preparation, previously expressed opinions, or expertise, explain to opposing counsel that your expert is not being called for those areas of inquiry or has not yet had an adequate opportunity to focus on them. As with the client, always object to improper questions. If there are matters that need further clarification after opposing counsel is finished with questioning, question the witness yourself.[2]

CONCLUSION

To prepare witnesses properly for deposition, you must be thorough. Instruct witnesses to prepare for meeting with you by reviewing all relevant documents and information. The prepared witness will be able to respond properly to any question asked.

After the deposition, send the witness a copy of the deposition with the original signature page so the witness can make necessary

---

2 Appendix C.2 demonstrates how to protect an expert during a deposition.

corrections and use the information in preparing for trial. If you have prepared your witnesses well, they will have few corrections to make in their depositions and will be confident and well equipped to testify at trial.

CHAPTER SIX

INTERROGATORIES AND DEPOSITION OF DEFENDANT-DOCTOR

There are two basic approaches to obtaining information from the defendant-doctor by written interrogatories. Your plans for the doctor's deposition and your trial strategy for cross-examining the defendant will determine which approach you take.

In the first approach, you use interrogatories to the doctor only to obtain general information and to identify witnesses and documents, and you reserve specific questions about the medical issues and your theory of the case for deposition. When you use the first approach, you discover the doctor's thinking process, theory of the case, and defenses during deposition and not by written interrogatories. You then use this information to prepare an effective cross-examination for trial, hoping to deliver the knockout blow in the courtroom.

In the second approach, you use interrogatories to the doctor to ask detailed questions concerning the medical issues and defenses.[1] With this approach, you seek to use the information obtained through interrogatories to deliver the knockout blow before trial, in cross-examination at the deposition.

To decide which approach to use, you must first decide whether to cross-examine the defendant-doctor on your theory of the case at deposition or to save it for trial. A devastating cross-examination at deposition may result in a favorable settlement before trial, but if settlement negotiations fail, the doctor is better prepared at trial to deal with your cross-examination on the medical issues. Therefore, the questions you ask at deposition and the questions you reserve for trial

---

1 See Appendix B.1 for sample interrogatories to individual doctors.

are a matter of individual preference and judgment. They may vary from case to case.

An advantage of detailed interrogatories is that they often provide ammunition for use in the deposition. A disadvantage is that they alert the doctor to your theory of the case before deposition and prepare the doctor for cross-examination. Another disadvantage is that your interrogatory questions may reveal your theory of the case and cross-examination plans in advance of the deposition. This eliminates the element of surprise at deposition and permits the doctor to be well prepared. Further, the doctor's lawyers may screen and refine the doctor's interrogatory responses so that you do not obtain the desired information.

Many lawyers therefore prefer to use general rather than detailed interrogatory questions and ask the more specific and detailed questions at deposition. This course of action leaves them with the option of effectively cross-examining either during the deposition or at trial.

DRAFTING INTERROGATORY QUESTIONS

You should serve interrogatories on the defendant as soon as the rules of your jurisdiction or court permit. If your jurisdiction limits the number of interrogatories, draft them carefully, using a series of general questions to elicit as much information as possible. For example, the following questions would be appropriate in an obstetrical negligence case:

- Describe your educational background, experience, and training as it relates to your profession or, if more convenient, attach your curriculum vitae or resume.
- Set forth verbatim all chart entries in your office records related to the care and treatment of the plaintiff, and for each entry explain the history you obtained, the examination you performed and its results, and the treatment you rendered.
- Set forth the date, time, place, and content of each conversation you had with the plaintiff before performing surgery on August 1, 1991.
- Attached as Exhibit 1 are the fetal monitor strips. Using the consecutive numbers located on the bottom of those strips, describe in detail your interpretation of each segment of the strips and comment specifically on whether the strips evidence any abnormalities, a reduction or loss in beat-to-beat variability, late or variable decelerations, tachycardia or bradycardia, or evidence of possible fetal stress or distress.
- Attached as Exhibit 2 is your operative report of August 1, 1991. Please describe in detail, using lay language when possible, what you did in the surgical procedure involved, what portion of the procedure

you performed and what portion was performed by others, and whether you encountered any problems during the procedure.

- Attached as Exhibit 3 are the hospital records for the August 1991 hospitalization. Pages have been consecutively numbered in the lower right-hand corner. Please identify, by page number, all charts and records that you authored. If any are in your handwriting, please translate them verbatim.

In jurisdictions that limit the number of interrogatories, defense counsel often will agree to respond to a more extensive set of well-drafted interrogatories because, unlike a deposition, interrogatories give the defendant-doctor time to analyze the records or diagnostic testing. When asked at deposition, doctors will frequently analyze fetal monitor strips, MRIs, X rays, or complicated diagnostic tests. They will also, however, qualify their opinions, citing the need for additional research or documents, and reserving the right to elaborate at trial. Interrogatories commit the defendant to firm opinions.

If you prefer general interrogatories, you may use form interrogatories, with slight modifications, in nearly every case. General interrogatories can be quickly drafted and served on the defendant. However, handcrafted interrogatories[2] require special attention. In drafting special handcrafted interrogatories, review your expert witness reports, medical research, summaries of records, and all other available information. During your preparation of interrogatories, as you review the defendant's office records, the hospital records, and the diagnostic test results, determine whether to seek clarification of these records by interrogatory or at deposition. For example, it may not be clear from the records whether the defendant-doctor was informed of medical history, diagnostic test results, or other information that would have resulted in the correct diagnosis. You may want to find out before the deposition whether the doctor received the information that would have resulted in the correct diagnosis. Draft interrogatories calling the doctor's attention to these types of information, and ask him when and how he first learned of each.

Hospital and medical records provide, at best, only a summary or skeleton of what actually transpired. Much of the rest of the story will emerge from answers to interrogatories. To complete the story, direct the doctor's attention to particular entries in the records, and then ask questions about these entries.[3]

---

2 See Appendix B (B.1 and B.2).

3 See Appendix B.1.

Don't look only for entries in the records that support your theory of the case; look for entries that may have been changed to provide the doctor with a defense, and try to identify the person who changed the entries. Similarly, look for signs of missing or destroyed records, and determine whether these documents could have supported your theory of the case. For example, the hospital records may refer to a diagnostic test, but the test results are missing. Draft interrogatories asking if the defendant remembers the missing records and when, how, and why they were lost or destroyed.[4]

Check the dates on which documents were typed or dictated. A doctor's defense may rely on a report that a consulting physician dictated before the doctor negligently performed surgery but that was not typed and placed in the medical records until after surgery. If, under your theory of the case, the surgeon would not have operated if he had been aware of the report, ask in your interrogatories whether the consultant gave the doctor an oral report before surgery and, if there was no oral report, why the surgeon operated before obtaining the results of the consultation.

Furthermore, in a case against a doctor and hospital, the delayed dictation of a report may have violated hospital rules. If an operative report was dictated days after the surgery instead of within 24 hours as required by hospital protocol, the lateness of the report might explain why nurses and staff physicians did not anticipate and treat postoperative complications promptly. Similarly, the dictation and typing dates on laboratory reports, radiology reports, and other diagnostic testing may show a delay in providing test results to a treating physician, causing misdiagnosis or improper treatment. Again, use interrogatories to ask about these matters.

In drafting interrogatories seeking background and general information as well as case-specific information, inquire into the following areas, where appropriate:

- the defendant's background, including education, experience and training in his profession, employment history, and medical articles he has authored;
- the defendant's staff privileges at hospitals and whether his application for staff privileges has ever been denied;
- lawsuits or claims filed against the defendant and whether the defendant has previously been deposed or given testimony in medical/legal matters;

---

4 See Appendix B (B.1 and B.2) for examples.

- the identity of the authors of all relevant records;[5]
- the medical history of the plaintiff obtained by the defendant;
- the physical examinations of the plaintiff and the findings on each examination;
- any diagnosis made;
- any treatment rendered;
- specific entries in charts and hospital records;
- information the defendant knew from the charts and records;
- information about the defendant's academic knowledge of the medical issues—for example, if a doctor failed to diagnose a ruptured appendix, ask him to itemize and describe the classic signs and symptoms of a ruptured appendix;
- causation—ask the doctor to list all possible causes of the plaintiff's condition, which of those he ruled out, and what he determined the most probable cause to be; you may also ask him what medical history, diagnostic testing, or other information he used in ruling out possible causes and in arriving at his opinion of the most probable cause;
- misdiagnosis—ask what the doctor relied on in arriving at the misdiagnosis, and ask why the proper diagnosis was not made;
- failure to obtain an informed consent—ask what information the doctor gave the plaintiff about treatment risks in obtaining the plaintiff's consent, and also ask what information he provided concerning alternative treatments and the nature of the procedure to be performed;
- negligent performance of a procedure—ask why the procedure was unsuccessful and, in retrospect, what could have made the procedure successful;
- failure to make a timely diagnosis—ask the doctor why there was a delay in diagnosis and whether the diagnosis could have been made earlier;
- the hospital—ask about the hospital's number of beds, its class or type for accreditation standards, and its staffing policies and any other internal policies or rules that could affect the case;[6]
- interpretation of diagnostic test results—ask specific questions about the equipment used for tests: ask the doctor to identify the equipment's manufacturer, date of purchase, operating instructions, and other information that could be useful in either confirming or

---

5 See Appendix B (B.1 and B.2).

6 See Appendix B.2.

crediting the diagnostic test results; also determine whether more advanced or appropriate equipment was available but not used; and

- the doctor's relationship to other health-care personnel involved in the care and treatment rendered—this information can be useful to you, and later to the jury, in judging the credibility of others' testimony and in weighing the relative fault of multiple defendants.

In summary, use your interrogatories to discover the defendant's defenses and theory of the case. What you discover will determine your approach to deposition and whether you will go for knockout blows at the deposition or later at trial. Review interrogatory answers with your consulting experts to identify the weaknesses and inconsistencies in the defendant's position. Gather medical literature with which to cross-examine the defendant on his defenses at deposition or trial.

DEPOSING THE DEFENDANT

Some lawyers would not depose a doctor who provides thorough and detailed answers to interrogatories.[7] Others might depose the doctor briefly to see how he reacts to questions and to decide how to cross-examine him at trial. Still others might cross-examine the doctor thoroughly in deposition, using interrogatory answers and other information to score points that they normally would reserve for trial. Lawyers generally use this last approach for settlement purposes; if the case does not settle, however, this approach better prepares the doctor for the cross-examination at trial.

General Points to Raise

At the deposition, begin by asking the defendant-doctor what documents and other resources he used in preparing for his deposition. Has he reviewed hospital records, clinical records, X rays, and other medical records? Did he bring them with him? Ask if he made notes on the records as he reviewed them. If so, mark the records with his notes on them as an exhibit and question him about the notes.

Ask him if he made other notes or written memoranda of any kind while reviewing the hospital charts and medical records, and ask if he reviewed these notes in preparing for his deposition. If so, ask for a copy of the notes, and mark it as an exhibit. Ask him to identify

---

7 See Appendix B.1 for an example.

or provide you with copies of all articles, papers, books, treatises, or journals he reviewed before the deposition. Mark these as exhibits, and ask the court reporter to make sure your copy of the deposition includes them.

Ask the defendant questions concerning the following miscellaneous topics, when appropriate:

- Do you believe that the negligence of a physician, nurse, or other health-care provider who is not named as a defendant in this lawsuit may have contributed to the patient's injuries? If so, please identify the person who contributed to the injuries, and state the reasons for your belief that this person contributed to them.
- Are you aware of any special investigation, incident report, or other inquiry that hospital staff made about this patient that is not in the hospital records?
- Are you aware of any personal notes or diary entries authored by a nurse or doctor involved in the care and treatment of this patient and not found in the hospital records?
- Has defense counsel previously represented you in medical negligence litigation? If so, please give the dates of the representation, the names of the parties to the litigation, the names of other lawyers involved in each case, a description of each case and its outcome, and copies of any depositions taken.

Following the deposition, carefully study all medical literature that the defendant reviewed to determine whether the literature contains information that you can use to cross-examine him at trial. If you ask him about medical literature at trial that he has admitted to using to prepare for his deposition, he will find it difficult to assert that the literature is not reliable or authoritative.

Ask the deponent if he is aware of any statistical study, article, paper, research document, textbook, or treatise containing information that he considers reliable concerning the general subject of the case. Ask whether he has any books on the subject of the case and whether he has read or examined any of these for the case.

Ask the defendant to clarify or explain any ambiguous interrogatory answers or to provide additional information regarding the interrogatory answers.

Get the defendant's curriculum vitae if you do not already have it. Ask the defendant the name of the hospital in which he did his residency and the name of the chief of the residency program. Also ask him which diagnostic equipment and testing methods used in this case were being used at the time of his residency.

Inquire about the defendant's medical licenses and hospital privileges. If there have been any hearings or disciplinary actions regarding the defendant's professional behavior, review them in detail.

Go over any changes you found in medical records that you obtained in discovery. Find out whether the defendant altered the records or knows who did and whether he knows why the records were altered.

Review the defendant's opinions about the case and the cause of injury. Start with the first entry in the plaintiff's medical records, and review the plaintiff's care from before her injury to the present. Ask the defendant to describe all examinations, tests, X rays, and their results in detail.

Review the defendant's diagnosis and treatment. Ask the following questions regarding the initial and the final diagnoses:

- Why and on what basis did you make your diagnosis?
- Did you consult others about your diagnosis and treatment and, if so, what were the opinions of those you consulted?
- Can you identify all tests or other studies that support your diagnosis?

Next, review the patient's treatment plan, and ask the doctor the following questions:

- Why did you make this treatment plan?
- Did you consult others about the patient's treatment plan and, if you did, what were the opinions of those you consulted?
- Can you identify all tests or other studies that support your treatment plan?
- Did you consider alternative treatment plans and, if you did, please explain the alternative plans and why you rejected them.

If there is an issue regarding the plaintiff's life expectancy, ask the defendant if he has an opinion based on reasonable medical certainty or probability about the plaintiff's life expectancy. If he has an opinion, ask him to state it and to identify all articles, books, papers, or other materials on which he bases his opinion. Mark these materials as exhibits.

Likewise, ask the defendant if he has an opinion about the plaintiff's prognosis based on reasonable medical certainty or probability. If he does, ask him to state his opinion and to identify all articles, books, papers, or other materials on which he bases his opinion. Mark these materials as exhibits. Ask if he believes that additional diagnostic testing or other studies could be used to form an opinion about the plaintiff's prognosis. If so, ask him to describe such testing or studies and how they would help him formulate a prognosis.

Ask the doctor when he last examined the plaintiff, and ask for the results of that examination.

To determine the defendant's theory of the case and the defenses he will raise to each allegation of negligence, ask him the following questions:

- What is your opinion about, and explanation of, each claim of negligence made by the plaintiff?
- What other explanations for the plaintiff's condition did you consider and reject or not consider at all, though they were possibilities? Please fully describe your reasons for rejecting these possibilities.
- Do you believe that there was a failure, by you or anyone else, to exercise "reasonable prudence" in this case?
- Are you aware of approaches different from yours that other competent physicians use under circumstances similar to those in this case?
- Have you discussed this case or your findings, opinions, or conclusions with any other physicians? If you have, please state fully the reasons for and the circumstances of these discussions.
- Are you aware of any other physicians who may have reviewed this case? If you are, please give their names and state the reasons for, and the circumstances of, their review. (Use the information elicited by these questions to determine whether any reviews conducted are discoverable, based on the law in your jurisdiction, or whether they are subject to a statutory privilege. If they are not privileged, obtain the results of the review.)

Questions in a Misdiagnosis Case

In a misdiagnosis case, ask questions that balance the signs and symptoms that favor the correct diagnosis against the signs and symptoms that favor the incorrect diagnosis. Make a list of the classic signs and symptoms contained in the hospital and medical records that support the correct diagnosis and use this list to question the doctor. He will concede either that he did consider the correct diagnosis or that he did not. If he did consider the correct diagnosis, he will concede either that he ruled it out, that he failed to confirm it or rule it out, or that he negligently misdiagnosed it.

If the doctor concedes that he did not consider the correct diagnosis, ask him to list the signs or symptoms present in the plaintiff and compare them with the classic signs and symptoms of the correct diagnosis that he learned in medical school. Go through the record, and establish that the plaintiff had the classic signs and symptoms of the condition that the doctor misdiagnosed.

Ask the following questions to clarify that there was ample evidence to support the correct diagnosis and little information or evidence to support the incorrect diagnosis that the doctor made, leading to the inescapable conclusion that the doctor was negligent:

- What signs or symptoms are present in the record or were present clinically that support the misdiagnosis? What diagnostic test results support the misdiagnosis?
- What would a reasonably careful and prudent physician look for in attempting to confirm or rule out the correct diagnosis?
- What diagnostic tests were available to confirm or rule out the correct diagnosis?
- What aspects of the plaintiff's medical history are important to confirm or to rule out the correct diagnosis?

In a misdiagnosis case, the defendant-doctor will rarely concede that his conduct fell below the accepted standards of practice or that he was negligent. He will know before the deposition that the accepted standard of practice is the legal test by which his conduct will be judged. The doctor may indirectly concede his negligence, however, when you use the approach of establishing that the plaintiff had all the symptoms of the correct diagnosis that the doctor did not make rather than the symptoms of the incorrect diagnosis that the doctor did make.

For example, if the doctor misdiagnosed septicemia and septic shock as the flu, thereby failing to treat the septic shock from which the patient died, make a list of all signs, symptoms, and diagnostic test results found in the office charts and emergency room hospital records that support the diagnosis of septicemia. During the deposition, ask the doctor to list all the classic signs and symptoms of septicemia. Then direct him to the medical records, and establish that this patient had all those signs and symptoms.

Ask the doctor if a reasonably careful and prudent physician would consider a diagnosis of septicemia when presented with all these signs, symptoms, and diagnostic test results. Ask if he would expect a reasonably careful and prudent physician, when confronted with the signs and symptoms, to do diagnostic testing to confirm or rule out septicemia. Establish that he did not consider that diagnosis and did not do additional testing to confirm or rule out that diagnosis.

You will be better able to recognize the areas into which you should inquire in deposition in a misdiagnosis case if you know the common reasons for misdiagnosis:

- The initial diagnosis was not reevaluated but was blindly followed by residents, emergency room personnel, the doctor himself, and others.
- Those making the diagnosis were not aware of all the facts; for example, the doctor did not read the nurses' notes.
- Information was not communicated at a shift change.
- Diagnostic test results were not available or were misinterpreted.
- Information was not recorded.
- The appropriate diagnostic tests were not ordered.
- The doctor failed to consult a specialist.
- The doctor failed to get a complete history.
- The doctor failed to do a thorough clinical examination.
- Authority was improperly delegated by the doctor to medical technicians or nurses, or by a registered nurse to a licensed practical nurse.
- The doctor was incompetent or negligent.
- The doctor disliked the patient but had to treat her.

Present Memory vs. Custom and Habit

When the defendant interprets medical records and describes events not contained in those records, you must determine if he has a present memory of those events, if he is speculating on what might have occurred, or if he is basing his testimony on his usual custom and habit.

If the defendant-doctor claims to have a present memory of the details of a surgical procedure or a conversation with the patient that is not recorded, a jury may discount his testimony if there is no apparent reason for his having a vivid recollection of such matters. Challenge his "present memory" by asking him how many patients he saw on the day that he remembers a particular event or how many surgical procedures he performed that month.

Remember that testimony based on custom and habit is admissible with a proper foundation. When this testimony has a proper foundation, the testimony is difficult for the plaintiff to overcome. One method of minimizing custom and habit testimony is to show that there is no standard custom and habit. Do this by obtaining the following concessions from the doctor:

> Dr. Smith, would you agree that the practice of medicine is an art and not a science? As such, every surgical procedure is subjective and unique because no two conditions and no two patients are pre-

cisely alike or identical; is that correct? For example, the conditions you find in performing surgery following a ruptured appendix will be somewhat different in each patient, depending on what you find when you do the exploratory; is that correct?

Although you might follow a general protocol or procedure in performing the surgery, the amount of material you remove and the damage you repair will vary from patient to patient; is that correct? Accordingly, doctor, you cannot describe the details of a specific surgical procedure based on custom and habit because what you do in each procedure will depend on the circumstances and will vary from patient to patient; is that correct?

Furthermore, Dr. Smith, in later dictating your summary of the surgical procedure, you generally use the same format for similar procedures and only dictate a general summary as you did in this case; is that correct? So, Dr. Smith, your custom and habit do not assist us in determining precisely what went wrong in this procedure, do they?

Questions about the Defendant's Experts

If you have the names of the defendant's expert witnesses when you take the defendant-doctor's deposition, explore the doctor's relationship with each expert. Determine whether the defendant knows any of the experts and whether he has reviewed any reports or letters from any of them about this case. If he knows any of the experts, determine whether he had any input in the selection of the expert he knows and determine why that expert was selected. Did he suggest anyone to defense counsel as a possible expert and, if so, what is his relationship to the person he suggested? For example, is the person a friend, a former partner, or a recipient of referrals or consultations? You may be able to obtain information that you can use to attack the credibility of the expert witness.

Ask the defendant what information he provided to the expert and whether the expert agreed to be a witness before receiving medical charts and records. If the defendant reviewed the reports authored by any of the experts, ask whether the reports were redrafted as a result of his suggestions. Ask why he reviewed the reports and whether he has made any attempt to conform his testimony and recollections to the material in the reports or to the experts' opinions.

Ask the defendant-doctor if anyone refused to be an expert witness in his case. If the defendant did not contact other physicians to request their assistance as experts, ask whom he considers highly qualified to be an expert in the case and whether, to his knowledge, any of the people he named as highly qualified have been consulted by anyone on his behalf concerning the medical-legal issues in this case.

CONCLUSION

The approach that you use in drafting interrogatories and in taking depositions may vary from case to case. For example, you may know in advance of discovery that the defendant-doctor refuses to give consent to settlement and insists on a trial. Under those circumstances, wait until trial to disclose your theory of the case, theme, ammunition for cross-examination, and knowledge of the weaknesses in the doctor's defense. On the other hand, if your client has decided not to face trial and to accept the defendant's top settlement offer, no matter what the amount, you will want to conduct discovery using all your ammunition to discredit the defendant and his theory of the case in order to achieve the maximum pretrial settlement.

Preparation and the careful and selective use of questions in interrogatories and depositions will determine whether you are successful in settlement negotiations or at trial. This is a critical part of the discovery and trial process and should be treated as such. When properly conducted, the discovery of the defendant-doctor allows you to use all your trial skills before trial. The results can make the time-consuming preparation well worthwhile.

CHAPTER SEVEN

PLANNING THE TRIAL: THEORY, WITNESSES, AND TRIAL STRATEGY

To be successful at trial, you must develop a case theory that the evidence supports and that the jury is likely to accept. Your case theory also must be supported by the law that is the least vulnerable to attack by the defense.

Identifying the defendant's case theory, defenses, and trial strategy, as well as the weaknesses in the defendant's position will help you to define your own theme and strategy. You can identify your opponent's strengths and weaknesses by mentally preparing the defendant's case. Putting yourself in the defendant's position will also help you detect weaknesses in your own case. Develop a trial strategy that will dramatize the weaknesses in the defendant's theory while highlighting the strengths of your theory. Your strategy should resolve or minimize weaknesses in your theory and prevent defense counsel from minimizing defense weaknesses.

DEVELOPING A CASE THEORY

The preparation and trial of a lawsuit is like a fascinating chess game, and the case is often won by the lawyer who asks and answers the question, "How many ways could I lose?"

The events that precipitate a lawsuit cannot be reconstructed with 100 percent accuracy; often you will have many competing explanations of what occurred. Work with the facts and the evidence to determine what probably occurred. Develop your theory during investigation, discovery, and trial preparation, and test the theory by conceiving and preparing a defense for every attack that can be made against it. Further test your theory with a healthy dose of common sense.

Consider using mock juries, focus groups, or other sources of feedback to identify problems and to suggest a theme. For example, you may present a summary of your evidence and the defense's evidence to members of the public who fit the jury profile you expect at trial. This presentation can be simple and inexpensive or elaborate and costly. To summarize the evidence that each witness will present at trial, you could make an inexpensive videotape presentation of the case using your office staff as witnesses. A focus group sitting as "jurors" could be selected to watch the videotape and then complete a questionnaire. The questionnaire should focus the group's attention on questions the jury will have to answer later, such as

- Was the doctor negligent? If so, what did she do or fail to do that was negligent?
- Did the doctor's negligence cause (describe the bad result here)? If not, what do you believe was the cause of (describe the bad result here)?
- Do you believe that the patient was at fault?
- Would you find in favor of the patient and against the doctor? If not, please explain why not.
- What amount of damages would you assess if you did find in favor of the patient and against the doctor? (Please answer this question even if you believe the doctor was not at fault.)

Each member of the focus group should complete the questionnaire after viewing the videotape but before the group discusses any of the issues of the case. After the questionnaire has been completed, videotape each member discussing his or her thoughts on the issues more fully. A focus group will often identify weaknesses in your theory of the case quickly, giving you the opportunity to overcome them before trial. The group also may suggest a theme for your case that you had not considered.

Conducting a mock trial is a more elaborate means of getting feedback about how a jury may respond to your case. It consists of a "mini-trial" before a jury with opening statements, the introduction of evidence, instructions, summation, and videotaped jury deliberations. However, a focus group can provide as much (if not more) helpful information as a mock trial at much less expense.

If you choose not to use a focus group or a mock trial to try out your case, you may obtain information that will help you identify problems and suggest a theme by presenting a summary of your case to a small group of neighbors and friends.

Dramatize your theory with a theme that runs throughout the case, such as the anesthesiologist who wasn't there, the uncaring caregiver, the greedy doctor, the missing fetal monitor strips, or the suffocated baby. Your theme should remind jurors of your overall theory of the case; it should be simple and should provoke an image.

DEVELOPING A TRIAL STRATEGY

You must be ready for the worst in any trial. Master each segment of the trial as a single entity, but do not prepare any portion of the trial in isolation. Consider each segment of the trial as a tool to disarm the defense and to resolve trial problems.[1] You may divide the trial process into the following segments:

- motions in limine on evidentiary matters;
- voir dire and jury selection;
- opening statement;
- selection and order of witnesses;
- direct, cross, and redirect examination of lay and expert witnesses;
- demonstrative evidence and exhibits;
- the court's instructions to the jury on the law; and
- summation.

Ask yourself how you can use each segment of the trial to resolve or minimize a problem in your case. You may discover that you can solve a problem in one segment of the trial, or you may need several segments.

Then develop your trial strategy. Ask yourself these questions:

- How can you best use each segment of the trial to explain your theory of the case, to minimize the weaknesses and problems in your case, and to dramatize the weaknesses in the defendant's theory and defenses?
- What prejudicial evidence can you eliminate by a motion in limine? Do you really want to preclude prejudicial evidence or can you use it to your advantage?
- How will the court rule on critical evidentiary matters?
- What types of jurors will identify with your theory of the case, and what types will identify with the defendant's theory and defenses?

---

1 See Chapter Twelve, "Applying Principles to Special Problems," for illustrations of how each segment of the trial can be used to resolve trial problems.

- Is your opening statement (theory of the case) reasonable and believable? Does the evidence support it? Is the jury more likely to believe this version of events than the defense's version?
- How can you enhance your own credibility as a trial lawyer in presenting this case to a jury?
- Who are your best witnesses on liability, causation, and damages? Which of your witnesses will the jury believe and accept as credible?
- In what order should you call your witnesses? What are the advantages and disadvantages of placing the witnesses in any particular order?
- In selecting witnesses and determining their order, how can you best present and sell your theory of the case to the jury?
- What aspects of each witness's testimony are potentially harmful to your case? How is each witness vulnerable to cross-examination? How can you eliminate or minimize the negative aspects of each witness's testimony?
- How can you enhance your witnesses' credibility? How can your witnesses bolster each other's credibility?
- Which of the defendant's witnesses will the jury believe and accept as credible? Can you blend their testimony with your theory of the case? If not, how can you best attack their credibility?
- Why is opposing counsel calling each witness?
- Why is opposing counsel introducing each exhibit listed?
- What is your strategy on objections during trial?
- How can you best use exhibits or demonstrative evidence to highlight your theory of the case and to dramatize the weaknesses in the defendant's theory and defenses?
- How can you simplify your case? Which witnesses and exhibits are absolutely necessary?
- How will the court rule on jury instructions, particularly instructions on the plaintiff's theory of the case, affirmative defenses, and evidence offered for limited purposes?
- What public policy arguments will persuade the jury to enforce the law that supports liability? What public policy arguments will minimize the defenses raised?
- What mental images and analogies will motivate the jury and explain your theory of the case?
- How can you best use analogies and visual images to dramatize the weaknesses in the defendant's theory and defenses?

- How can you use summation to develop your theory of the case further in a persuasive and intriguing manner, offering new insight into the evidence that the jurors may have overlooked?
- How can you best use the law in summation to persuade the jurors that the facts, when applied to the law, mandate a verdict for the plaintiff?

Overcoming the Weaknesses in Your Case

To develop a strategy to minimize or overcome weaknesses in your case, you must first identify the weaknesses. Examples of problems that may complicate your case include the following:

- The plaintiff's theory of the case may be subject to attack if the theory is based largely on subjective medical symptoms.
- Often a number of health-care professionals missed the correct diagnosis; this supports the defendant's theory that there was no negligence and that your client's condition was difficult to diagnose.
- The plaintiff may have a preexisting condition that made a proper diagnosis or treatment very difficult.
- A client may exaggerate or appear to exaggerate his injuries.
- The defendant may be likable, credible, and a well-known, reputable physician. If so, you may have difficulty getting expert witnesses to testify against the defendant, and the jury will give great weight to the defendant's testimony.
- The jury may perceive the plaintiff's injuries to be the aggravation of preexisting conditions for which the defendant is not responsible.
- Your expert witness may be perceived as a "hired gun" from out of state and may lack credibility with the jury.
- Physicians who treated the plaintiff may know and want to help the defendant-doctor.
- The jury may have been influenced by media coverage favorable to the medical profession and by paid advertisements about the "insurance crisis."
- The defendant may introduce evidence that medical intervention may not have made a difference in the plaintiff's outcome.
- The facts may support causation only remotely.
- Even if you establish negligence, the defense may present evidence that the negligence did not cause additional injury.
- The plaintiff may have signed a consent form.
- The plaintiff's medical damages may seem nominal or moderate to the jury.
- There may be evidence of comparative fault.

- The defendant may practice in a subspecialty composed of very few physicians nationwide who are familiar with the procedure involved, making it extremely difficult to obtain expert testimony on negligence. Examples of such subspecialties and procedures include a neuroradiologist using an intravenous catheter for a glue embolization procedure, or a urologist doing a penile implant.

Once you have identified the weaknesses or problems in your case, you must carefully plan to minimize or overcome these problems during trial.[2]

SELECTING WITNESSES

Select your witnesses carefully. Call only those witnesses necessary to establish the important elements of your theory. If several witnesses are available to make the same point, choose only the most helpful and persuasive one. Ask yourself if one witness establishes more of your theory of the case than another. Also ask which witnesses have information that might be helpful to the defense if elicited on cross-examination. Which witness will create the best impression and be the most credible? Which witness is the most cooperative, friendly, and trustworthy?

You may want to use a witness whose testimony favors the defendant to establish a specific point that only this witness can make. The defense will probably call this witness, enabling you to both question the witness on the point you wish to make and cross-examine the witness on the rest of the testimony favoring the defense. If the point you wish the witness to make is critical to your case, you must decide whether the defense will in fact call the witness if you do not.

Using more than one witness to establish the same point can be dangerous, unless you need to have the point corroborated. Witnesses may give inconsistent testimony and impeach one another, or repetition may destroy the momentum of your case and bore the jury.

Selecting witnesses is a difficult tactical aspect of trial preparation. Witness 1 may be able to establish three evidentiary points (A, B, and C) convincingly but also may have information that is helpful to the defense. Witness 2 may be able to establish evidentiary point A; witness 3, point B; and witness 4, point C. Though none of these witnesses has information helpful to the defense, none is as credible and trustworthy as witness 1. Whom should you call to testify? Only you can make this judgment, and it differs for every case.

---

2 See Chapter Twelve, "Applying Principles to Special Problems," for an example.

Order of Witnesses

Consider the overall structure of the trial in determining the order of your witnesses. As you establish an order of witnesses for the trial as a whole as well as for each day, remember that jurors generally remember emotional material longer than they do factual material. You can use emotional evidence early in the trial with some confidence that jurors will remember it two or three weeks later in the jury room. However, the impact of this emotional evidence will dissipate to some extent during that time, and you may want to introduce dramatic emotional evidence, such as a day-in-the-life film, closer to jury deliberation. Save important factual material for later in the trial; jurors have a shorter memory for facts.

Should you start the trial with evidence of liability or evidence related to injuries and damages? Again, you will find that experienced lawyers have differing opinions. However, if you have evidence of aggravated conduct by the defendant, such as in the case of an intoxicated doctor who removes the wrong body part, you should introduce this evidence first because it will make the jury more receptive to the evidence on damages later. If you introduce the evidence on damages first, the jurors may listen to it with some skepticism because they have not yet heard about the cause of the damages. Similarly, when causation is disputed, introducing evidence of aggravated conduct first will make the jury more receptive to the plaintiff's theory of causation. On the other hand, when liability is borderline and the jury could go either way on that issue, it is sometimes helpful to introduce evidence of the catastrophic injuries caused by the doctor's negligence first. The emotional impact of the injuries may make the jury more receptive to the plaintiff's theory of the case.

Organize your case to begin and end with an "impact" witness, and begin and end each day with an impact witness. Do not dilute the effectiveness of impact witnesses by calling two back to back; camouflage the testimony of a necessary but weak witness by placing that witness between two good witnesses. The order of your witnesses should emphasize the weaknesses and inconsistencies of the defendant's testimony. Begin the testimony of each witness with the key points that that witness will make, and end on a dramatic note.

Defendant-Doctor as a Witness

You may want to call the defendant as an adverse witness to impeach her or other witnesses dramatically with her deposition or with other evidence. The impeachment is often ineffective if several days or even weeks separate it from the defendant's testimony.

If you have impeachment evidence to be used against the defendant-physician, consider calling her first or early in your case, before offering impeachment testimony. Some of the reasons to call the doctor to the stand early include the following:

- If you call the doctor early and then immediately impeach her with her deposition, with other witnesses, or with other evidence, the jury is more likely to grasp the significance of the impeachment than if it comes long after the testimony. The impeachment evidence will be dramatized by the contrast between the doctor's testimony and the evidence used to impeach. Do not put on impeachment testimony before the doctor's testimony; if you do, the jurors may not understand the impeachment testimony's relevance, and its impact will be lost.
- By calling the doctor early, you avoid giving her an opportunity to perfect her explanations or excuses and to prepare for her cross-examination. If you do not call the doctor as a witness in your case, or do not call her early, she will be better able to distinguish and minimize your expert's testimony or find loopholes in your theories of liability.
- Doctors usually do not like being cross-examined and may create a bad first impression with the jury.
- Your best chance to show that the doctor is dishonest, incompetent, or uncaring is on cross-examination. It is difficult to bring this out if the doctor first takes the stand on direct examination, and defense counsel goes to elaborate means to humanize the doctor and to show that she is a warm and caring person.

If you do call the defendant as an adverse witness, be careful that you and your client remain the underdogs. Let the jury know that the plaintiff is not on equal footing with the defendant. Your client did not have equal access to hospital records and diagnostic testing when the negligence occurred and does not have equal knowledge of the medicine and the facts and circumstances surrounding the defendant's negligence.

Do not call the defendant until and unless the jury has been conditioned to receive favorably the "treatment" that you intend to render during the examination. If your timing is off, jurors will view a devastating examination as premature or as overkill and may feel sympathy for the defendant and animosity toward you. Jurors expect a critical cross-examination following a defendant's lengthy self-serving direct examination, but a cross-examination that prevents the defendant from first telling her story may offend them.

Therefore, if you do call the doctor as your first witness, prepare the jurors during voir dire by explaining that you have the right to call the doctor for this purpose, just as the defense may call your client for cross-examination. Explain that the law permits you to do this, and ask the jurors if your calling the doctor as your first witness would trouble them.

Identify facts and circumstances in your case that you can use in the examination to show that the doctor is not a warm and caring person. For example, show that the doctor did not respond to telephone calls in a timely fashion or did not meet your client at the hospital as promised. Tell the jury that the doctor failed to go to the hospital two or three hours after delivery to see how the baby was doing, and after attending to the birth of this brain-injured baby the doctor did not visit the mother to help her through her grief, even though the doctor knew the baby was flaccid at birth and was in trouble. Explain that when the mother went in for her six-week checkup, the doctor failed to ask how the baby was doing.

Beware of a danger in calling the defendant-doctor: defense counsel may conduct a lengthy, self-serving cross-examination of the defendant or elicit lengthy defense testimony following your direct examination, breaking the momentum of your case. On the other hand, you may be able to examine the defendant-doctor so dramatically and effectively during your case that defense counsel will have few or no questions and will probably not call the defendant later in the trial for fear of a repeat performance of your examination. The reason that defense counsel asks few or no questions of the defendant-doctor under these circumstances is to prevent you from again effectively questioning the doctor on redirect examination.If you intend to call the defendant as an adverse witness, but you want to discourage defense counsel from conducting a self-serving cross-examination of the defendant, you should call your best expert on liability and causation as your first witness so that the expert can describe all the treatment and medical care the defendant rendered. Have your expert reconstruct the defendant's care and treatment using hospital records, diagnostic test results, the defendant's office charts, and all other information available. Often the defendant's negligence will become clear during the expert's description of the care and treatment rendered—before any opinions are elicited. You can then ask the witness to give opinions on standards of care and causation and to explain the bases for those opinions.

When your expert witness reconstructs for the jury the care rendered and explains the medical history using models, diagrams, and other demonstrative evidence, the jury will see that the witness is truly an expert. The witness will have the opportunity to teach as well as to explain what happened. This takes the thunder out of the defendant's testimony, and if the defendant later attempts to cover the same ground to enhance her own credibility, the jury will be bored with the repetition.

This approach is particularly helpful when the plaintiff's treating physicians cannot be called as witnesses for the plaintiff because they are uncooperative, because they are friends of the defendant, or because they are apt to give information or opinions on cross-examination that will help the defendant. On the other hand, if the treating physicians' testimony will be neutral and will not damage the plaintiff's case, you can call the treating physicians as witnesses after your expert witness.

You may sometimes want to call hospital nurses as witnesses before calling the defendant-doctor. This is particularly helpful when the nurses have a level of experience, training, or knowledge that the doctor lacked or claims to have lacked at the time of her negligent act. For example, in a misdiagnosis case, hospital nurses who correctly identified the cause of the patient's condition may be called as witnesses when the doctor now claims that there was inadequate information to make a correct diagnosis of the condition. Likewise, a doctor's testimony that she could not detect symptoms that were easily detected by nurses dramatically supports the plaintiff's expert testimony that the doctor was negligent. Whenever nurses, who are perceived by jurors as having less experience, training, and education than a doctor, perform at a higher level than the doctor, the defendant-doctor's negligence is self-evident. Accordingly, the doctor's testimony that she did not know, or did not recognize, the classic symptoms of the plaintiff's condition will fall on deaf ears when the jury hears testimony that the nurses made the correct assessment.

If you intend to call the defendant during your case in chief, and if the plaintiff is unlikely to be cross-examined or will not be damaged by cross-examination, consider putting the plaintiff on the stand before the defendant. If the jurors identify with the plaintiff as a result of the plaintiff's testimony, they will be more offended later when they hear the testimony of the defendant who injured this "nice person." Jurors who identify with the plaintiff will be more inclined to look at the defendant's testimony critically and less inclined to be offended by an aggressive cross-examination of the defendant.

Your Client as a Witness

Do not allow your client to shoulder the burden of proving the whole case. Although he may have information about every aspect of the case, other witnesses who have similar and perhaps better knowledge of the facts should testify first and relieve him of that obligation. Usually, you can present all damages and establish nearly all elements of liability and causation through witnesses other than the plaintiff. Your client should testify only about elements of the case that he alone can establish.

In determining when to call your client as a witness, ask yourself the following questions:

- Will my client be a strong witness or a weak witness needing substantial support from other witnesses?
- At what point in the trial will my client's testimony best support a chronology that will explain logically what happened?
- At what point in the trial will my client's testimony have the greatest impact on the jury—and leave the least opportunity for impeachment or effective cross-examination?
- Which witnesses can give more effective testimony than my client?
- To what extent can other witnesses minimize possible weaknesses and problems in my client's testimony by testifying before my client?
- Will my client's testimony strengthen the testimony of any other witness if he testifies before them?

When the facts used by your expert witness are disputed, you need to persuade the jurors that the facts on which the expert relies are correct. One way to do this is to present your client's testimony before calling the expert. If your client describes his condition in detail and corroborates the testimony of the expert to follow, the jurors will be more likely to trust the expert's opinions and testimony. In addition, often your expert will not have a complete current history of your client's physical and mental damages because hospital charts and records provided to the expert are often not current or complete, or they may have erroneous entries. In this situation, if your client testifies first, the expert may be able to draw on the testimony.

Although circumstances may necessitate your calling your client early in the trial to lay a foundation for the testimony of experts or other witnesses, it is often wise to call him as the last witness. That is when he is usually least vulnerable to cross-examination and when his testimony will have the greatest impact on the jury.

Resolving Client Weaknesses

If your client is likely to recall events incorrectly, let eyewitness testimony both resolve the facts of liability and explain why the client's recollection is inaccurate. Present the eyewitness testimony to the jury before the client's incorrect recollection.

Use lay and expert testimony to humanize a problem client—for example, a client who is psychologically disturbed, who is an alcoholic, or who has a repulsive personality or unfavorable background—before you present him to the jury. You can accomplish this through the testimony of relatives, friends, coworkers, psychologists, psychiatrists, social workers, and physicians. Every client was once a baby that anyone would adore. The jury should understand, before the client testifies, how environmental factors caused the client's present condition. If you introduce a problem client properly, he will have the respect or sympathy of the jury before he testifies.

The plaintiff will be more credible if his testimony is less adversarial, so use health-care witnesses, not the plaintiff, to introduce photographs of injuries, day-in-the-life movies, medical bills, or other exhibits to establish damages. Do not have your client testify until the weaknesses in his testimony have been minimized by other witnesses. Otherwise, the jurors will analyze those weaknesses critically and may form an unfavorable impression of him.

Other Witnesses

When one or more of the defendant's expert witnesses have given deposition testimony favorable to the plaintiff, you may want the jury to hear that testimony. You may accomplish this objective in several ways.

You may subpoena the defendant's experts in case the defendant does not call them. If the expert witnesses are not subject to subpoena, you may describe the experts' favorable testimony during your opening statement, hoping that this tactic will force the defendant to call the experts as witnesses. If the defendant fails to call the expert, you may use the "missing witness" strategy during summation by informing the jury that expert witnesses named by the defendant were not called to testify on the defendant's behalf, "and we can only assume that the testimony would not have been favorable to the defendant." Further, "I informed you during opening statement that my cross-examination of these experts would support our case against the defendant, so I am not surprised that defense counsel decided not to put them on the witness stand. These out-of-state experts are not subject to subpoena in Colorado but could have voluntarily appeared to testify at the defendant's request."

You may read a portion of the expert's deposition during your case or threaten to read the deposition unless the defendant stipulates that the expert witness will be called by the defense and thus will be available for cross-examination. The court should approve the stipulation and should provide that you are not limited in cross-examination to the scope of the direct examination. Further, the stipulation should provide that if the defendant is unable to produce the expert when putting on the defense testimony, you may then read the deposition.

In proving damages, prove as many elements of damages as possible through witnesses other than the plaintiff, such as family, nurses, friends, physicians, economists, and life-care planners. Consider using a life-care planner, rehabilitation expert, and economist toward the end of the trial after liability has been established. During their deliberations, jurors will remember damages testimony that you offered at the end of the trial more clearly than they will remember earlier testimony. At the end of your case, consider putting on witnesses who can discuss the plaintiff's present condition and needs. If you do not call the plaintiff as your last witness, consider closing with the attendant-care person or nurse who cares for the plaintiff now and having that person narrate a day-in-the-life film. Show the jury what life has become for the plaintiff as a result of the negligence of the health-care people in whom he placed his trust.

CONCLUSION

Planning the trial and developing your trial strategy begins with the first client interview and is an ongoing process throughout informal and formal discovery. The final planning occurs after formal discovery, in the days and weeks immediately before trial. During this time, you should finalize the selection and order of your witnesses, prepare them for trial, and finish the preparation of all segments of the trial. Also use this time to prepare your opening statement and voir dire of the jury, and think about your summation. Now you are prepared to commence trial.

During the trial, you should be prepared to periodically reevaluate the pretrial game plan or trial strategy and make changes as new developments occur. It may be necessary to alter the order of witnesses, arrange for additional demonstrative evidence, put greater emphasis on certain evidence, or make other adjustments.

Keep in mind the direct relationship between the number of surprises during a trial and the amount of preparation, and remember that unexpected, potentially damaging incidents during trial generally require a change in trial tactics or strategy. Though there are some problems you cannot overcome during trial, there are many you can prevent by thorough and careful pretrial preparation. You cannot overprepare a case.

CHAPTER EIGHT

VOIR DIRE

An English barrister once told an American lawyer that a trial in England begins when the jury is accepted by counsel and sworn to try the case. The American lawyer replied, "Hell, in the United States, the trial is all over by that time."

IDENTIFYING UNFAVORABLE JURORS

The questions you ask potential jurors during the voir dire examination and the answers the jurors provide allow you to identify jurors who will look either favorably or unfavorably on your case. For this reason, voir dire is a critical component of trial. Voir dire allows you to weed out jurors who will decide the case against your client on limited emotional issues, without regard to the law or the facts. In short, it helps you uncover jurors who will so identify with some adverse factor in the case that they will decide the case on only that factor, ignoring the rest of the evidence.

To detect juror bias, prejudice, or adverse attitudes, you must prepare carefully for voir dire. Your goal is to detect unfavorable jurors and challenge or neutralize them.[1] After you have challenged for cause and eliminated the most undesirable jurors, you can concentrate on establishing credibility with the remaining jurors while soliciting additional information that will enable you to exercise your peremptory challenges wisely.

Identify favorable jurors without tipping off opposing counsel. To do this, you must have a thorough knowledge of all evidence—including evidence unfavorable to your case—and detailed background information on your client and your client's family. For example, the voir dire may reveal that a juror's favorite recreational activity is mountain climbing, which is

---

[1] For further information and an illustration of how this is accomplished, see Chapter Twelve, "Applying Principles to Special Problems."

also the favorite activity of your key expert witness, although that fact is unknown to the defense. If that juror seems otherwise favorable to the plaintiff or is at least neutral, your expert witness can later disclose in testimony that when he is not practicing medicine, he is an avid mountain climber. Often, by obtaining detailed background information about your client and your witnesses, which the defendant often does not do in formal discovery, you may discover facts about a juror's background that would cause a juror to identify in a friendly way with your client or an important witness.

Similarly, you should identify jurors—again without tipping off opposing counsel—who will react unfavorably to the defense when information you elicit during the trial triggers an emotional response in them. For example, a juror may disclose that he is an animal-rights activist, and you know that one of the defendant's expert witnesses is a big-game hunter. The fact that the expert is a big-game hunter may come to light during trial. You may know that defense counsel is a chauvinist who badgers or patronizes expert witnesses who are women. Based on this knowledge you may select as expert witnesses an economist and a pediatrician who are women, and you may select women as jurors because defense counsel's chauvinism toward the experts will offend the jurors.

Accept the fact that you cannot change the jurors' attitudes during voir dire. Instead of brainwashing the jury, you must discover the attitudes they already have and use them to your client's advantage.

Do not ask questions during voir dire that will help the defense identify jurors who may favor the plaintiff. For example, do not ask the jurors, "Have any of you or any members of your families been subjected to substandard medical care that would make it difficult for you to render a verdict for the doctor in this case?" If your questions expose jurors who may favor the plaintiff, the defense will challenge those jurors. If you don't ask questions that would benefit the defendant in identifying jurors who favor the plaintiff, defense counsel may overlook the areas of inquiry that would help identify these jurors.

Use your intuition and common sense to distinguish between the jurors who will probably favor the plaintiff and those who will probably favor the defendant. After you identify and challenge jurors who will favor the defendant, you can assume that the remaining jurors either will be neutral or will favor the plaintiff. During your opponent's voir dire, carefully observe the interaction between opposing counsel and the jurors and continue to evaluate your preliminary feelings about each juror. A juror who seems warm and friendly during your questions and whom you therefore judge to be favorable may be equally warm and friendly to the defense. On the other hand, a juror who seemed to favor the plaintiff during your voir dire may show an unfriendly attitude toward the defendant when questioned by the defense, confirming your initial impression.

ESTABLISHING A RAPPORT WITH JURORS

You should establish a rapport with the jurors and "get acquainted." To do this, you must "visit" with the jurors rather than just talk to them. Be pleasant and genuine. You cannot expect jurors to communicate candidly and openly unless you are sincere with them. Each juror is important, and you should treat each accordingly. Establish eye contact with each juror and listen attentively, asking appropriate follow-up questions or making comments. Let the jurors know that it is okay to have attitudes, feelings, biases, or even prejudices, and encourage them to speak freely on these topics. Respect the jurors' individual views; thank the first juror who openly discloses attitudes and opinions unfavorable to your case, and encourage others to respond likewise. Other jurors will observe carefully your first interaction with a juror who talks to you frankly. If they see that you are receptive to the juror's views and sincerely interested, they too will answer openly.

Remember, even though the jurors are strangers to one another and first learn about each other during voir dire, it is easier for them to identify with one another than to identify with the attorneys, the plaintiff and defendant, the judge, or other strangers in the courtroom. Accordingly, the entire jury panel will be alert and sensitive to how you treat another "one of them." They will identify with each other before identifying with anyone else in the courtroom. Thus, if you embarrass one juror, you may damage your relationship with the others as well.

Always show respect for the jury. Do not argue or become defensive if a juror says something you do not like. Do not lecture a juror. Do not pose difficult questions that test a juror, as in school, causing anxiety and embarrassment. Do not cross-examine a juror or make disagreeing with you uncomfortable. Instead, be respectful and courteous, and use jurors' names when addressing them.

Do not offend jurors by asking invasive questions about personal matters or beliefs; if it is necessary to ask these questions, explain your reasons for inquiring into these matters. Sometimes it is helpful to have the court ask "sensitive" questions that might be embarrassing or offensive, such as questions regarding sexual or criminal conduct. Jurors will not hold you responsible for questions the judge asks. The judge often asks these questions individually in chambers, outside the presence of the other jurors and spectators.

In short, your success in establishing a rapport with the jury is related directly to your sincerity, credibility, and honesty, and how you make the jurors feel important and respected.

EXERCISING CHALLENGES FOR CAUSE

Do not challenge the first juror who displays a bias that would justify a challenge for cause, thus punishing the juror for being candid; this will only silence others with similar views. Challenges can be made at the conclusion of the voir dire or after all "sensitive" areas have been fully explored. Many experienced lawyers prefer to question the panel on "sensitive issues" in open court rather than in chambers because they want to observe jurors' interaction and see how each reacts to the comments made by the others. They want the jurors as a group to open up and discuss sensitive issues. Whether it is desirable to question the jurors in open court or in chambers depends on the sensitivity of the issue. Sometimes it is wise to encourage an in camera hearing at a juror's request. However, remember that unless a juror requests the in camera examination himself, he may be intimidated by it. An in camera examination of each juror on all issues should absolutely be avoided.

QUESTIONING JURORS ABOUT THE LAW

Your voir dire should deal with the relevant law—not to educate the jury—the court will do that—but to identify jurors who disagree with the law that helps your client; if they disagree with the law, they may not apply it. For example, in a claim based on a medical assault and battery, ask the potential jurors the following questions:

> I am sure that you each have your own concept of assault and battery. You probably think of it as one person striking another, without the other's consent, am I correct? You will learn during this trial that there is another type of assault and battery that makes it unlawful to injure a person by performing surgery without consent. Is there anything about that type of assault and battery that bothers you? Do you have any quarrel with the proposition that a physician commits an assault and battery if he performs surgery on the wrong leg, even though the surgery was perfectly performed, and even if he was not negligent in performing the surgery? Do you have any quarrel with the proposition that the failure of a physician to obtain consent from a patient to perform the surgery constitutes an assault and battery? Is that contrary to what you believe the law should be? If the court instructs you that under the law a physician com-

mits an assault and battery if he performs surgery on the wrong leg, even though the surgery was performed perfectly, would any of you refuse to apply that law for any reason?

If there are jurors who do not like the law, but who cannot be successfully challenged for cause, you can neutralize them by obtaining a commitment from them to set aside unfavorable attitudes, prejudices, or biases, and to apply the law even when they have reservations. It is important to have the jurors make this commitment by promising under oath to apply the law. Conscientious jurors take their job seriously; even though jurors may disagree with the law, they generally will apply it if they have promised under oath to do so.

Furthermore, once jurors have committed in front of the other jurors and the judge to set aside unfavorable attitudes, they will often react more favorably to the plaintiff during jury deliberations to show the other jurors that they are honoring the commitment. On the other hand, if a juror makes such a commitment under oath and then later shows bias or prejudice during jury deliberations, often the other jurors will remind that juror of the commitment. Thus you should secure the jurors' commitment both to set aside bias and to follow the court's instructions on points of law with which they disagree.

USING VOIR DIRE TO MINIMIZE PROBLEMS

Use voir dire to preclude problems that may arise during trial. For example, if you intend to call the defendant-doctor as your first witness, or early in the case for cross-examination, prepare the jurors during voir dire by explaining, "Mrs. Jones, the law gives me the right to call Dr. Smith for cross-examination; do you object to that? Do you understand that the defendant can call my client as a witness for cross-examination during the defendant's case? This is a perfectly appropriate procedure and well-recognized in the law. Does that trouble you?" You have then set the stage for addressing this problem again in your opening statement.

In opening statement, you want to be the professor and teacher for the jury when it comes to explaining the medical testimony and issues. Do not use the defendant-doctor for that purpose if you call him as your first witness; you do not want to enhance the defendant's credibility by permitting him to be the professor and teacher.

PREPARING FOR VOIR DIRE

Determine before trial whether the judge will conduct a preliminary voir dire and, if so, determine the nature and extent of the judge's examination. Also determine the ways in which the judge will restrict the content or duration of your voir dire. For example, in some jurisdictions the court may caution counsel not to anticipate the court's instructions or to mention the applicable law to the jury. The court also may tell you not to mention issues or evidence that are subject to motions in limine.

If the court severely restricts your voir dire time, have the court ask questions to obtain preliminary background information and to explain the purpose of voir dire and the jury's function.

The judge may conduct the entire voir dire. When this happens, you often may submit written questions or areas of inquiry for the judge to include in the examination. Carefully prepare your questions so that the judge accepts and uses them; it may help to explain to the judge your reasons for wanting these questions asked.

Obtain a list of the prospective jurors before trial in jurisdictions in which this is allowed. After you have the list, get information about the jurors from city directories, voter registration lists of political party affiliation, questionnaires completed for the court, or other available materials.

In major cases, some lawyers use investigative services to learn more about prospective jurors. In conducting your investigations, avoid conduct that could be improper or even unethical, such as indirect contact with a juror through the juror's family, friends, fellow employees, and others. If a juror should learn of the investigation, you could be charged with jury tampering or invasion of privacy and the investigation could result in a mistrial. These violations of law may occur if you or your investigator questions neighbors, friends, or relatives of a prospective juror about the juror's finances, lifestyle, employment, or other personal matters. Even if no charges are brought against you, a juror who learns of such an investigation may justifiably feel angry and intimidated and may blame one or more of the parties and the judicial process. The juror would find it difficult to be fair and impartial.

There are less intrusive ways of investigating potential jurors. For example, an investigator can drive by potential jurors' residences, noting the type of neighborhood, the automobiles in the driveway, any bumper-sticker language, the condition of the yard and home, and other objects in or about the yard and home that provide information about the juror and the juror's family. Hiring a cab driver familiar with all the neighborhoods in a city is an inexpensive way to obtain generic information about the neighborhood in which each potential juror lives.

In preparing for voir dire, it is helpful to create a composite of the ideal juror, perhaps with the help of a psychologist. List characteristics that you believe would cause a juror to identify with your client and your case. Do a similar composite of the unfavorable juror whom you would challenge. List factors that you believe would cause a juror to identify with the defendant and the defendant's case.

Also, for help in creating a composite of the ideal juror, consider using a random survey of people in the community to obtain more information about possible bias or attitudes concerning the issues in your case. The survey can be conducted by calling on people in their homes or by telephone. The survey questions must be carefully drafted, perhaps with the help of a psychologist.[2]

Observe prospective jurors in the courthouse, as they enter the courtroom, as their names are called, and as they enter the jury box. Note their dress and what they bring with them, such as reading materials, crossword puzzles, work from the office, or needlework. Note their reactions to any introductory comments the judge makes about the case. Note the interaction among jurors and their body language. Look for juror familiarity with defense counsel, the defendant, or prospective witnesses in the courtroom. If a juror denies knowing the defendant and then warmly greets the defendant in the hallway, it brings the juror's honesty and integrity into question.

USING JUROR QUESTIONNAIRES

Questionnaires prepared by counsel and submitted to the court before trial often elicit information not otherwise disclosed. When the prospective jurors are called to the courtroom, the judge places them under oath and instructs them to complete and sign the questionnaire. The jurors complete the questionnaires before the judge or lawyers provide them with any information about the case. The bailiff collects the questionnaires and distributes copies to counsel and the court before voir dire.

The use of juror questionnaires has several advantages:

- Questionnaires solicit information from the jurors before the jurors are contaminated by the court's preliminary remarks, the remarks of counsel, or remarks made by other jurors during the voir dire examination.
- Jurors who may not voice their opinions in open court may express them in the questionnaire. They may also respond more candidly to sensitive questions.

---

2 Appendix D.1 is a sample of such a survey.

- The court instructs the jurors to complete the questionnaires, whereas the attorneys ask questions orally in voir dire. Jurors take the judge more seriously than they take the lawyers, and they may feel obligated to fully answer all questionnaire questions.
- Since jurors will more often express strong opinions in the privacy of a questionnaire than they will in court, the information provided in the questionnaire sometimes supports a challenge for cause as well as opens additional doors for examination during voir dire. For example, a juror's statement that "I do not believe that medical negligence lawsuits should be brought against doctors, and I could not be fair to anyone who brought such a lawsuit" could lead to a successful challenge for cause.

The questionnaire is not a substitute for voir dire: voir dire is conducted following a review of the questionnaires.

A sample questionnaire used in a medical negligence case and a summary of jurors' responses to specific questions have been provided.[3] As you can see from the summary, a great deal of important information was obtained on the morning of the first day of trial, before voir dire commenced. For example, seven prospective jurors were concerned about medical negligence lawsuits because they believed that such lawsuits increase insurance rates and health-care costs and "drive doctors out of practice." Many jurors expressed the opinion that suits are brought too frequently as an easy way to get money. Some prospective jurors felt that a verdict for the plaintiff would have an economic impact on them. The value of jurors' answers to a juror questionnaire is that the answers often measure how strongly the jurors feel about particular issues. For example, when asked how she felt about people who file personal injury lawsuits, one potential juror responded, "I think they are encouraged by disreputable, unprofessional attorneys."

In many jurisdictions, only the jurors called to the jury box are questioned during voir dire and those who are challenged are replaced by jurors who have not yet been questioned. The information obtained in questionnaires is helpful in deciding whether to challenge jurors--who would then be replaced by those who remain--because the questionnaire provides a great deal of information about the remaining jurors. Without the questionnaire information, a juror might be challenged, only to be replaced by someone even more adverse to the plaintiff's case.

---

[3] See Appendix D (D.2 and D.3).

EMPLOYING VOIR DIRE TECHNIQUES

One method of detecting bias, prejudice, or attitudes of jurors is to present the evidence in the light most favorable to the defense and ask detailed questions about each juror's attitude or feeling about that evidence.[4] For example:

> My client, Pete Smith, had a car accident because he was driving while intoxicated. He was brought to the hospital by ambulance, and Dr. Jones came to the hospital from his home in the middle of the night and saved my client's life. We allege that, at a later date, Dr. Jones was negligent in treating Mr. Smith. Now it would be natural for some people to assume that if you save a person's life you should not be held legally responsible if you later negligently injure that same person. Ms. Juror, how do you feel about that? How many of you other jurors share the feeling that a doctor who gets out of bed in the middle of the night and saves a life should be legally excused if he is later negligent and, by his negligence, injures the life he saved?

Your areas of inquiry in voir dire are an important means of finding jurors who may identify with the defendant rather than the plaintiff.[5] Inquire into the following areas:

- Do any of the jurors have any education, training, experience, employment, or financial interest in the health-care profession?
- Do any of the jurors have a member of their immediate family, a close friend, or a neighbor who, through education, training, employment, or financial interest, is involved with the health-care profession?
- Where do the jurors and members of their immediate families obtain health care? Are they satisfied or dissatisfied with the care they have received?
- Do any of the jurors have a warm and friendly relationship with a health-care provider, including their treating physicians?
- Have any of the jurors or members of the jurors' immediate families received extraordinary care from a health-care provider that saved a life, cured a disease or illness, or caused the juror to feel indebted to the health-care industry?
- Are any of the jurors acquainted with anyone in the health-care industry? If so, inquire into the relationship. If a hospital is involved as a defendant, determine whether any juror has ever been a patient at the

---

4 For a more detailed discussion of this technique, see Chapter Twelve, Case Example II.

5 See Appendix D.4 for a sample voir dire outline.

hospital, has been involved in fund-raising for the hospital, or has a close friend or relative who is presently a patient at the hospital.

- Are the jurors familiar with any of the diagnostic testing, medical procedures, or medical devices that will be the subject of testimony during the trial?
- Are any of the jurors members of civic or social groups to which the defendant also belongs? (You will have obtained a list of such groups in discovery.)
- Are the jurors familiar with the events involved in the litigation or with similar events?

In selecting jurors, also consider whether a juror might consciously or subconsciously favor the defendant or be reluctant to render a verdict against the defendant because of the subtle influence of family, friends, employment, economics, or politics. For example, a juror may be reluctant to enter a verdict against a health-care provider if such a verdict could later subject the juror to criticism by a loved one, fellow employees, members of organizations to which the juror belongs, a close friend, neighbors, or someone that the juror respects. Likewise, the juror's participation in a verdict against a physician might be viewed by the juror as an act that could jeopardize the juror's social, political, or economic goals. Accordingly, you should obtain additional information needed to evaluate the jurors in this light:

- Are any of the jurors in a socioeconomic group that receives better health care than the average patient or that has a high incidence of conflicts with the health-care profession?
- Do any of the jurors have political, social, business, or financial aspirations that they believe could be jeopardized by a verdict that offends the health-care industry? The fact that such fears or concerns may be without foundation is irrelevant; they may still affect a juror's judgment.
- Would the jurors' families, fellow employees, employers, and peers accept a verdict for the plaintiff? A juror may not want to render a verdict that will offend people that the juror holds in high regard or that might cause the loss of respect of those who are important to the juror.

Also consider how jurors will relate to each other. Select jurors who will favor the plaintiff, but who will also command the respect of the remaining jurors. You may not want to select a juror who may be a strong and biased advocate for the plaintiff if that juror has character flaws or personality defects that will offend the other jurors. With such a juror on the jury, even jurors who favor the plaintiff may lean toward the defense rather than side with the offensive juror.

As you select jurors, for each prospective juror you consider, think about what impact the evidence might have on that juror and how the juror might react to your trial strategy, to the defense strategy, and to the witnesses who will be called to testify. Likewise, evaluate your own interaction with the juror and your prospects of establishing an appropriate relationship with the juror during the trial process. You should ask yourself the following questions about each juror:

- Will you be able to establish a rapport with the juror during trial and effectively relate to the juror in a persuasive fashion?
- Will you and your client be able to establish credibility with the juror? Will the juror respect you and look to you for guidance?
- How will the prospective juror react to the witnesses and to your cross-examination of the witnesses and of the defendant?
- How will the juror react to your trial tactics, your demonstrative evidence, the court's instructions, and your summation?

At the conclusion of the voir dire, ask if the prospective jurors have anything to add to their responses to any of the previously asked questions. Tell the jurors that anything that would make them feel uncomfortable sitting as a juror in the case, or anything that they believe, in good conscience, should be disclosed to the court, should be mentioned at this time.

In conducting the voir dire, communicate on an "adult to adult" basis. Don't be overly solicitous. Don't curry favor, never use a juror's first name, and carefully observe all nonverbal communications.

CONCLUSION

Jury selection is a critical phase of the trial process. The best case presented by the best lawyer will fall on deaf ears with the wrong jury. To avoid the wrong jury, you must intelligently exercise peremptory challenges and eliminate unfavorable jurors by challenges for cause. To do this, you must know as much as possible about what each prospective juror thinks of the critical issues of the litigation and related issues. The selection of a jury is a highly subjective process and is necessarily more of an art than a science. Therefore, you must also rely on your gut instincts and common sense. Further, "selecting" a jury is a misnomer; the heart of jury selection is eliminating the jurors you fear rather than picking the jurors you want. This can be accomplished by exercising all of the techniques and skills necessary to conduct a successful voir dire examination.

CHAPTER NINE

OPENING STATEMENT

SCORING POINTS IN OPENING

A good opening statement will capture the jury's attention at the outset, tell the story factually and persuasively, and communicate your confidence, knowledge, and sincerity to the jury.[1] The statement should be brief, clear, well organized, and interesting, and it should develop your theory of the case by telling a simple story with simple concepts. Simplify complex scientific or medical concepts, and do not describe the detailed testimony of each witness.

The opening statement can achieve multiple ends besides persuading the jurors. Often the opening helps the client who, in listening to it, may understand for the first time the theory of the case and his role in the trial process. Sometimes it gives your client the confidence he will need to testify well. The opening should also give the court a favorable framework for difficult evidentiary rulings. In addition, the opening statement can have a psychologically devastating effect on the defendant or any of the defendant's expert witnesses who are present during the opening. It also gives you the opportunity to disclose and minimize the weaknesses in your case and dramatize the weaknesses in the defendant's case before the defense has an opportunity to present its side of the case.

The opening statement gives you an important opportunity to establish your credibility. Adhere to the following rules:

- Do not overstate or misstate; when in doubt, understate.
- Do not include anything in the opening statement that the evidence does not support.

---

1 See Appendix E for a sample opening statement.

- Use your strongest and most credible evidence in opening statement. Do not rely on evidence the jury may discount or find untrue, and certainly do not rely on testimony that you know will be impeached or discredited.
- Though you should mention all the weaknesses in your case, do not mention all its strengths. For example, do not mention all of the defendant's aggravated conduct. Let the jury discover during trial that your case is even stronger than you mentioned in your opening statement.

When the jurors later hear the evidence they will know that you were fair and honest when you earlier spoke to them; their initial impression of you will be reinforced and your credibility further enhanced.

Use your opening to let the jury know that you are an expert in this case and that you are trustworthy. Positive, powerful, and convincing language is most effective. A powerless style—indicated by the frequent use of such expressions as "I think," "I guess," "perhaps," and "maybe"—projects uncertainty. Powerful speech, on the other hand, provides a direct description of what occurred and establishes that you have both confidence and expertise. Get directly to the point, and do not hedge. If you believe that yours is a winning case, show it!

It is important that you use a matter-of-fact tone. Your language can be persuasive and compelling, but save argument and emotion for summation. Some jurors, influenced by the news media and Perry Mason, expect to observe a deceptive lawyer who will unfairly appeal to their emotions in the hope that they will overlook the facts. These jurors will be more likely to believe you if your demeanor is calm and unemotional.

CAPTURING THE JURORS' ATTENTION

The first step in motivating jurors to render a verdict for your client is to capture their attention. The following are examples of openings that draw the jurors' interest quickly.

Fetal Asphyxia

In a case about a brain-damaged baby, you could focus the jurors on a seemingly everyday house and family.

> Ladies and gentlemen, in the block off Arapahoe and Broadway Road there is a small frame house that is the residence of the Jones family: the parents, John and Ann; Bruce, who is 11; Cindy, who is 1; and Michael, who is 3½. It looks like a normal house lived in by a normal family, but you will discover during the course of this

> trial that the lifestyle and daily activities of the Jones family are far from normal because Michael is blind and severely brain damaged. That's what this case is all about. You might say it all started on January 29, 1986 . . .

Delayed Breast Cancer Diagnosis

In the following delayed diagnosis case, the jurors' attention is captured by the startling statistics about breast cancer and early diagnosis.

> One of every 10 or 11 women in the United States of childbearing age will develop cancer of the breast. Not all of these women will die. In fact, a very large percentage of these women will survive because their cancer will be discovered early enough to be treated successfully. Betsy Zinn did die in 1990, however, and the evidence will show that she was deprived of the opportunity to live a longer life because her cancer was not detected and treated by the defendants when she went to them for help in 1987.

Negligent Surgical Treatment

The jury is likely to be interested immediately in the story of a young girl who was harmed when her doctor performed an incorrect procedure on her foot.

> In this case you are going to find out what happened when a doctor performed the wrong surgery on a young girl's foot, and why it took four years for this young girl to partially overcome the results of that unnecessary medical mistake. To understand how and why Dr. Smith performed the wrong surgery, you will have to become familiar with two medical concepts . . .

Uninformed Consent

In this case, the plaintiff, Bill Bloom, relied on his doctor's advice to make what turned out to be a tragic decision. The jurors' interest is captured by focusing on Bill Bloom's decision—"one of the most important decisions of his life."

> On September 19, 1974, Bill Bloom, age 55, made one of the most important decisions of his life. It turned out to be the wrong decision because it was based on erroneous medical information provided to him that day by Dr. Jones, who recommended that Bill undergo a total ankle replacement with plastic and steel, rather than an ankle fusion.
>
> Later, to save his life, Bill Bloom had to have his right leg amputated below the knee because earlier he had followed the advice and recommendations of Dr. Jones. What Dr. Jones said to Mr. and

> Mrs. Bloom on September 18, 1974, is the subject of this lawsuit. During the trial, you will learn . . .

After you capture the jury's attention, weave a persuasive and dynamic opening statement that anticipates the evidence. Unfold the plaintiff's story, first describing liability (how the plaintiff received the injuries) and then describing damages (the impact of the injuries on the plaintiff's life).

MITIGATING THE WEAKNESSES IN YOUR CASE

Mitigate the weaknesses in your case, drawing on your answers to the questions you asked yourself when you tested the theory of your case.[2] Identify the factors of your case that will cause a jury to react unfavorably toward your client, and minimize the impact of the factors while emphasizing the tortious conduct of the other party. The following sections illustrate how you can overcome or minimize case weaknesses.

Plaintiff's Family Background

If there are aspects of the plaintiff's conduct that may help the defense, humanize that conduct by weaving all the mitigating and explanatory circumstances into your opening statement. The following example is from an outrageous conduct suit against a physician for racial remarks directed at a white mother and her black child. Plaintiff's counsel realized that the defense would try to use the mother's early interracial marriage, single parenthood, and other problems against her. This opening illustrates the strategy of mitigating those weaknesses in plaintiff's case by humanizing the plaintiff.

> When Nancy was a teenager, she made a mistake—she married at the earliest opportunity. It happened that her husband was black. The marriage was an error in judgment; it ended in divorce shortly after two darling children were born, and she and the children then moved to Colorado to start a new life. Nancy learned to cope with the problem of raising the children of an interracial marriage. There were difficulties, but she protected and loved her children, and they handled their day-to-day problems together. The family had no serious difficulties until August 23, 1989. On that date, an unnecessary and emotionally devastating incident occurred that is etched forever in the memory of Nancy and her son, Steven. What happened on August 23, 1989, in Dr. Jones's office?

---

2 See Chapter Seven, "Planning the Trial: Theory, Witnesses, and Trial Strategy."

Difficulty in Proving Causation

You frequently must address the issue of causation in opening statement. For example, in a case against an obstetrician for failing to perform a timely cesarean section when confronted with evidence of fetal hypoxia, the defendants claimed that the fetus could have been damaged before the mother was admitted to the hospital. The following portion of the opening statement was prepared specifically to anticipate and neutralize this defense claim.

> You will learn during trial that the mother had no symptoms until she began bleeding shortly before she was admitted to the hospital, that Mother Nature provides a pregnant woman with 70 percent more blood during pregnancy than she would otherwise have and therefore a 70 percent greater oxygen supply to protect the mother and fetus, that the vital organs of the fetus, including the heart and brain, are protected further because the fetal body withdraws blood from its extremities to protect the brain as the oxygen supply diminishes, and that the fetal monitor used at the hospital showed no significant fetal distress until three hours before the c-section was performed. Furthermore, you will hear testimony that Dr. Anderson redictated hospital records once he discovered the severity of the infant's brain injury and that in the redictated records he blamed the anesthesiologist for the baby's injuries. There would have been no reason to redictate records if the fetus had been injured before the mother's admission to the hospital.

Negative Attitudes toward Experts

When you retain out-of-state expert witnesses, it is sometimes necessary to overcome the implication that you needed "hired guns" because local experts did not believe your case had merit. The following example from a trial in Wyoming illustrates how you can mitigate this problem in your opening statement:

> You will hear testimony from two expert witnesses whom the defendants hired just a few months ago. These expert witnesses are from Texas and Colorado, and there is nothing wrong with that; they are highly qualified. They are former teachers and friends of the defendants, however. We will call expert witnesses from Ohio and California, and you will learn that after the plaintiffs came to my office in Boulder, Colorado, these experts carefully reviewed every piece of information available before expressing an opinion, and they arrived at their opinions before this lawsuit was filed.

When it is appropriate, subtly impeach the defendant's lay or expert witnesses during your opening statement. Use some of the same information you intend to use in your closing argument or in your cross-examination of the defense experts. For example, if the defense expert overlooked certain diagnostic test results in arriving at opinions, highlight those test results in your opening statement and explain their importance. Whenever the defense expert relies on inadequate or erroneous information to support opinions, tell your story of the facts in a manner that makes this clear. Later, you can cross-examine the expert to demonstrate that the expert relied on erroneous information. If the jurors reject the expert's basis for the opinions she renders, they will reject the expert's opinions.

Overcoming Evidentiary Problems

Use opening statement to minimize any evidentiary problems. If you expect a challenge from opposing counsel or the court on the admissibility of particular evidence, use your opening statement to describe the facts in a way that clarifies their relevance for the judge. On the other hand, if you seek to preclude the admissibility of certain evidence favorable to the defense by a motion in limine and the court reserves its ruling until the defense tries to introduce the evidence, you are on the horns of a dilemma.

If you believe the court will probably allow the evidence during trial, you must decide whether to mention the evidence in opening statement or to gamble that it will not be allowed. If you mention the damaging evidence and the court later rules in your favor, the jury will not hear the unfavorable evidence, so you need not have mentioned it. But if you fail to minimize the impact of the evidence during opening statement and the court allows the evidence during trial, the evidence could cause more damage than it would otherwise.

Occasionally a court will forbid both sides from referring to questionable evidence during trial, until after a party seeks the evidence's admission. In that situation, if you believe that the court will probably allow the evidence during trial, withdraw your motion in limine so that you can minimize the impact of the evidence during opening statement.

Similarly, if you are aware of evidence that is potentially devastating to the plaintiff, and you realize that opposing counsel may discover the evidence for the first time during trial, you must decide whether to bring the evidence to the attention of the jury and the defense in your opening statement to minimize it, or to gamble that the evidence will not be disclosed during trial.

USING YOUR OPPONENT'S WEAKNESSES

Use your opponent's weaknesses to your advantage. In opening statement, you, as the plaintiff's lawyer, have the unique opportunity to dramatize weaknesses in the defendant's position before the defendant has a chance to mitigate them. You can minimize your weaknesses and lessen their impact on the jury while describing—without mitigating—the facts or events that damage the defendant's position. Use this technique cautiously. If the defendant is unaware of devastating testimony that you plan to use to impeach, do not tip him off. Only when it is obvious that the defense counsel is aware of weaknesses in his own case and is prepared to explain them in his opening statement should you beat him to the punch.

Weaknesses in a Defense Expert

Consider the situation in which the defense has an expert witness whose credibility you must attack because you cannot attack the substance of her testimony. The following passage illustrates one way of dealing with the problem:

> Listen carefully when I cross-examine the defendant's expert witness, Dr. Jones. As you listen, ask yourself, "Why does she agree with the testimony of the plaintiff's expert witnesses that the cancer could have been detected by the defendant at an earlier date and could have been treated at that time, yet conclude that the defendant was not negligent in failing to detect and treat the cancer?" The answer to this question will be provided to you during cross-examination.

Then during cross-examination establish that the expert witness and defendant are close friends, that they refer patients to each other, and that the expert volunteered to testify on her friend's behalf.

Document Destruction

You can highlight any aggravated conduct by the defendant-doctor, such as altered records, and dramatize the doctor's conduct before the doctor or defense counsel has an opportunity to minimize or explain it. For example,

> You will learn that after this lawsuit was filed, the defendant, Dr. Johnson, redictated some of the hospital records. He claims he did this because the hospital lost the records. However, the records that he redictated are those concerning the crucial issues in this case. We will call as witnesses hospital employees who will testify that the original records were not lost or destroyed, that the hospital did not ask Dr. Johnson to redictate records, and that Dr. Johnson violated hospital rules and regulations in redictating these records after the plaintiff filed this lawsuit. The question is, "What information was in the original records?" Please listen carefully to the testimony, and

we may be able to provide you with an answer to that question during trial.

RESOLVING DAMAGES ISSUES AND PROBLEMS

If your opening statement motivates the jurors to resolve the liability issues in your client's favor, the jurors will be more attentive to your remarks on injuries and damages. Therefore, you should organize the damages portion of your opening statement carefully to capture the jurors' attention and leave them with a mental image of the plaintiff's injuries that stays with them throughout the trial.

Should you refer to a specific sum in your opening statement? This depends on the case, your style of case presentation, the nature of the damages, and the trial tactics. In some cases, you can enhance your credibility with the jury by not mentioning in opening statement the amount of damages you will request in summation. Some lawyers make it a rule never to request a specific amount in either opening statement or summation.

In a case with large damages, jurors are sometimes questioned on voir dire about their willingness to assess "very substantial damages," perhaps even "millions of dollars," if the evidence supports these damages. If you properly cover the issue on voir dire, you might choose not to mention an amount in the opening statement or, consistent with voir dire, you might conclude the opening statement by telling the jurors that at the end of the trial the plaintiff will ask them to assess "fair and reasonable damages which, in this case, are substantial."

Many lawyers describe the damages as a "debt due and owing" and carefully avoid referring to damages as an "award." They believe that the term "award" implies a gift or undeserved proceeds, such as those one might win in a game or lottery.

Also avoid creating an impression during the opening statement that the plaintiff is overreaching. This helps to counter the defense tactic of weaving evidence of plaintiff "greed" into defense counsel's opening statement, such as evidence that the plaintiff is exaggerating the nature and extent of the injuries or that the plaintiff is unfairly claiming that the defendant caused unrelated injuries or damages. If the case lends itself to these defense tactics, you should mitigate claims of greed in your opening. The following examples illustrate ways to demonstrate to jurors that the plaintiff is only seeking fair compensation for injuries the defendant inflicted.

Hypochondriac with No Permanent Injury

The following is a good way to anticipate a defense argument that the plaintiff is a greedy hypochondriac who exaggerates her injuries.

> Due to her own determination and the help of her treating physicians, Mrs. Gardner has made a good recovery, and her life is now pretty much back to normal. This is not a case with large damages, and she is not entitled to substantial damages. A debt is due and owing for each item of injury and damage that she sustained, but she is not interested in, nor is she entitled to, a verdict for more than the law permits for her injuries and damages. Accordingly, at the conclusion of this trial you will be asked to determine the amount of that debt and to make certain that you are satisfied that your verdict fairly and reasonably compensates the plaintiff for her injuries and damages.

Preexisting Condition

If your client has a preexisting condition, you should acknowledge that from the beginning and clarify what damages are being claimed. In the following case, improper surgery was performed in an attempt to correct a congenital defect.

> At the conclusion of this case, we will ask you to assess damages only for those problems resulting from the wrong surgery performed by Dr. Smith and for the complications resulting from that surgery. Sarah Jones is not entitled to damages for the congenital defect that Dr. Smith failed to correct with his improper surgery, nor is she entitled to damages for the surgery performed when Dr. Coleman subsequently corrected the congenital defect with proper surgery. Likewise, if you can separate the damages the hospital nurses caused from the damages Dr. Smith caused, please do so, because we want to be fair to every party involved in this litigation.

Wrongful Death of an Adult Child with No Dependents

In a breast cancer medical negligence case, Anita Sanchez brought suit for the wrongful death of her adult unmarried daughter.

> What about damages in this case? You will learn that Theresa died where she was born, in her mother's small adobe house in New Mexico. Anita raised Theresa and her brother and sister, who never knew their father. They were raised as an extended family with their grandparents, who lived next door. Anita has an eighth-grade education and has lived in poverty all her life. Her children all worked hard, finished high school, and went to college. Theresa was always employed, always helped provide for her mother and

> assisted the rest of the family financially. You will learn that Theresa purchased a new roof for her mother's house and bought her mother furniture and that, at the time of Theresa's death, Theresa's automobile was co-owned by her mother. Theresa also purchased food and clothing for her mother.
>
> Had Theresa survived, she would have continued to pay the enormous debt she owed to her mother for her mother's unselfish care and devotion. An economist will give an opinion on the future value of Theresa's services to her mother, and you may use this opinion for guidance if you find it helpful. In addition to Anita's economic losses, you will be asked to judge the worth of Theresa's life and to place a monetary value on it.

In wrongful death cases with limited economic losses, defense counsel will often describe the facts in a manner that minimizes the economic losses. You should use the evidence available to you in your opening statement to maximize damages in order to negate this tactic.

Testimony of Economist

Defense counsel will often refer to the testimony of an economist as a cap on damages that the jury cannot exceed, or he may insinuate that the economist's testimony exaggerates the damages. To minimize the defendant's opening statement, you should emphasize fairness and the fact that the jury can assess damages in excess of the amount the economist suggests. For example,

> Susan Milo is now a widow. She and Gary did not have children, and she has not remarried. At the conclusion of this case, you will learn that you must assess damages for a wrongful death based on the net monetary loss to Susan Milo. To fairly and accurately estimate this loss, we will provide you with the testimony of Dr. Evenson, an economist. He places the value of Susan Milo's loss at approximately $950,000. You are not bound by Dr. Evenson's opinion; however, you may find his calculations and approach informative and useful. You may assess greater or lesser damages than the amount Dr. Evenson calculates. You will be asked to assess the damages and render a verdict for an amount that you believe the evidence supports.

USING DEMONSTRATIVE EXHIBITS AND EVIDENCE

Occasionally, you may want to use during opening statement an exhibit that was admitted as evidence before the trial. If a particular exhibit has not been previously admitted as evidence, opposing counsel will often stipulate to its use during opening statements. It is likewise sometimes advantageous to use the blackboard or a previously prepared drawing or chart to help the jury understand the evidence. The court will often permit counsel to proceed in this fashion if the use of the evidence assists the jury and does not otherwise violate the rules governing opening statements.

Use demonstrative evidence or aids in your opening statement only if they make the statement easier to understand. Before using such evidence, consider the following:

- Will the evidence complicate, rather than simplify, your narrative?
- Could you use the information conveyed by the demonstrative item more effectively during the trial or in summation?
- Could you present the information in the demonstrative aid more effectively in some other form?

If you determine that the demonstrative evidence will not accomplish its desired purpose in opening statement, do not use it at that time.

The following paragraphs provide examples of the dramatic and effective use of demonstrative aids in opening statement.

Hospital and Medical Charts and Records

Consider a case where the plaintiff claims that a physician performed the wrong surgery and should have done a triple arthrodesis. During your opening statement, you could note,

> When Dr. Brown testifies, we expect her to deny that she should have performed a triple arthrodesis at the outset. But we will introduce a letter she wrote to another physician, marked as exhibit 23, in which she states, "I am referring Jane Parker to you for consultation. . . . My recommendation is for a triple arthrodesis, which I should have done in the first place. . . ."

Another way of approaching the use of that exhibit in opening statement would be

> We expect Dr. Brown to testify that she was correct in not performing a triple arthrodesis. However, we will show you a document as evidence that Dr. Brown herself is of the opinion that she performed the wrong surgery and should have performed a triple arthrodesis. We do not expect Dr. Brown to testify that the document is unreliable, because she authored and signed it.

Medical Illustrations and Models

When your case involves a complicated medical concept, you often may use in opening statement a simplified medical illustration, an X ray, or a medical model to describe how the plaintiff sustained injury through the doctor's negligence. As a rule of thumb, if you cannot describe the negligent conduct and its harmful consequences in simple language that gives the jury a mental image, you should consider using exhibits or demonstrative aids.

Simple Demonstrative Aids

When possible, you should use your hands, your arms, your body, the courtroom, and objects in the courtroom as demonstrative aids. These "aids" are often more effective in communicating ideas to the jury than a previously prepared chart or exhibit.

DISCLOSING INFORMATION IN OPENING STATEMENT

Your opening statement should be well reasoned and calm, yet persuasive. It should not be emotional, flamboyant, or comical. Make your opening statement a short and powerful description of the essential facts you must prove to win. Although you should refute the anticipated defenses by emphasizing the reasonableness of the plaintiff's conduct, your opening statement should not resemble your summation. Accordingly, leave your attack on witnesses' credibility for cross-examination, and save policy arguments for summation.

It is best not to disclose all significant evidence in opening statement. The evidence itself will often be far more dramatic than your description of it. For example, showing a day-in-the-life movie later in trial is more effective than describing an average day in the plaintiff's life during opening statement. Rather than teaching the jurors everything in your opening statement, allow them to "complete the puzzle" themselves during the trial. Let the jurors "discover" further evidence to support their first impression that the plaintiff should prevail.

Describe the factual disputes to the jury. Doing this accurately in the opening statement will enhance your credibility during the trial as the jury hears the evidence and will also enhance your credibility during closing argument. At that time you can remind the jury of your accuracy during opening statement, and you will be able to point out any significant misstatements made by the defense.

Do not compose your opening statement until you have completed all other phases of trial preparation; it must mesh with your overall strategy for trial. Accordingly, each portion of your opening statement must be consistent with all the other segments of the trial.

CONCLUSION

When you conclude a successful opening statement, if what you said is an accurate description of what the evidence will prove, the jurors will be thinking that you should win the case. Further, since what you said sounded reasonable, they will be thinking that you can probably prove your case.

At the conclusion of your opening statement, the jurors will probably expect the defense to strongly contest your claims, but they should already have serious doubts about the defense's ability to do so.

Finally, the jurors should be developing some respect for you and be impressed with your knowledge, fairness, and sincerity.

If your opening statement has been successful, the jurors will not be surprised by statements or evidence described by the defense during the defendant's opening statement, and you will have the advantage as you begin calling witnesses to testify on your client's behalf. You develop momentum and score points in opening statement; you must continue with that momentum as the trial progresses.

CHAPTER TEN

EXAMINING WITNESSES

DIRECT EXAMINATION

Planning Direct

There are four important goals of direct examination:

- Support your overall trial strategy and tie together your opening statement and closing arguments. Your direct examination of your witnesses should lend credibility to your opening statement and mesh with the total trial structure and strategy. For instance, if you explain in opening statement that your client was cautious in operating his motorcycle when he was injured in a collision with a car, then you should elicit direct testimony that he is a good motorcyclist and not a motorcycle gang member or a trail rider who destroys the environment. Also emphasize that he always keeps within the speed limit, wears a helmet, and operates the cycle only to and from work, both for economic and environmental reasons.
- Minimize issues that may cause a jury to react unfavorably to your client. For instance, explain how your client became addicted to drugs while recovering from injuries sustained in Vietnam.
- Dramatize weaknesses in the defendant's position; reiterate and underscore them through your witnesses' testimony. Relate your direct examination to your intended summation. In preparing your witnesses' testimony, consider how your summation will further dramatize any weaknesses in the defendant's position, and then lay a proper foundation for that summation during the direct examination. For example, consider a medical negligence case brought against an obstetrician for failure to timely perform a cesarean section, which resulted in a brain-damaged baby. Assume hypothetically that the obstetrician's late arrival at the hospital caused the delay in surgery, and he never visited the baby or the mother following surgery. You intend to present the obstetrician as the "uncaring doctor" during summation. On direct examination, the mother should factually describe the fear and concern

she had for the baby as the surgery was delayed because of the doctor's absence. She should also make a simple statement, without anger, that the doctor never visited her or the baby following delivery. You should save the accusation that the doctor is a cold and uncaring person for summation.

- Minimize the impact of points the defense counsel probably intends to score on cross-examination. First disclose all weaknesses and problems in your client's case, and then elicit satisfactory explanations from your witnesses.

Start working toward these goals by returning to the theme or basic concept of the case. Thoroughly review the facts, the deposition testimony, the medical records, the expert consultant's information, and any other important information. Prepare a basic fact outline, and identify all of the relevant factual issues in the case.[1] Carefully evaluate the testimony available to you from the witnesses and determine which of the witnesses can best address each issue. Determine how you are going to use witnesses and evidence to logically present your story to the jury during the direct examination part of the trial, and decide how you can best present your case themes. These decisions then becomes the basis for determining the order in which you will call witnesses during the trial. (Remember that the normal complications of trial may prevent you from strictly adhering to your planned order.)[2]

As part of your planning, review the exhibits that you will introduce and the witnesses you will need to introduce them. If your jurisdiction requires that exhibits be authenticated and introduced in a particular manner, research the necessary procedures. Be sure that your exhibits are organized for easy access and use with witnesses during trial.[3]

Prepare an outline for each witness so you can be sure that you establish all relevant points that you intend to make during the direct examination of that witness. The outline can consist of detailed, written questions, a list of points you need to make and exhibits you need to introduce with each witness, or a simple outline of the areas in which you will ask questions.[4] The witness outline may also include a

---

1 See Appendix F.1 for a sample case summary.

2 See Appendix F.2 for a sample schedule.

3 See Appendix F.3 for a sample exhibit list.

4 See Appendix F (F.4–F.6) for sample outlines of direct examinations.

checklist of damages elements to assist in questioning witnesses on the subject of injury and damages. The outline is for your use only in preparing your witness for direct examination and in conducting the direct examination during trial. The outline should not be provided to the witness because it could then be discovered by defense counsel and used to embarrass or discredit the witness during cross-examination.[5]

Handling Direct

During direct examination, you should

- Elicit background information from your client. This will humanize your client and lay a foundation for subsequent testimony on both liability and damages.
- Given the information you got during voir dire about the jurors, include any items you think will establish a rapport between your client and the jurors and cause the jurors to identify with your client.
- Let your witness explain the critical events after he has relaxed and is no longer a stranger to the jury. His description of the events should be chronological and factual. His testimony should be persuasive and told as a story, using language intended to help the jurors paint a mental picture of the events. If your client is the one telling the story, do not interrupt this portion of his testimony. You can always go back and fill in any gaps after your client is done telling the story.
- Weave into the chronology facts that will further your goals of direct. Remember, you are aiming to defuse affirmative defenses, minimize problems or weaknesses in your client's claim, and impeach the defendant or the defendant's witnesses.
- Have witnesses other than your client describe your client's injuries to the jury, or use exhibits to depict the injuries. Most jurors do not like to hear a client's self-serving complaints about injuries and a description of his own ailments. Introduce films, photographs, and demonstrative evidence to speak for your client.

Helping Witnesses

Use the following techniques to help the witness tell a story that creates images—a story that the jury can relive.

- Assist the witness in retelling the story by using short questions, such as "Who?", "What?", "Where?", "Why?", and "When?", rather than complicated and lengthy questions. Juries find a witness's narrative ac-

---

5 See Appendix F (F.7 and F.8) for sample outlines regarding damages.

count more believable than an account that emerges from a lawyer's close questioning.

- Keep your questions and tone of voice inconspicuous; the focus should be on the witness. In effective direct examination, the jurors are almost unaware of the examining lawyer's presence, despite the frequency of the questions. Like the baton in the hand of an orchestra conductor, your questions should go virtually unnoticed as the jury focuses on the witness. This contrasts with cross-examination, in which the focus of attention alternates between the lawyer and the witness, and the jurors' heads move back and forth between the two combatants.
- Use simple but descriptive language that the jury can understand, and prepare your client to do the same.
- Use your demeanor, tone of voice, and position in the courtroom to highlight the emotion and drama of your witness's story.
- Use your questions to set the pace and maintain the momentum of the examination. Guide and control the emotions of the witness with your demeanor, your tone of voice, and the information your question supplies.
- Prevent the witness from fumbling with exhibits or other demonstrative evidence; such a distraction can break the momentum of the testimony. Always give the witness the appropriate page of a complex exhibit rather than ask him to search through the document. Project critical documents using an overhead viewer, or give each juror a copy to follow as the witness testifies.
- Avoid defense objections, interruptions by the court, and recesses during the critical part of a witness's testimony, when pace and momentum are important.

The following example illustrates the use of some of these techniques to elicit information from a widow in a wrongful death case:

Q: Mrs. Brown, your neighbor testified earlier that you looked thin, frail, and sick after your husband's death. Did you lose weight?

A: I guess I did, but I wasn't aware of it at the time. I don't remember much of those first few weeks. I wasn't sleeping well, and it seemed like I was always crying and couldn't control myself.

Q: (Looking concerned and sympathetic) Were you alone in the house at night?

A: (Hesitating) Well, yes.

Q: (Looking perplexed) You hesitated; was there a problem?

A: (Starting to cry) John [her deceased husband] was always there at night. At first I knew I was dreaming, or thought I was, but then I didn't know, and it was happening so much I couldn't tell whether I was dreaming or whether he was really there. After a while I thought I was going crazy, but I didn't care so long as he would come back at night. (Crying)

Q: (In a soft tone of voice) You must miss him very much. Your Honor, could we have a short recess?

CROSS-EXAMINATION

One author has suggested that the objectives of cross-examination should include the following:[6]

(1) To establish that the witness is lying on a material point;

(2) To show that the witness is prejudiced—this will establish a motive for coloring testimony;

(3) To show that his testimony is improbable;

(4) To force the witness to admit certain facts;

(5) To supplement testimony that the witness has already given;

(6) To weaken the testimony of the witness by showing his opinion is questionable because of his inability to observe, to hear a conversation, or to see because of poor lighting conditions, or by showing other facts to reduce the value of his opinion;

(7) To show that an expert witness or even a lay witness who has testified to an opinion is not competent or qualified because he lacks the training or experience (the purpose is to negate or reduce the probative value of his opinion);

(8) To impeach a witness by showing that he has given a contrary statement at another time;

(9) To show that a witness has been convicted of an infamous crime in order to cast doubt on his credibility;

(10) To obtain necessary evidence to establish the case through examination of an adverse witness during the case in chief.

Other goals of cross-examination include:

---

6 A. E. MORRILL, TRIAL DIPLOMACY 55 (2d ed. 1979).

- Destroying or weakening the jurors' favorable impressions of the adverse witness;
- Discrediting the witness because of bias, prejudice, lack of qualifications or other deficiencies;
- Eliciting contradictions, modifications, or retractions of material testimony given;
- Exposing fabrication or exaggeration;
- Testing the truth of the statements of a witness;
- Eliciting damaging admissions from the witness that will discredit him and the party calling him;
- Weakening or disproving the case of your adversary;
- Separating falsehood from truth, hearsay from actual knowledge, things imaginary from things real, opinion from fact, and inference from recollection;
- Discrediting the witness personally;
- Destroying all or a portion of the direct testimony of a witness; and
- Forcing the witness to admit certain facts.

Apart from the negative goals of discrediting, destroying, or weakening the witness's testimony, there are affirmative goals of cross-examination. One such goal is to get the witness to make statements that help the plaintiff's case, for example, statements that narrow the issues or amount to concessions that favor the plaintiff. The late John Appleman said that the following were the seven primary purposes of cross-examination:

- To destroy testimony;
- To minimize testimony;
- To minimize the witness as a witness;
- To minimize the witness as a person;
- To destroy or damage other testimony of the adversary;
- To corroborate other testimony on your side of the case;
- To build up your witness(es).

In summary, cross-examination has a twofold purpose: (1) to discredit the testimony previously given by the witness on direct examination, and (2) to draw out facts and opinions favorable to the position of the cross-examiner.

Planning Cross

The planning required for proper cross-examination should reflect basic principles of trial preparation, some of which are discussed later in this chapter. Know the subject matter of your case. Use your resources; you may need to research the general subject matter in the library in addition to studying the material generated by your case.

Plan and outline the cross-examination. Plan a step-by-step attack; build slowly, permit no retreat, and force an ultimately unavoidable conclusion.

Your outline can be merely a summary of the claims of negligence, based on the facts on which the plaintiff is relying. Using this outline as a checklist, you can formulate your cross-examination into something more precise. You can also use more detailed outlines. You may choose to create an extensive outline that includes each complete question that you plan to ask.[7]

Remember, however, that although it is important that you outline the overall procedure for your cross-examination, you should not simply read from your outline in conducting the cross-examination. You must listen carefully when the witness answers your questions. Too often, examiners are so preoccupied with asking the next question that they don't listen to the answer being given to their last question. If you follow your cross-examination outline too rigidly, you may miss an important line of inquiry that the witness may have opened in response to one of your questions.

Handling Cross

An effective cross-examination should immediately follow the direct examination. If possible, avoid a delay in cross-examination because of evening recess or the calling of another witness out of order.

Your cross-examination should start strong; that is, you should attempt to make an important point early in your examination. For instance, this is a prime opportunity to attack a witness's credibility. Under the principles of primacy, an early attack has a significant effect on the jury. At the same time, the principles of recency dictate that cross should end on a strong note; therefore, save a significant point for the final question in cross-examination.

Cross-examine for the jury. Think of yourself as a lay person in the jury box, and listen to every question and answer during cross-ex-

---

7 See Appendix F (F.9–F.11) for sample outlines regarding cross-examination.

amination as if you are a juror: make the observations the jurors are making, and answer the questions the jurors are asking. Do not allow the cross-examination to bore the jury. Alter the pace and content of the cross-examination to keep it interesting and effective. Use humor to control the momentum and maintain the jury's interest; a good cross-examination is entertaining, and occasional humor can both entertain the jurors and score points.

Cross-examination is most effective when it is conducted in a professional, calm, and rational manner. An overly aggressive or demeaning approach to the witness will have an adverse impact on the jury; you should not ask questions in such a way that the jurors resent your "attack" on the witness. For example, do not storm around the courtroom pointing your finger at a terrified witness. Also avoid academic nitpicking; it will confuse the jurors, and they will resent your browbeating technique. It is crucial that you not lose your temper, and it is equally important that you apologize when necessary.

Do not give the jurors the opportunity to feel empathy or sympathy for the witness. Your goal is not to help the jurors vent their anger through your cross-examination but to make them show that anger later through the size of their verdict. Cross-examination enables the jurors to identify with you as the underdog. In so doing, the jurors will root for you and cheer inwardly when you overcome the defense witness and conclude your cross-examination in victory.

Uphold your credibility and reputation for fairness in the eyes of the jury. The jurors must understand the words you use, and your sentences must be clear so that they are not misunderstood. Reduce highly technical and complex analyses to a level the jurors can understand. Use illustrations, analogies, and simple statements of fundamental concepts. Make your questions short so that the witness has no room to evade them. Your questions must not appear to be "trick questions," or the jurors will think that you are being unfair to the witness. Ensure that your questions are actually fair in context; in other words, do not misstate the facts or prior testimony. Fairness also requires that you follow up on the directions or leads that the witness suggests, if they are relevant. Ask the witness questions in such a way that if the witness doesn't give the desired answer, he appears unfair or dishonest.

Remember that leading questions are permitted on cross-examination. The use of leading questions is one of the most effective techniques for you to control the witness in cross-examination. Be careful, however, not to ask leading questions that appear to "hammer" the witness into a position; this may cause the jury to feel sorry for him.

Whenever possible, properly framed leading questions should require the witness to answer with a yes or no. Typical cross-examination questions such as: "Do you agree?", "You will concede, won't you?", and "Isn't it true that . . . ?" all call for yes or no answers. A high percentage of "yes" answers frequently characterizes a successful cross-examination.[8] For this reason, only in extraordinary circumstances should you ask the witness "why" or "how" questions, which invite explanation or description.

You will frequently encounter witnesses who refuse to respond with a yes or no and who evade answering your questions or insist on explaining every answer. You may handle this problem in two ways. First, you could ask the trial judge to assist you, for example, by directing the witness to answer your questions. Studies have shown, however, that jurors believe that lawyers who ask the judge for help are ineffective lawyers. Second, you could tell the witness that your question calls for a simple yes or no answer, and that the witness will have the opportunity to testify further on redirect examination.

Do not lead the witness all the time; rather, lead him when appropriate, and limit the witness by the form of your question to give the illusion of freedom.

Force direct responses when the witness tries to sidetrack or hedge. Prevent him from changing the subject. If he does not respond directly to a question, give him the benefit of the doubt; perhaps he misunderstood the question. If he continues to be evasive and unresponsive, show some frustration to the jury as you press for your answer. Have the question read back by the court reporter, and then ask the witness again for a direct response. Finally, show disappointment and increasing frustration. If the court then becomes angry at the witness, the jury will question the witness's credibility.

If the witness's responses are weak, use voice inflection to emphasize the weakness. When the testimony sounds incredible, reinforce the jury's impression with your own facial expression and voice inflection in the next question. Emphasize the confusing nature of the testimony, inconsistencies, erroneous calculations, or other weaknesses in the same way. Once the jurors realize that your reaction to the testimony is the same as theirs, you can subtly influence them by exploit-

---

8 See Appendix F.12 for a sample examination and cross-examination of a defense medical expert. It illustrates this technique of cross-examination as well as the other techniques described in this chapter.

ing that rapport and your credibility. Ways to remark on the witness' behavior without appearing to pick on him include:

"You hesitated—I gather that you are uncertain?"

"Why are you angry? Did I do something to offend you?"

"I'm sorry, I didn't hear that answer. Would you repeat it?" (A devastating answer in a low tone of voice.)

"You seem to be choking. May I get you a cup of water?"

"Is there some reason for glancing at defense counsel before answering these questions?"

Federal Rule of Evidence 607 permits any party to attack the credibility of a witness.[9] If you think the witness is being dishonest, first try to determine if the witness is mistaken. For example, few witnesses are capable of describing exactly what occurred. Most of them reconstruct what they believe to have happened, and they have in their minds a mental image from which they testify.

Furthermore, the witness's interpretation may be subconsciously shaded by conversations he has had with one of the other parties or perhaps by interviews with attorneys or adjusters. Carefully observe the witness at all times. His expression and nonverbal communication, perhaps in looking to the other attorney for help, can signal you and the jury that you are exploring an important area.

Watch the witness carefully and, when appropriate, remark on the information obtained to alert the jury of its significance. However, do not emphasize the importance of information when its significance is obvious to the jury and it is clear that they have already taken notice. The jurors could be offended by a perception that you have underestimated their intelligence.

If necessary, the testimony of a witness may be discredited by showing, among other things:

- That the witness is incompetent to testify to the events;
- That the passage of time and the suggestions of others have changed or exaggerated the witness's recollection;
- That the witness's testimony contradicts itself;
- That the witness admits uncertainty about a statement made on direct examination;

---

[9] Rule 607 provides: "The credibility of a witness may be attacked by any party, including the party calling the witness."

- That the witness is biased or prejudiced; or
- That the witness's character may be impeached under Federal Rule of Evidence 608.

To prepare for cross-examination, ask yourself the following questions:

- Is the witness biased or prejudiced?[10]
- What is the witness's motive for exaggeration or distortion?
- Has the witness previously been convicted of a crime while represented by counsel?[11]
- Are there lapses or failures in the witness's memory?
- Does the witness lack the mental faculties to testify?
- What deficiencies existed in the witness's opportunity for observation of the negligent act?
- Is any prior testimony or statement of the witness in conflict with the testimony at trial?[12]
- What memoranda did the witness use on direct testimony?
- Was the witness coached?

During cross-examination, use analogies or strong comparisons to illustrate that an opinion may not be based on reality. For example:

> "A blood alcohol content of .999 percent means Mr. Jones is capable of driving a car, but 1.0 percent means he is not capable of driving a car; is that correct?"

If you "score" with an answer, stop the line of questioning, and do not repeat the question. Go on to another subject quickly before the witness can recover and change the testimony. Prevent the witness from qualifying an answer with a "perhaps" or a "maybe" when you know that you can elicit a favorable, unqualified answer.

Of course, you should never approach cross-examination without a plan. Never ask a question if you are unsure of the answer. Never lose sight of your objectives in cross, but do not reveal them either. If the witness knows your objectives early in the questioning, he may be able to avoid conceding facts that your questions would have otherwise caused him to concede. Generally speaking, your questions

---

10 Evidence of the witness's religious beliefs or opinions is inadmissible for this purpose under FED. R. EVID. 610.

11 FED. R. EVID. 609.

12 FED. R. EVID. 608(a) & 613.

should appear harmless. Some of the best cross-examinations involve a step-by-step process in which the witness is ultimately compelled to concede certain facts because his previous answers make a certain conclusion inescapable.

Impeaching Witnesses

Impeach a witness's testimony appropriately and quickly. When you cite inconsistent statements, you should be clear and convincing, and you should quote verbatim. Your impeachment should immediately follow the answer being impeached, with no delay for asking foundation questions or fumbling through a deposition. Highlight instances in which a witness is not responding directly to questions, not answering questions, or not conceding what, in all fairness, should be conceded.

Discredit or impeach only testimony that is harmful to your client's case. If a witness gives surprisingly favorable testimony that is contrary to unfavorable testimony he gave in deposition or in prior statements, do not impeach the witness with the prior unfavorable statements. Do not impeach on relatively minor points if you can destroy the effectiveness of the testimony by impeaching on major points.

The use of a contradictory statement that impeaches the witness is effective only if the contradiction is direct and the witness's testimony is significant. If you impeach on a minor issue, or if the claimed contradiction is in fact ambiguous and is not clearly a contradiction, you may lose ground. If you are having trouble controlling the witness, impeachment is an effective device to bring him into line. If you are going to impeach with a written document, such as a deposition or statement, you need to refer to the specific time and place and have the witness acknowledge that he made the statement. Each question you ask should call for a yes or no answer. If the witness admits the contradiction, the impeachment is complete. If the witness denies making the statement or says that he cannot remember it, you will need further proof.

With regard to prior inconsistent writings of a witness, normally, if the writing contains nothing except the contradictory facts, the entire writing will be admitted into evidence when the witness denies the statement. If the witness admits the statement, the writing normally will not be introduced into evidence unless it is an admission of a part. Usually, you must lay a foundation for the witness's oral statements by calling his attention to the time, place, and circumstances in which he made the statements.

After the witness has been impeached, you will find it easier to elicit the more difficult concessions from him. A witness who has been "burned" in this fashion early in cross-examination may concede far more as the cross-examination progresses, particularly if he becomes confused or does not remember what he said earlier in his deposition. Sometimes merely reaching for the deposition when the witness hesitates will bring a favorable response.

Make it easy for the witness to give a favorable response, and make it difficult for him to stray from the script and give an unfavorable response. If you challenge and accuse the witness, do not expect him to respond favorably; he will accept the challenge. To maintain control, punish a witness who is bad: make him look foolish, biased, prejudiced, incompetent, or otherwise weak. Reward him when he is good: be courteous and respectful, and restrain yourself from embarrassing him in front of the jury. Once you have conditioned a witness to respond to punishment or rewards, let him know by your tone of voice, your facial expression, and the form of your question whether you expect him to respond favorably or whether you are giving him the option of offering an unfavorable response. To control the witness through punishment and rewards, be consistent and fair. Do not embarrass him unnecessarily or attack his credibility when he reacts appropriately and concedes everything he should concede. Be consistent in case you meet the witness in a future trial.

A technique that works well when the defendant has more than one witness is to impeach one witness with the testimony of another. This is particularly effective when you have only one strong witness whose testimony is not weakened by inconsistencies, and when each defense witness has been unable to hear the testimony of the other and is therefore unaware that he is impeaching the testimony of the other.

The opinions of opposing experts will often be the same, provided they are based on the same assumed facts or variables. If you have a situation where experts on both sides agree once the proper facts or variables have been established, ask the opposing expert to assume that the facts that support your theory or your expert's conclusions are correct and to render opinions based on those facts. This lays the foundation for arguing in summation that only the facts are in dispute, and that the expert witnesses on both sides agree once the facts on which they are relying have been properly established. You should argue further that the experts' opinions compel the jury to render a verdict for your client if the jury agrees with your rendition of the facts. Keep in mind that this approach is not effective unless you persuade the jury that your facts are the correct ones.

Cross-Examining Experts

Careful preparation for the cross-examination of the defendant's expert is essential; never attempt to cross-examine an experienced expert witness without doing the necessary groundwork first. This groundwork includes reviewing the material you obtained in discovery, such as in interrogatories and depositions; studying the relevant literature; and deciding your angle of attack.

Also examine the following information in preparing for the cross:

- The material obtained from, or considered by, the expert in forming her opinions;
- The witness's education, experience, and claimed qualifications;
- The general principles of the art or science on which the expert is giving an opinion as compared with the expert's opinion;
- The facts assumed by the expert and their accuracy. You will be able to use any inaccuracy you uncover to later impeach the expert;
- Any admitted material that might prove helpful at trial;
- The written material, articles, or testimony by the witness offered in other cases as well as material generated in discovery; and
- The evidence of possible bias, such as the expert's relationship with the defendant, the number of times the expert has testified in court, the number of times the expert has testified exclusively for one side or the other, whether she has given consistent opinions in every case, the amount paid to her, or opinions that are so ridiculous that they demonstrate bias.

Plan an attack that attempts to get the expert to water down or back down from her opinions so that they appear to be conjecture and speculation. Try to get the expert to point the finger of blame at any other defendant in the action, even if the expert will not be critical of the defendant who hired her.

In general, your cross-examination of the expert witness should carefully show the jury the expert's role, demonstrate any implied or actual biases, and capitalize on admissions or helpful affirmative statements.[13]

Lead the expert witness down the primrose path. Have her concede all the established points that logically lead to the conclusion favorable to your case. That way if she does not concede the conclusion you suggest, she will appear unfair, biased, and incredible. Be careful not to warn the expert in advance of the trap you are setting. Your

---

13 Appendix F.12 illustrates the technique of demonstrating implied biases and also shows how to elicit admissions and helpful statements.

concluding questions, like the one that follows, should be safe but helpful:

> "Certainly, doctor, you are not claiming to be a person who has never made a mistake? This is simply your opinion and you might be wrong; isn't that correct?"

Elicit the concessions you know the expert will make based on her deposition. Begin by framing questions in the precise language of the deposition and, if the witness deviates from the answers she gave at deposition, impeach her.

The technique for impeachment with a deposition should be well known to all counsel; however, many lawyers do not know how to use this important impeachment device. First, establish for the jury what a deposition is. Next, make the following points clear to the jury: (1) the witness was under oath during the deposition, (2) the defendant's attorney was present at the deposition, and (3) the court reporter recorded everything the witness said at the deposition.

In some cases, you should refer to sections of the deposition in which you may have given the expert the opportunity to change any other answer or reflect on an answer to show that the witness was treated fairly.

After doing this, call the witness's attention to inconsistent testimony. In all cases, preface your questions with the page and line number to which you are referring in the deposition. For example, you might say: "Referring to page 37, line 17 of the deposition of Dr. Halpert . . . do you recall, Doctor, my asking you this question and your giving this answer. . . ." [Read the question and answer.]

After reading the question and answer to the witness, ask several questions, including:

- Did I read that correctly?
- Is that a correct answer?
- Was that the answer you gave to that question at the time of your deposition?
- Were you telling the truth when you gave that testimony?

Using expert literature in cross-examination can be very effective. Depending on the rules under which you are operating, normally you must establish that the text or literature is reliable, or that it is information on which this witness has relied. Following that, identify the text and section to which you are referring, just as in a deposition.

As a practical matter, most attorneys prepare an extra copy of the material for the witness to look at. Some even project enlargements on a screen or have enlargements of the literature made for the witness and the jury to see during the examination.

You must be concerned about the jurors' attitudes regarding what is happening as the examination takes place. For example, the jury will generally be on the side of all witnesses, including expert witnesses. Some judges are awed by experts such as physicians, and they are frequently protective of them. Other judges, however, require experts to answer questions directly. Consider the court's attitude regarding the expert witness.

You must use the proper demeanor. For example, don't treat the expert with sarcasm and contempt. Persistent and respectful interrogation is much more effective. However, it may be appropriate to alter your attitude if the witness becomes hostile, arrogant, or untruthful. When this occurs, you may want to appear to be disbelieving, perplexed, dismayed, frustrated, or concerned. When and how to alter your demeanor to effectively react to a change in the witness's attitude is something that is only learned by experience.

Keeping a "poker face" is a good technique that should be developed. On the other hand, if it is a time to laugh, even at yourself, do that. Losing your temper, though, is always a bad tactic.

Know what your goals or objectives are before you start, and be prepared to work toward them. Do not simply ask questions hoping that something will develop.

The pace at which you move depends on your tactics and your approach to the problem. While changing rapidly from one issue to another or one topic to another may be an effective device to keep a witness off balance, it sometimes results in the jury's losing context, and they may perceive you as being tricky.

Decide on a case-by-case basis whether you should use a question on cross or save it for summation. Keep in mind though, that one of the keys to persuasion is repetition; if you can make the point early in the trial during cross-examination and perhaps make it again later, do that.

If demonstrative evidence will help during cross-examination, use it. Use enlarged photographs of reports, copies of depositions, charts, photographs, and the like. Writing on poster-size paper during cross-examination can be an effective tool when outlining the testimony of a witness or perhaps identifying the signs of a particular symptom in a medical negligence case so that everyone can see it in writing as well as hear it out loud.

Although most trial judges don't interfere during cross-examination, some do. If the interference is excessive and inappropriate, a respectful objection should be made outside the presence of the jury to protect the record. Usually, this can be handled tactfully, and judges are sensitive to the problem of prejudice under such an arrangement.

In summary, the cross-examination of experts, like everything else relating to the trial of a case, is an art and not a science. It requires experience, skill, preparation, hard work, and, to be successful, a lot of luck.

REDIRECT EXAMINATION

Use redirect examination to rehabilitate a witness. The procedure is similar to using a deposition for impeachment: first call the witness's attention to testimony rendered during cross-examination; summarize and restate that testimony precisely. Then guide the witness through an explanation of the admissions or concessions he made during cross. Do this only on critical items that go to the heart of the case, not on items that are inconsequential.

Redirect examination, unlike direct examination,is a time when the jury's attention is on the lawyer as well as on the client. You may now ask leading questions, but you absolutely must preface each question with a recitation of earlier testimony. If opposing counsel has tricked the witness or misstated the facts during cross-examination, you can call it to the jury's attention during redirect examination. If the defendant's lawyer used impeachment materials unfairly during cross-examination (for example, by lifting portions of a deposition out of context), you can rehabilitate your client by reading additional materials. This technique not only rehabilitates your client but also attacks the credibility of opposing counsel.

CONCLUSION

It is imperative that you plan and prepare for the direct and cross-examination of witnesses as early as possible using the information you obtain through formal and informal discovery.

Appropriate outlines for the examination of each witness must be carefully prepared with references to exhibits and impeachment materials. Having done this, you must skillfully use the techniques available to conduct a successful examination in the courtroom.

The direct examination, cross-examination, and redirect examination of witnesses involve skills that are only acquired through experience. Medical negligence cases are particularly difficult and require your maximum effort, but the thrill of conducting successful examinations makes the time and effort worthwhile.

CHAPTER ELEVEN

SUMMATION

MOTIVATING THE JURY

Summation offers you the opportunity to persuade the unconvinced, to give those jurors who are convinced the ammunition with which to persuade others, and to fortify your assertions that from the beginning your presentation of the case has been sincere and based on the facts. Summation is also an opportunity to maximize the jury's assessment of damages for your client.[1]

Although this chapter focuses on using summation to maximize damages, you must decide in each case whether you should start the substantive part of summation with a discussion of the facts as they relate to the law of liability and then progress to the facts as they relate to the law of damages, or discuss damages first, then liability.[2] Generally, jurors will be more receptive to your summation on damages if you first dispel any concerns that they may still have about liability. Likewise, when a doctor is guilty of gross misconduct or abusive behavior, a persuasive reminder of that misconduct at the outset can motivate jurors to be more attentive when you then focus their attention on injuries and damages. However, when you are representing a catastrophically injured person and liability based on simple negligence is a close call, you should consider discussing damages before liability. In doing so, realize that a captivating summation of damages can sometimes motivate the jurors to be more receptive in resolving the liability issues in your client's favor.

---

1 Appendix G is a sample summation in a brain-damaged baby case brought against obstetricians and a hospital.

2 For an excellent discussion of this topic, see Philip H. Corboy, Sr., *Final Argument—Earning the Jury's Trust*, 28 TRIAL, Feb. 1992, at 61, 64.

You must shape the jurors' expectations throughout the trial so the jurors will anticipate the drama of your summation and respond favorably to it. Motivate the jurors with your credibility as well as the respect and rapport you have earned during the trial. The jurors will have high expectations and positive responses if your game plan for trial has been successful[3] and you have presented your case in an honest and forthright manner. The trial process gives you the opportunity to shape jurors' expectations and reactions; use it to "grease the wheels" for a successful summation. Consider the following questions and what they suggest about how our expectations influence our reactions:

- Why do we smile before a well-known comedian gives us the punch line?
- Why do we applaud when a theatrical star first enters the scene?
- Why do we sit in anticipation at a formal gathering to hear a speech by someone we know, like, and respect?

Our expectations color our reactions, and past experiences condition us to react either favorably or unfavorably to new experiences.

Use stories to make your point occasionally. Tell simple stories that serve the dual purpose of humanizing the lawyer and scoring a point on damages. Continue to seek jury kinship and identification throughout summation, even though you established them earlier in the trial.

Motivate the jurors to listen to your summation by playing on their patriotism and their important role in our democratic civil justice system. Make them aware of the importance of their verdict; stress the power each juror has to change the plaintiff's life and the defendant's conduct, thereby protecting others from the kind of harm suffered by the plaintiff. The following passages convey to jurors their importance and power in rendering a verdict:

> Ladies and gentlemen, you are participating in something dear to all of us, something dear and priceless in a democracy: trial by jury. For most of you, this is the first rare opportunity to sit as jurors. As Americans, we value the justice provided by this unique feature of democracy. All of you came to this courtroom as strangers from all walks of life with varying experiences and backgrounds, and you brought with you your collective wisdom, knowledge, and experience. Each of you has something to contribute, and because your

---

3 The planning and techniques involved in creating and implementing a successful game plan are discussed in Chapter Seven, "Planning the Trial: Theory, Witnesses, and Trial Strategy."

verdict must be unanimous, it will represent a melting pot of your combined experience and wisdom.

Ladies and gentlemen, remember when this trial began and you were asked to raise your hands and take an oath? You may recall that you all swore to render a "true verdict according to the evidence." You may not then have realized the magnitude of that serious undertaking. You now know that the Smith family has struggled with the burden of this disaster for three-and-one-half years. I have shouldered my responsibility for this case for two years and it weighs heavily on my mind. I have had many sleepless nights seeking justice for this family. Now, as I turn this case over to you, the magnitude of the responsibility you first assumed when you took that oath must likewise weigh heavily on your minds. My job has ended and yours has begun. The future of my client is now in your hands.

Ladies and gentlemen, when you render your verdict in this case, it becomes a permanent court record—a document that will remain long after everyone who has participated in this trial has passed on, and a document that will mark a historic moment in time when six people were called together, as strangers, to do justice.

Folks, I am reminded of the words engraved above the entrance to the University of Colorado library: "I shall study and prepare myself, and someday my chance will come."

Why does that remind me of you? Each of you has studied and become experienced and knowledgeable in particular occupations or aspects of life, and each of you brings the totality of that knowledge and experience to this courtroom. You now have the rare opportunity to best use the totality of that wisdom and experience in serving as jurors and in rendering a verdict.

"I shall study and prepare myself, and someday my chance will come." This is that day. You have been called on to do justice.

A famous philosopher once said, "The things you say and the things you do can change your destiny, and the results are eternal." You will soon arrive at a unanimous jury verdict and, in doing so, have the opportunity to change Tom Brown's despair to hope . . . to remove him from his injury-laden prison and give him the free-

> dom of independence . . . and to offer him a new life. In rendering your verdict, you do have the power to change Tom Brown's destiny, and in doing so, be sure that for Tom Brown the results will be eternal.
>
> Let me speak to you now about the precious freedoms of a democracy—freedoms that we too often take for granted. In the United States you are not born to poverty with absolutely no opportunity to escape. You are not committed to a job from which you can never escape. You are not bound to a neighborhood or a community, or unable to travel about freely. In America we have precious freedoms of choice, and we protect those freedoms dearly. In the United States if someone unlawfully deprives us of the opportunity to seek better employment or to travel about freely and be independent, that person must pay for the consequences.
>
> Under our law, we are entitled to the integrity of our bodies, to our self-respect, our independence, our personalities, and our lifestyles. Nowhere else in the world are citizens offered as much protection of these rights and freedoms by law. Likewise, in America we do not send people like Dr. Smith, the defendant, to jail because he was negligent and caused injury to my client. To send Dr. Smith to jail would deprive him of his independence and self-esteem and would invade his dignity and lifestyle. It could interfere with his employment.
>
> But the law does require that a negligent person pay back what he has taken away. Dr. Smith must pay an indebtedness for causing my client to lose freedoms and rights.
>
> I am sure that Dr. Smith feels guilty of depriving my client of rights that we all cherish. He must feel guilty knowing that he cannot totally replace my client's losses with money. The payment of the debt that he owes is necessary, and it will help. A just verdict in this case will accomplish two things: first, full payment of the debt owed will help restore my client's dignity, self-esteem, independence, and freedom of choice; second, full payment will reduce the defendant's guilt. Pure justice should satisfy everyone in the courtroom. Less than full and complete justice benefits no one.

Demonstrative tools are particularly effective in motivating the jury during summation. Carefully prepare some demonstrative aids solely for use in summation. These aids can effectively illustrate your theory of the case, summarize relevant evidence and exhibits, and refute the defenses being asserted. Use diagrams or charts during summation to simplify complex material. Use overlays to explain the sequence of critical events by time and date and to demonstrate any inconsistencies in testimony. You may also use overhead viewers to present a sentence or two from hospital records, office charts, or deposition testimony.

If the defendant-doctor had five separate opportunities to save your client's life, and on each occasion she negligently failed to do so, prepare a separate numbered chart to describe each opportunity. Each chart should have a title that describes the event, such as "wrong diagnosis," "wrong medicine," or "no consultations." List on each chart the critical exhibit or witness you have used to establish the negligent act.

You can prepare another chart to demonstrate causation. This chart should list all five opportunities, in graph form, with a line drawn from each opportunity to the word "death."

These charts will help you explain to the jury that according to the law, if you prove just one act of negligence that could have caused death, your client is entitled to damages. The charts will also help you explain that in this case you have proven five separate acts of negligence, although you were only obligated to prove one, and that any one of those individual acts could have caused the death.

When you have evidence of multiple acts of negligence by the defendant and you can prove that any of those acts standing alone could have caused the damages claimed, you should still prove all of the acts. By using all the evidence of negligence, you increase your odds of persuading the jury that the plaintiff should prevail and that the jury should assess adequate damages. Jurors are not as inclined to excuse multiple acts of negligence as they are a single act; they are more inclined to assess adequate damages if they view the defendant's conduct as aggravated or gross. However, in hearing evidence of multiple acts of negligence, jurors may erroneously believe that the plaintiff is only entitled to recover if you have proved all of the acts. Therefore, make sure that your opening statement, your evidence, and the court's instructions clarify that this is not the case. To further drive this point home, list all of the defendant's 10 or 15 acts of negligence in your summation, and explain that if you have established even one of these, the jury's verdict must be for your client. Add that you believe that the evidence establishes that all the acts of negligence occurred.

ARGUING DAMAGES

Loss of Enjoyment

In your pleas for general damages, stress the plaintiff's loss of enjoyment of a full and complete life, using concrete examples with which the jury can identify. Emphasize such intangibles as the value of good health and the right to enjoy the "autumn" of one's life:

> Ladies and gentlemen, what do we value most in life? We all grow up wanting to be loved and respected by those whom we love and respect. If someone interfered with our ability to be loved and respected, we would consider that a substantial loss.
>
> What else do we value? We strive to do at least one thing well. It gives us satisfaction, dignity, and reputation. A loss of the ability to do the one thing in which we take pride is a loss of self-respect, dignity, and reputation. It is a loss of the inner peace and pleasure that nourish life. Life without occasional inner peace and pleasure is not worth living.

> The loss of the ability to earn a living is far more than just a loss of income and wages. How often have you heard the expression "If he retires he'll probably die"? Why is a job important to us? If we do it well, we are respected for our work. We feel needed and important if we are able to provide for our family and loved ones. The earnings from a job give us independence and thus self-esteem and dignity. No wonder, then, that people often fear retiring, and when some retire, they vegetate and die. My client has been deprived of far more than lost earnings and wages. He has been deprived of his enjoyment of life itself.

> Folks, I told you earlier that the law tries to put people back in the position they were in before the negligence occurred. The law tries to restore the injured person to his previous status quo. This is easy to do when property is damaged. When a house burns down, you can use money to rebuild it. But you cannot give Matthew back his brain—it's gone. Folks, the brain is unique. The finest computer in the world cannot replace the brain. It's irreplaceable and thus invaluable. No value can be placed on it because you cannot buy one anywhere.
>
> I don't know what it's like to be Matthew—to be a child in a growing boy's body, and then a child in a man's body. We all know what Matthew feels: he feels hunger, he feels cold, heat, pain; he hears his mother's voice. We know that, as a human being, he relies totally on his mother for infant care. We know that he is a helpless child in a growing body. There is no amount of money that can adequately compensate him for his loss of the opportunity to see, to love, to create, and to live a full and productive life. But I will now

outline the items of indebtedness that should be paid to arrive at a fair and reasonable verdict . . .

Sarah, at age 21, has a permanently crippled foot. The court has informed you that she has an average life expectancy of 51 years. Many people live longer than that, and some do not live that long. But Sarah is legally entitled to damages as long as she must live with her injury.

When you go into the jury room to deliberate, each of you will have thoughts and suggestions on how this injury will affect Sarah in the future. I will outline a few items that immediately come to mind, and I am sure that the six of you, using your collective wisdom and experience, will consider many more.

For example, Sarah is not very athletic. My wife and I began running at age 47. Many of us begin recreational activities at various stages of our lives. Many of us commence new hobbies later in life that require the full use of our legs and feet.

Sarah will probably marry. She will probably have children. How will her injury affect her relationship with her children? A parent with young children must be physically active. In a successful and happy marriage, the husband and wife have common interests and often participate in activities together, such as skiing, dancing, family picnics, or other activities that require the use of a healthy body. How often will Sarah have to disappoint her children or husband? How will this injury affect her ability to make new friends who ask her to participate in activities that cannot be a part of her life?

As Sarah grows older—and our bodies do start wearing out as we get older—how will this crippling injury, superimposed on the aging process, affect Sarah's lifestyle and activities? Yes, Sarah has been deprived of the benefits and joys of a full and complete life.

Folks, my relatives on Mom's side of the family were all coal miners, and Dad worked on the railroad. I remember how they looked forward to vacations or a day off work—looked forward to an escape from hard work and the boring drudgery of working at the same job for 20 or 30 years. Dad used to tell me that it doesn't make any difference what your occupation is, you eventually get tired of it. And the older you get, the more you look forward to leisure time and the more you enjoy your family—first your children and then your grandchildren.

How true that is! We work hard all day, every week, every year, and what makes it bearable? We work hard and look forward to the few hours of leisure time remaining.

John worked hard all of his life. He still works, with great pain. He is so exhausted at the end of the day that he can no longer enjoy those precious few remaining hours. He can no longer enjoy his grandchildren. The defendant took this away from John. As a result, there is a debt due and owing, and the defendant must now pay John for depriving him of his leisure time, for depriving him of the benefits and joy of a full and complete life.

Molly Jefferson had worked hard her entire life. In the early years, she assisted her husband in running a filling station and later a cafe. She worked as a fabric maker. She had never been on a vacation, and finally at age 63 she retired after her husband's death.

It was finally time to relax—she had earned it. And oh, how she was looking forward to the autumn of her life after long and arduous years of raising a family and working full-time. Her mother lived to age 85. Molly probably had 20 years left to enjoy playing with her grandchildren, puttering in the garden, and savoring the other pleasures that she had so looked forward to before the defendant crippled her.

There is no amount of money that can possibly compensate her for the destruction of those joyful benefits available only in the autumn of one's life. The debt that results—the debt the defendant now owes Molly—is a substantial one. Molly was on her first vacation when the defendant injured her, and she is now paying for that vacation in rare coin. Yet the defendant will only have to pay his indebtedness to Molly in money damages.

There are some things in life that are difficult to place a value on, such as morality, religion, art, music, and a good education. What is the value of good health, the freedom to do what you enjoy? You would never give up your favorite pastimes—whatever they are—for the rest of your life, for any amount of money, because they are too valuable to you. Yet you must place a value on Mrs. Jefferson's good health and all the benefits that would have flowed from her good health.

Pain and Suffering

Emphasize the importance of compensating the injured client for pain and suffering.

> The next item of damages on this chart is Sally's physical and mental pain and suffering. Fancy words, but how do they relate to Sally's injury? We now know that her teenage years were shattered by this injury. The teenage years are fragile years. These are the years when we are self-conscious; we are forming our personal identity. Just discovering a pimple on your face can be a devastating source of embarrassment. A teenager's hairstyle and clothes can be the most important thing in the world. It is understandable and natural that Sally, at age 17, was shattered by this injury, which was a source of extreme embarrassment and emotional pain.

> When physical pain is inflicted on another person, how do you evaluate the debt owed for inflicting that pain? Physical pain is something that we avoid like the plague. We will spend an additional $75 for a local anesthetic just to have a tooth pulled. We will spend $200 a month for pain medications that do not eliminate the pain, but only reduce it to some extent. One of the first questions we ask a doctor about proposed treatment is: "Will it be painful?"
>
> The defendant inflicted this pain on my client, and for the payment of that debt I have suggested the sum of $500 per day.

> Our society has become desensitized to pain. We see violence and pain on television and in movies, and we read about it in newspapers and hear it on the radio. This courtroom has been filled with evidence of pain and suffering. We don't like to think about our own pain, and in fact, our bodies will block severe pain from our minds through amnesia.
>
> Defense counsel stated that Sam has adjusted nicely to his pain. What does that mean? It means that his personality has changed, that his personality has been scarred by pain, just as a body becomes scarred from burn injuries. We have all heard statements like, "He didn't become an alcoholic until his wife died," or "She's not the same person since her mother died," or "He's not much fun to be around since he was injured." Sure, Sam has adjusted to pain: His life has changed, and his personality is scarred. You now have a duty to become sensitive to Sam's pain and suffering and to recognize that each of you may have been desensitized by mass media

and your own life experiences. You must now cast those influences aside and look into Sam's life, spirit, and soul, as painful as that might be, and assess the nature and extent of his suffering.

What distinguishes each of us from every other person in the world? How can friends and family identify us? Each person's face is uniquely his or her own, and there is none other like it in the world. To disfigure a person's face is to rob that person of his or her singular identity.

No wonder, then, that the practice of cosmetic surgery has flourished. In order to combat the aging process, people will spend exorbitant sums of money to preserve their appearance and hence their identity—whether it be with hair implants, face-lifts, or reconstructive surgery.

The defendant has inflicted terribly disfiguring scars on Tom Jones. In doing so, he has destroyed Tom's identity. Tom's grandchildren were bewildered and repulsed; they treated him as a stranger. He fought the temptation to become a recluse. Friends did not recognize him on the street, and fellow employees avoided him. If before he was injured he had had a dream that all of this would come to pass, it would have been a nightmare that would have awakened him. For Tom, it has now become a living nightmare.

There is a conflict in the testimony on how long Jerry Smith will live and need attendant care. In all fairness, you should resolve that conflict in favor of Jerry and give the Smith family the benefit of the doubt. If, by your verdict, you tell the defendant-doctors to pay for only 20 years, you are permitting these doctors to benefit financially from their own mistakes and negligence.

Defense counsel has argued that we cannot prove that Jerry will live a full life and that he will probably live only 10 years. These doctors should not be permitted to say, "I did not render proper treatment in this case, so you cannot now prove how many years of this child's life I destroyed!" Because of these doctors, we do not know precisely how long Jerry will require attendant care. Therefore, it is only fair that you resolve any doubts about the amount of the indebtedness owed in favor of Jerry and his parents.

What distinguishes us from animals is the ability to be humane. Our humanity causes us to want to help a bird with a broken wing or to help the other defenseless creatures of the world. We sometimes spend large sums of money taking our pets to animal doctors.

It is this uniquely human kindness that would compel us to render assistance for the rest of Jerry's natural life. However, in this case we are not asking for kindness because the law requires that the defendants provide this care in payment of the debt they incurred when they reduced this child to a helpless, brain-injured, cortically blind infant.

Jerry's parents, John and Ann Smith, also have the freedom to live and work where they choose and the right to be near their son. When Jerry has grown so large that Ann can no longer care for him, John and Ann have the right to provide the best possible care for Jerry, if that will help Jerry and ease Ann's burdens. I am asking you, by your verdict, to give Ann and John Smith peace of mind.

Now what do I mean, and how do you do that? Well, much has been written about a parent's instinctive need to care for his or her child until it is time to "cut the apron strings." A parent instinctively knows when a child is ready for some freedom and independence, and just as a bird first teaches its young to fly and then kicks them out of the nest, so a parent will protect, nurture, and raise his or her children until they can safely venture into the world. Parents know when a child is ready to leave, and they feel comfortable knowing their task is finished.

But Ann and John will be forever saddled with this "gift" of Mother Nature because they will forever worry about Jerry and will forever have the instinctive need to care for him as a child. Parents can never psychologically abandon a child, and Jerry will forever remain a child in a man's body.

Therefore, if Jerry is to be placed in a residential care facility, it will have to be a facility where Ann and John don't worry "Is he in pain? Is someone holding him during his seizures? Is he being fed properly? Is he being given enough liquids? Is someone easing his pain?" It will have to be a facility so close that they can frequently visit Jerry and be reassured that he is being given proper care. Ann and John must also be given their freedom and peace of mind so they can devote their thoughts and energy to their other children, knowing that Jerry is not in pain and discomfort.

Localized pain affects our entire body and everything we do. We have all experienced something like a severe toothache or a migraine headache. Such pain affects our activities, employment, relationships with others, and our personality and disposition. Such pain detracts from everything we do.

Remind the jury of one dramatic incident that was described in the testimony. Then use mental images and analogies to compare that incident to an iceberg: "You see only the tip of the iceberg and know from the tip that the great bulk of the iceberg is hidden from view; likewise, from a witness's description of only one traumatic example of pain and suffering, you know what massive additional suffering has occurred."

Loss of Earning Capacity

In stressing the loss of earning capacity, show how the injury will affect future earning capacity, even though the plaintiff is presently employed.

> Jack Williams is a 43-year-old construction superintendent who has lost his only good eye. He must wear a prosthesis for the rest of his life. His body has been unnecessarily maimed and scarred, and so has his mind. He is humiliated and embarrassed. He will be reminded daily of this incident, and he will be reminded of his disability for the rest of his life. He will live in fear of losing his remaining eyesight, for if he should have an industrial accident or disease that destroys his remaining eye, he will be totally blind.
>
> And what is the possibility of companies refusing him work as he grows older? He has at least 22 years of work expectancy until age 65. Do companies discriminate against the handicapped in employment? You bet they do. Do companies discriminate against the elderly in employment? You bet they do. How many young, healthy men are competing for $40,000-a-year construction superintendent jobs?

Wrongful Death

You can argue damages for wrongful death in a variety of ways, depending on the circumstances of the case. Speak directly of grief and mental anguish. As one court has said: "No loss is greater than the loss of a loved one, and no tragedy is more wrenching than the helpless apprehension of the death or serious injury of one whose very existence is a precious treasure."[4]

Death of a Child

> Ladies and gentlemen, it's difficult to describe intangibles like comfort and society. It's hard to explain that special moment when a

---

[4] *Portee v. Jaffee*, 417 A.2d 521, 526 (N.J. 1980).

three-year-old child has just bathed and smells of talcum powder and bath water. He runs across the room in his pajamas with that special excitement and laughter and jumps into your arms to kiss you goodnight with his arms and legs wrapped around you. It's hard to describe the comfort of that moment—it can lift your spirits and make your whole day. Or, in later years, when you come home from work and have a son in junior high school catch you by surprise, throwing a basketball at you, saying with a big grin, "Come on, Dad, let's shoot a few." Or later in life, when one of your own parents has died, it's a special thing to have a grown son reach out and touch you, saying, "Don't cry, Dad—it's all right."

My client, John Smith, has lost his only child, a son, and that loss cannot be restored no matter how substantial your verdict might be. The debt owed is astronomical.

Here we do not have a child who is burying his father, as it should be under the law of nature, but a father who must bury his child.

John and Judy will live the rest of their lives knowing that their little girl should have had the opportunity to live a long time in this world. She should have been able to experience a lot of its wonders, and not too much of its pain. They know she will never experience the wonders and excitement of growing up, of birthdays and holidays, of falling in love and being loved, and they will never know what contributions she might have made to society and to those she would have touched during her lifetime. You have seen a photograph of the happy and radiant face of this small girl—when we look at that photograph, we all understand why the anguish and grief of parents is everlasting when they lose a small child that they dearly love. It is the premature death of this child that has brought us all together in this courtroom, and the only contribution she can now make to society will be through your verdict. By publicly revealing the negligence of the doctor in this case and by assessing the damages that are due, you can help ensure that the negligence that caused this death will never be repeated.

Death of a Mother

Defense counsel would have you believe that Sally Jones, a mother and homemaker, can be replaced by hiring a substitute mother for these young children. When Sally Jones was alive and cared for her children and husband, she worked full-time during the day, and occasionally at night, and she became a specialist in several occupations. She became a landscape artist and gardener for the family home. She took care of the family's finances and became a bookkeeper and accountant. She became a marketing expert and purchased food and clothing and took care of the family's needs. She became a teacher and tutored the children, helping them with their homework. She became a nurse and cared for her children and husband when they became ill. She became an amateur psychologist and raised her children, gave them counseling, resolved their disputes, and ministered to their emotional needs. She became a chauffeur and spent countless hours taking the children to school activities, to recreational activities, and to medical and dental appointments. She was not only a cook but also a dietitian. She was anxious that the children have a well-rounded and healthy diet. She was a house-cleaner and maid, repair-person and jack-of-all-trades. No one person could be hired to perform all of these services, 14 hours a day, seven days a week.

Several people could be hired: a gardener, a cook, a nursemaid, a cleaning person, a part-time bookkeeper. But no one will replace Sally Jones because she is irreplaceable. A mother who loves and cares for her children is irreplaceable, and the best substitutes cannot do the same job. You cannot purchase love, kindness, and dedication. You cannot purchase a mother. If you render a verdict for all of these amounts I have placed on the board, only a portion of the debt owed this family by the defendant will be paid. The defendant knows that this amount is only partial payment of the debt he owes because there will never be another Sally Jones.

Death of a Spouse

We have all known couples who did everything together and relied and depended totally on one another. When death struck one, the survivor also soon died. Betty Smith is fortunate to have a supportive family and friends, but none of them can be to her what Jim was. When he died, part of her died—the will to do alone what they had done together, to reach out to life as she had done before.

She should have been free to love her husband, raise children of her own, and fill their lives with joy and music and laughter and art.

Amount of Damages

Anticipate the defendant's summation; use arguments that dismiss the value of sympathy and stress the debt the defendant owes rather than the pity the jury could give. Explain that the injured plaintiff does not want sympathy but is entitled to payment of a debt. "The plaintiff received sympathy, and still receives sympathy, from family and friends; if he wanted sympathy, he could get that by staying home and not by coming to court."

In a small town in a case with a conservative jury, convince the jury to award the same damages that a jury in a big city or in other communities would award. Urge the jury to do this to announce to the world, "This small community places great value on human life and dignity." Challenge the jury to let other communities know, by its verdict, that it places great value on self-esteem, independence, the ability to work, and the value of life.

Emphasize inflation. Remind the jurors of the cost of groceries and other items with which they are familiar, and of the cost of those same items 10 and 50 years ago. Ask "What will medical services, housing, utilities, and groceries cost 20 years in the future?"

Show some humility when you suggest the amount of damages.

> It would be presumptuous of me or defense counsel to tell you what your verdict on damages should be. This is exclusively within your province and, after fully discussing each and every item of damage, you must collectively and unanimously determine the debt owed. However, I would not be doing my duty as an officer of the court and as an advocate for my client if I did not give you the benefit of my knowledge and experience and my recommendations. If my recommendations seem appropriate, logical, and based on the evidence, you should consider them. If not, you should disregard them."

REBUTTING SPECIAL DEFENSE ARGUMENTS

Strongly rebut special defense arguments. To the contention that "doctors save lives," argue:

> I get tired of hearing how doctors save lives and therefore should never be sued. What does that have to do with this case? I suggest the defendant is trying to play on your sympathy, contrary to the court's instruction and the law. Besides, doctors are paid to save lives and, in this case, they were handsomely paid and now have the legal obligation to pay the plaintiffs for the damages caused by their negligence.

Against the argument that the state will care for the brain-injured child and therefore damages for private institutional care are unnecessary, argue:

> Apparently, there is an excellent state institution in Wyoming, perhaps the finest in the nation. But it is still a state institution operated by the taxpayers; therefore, it is subject to the whims of

> the government and the legislature. It may or may not get adequate funds in the future. Look at Exhibit 21, introduced by the defendant, which indicates the institution's desperate need for additional funds in the future. The state institution may or may not be in existence in 20 years. There is a trend to eliminate this sort of facility.
>
> Folks, we give our elderly the freedom of choice—the freedom to look about and select the best available care facility or nursing home, and often the choice to live with relatives when they are no longer able to care for themselves. No one tells us that a feeble, senile grandfather must be incarcerated in a state institution. Apparently, the defendants would have you deprive the Smiths of their freedom of choice by depriving them of the financial freedom necessary to choose. Ladies and gentlemen, the defendants, not the state of Wyoming, are responsible for Michael's condition. They tried to shift the blame to the anesthesiologists, then to the parents, then to the ultrasound, and having failed at all of that, they now try to shift the responsibility to the taxpayers of this state.

A strong and sometimes effective defense tactic is to argue that the plaintiff is charging the defendant with malpractice or something akin to a crime. You must debunk that myth.

> Defense counsel keeps talking about "malpractice" as if we have accused his clients of a crime. You will note that I never used that term throughout this trial because it would have been improper. You will also note that nowhere in the court's instructions on the law is that term used, and that the law applicable to this case involves simple negligence. The defendant is charged with simple negligence.
>
> If you negligently operate your automobile and injure another person, you are liable under the law for the injuries you cause. If I negligently fail to place a trial date on my calendar and my client loses his case because of it, I am liable for his damages in the eyes of the law. We are all equal under the law: carpenters, salespersons, homemakers, lawyers, and doctors. A doctor is not one of the chosen few, and this is a case of simple negligence. So let's forget the word "malpractice," which is not a legal term and means nothing in the law.

You must also debunk the idea that doctors should be immune from suit.

> Immunity breeds irresponsibility, and doctors are not immune from suit. Don't give them immunity by your verdict. Dr. Smith is highly qualified and extremely competent, and that is why he is liable in this particular case. He of all people should not have overlooked this problem.

Strongly rebut the defense argument that "the patient would have died anyway."

> Defense counsel tells you that Mr. Garcia would have died anyway. He tells you that Mr. Garcia's heart disease was so severe that he didn't have long to live. He tells you that it doesn't matter that his client was negligent in failing to diagnose and treat Mr. Garcia's heart condition.
>
> But the expert witnesses unanimously agreed that Mr. Garcia might have lived a full life had he been properly treated. He had a one percent to 25 percent chance of living a full life. We don't know whether he would have lived a full life because he was robbed of that opportunity by the defendant's negligence. If Mr. Garcia were here to speak and to testify, I am sure that he would tearfully state, "It would not have happened to me: I would have lived." Give him the benefit of the doubt. He deserves at least that.

Defense counsel may argue that a physician complied with local community standards, even though those standards were not comparable to the standards of a teaching institution in a large city. You must show that this argument is unreasonable and without merit.

> Ladies and gentlemen, is it reasonable to expect a physician to read the latest medical journals in his field of practice and keep up-to-date? To know what advances have been made in medicine in recent years? Is it reasonable to ask him to do this when lives are at stake and people in the community are placing their lives in his hands with faith and trust? Why should the standards of practice in Montrose, Colorado, be lower than those elsewhere? Don't tell Dr. Jones and other physicians in the community, by your verdict, that you will tolerate a lower standard of practice than that enjoyed by citizens in similar communities.

Defuse the defense's attempt to minimize damages on the basis of preexisting conditions:

> Defense counsel would have you reduce the amount owed to Jeni because she was not in perfect health when the defendant inflicted her injury. Let me ask you this: Who is more seriously injured by the loss of an eye—the person in good health who had two eyes when the injury occurred, or the person who had only one? Who is the more seriously injured or damaged by the loss of a leg—the person in good health who had two legs when the injury occurred, or the person who had only one? This injury was more devastating to Jeni than it would have been to a healthy person. So the defendant's debt to Jeni is far greater than it would have been had he inflicted this injury on a healthy person.

> If this were a property damage case and the defendant had damaged a farmer's truck loaded with fresh eggs, breaking all the eggs, you would not hesitate to reimburse the farmer for his losses. Say the farmer would have been able to sell the eggs wholesale for 50 cents a dozen. His loss then would have equaled 50 cents for every dozen he carried, and the debt of that amount would have to be paid. If the cost to repair his truck were $5,000, that is the debt that would have to be paid. It would be no defense for the defendant to argue that there would have been no damage had the truck been loaded with golf balls. The truck was not loaded with golf balls; it was loaded with eggs. The defendant in this case cannot argue that there would have been very little damage if the plaintiff had had a healthy back. The plaintiff did not have a healthy back and is now permanently crippled because of the defendant.

If hospital records have been altered, emphasize that fact, noting, "Ladies and gentlemen, we have established in this case that the hospital records were doctored more than the patient was."

CONCLUSION

Your summation should be a well-organized, logical, and persuasive presentation that captivates and empowers the jurors, clarifies the issues, and finally motivates the jurors to adequately and fairly compensate your client.

Remember, no two summations are alike because no two cases are alike. Tailor the structure and content of each summation to fit the case. Use summation to paint a picture that, when viewed in its entirety, leads the jury to the inescapable conclusion that the plaintiff has won the case, deserved to win it, and is entitled to the maximum damages permitted by the court's instructions on the law.

CHAPTER TWELVE

APPLYING PRINCIPLES TO SPECIAL PROBLEMS

It is important to identify problems in your case and to determine which segments of the trial are best suited to minimize or resolve those problems. Often, the identified problems cannot be addressed in every segment of the trial. You must carefully analyze each problem and determine how and when you can deal with it most effectively. Through four case examples, this chapter illustrates many of the problems you may confront and the issues that these problems present; it also explains how to deal with them at appropriate times during the trial.

CASE EXAMPLE I

In Case Example I, Dr. Black, chairperson of the department of pediatric-orthopedic surgery at Children's Hospital, performed elective surgery on a teenage girl, Shirley Lara, to correct a congenital defect. The surgery was unsuccessful. Additional surgery, attempted at another hospital (Shriners) by another surgeon, met with only partial success. The girl sued Dr. Black, alleging that he performed the wrong procedure and that he should have originally performed the type of procedure that was eventually used at Shriners Hospital. The problems created by Dr. Black during the first surgery prevented the second surgery from being completely successful.

The defendant names all the plaintiff's treating physicians as expert witnesses for the defense. The four expert witnesses include the chairperson of the department of orthopedic surgery at the University of Colorado, Shirley Lara's surgeon at Shriners Hospital, and two orthopedic surgeons in Denver who referred Shirley to Dr. Black.

You have difficulty getting a physician of the defendant's high caliber to testify for the plaintiff. Your lone expert witness is an orthopedic surgeon from another state who still maintains an office practice but who has not performed surgery in five years and has not performed the surgical procedure in question in more than 20 years. He is knowledgeable about the procedure, but in recent years he has earned his living primarily by testifying rather than by practicing medicine.

Representing the defendant in this case is a lawyer who is also a physician. She prefers to be called "Doctor" in the courtroom.

The trial will take place in a jurisdiction bombarded by lawyer advertising for personal injury cases. Although potential jurors have seen many such advertisements, you do not advertise. Potential jurors are also influenced by public perceptions of litigation abuse, rising health-care costs, and a medical negligence "insurance crisis," making it difficult to find unbiased jurors and to persuade them of the merits of your case.

Problems

The problems and issues raised in this fact pattern include:

- How can you enhance your expert witness's credibility so jurors do not perceive the expert as lacking the experience and qualifications of the defense's experts?
- How can you overcome the testimony of the treating physicians called as expert witnesses for the defense?
- Should you try to hide the fact that the defense lawyer is a doctor for fear that the jury will give greater weight to her opening statement, cross-examinations, and summation? Or should you call the jury's attention to the fact that she is a doctor and use that fact to establish an underdog theme that the doctors and defense counsel are ganging up on your client?
- How can you eliminate potential jurors who would identify with the doctors or hospitals and who would not side with you unless you could show beyond a reasonable doubt that the defendant's misconduct was wanton and reckless?
- How can you handle the potential juror sympathy if the defendant is perceived as a victim of litigation abuse and the insurance crisis?
- Should you meet the medical negligence insurance crisis/litigation explosion issue head-on, not address the issue, or attempt to hide it?

To resolve or minimize these issues and problems, analyze each in the context of the different segments of the trial. Start by considering the use of motions in limine.

Motions in Limine

It is an important segment of the trial process to determine whether any identified problems can be overcome by the use of pretrial motions in limine. In considering the use of such motions, you must always question whether it is in your client's best interest to attempt to hide the problems or to meet them head-on during trial. As a rule of thumb, even if the court rules in favor of your motion in limine, do not attempt to hide facts or issues from the jurors that they are likely to see anyway. In this case example, consider the following questions:

- Should you make a motion in limine to try to limit the number of defense experts?
- Will the motion be successful if all the experts are also treating physicians?
- Should the motion be used to try to exclude references to the increase in insurance premiums, damage to the defendant's reputation, the defendant's possible loss of his license to practice medicine, or the "insurance crisis" in general?
- Should it be used to exclude references to defense counsel as "Doctor," even though she is also a physician?
- Should it be used to exclude references to your expert's income from testifying?

When, as in this case, the defense has no independent expert witnesses and intends to call all of the plaintiff's treating physicians as expert witnesses on liability issues, it is unlikely that the court would exclude any of this expert testimony by granting a motion in limine. Further, by showing that all of the treating physicians are acquainted with the defendant-doctor and with one another, you know that you can impeach their credibility during trial and also create an impression that the treating physicians are being disloyal to their patient in order to protect their brethren in the profession. In addition, with all of the treating physicians testifying against your client, you are enhancing your role as the underdog in protecting the rights of this teenage girl.

The motion should not be used to exclude references to a perceived increase in insurance premiums, possible damage to the defendant's reputation, the defendant's possible loss of his license to practice medicine, or the "insurance crisis" in general. These issues are present in the minds of jurors whether or not mentioned during trial, and these issues must be met head-on during the voir dire examination. In some cases, you may want to refer to them again during summation.

It is highly unlikely that the court would exclude evidence of your expert's income derived from testifying in medical negligence cases. You may want to introduce such evidence concerning the defendant's experts, particularly if they are being paid far more than your own expert. However, be aware that if jurors accept an expert witness's testimony and relate higher fees to enhanced expertise, they may believe that the expert's fees are justified.

Whether you use a motion in limine to exclude references to defense counsel as "Doctor" during trial will be determined by your overall trial strategy and game plan. In this case, there are distinct advantages in informing the jury that the defense lawyer is a doctor. The defense lawyer's objectivity becomes suspect: Is defense counsel, as a doctor, participating in a conspiracy to protect a fellow member of the profession? Is defense counsel acting as an officer of the court or as a puppet of the medical profession? Is defense counsel joining the treating physicians in ganging up on this poor teenage girl?

In summary, although you should consider motions in limine in every case when attempting to resolve problems and issues, this segment of the trial process would not be the time to effectively solve the problems raised by this case example. However, several of the identified problems can be dealt with effectively on voir dire.

Voir Dire

This segment of the trial can be used to diffuse the problem concerning jury sympathy for the defendant, the problem of defense counsel being a doctor, credibility problems regarding the plaintiff's expert witness, and problems created by the climate of perceived litigation abuse and lawyer advertising.

Overcoming Jury Sympathy for the Defendant

Defense counsel will do her best to make the defendant an object of the jurors' sympathy. The following questions illustrate ways of turning that sympathy away from the defendant and toward the plaintiff.

> Ms. Juror, do you understand that Dr. Black is not being accused of committing a criminal act or of doing something reckless; he is being sued for simple negligence as the law allows? Would you follow the court's instructions that you must return a verdict for the plaintiff if you determine that Dr. Black was simply negligent and caused the plaintiff's damages?

> There will be testimony that could cause you to feel sympathy for Shirley Lara. If you are selected as a juror, the court will instruct you at the conclusion of the trial that you cannot base your verdict on sympathy because that would violate the law. Ms. Lara does not want a verdict based on sympathy because that would not be fair to Dr. Black. Will all of you promise me that, if selected, you will render a verdict based on the evidence and the law, not on sympathy?
>
> Just as it would be improper for you to base your verdict on sympathy for Shirley Lara, it would also be improper for you to render a verdict for Dr. Black out of sympathy for him because he is being sued and is here in the courtroom, or because you believe that this lawsuit will somehow harm his reputation or affect his medical license. This is neither a criminal case nor a case involving the doctor's reputation or license to practice. Will you also promise me that you will follow the court's instructions and not base your verdict on sympathy for Dr. Black? Basing your verdict on sympathy for him would not be fair to Ms. Lara and would violate the court's instructions. Would you all follow the court's instructions in this regard?
>
> Ms. Juror, if you went to an auto mechanic who told you what was wrong with your car, made the repairs and charged you for them, but made the wrong diagnosis and the wrong repairs, would you be upset? Do you believe there is anything different about a physician who performs the wrong surgery and does not correct the problem?
>
> Mr. Juror, if the driver of a car ran a red light and struck your car, would you hold that driver responsible? If a physician ran a medical red light and caused a patient harm, would you hold that physician responsible if the evidence proved that the physician was negligent?

Dealing with the Problem of Defense Counsel's Being a Doctor

The following questions would help you identify jurors who would give the doctor-lawyer defense counsel's remarks greater weight than yours.

> Ms. Juror, Dr. Black is represented in this case by Jane Smith, who is both a lawyer and a doctor. The court will instruct you that the comments of counsel during the trial are not evidence and that you may not favor Jane Smith when she speaks to you because she is a doctor and I am not. However, would you give her statements greater weight than my statements because she is a doctor?

> Are my client and I at a disadvantage with any of you because we do not have a doctor seated at our table, while both Dr. Black and his lawyer are doctors, and all of their witnesses will be doctors and nurses? Do any of you believe at this time, without having heard the evidence, that Shirley Lara will not be able to prove her claim because there are no doctors seated at our table to assist us during the trial? Do you understand that we will have the opportunity to prove that Dr. Black was negligent by calling a doctor as our expert witness during trial and by cross-examining Dr. Black and all his medical witnesses? Will you keep an open mind about these issues until we have had an opportunity to present our evidence and cross-examine all the doctors called by the defendant, even though we may be at a disadvantage in not having a doctor seated at our table with whom to consult during trial?

Dealing with Your Expert Witness's Credibility Problems

Defense counsel will attack your expert's credibility by showing that he is not familiar with the surgery performed by Dr. Black, yet he is criticizing the surgical procedures. Also, defense counsel will attack his credibility by showing that he more frequently testifies for the plaintiff than for the defense. You intend to attack the credibility of the defendant's experts during trial by showing that they are all friends or acquaintances of the defendant. The following questions are used to defuse the defense counsel's attack and to lay a foundation for your strategy during trial.

> Several of the doctors who will be testifying in this case have not in recent years performed the precise surgery that Dr. Black performed on Shirley Lara, including Dr. Jones, who will testify as an expert witness for Shirley Lara. Dr. Jones lives in Wichita, Kansas. Would any of you be inclined to give less weight or credence to the testimony of these doctors simply because they have not in recent years performed the type of surgery that Dr. Black used? Ms. Juror, Shirley Lara's claim is not based on Dr. Black having incorrectly performed the surgery; our claim is that the type of surgery performed should not have been performed at all. Instead, the corrective surgery later performed at Shriners hospital in Salt Lake City should have been used in the first place by Dr. Black. Do you understand that?
>
> Would you carefully listen to the testimony of all expert witnesses on both sides of this case before deciding which testimony is more persuasive and believable?

> Dr. Jones, the orthopedic surgeon from Wichita, Kansas, who will appear as an expert witness on Shirley Lara's behalf, will testify that he is willing to travel to another state such as Colorado to testify against a physician whom he believes to be negligent, but seldom testifies against physicians who are personal friends or acquaintances of his in Kansas. Ms. Juror, do you understand why he would be reluctant to testify against a physician who is a personal friend or acquaintance? Do you understand that it would be difficult for him to be objective in evaluating the work of a friend? In like fashion, we expect the defendant's expert witnesses from Colorado to testify that they have never appeared in court against a Colorado physician but are not reluctant to testify against a physician outside Colorado if they believe that physician was negligent. Would any of you hold these attitudes against the doctors?

Dealing with the Climate of Perceived Litigation Abuse

Use pretrial juror questionnaires to obtain information about the jurors' attitudes and opinions about perceived litigation abuse. Then, meet this issue head-on, discussing it openly in voir dire.[1]

If necessary, remind jurors in summation of the promises they made in voir dire to judge your case objectively. During voir dire, ask the following questions:

> Much has been written and said about a litigation crisis—that too many lawsuits are being filed against the medical profession and health-care providers generally. How many of you feel that way? Of those who raised your hands, how many of you believe that everything is accurately reported by the press or the news media? How many of you question whether there really is a litigation crisis? Of those of you who have voiced an opinion that there is litigation abuse and that there are too many lawsuits, do any of you feel that every lawsuit filed against a physician is unfounded and that doctors are never negligent?
>
> Ms. Juror, as you sit here today, do you have any reason to believe that Shirley Lara's claim against Dr. Black is unfounded and that this is one of those lawsuits that should never have been filed? Do you all agree, having heard none of the evidence and knowing nothing about this incident, that Shirley Lara's claim against Dr. Black could well be one of those lawsuits that is well founded and supported by the evidence? Have any of you prejudged this case, without having heard the facts, or do any of you believe that it is frivolous and that it contributes to a litigation explosion? Mr. Juror,

---

1 See Chapter Eight, "Voir Dire," for further discussion.

do you understand that it would be improper and would violate your oath as a juror to judge this case before hearing the evidence?

Of those of you who have strong feelings that there is widespread litigation abuse and that there are many unfounded cases filed against doctors, can you accept that this case could be justified and render a verdict against Dr. Black if the plaintiff establishes that he was negligent and caused Shirley Lara's damages?

Do any of you believe that rising health-care costs have been caused solely, or primarily, by lawsuits filed against the health-care industry? Ms. Juror, please tell us why you believe that. Of those of you who have voiced such an opinion, would any of you find it difficult to render a verdict against Dr. Black, even if you decided he was negligent, because you believe that verdicts such as yours might increase the amount that you personally pay for health care or health insurance? Could I please see the hands of those who believe that there are multiple reasons for increased health-care costs, unrelated to lawsuits against health-care professionals? Mr. Juror, did you know that the insurance company providing health-care coverage for Shirley Lara must be reimbursed in full by Shirley Lara from any verdict she might receive in this case? That is why we will introduce evidence of the health-care costs. Is there anyone who did not know that most health-care providers have what is called a 'subrogation claim' that requires people who recover damages in a suit like this to reimburse the health-care insurance carrier? Ms. Juror, you indicated earlier that you believe that verdicts against doctors might have an impact on the amount that you personally pay for health care or health insurance. Do you now understand that the impact could be a reduction in the amount that you pay because of the reimbursement that sometimes results from litigation like this?

If you determined that Dr. Black was negligent and caused Shirley Lara damages, would any of you be unwilling or unable to render a verdict assessing fair and reasonable damages to Shirley Lara because of any concern you might have about rising health-care costs? Do you all realize that that would be unfair and would not only deprive Shirley Lara of her rights but would violate your civic duty and oath as jurors?

Dealing with the Problem of Lawyer Advertising

The problem of lawyer advertising is another issue to address on the jury questionnaire. Use the following questions during voir dire and what you learn from juror responses to the questionnaire to identify jurors who have a problem with this issue. Let the jurors know that neither you nor your law firm advertises.

> How many of you have seen or read lawyer advertising, perhaps on television, soliciting clients for personal injury lawsuits? How many of you have been offended by such advertising or have developed a negative impression of those who advertise?
>
> Neither I nor my law firm has ever advertised. Would any of you hold it against me and my client because other lawyers have offended some of you with their advertising? Do you all agree that it would be unfair to punish me and my client, through your attitude or verdict, for the conduct of others? Would any of you be inclined to do this?

Opening Statement

Opening statement is not an appropriate segment of the trial to deal with lawyer advertising, the perceived litigation crisis, or the defense lawyer's being a doctor. These are not evidentiary matters that can be dealt with in opening statement; furthermore, they have already been diffused during voir dire. However, you should use opening statement to further address credibility problems regarding the plaintiff's expert witness and to deal with the problem of multiple defense experts and sympathy for Dr. Black.

Dealing with Your Expert Witness's Credibility Problems

Explain in your opening statement that the surgery performed by Dr. Black was once the preferred treatment but had been discarded because of a high failure rate. Explain that the type of surgery performed in Salt Lake City is now favored. Inform the jurors that the plaintiff's expert has not performed the surgery used by Dr. Black for 20 years because of its high failure rate; he used a safer alternative procedure. Explain that the plaintiff's expert stopped performing surgery five years ago because orthopedic surgery requires a strong, healthy body as well as knowledge and skill, and the expert no longer had the physical strength to do some surgical procedures and did not want to subject a patient to any risks during surgery. Emphasize the fact that the expert is highly skilled, knowledgeable, and competent, and that he continues to teach, author medical articles, maintain a practice, and frequently provides consultation to younger members of the profession.

Explain that he will be called as the first witness to describe the surgery performed by Dr. Black and tell why it was the wrong surgery; that he will be asked to explain why the surgery later performed in Salt Lake City was the preferred surgery and should have been done initially by Dr. Black; and that he will show how Dr. Black's surgery contributed to the failure of the second surgery performed in Salt Lake City.

Explain that you expect one or more of the defendant's own expert witnesses to agree with plaintiff's expert that the first surgery failed but the second surgery would have been successful had the first surgery not been used; that the first surgery was no longer accepted as the preferred treatment for this congenital defect because of the high failure rate; and that the expert witnesses only disagree over whether Dr. Black was negligent in using that procedure.

Dealing with Multiple Defense Experts and Sympathy for the Defendant

Explain that the two orthopedic surgeons who treated Shirley Lara for her congenital defect and who referred her to Dr. Black will be called as witnesses for Dr. Black. Tell the jurors that you expect them to testify that Dr. Black was not negligent. Likewise, tell the jurors that you expect both the chairperson of the department of orthopedic surgery at the University of Colorado, where Dr. Black performed his residency in orthopedic surgery, and the surgeon at Shriners Hospital in Salt Lake City, who performed the second procedure on Shirley Lara, to testify that Dr. Black was not negligent. The surgeon at Shriners is Dr. Black's friend; they are in the same subspecialty of pediatric orthopedic surgery. Then tell the jury

> It is expected that all of these doctors will testify that Dr. Black was not negligent, yet we expect all of them to testify that if Dr. Black had performed the surgery used in Salt Lake City instead of another procedure, the surgery probably would have been successful. The correct procedure failed in Salt Lake City only because Dr. Black's earlier surgery made its success nearly impossible. The defendant's expert witness will agree that the surgery performed by Dr. Black had a high failure rate and that most surgeons no longer use it to correct this congenital defect.
>
> You might ask yourself as you listen carefully to the testimony of the defendant's experts why they agree with all of the plaintiff's expert opinions, yet arrive at a different conclusion in deciding that Dr. Black was not negligent. This question will be answered during the cross-examination of these witnesses.

The next segment of the trial to be considered in defusing the identified problems is the use of witnesses.

Witnesses

The order in which you examine witnesses and the testimony provided by each witness can be used to help you overcome problems. Also, you can effectively use your cross-examination of defendant's experts to help overcome the problems.

The following suggestions will help you address your expert witness's credibility problems and overcome the testimony of the defense's expert witnesses.

- Enhance your expert's credibility by having him testify before any other physicians do, thereby permitting him to demonstrate his expertise and knowledge of the facts first, when the jury is most attentive and receptive.[2] Your expert should become the teacher, explaining in detail the surgical procedures, X rays, and other tests performed on the plaintiff. He should use models, charts, an overhead viewer, and other visual aids.
- Establish your expert's knowledge of the prevailing standards of practice.
- Elicit all the unfavorable testimony that defense counsel could use in cross-examining your expert, for example, testimony that he has not performed surgery for five years and the reasons he has not performed surgery; testimony that he has not performed the surgery in question in more than 20 years and the reasons he has not performed it; testimony that he derives a substantial part of his income from testifying; and testimony that he more often testifies for the plaintiff than for the defendant. Your expert can explain that he now has more time to testify because he no longer performs surgery. He no longer has the physical strength to do some of the surgical procedures and does not want to subject a patient to any risks during surgery, and he has not performed the surgery used by Dr. Black for more than 20 years because of its high failure rate and because safer alternative procedures are available. He can explain that he more often testifies for the plaintiff because he chooses not to testify for physicians who are friends or acquaintances in his home state. He believes it is inappropriate to testify for or against a physician who is a friend or acquaintance because it is difficult to be objective and fair.
- Use medical literature to establish the low success rate for the surgery Dr. Black used at Children's Hospital as opposed to the high success rate for the procedure used at Shriners, thus reinforcing your expert's

---

2 See Chapter Seven, "Planning the Trial: Theory, Witnesses, and Trial Strategy," for a detailed discussion of this tactic.

opinion. Mention the diagnostic indications and contraindications from the literature for either procedure and compare them with the facts in Shirley Lara's case.

- In cross-examining the defendant and the defendant's expert witnesses, secure all concessions that lead to liability and suggest that any testimony favorable to the defendant is suspect because of the relationship between each of the defendant's expert witnesses and the defendant.

Summation

In summation, you should again address the identified problems, further defusing and overcoming them.

Dealing with the Problem of Treating Physicians and Other Experts Testifying for the Defendant

One of your objectives in summation will be to counter the effectiveness of the testimony of the treating physicians and other experts who have testified for the defendant. The following sample from a summation illustrates how you can use the defense experts' testimony to support your theory of the case and to explain why those experts have erroneously concluded that the defendant was not negligent.

> You may have wondered why all of the physicians who testified for Dr. Black were willing to concede, on cross-examination, that the surgery he performed was outdated and high risk, and that the later surgery used in Salt Lake City was preferred, yet those doctors were unwilling to testify that Dr. Black was negligent in performing a surgery that is no longer used by most doctors.

> I told you in my opening statement that if you listened carefully to the cross-examination of these witnesses you would learn why they agreed with our expert yet were unwilling to concede that Dr. Black was negligent. You heard the orthopedic surgeons who referred Shirley Lara to Dr. Black testify that they frequently refer patients to Dr. Black and have a close professional relationship with him. It is not surprising that they would agree with our expert on everything except the conclusion that Dr. Black was negligent. Likewise, you would expect the chairman of the department of orthopedic surgery to support Dr. Black, a resident that he supervised and trained, even though he agreed with our expert that the surgery Dr. Black performed on Shirley Lara is outmoded and has a high failure rate. It is also not surprising that the Salt Lake City doctor who performed the second surgery, a friend and colleague of Dr. Black, testified that Dr. Black was not negligent. Had he been given the

> opportunity to perform the first surgery on Shirley Lara, this doctor said that he would have used the surgical procedure he performed after Dr. Black's surgery rather than the one performed by Dr. Black.
>
> In short, if you discount the opinions rendered by all of the defense doctors that Dr. Black was not negligent and consider all of the rest of their testimony, all of the physicians who testified in this case agree with our expert witness. The obvious conclusion is that Dr. Black was negligent. If the defendant's experts did not have a relationship with Dr. Black and were free to express an objective opinion about negligence, there would have been no dispute over that issue. The plaintiff's expert was not acquainted with Dr. Black prior to trial, did not know the plaintiff and her family, and was better able than the defense experts to render a fair and objective opinion.

Explain how all the concessions made by the defense experts during cross-examination are consistent with the testimony of your expert and hence only the ultimate conclusions reached by the experts are inconsistent. Those inconsistent conclusions can be explained by the relationships existing between the defense doctors and the defendant.

Overcoming Jury Sympathy for the Defendant

If the jurors have developed any sympathy for the defendant-doctor over the course of the trial, you will need to address that in your summation. A comparison between the doctor and an auto mechanic can be an effective way of making jurors feel more empathy for the plaintiff:

> Folks, when I questioned you on voir dire at the beginning of this trial, you all stated that you would not be influenced in your verdict by sympathy for either Shirley Lara or Dr. Black because that would be improper. Some of you may feel some sympathy for Dr. Black, thinking that orthopedic surgery is a complicated matter and because it is complicated, perhaps that should somehow excuse Dr. Black's use of the wrong surgery.
>
> If that thought has crossed your mind, I ask you to consider the work of an auto mechanic because the mechanic's situation is in many ways analogous to that of Dr. Black. When a troubled customer brings a vehicle to an auto mechanic for repairs, the mechanic, just like a doctor, must take a history. When did the trouble start? How does it sound? When does it happen? Then the mechanic, like a doctor, must make a diagnosis and decide what is causing the problem. However, consider the mechanic's plight: he

> must deal with autos manufactured by many companies in all parts of the world, with thousands of parts that are constantly being changed with every new model. Did you know that there are only 206 bones in the human body, and they stay the same—they never change. The auto mechanic often works on his back under the vehicle with poor lighting, with no help, and with grease dripping onto his face or in his eyes. The orthopedic surgeon works in a well-lit, clean room with as many assistants as necessary. If the auto mechanic negligently performs the wrong procedure and doesn't correct the problem, he is held responsible. In this case, Dr. Black performed the wrong procedure, was negligent, and should likewise be held responsible. He is all the more responsible because he has been well trained and educated, and he has a subspecialty limited to only the 206 bones in children. He has excluded orthopedic surgery involving adults from his practice. He, of all people, should have performed the proper surgery.
>
> Although an auto mechanic might be excused for not carefully reading every new maintenance manual that accompanies every new model vehicle, unlike the auto mechanic, Dr. Black is expected to read all current literature and know when a surgical procedure is outdated and has been replaced by new techniques that are more successful. After all, if you look at the medical expenses in evidence, Dr. Black was well paid for the services he rendered. For this payment, Shirley Lara was entitled to receive good medical care and treatment. The debt to Dr. Black was paid, now he must pay to Shirley the debt created by his negligence. You will determine that indebtedness by the damages you assess in your verdict.
>
> Doctors are liable for their negligence just as lawyers, accountants, and all members of our society are responsible for negligently harming other people. Doctors are not immune from suit, and they should not be.

Case Example I presents problems and issues that frequently occur in medical negligence cases. All too often we encounter treating physicians who believe that the defendant-doctor was negligent but are unwilling to express that opinion in court. Some of those treating physicians are persuaded, or feel compelled, to testify for the defense. As the medical profession has unified in efforts to close the courthouse doors to victims of medical negligence, it has become increasingly difficult to find highly qualified expert witnesses who are willing to testify for the plaintiff in meritorious cases.

Likewise, many potential jurors enter the courthouse with sympathy for the defendant-physician who is perceived as a victim of litigation abuse, elevated insurance premiums, and an unwarranted litigation explosion. These are difficult problems and issues, but they can be overcome or substantially mitigated in one or more of the segments of trial as demonstrated in Case Example I.

The next case example raises other problems and issues that are also frequently encountered in medical negligence cases.

CASE EXAMPLE II

The plaintiff in Case Example II is a physically filthy member of a motorcycle gang who abuses alcohol and drugs. He wears a chain on his leather belt, he has been convicted of theft, and he has seldom been employed. When he has been employed, he has never filed an income-tax return. He has been injured in a collision that was not his fault and has been further injured by the negligence of the defendant-doctor.

Problems

The problems raised by the facts in this example include the following:

- How do you identify and eliminate jurors who will find the plaintiff so socially unacceptable that they could not render a verdict for the plaintiff, even if the plaintiff established negligence beyond a reasonable doubt?
- When you have evidence to explain the plaintiff's lifestyle and you can humanize him, how do you use the trial process to gain the jurors' sympathy and understanding?
- How do you identify jurors who have sympathy for the defendant, who made good faith attempts to properly treat the plaintiff in an emergency situation at the hospital with no choice in accepting him as a patient? Then, how do you overcome this sympathy during trial?
- Should the plaintiff seek damages for future loss of earning capacity when he has a history of only sparse earnings?

Again, to resolve or minimize these issues and problems, analyze each problem against each segment of the trial and determine which segments of the trial can be best utilized to minimize or overcome the problems. For example, you can first address the problem of jury sympathy for the doctor during the voir dire examination of jurors by identifying those who feel strongly that when a doctor is called in the middle of the night to render emergency treatment, he should not be held legally responsible if he later negligently injures the patient. After identifying these jurors, you can exercise peremptory challenges to eliminate some of them.

Next, during opening statement, you can minimize the sympathy factor by emphasizing that the doctor was well paid for coming to the hospital in the middle of the night and that he did so for economic reasons, not out of kindness.

In summation, you should refer the jurors to the court's instruction prohibiting them from considering sympathy in arriving at a verdict, and you should also remind them of the individual promises they made during voir dire that they would not be influenced in their deliberations by any sympathy that they might have had for the doctor.

Likewise, you must consider which segments of the trial process to use in addressing the problem of the plaintiff's sparse history of earnings and his failure to file income tax returns. Should the plaintiff seek damages for future loss of earning capacity and face a probable court ruling that the failure to file income tax returns is admissible evidence, or should the plaintiff waive this element of damages and seek to prevent the introduction of such evidence by a motion in limine?

To resolve this issue, you must know whether your evidence will overcome the facts that make the plaintiff a socially unacceptable person and, in addition, whether you have evidence that would persuade the jury that the plaintiff would have overcome his lifestyle problems and become a productive member of society had he not been crippled by the defendant's negligence.

If you have such evidence, then consider confronting the issue head-on by disclosing to the jury during voir dire that he has never filed an income tax return, before defense counsel has an opportunity to reveal it in a dramatic way. Again, identify jurors who have a strong negative reaction to the plaintiff as a result of this disclosure and exercise appropriate peremptory challenges. Then use opening statement to describe the evidence showing that the plaintiff would have overcome his lifestyle problems and become a productive member of society. You must then carefully consider how this evidence should be presented during the trial and how best to address this issue during summation.

In a similar fashion, the problem of identifying and eliminating jurors who find the plaintiff to be so socially unacceptable that they could not render a verdict for the plaintiff must be addressed during voir dire and opening statement. If you elect not to file a motion in limine to prevent the introduction of unfavorable evidence, or if the motion is denied, you will also need to address the problem throughout the trial. Accordingly, you must first make a threshold decision of whether to file a motion in limine. The factors involved in making that decision must be carefully evaluated as explained in the next section.

The segments of the trial process that should be used to overcome or minimize the problems in this case example are motions in limine, voir dire, opening statement, witness examination, and summation.

Motions in Limine

In considering the problems raised by the plaintiff's background and lifestyle, you must first decide whether to use a motion in limine in an attempt to keep this information from the jury or to use other segments of the trial process to lessen the information's adverse affects. To resolve this issue you must first know what evidence, if any, you can use in trial to humanize the plaintiff and explain his conduct and lifestyle. You must also know whether the jury will react favorably to your explanation.[3]

If there is no satisfactory explanation, then you should make a motion in limine to exclude the testimony. However, if you can humanize the plaintiff and create understanding and sympathy for him by explaining his lifestyle, you may want to meet the issue head-on in trial and fully disclose the facts that make him socially unacceptable.

If you do not have evidence to explain the plaintiff's lifestyle and his failure to file income-tax returns, it is imperative that you attempt to exclude references to this information during trial by a motion in limine. You must persuasively argue that this information is so prejudicial that it outweighs any probative value. To prevent disclosure of the plaintiff's failure to file income-tax returns, it will be necessary to withdraw or not assert a claim for lost earnings or loss of earning capacity, which could open the door to this damaging evidence.

Consider filing a motion in limine to prevent the doctor from talking about all the good things he has done, such as saving hundreds of lives and performing thousands of surgeries without being sued for negligence, serving as chairperson of charitable organizations or drives, participating in civic activities, and being a generous person. This testimony is not relevant and would only be introduced to gain sympathy and to distract the jury from the issues of the case.

When the plaintiff is involved in similar positive activities, evidence of those activities may be relevant to the plaintiff's claim, such

---

3 Chapter Seven, "Planning the Trial: Theory, Witnesses, and Trial Strategy," describes how you can determine a jury's probable reaction by using focus groups in combination with your own experience and a healthy dose of common sense.

as in a claim for loss of enjoyment of life and inability to engage in activities previously enjoyed. Evidence of the defendant's activities has no relevance to the defenses raised by defendant, whereas evidence of the plaintiff's activities may be relevant in establishing damages.

Voir Dire

Use voir dire to identify and to excuse jurors who are so offended by your client's lifestyle that they will not be persuaded by evidence that explains the lifestyle or by attempts to humanize the plaintiff. To do this, describe the plaintiff's background without couching it in explanations or humanizing evidence. In other words, present the evidence in the light most favorable to the defense. This approach makes it easier to excuse one or more of the most biased jurors for cause:

> Ladies and gentlemen, my client appears here in court physically crippled, but otherwise clean and presentable. He is well dressed and clean shaven. You will hear testimony that at the time of his motorcycle-auto collision, he was a filthy member of a motorcycle gang. When he arrived at the hospital, he was wearing a chain on his leather belt, and he had long hair and a beard. He smelled. He had a history of alcohol and drug abuse, had been convicted of theft, and had never filed an income-tax return. He was injured in that collision and is here suing Dr. Smith, who was called out of his bed in the middle of the night to treat the plaintiff. Now, having heard this information, I can understand why some or all of you might feel strongly that you could not render a verdict for the plaintiff, no matter what the evidence is regarding Dr. Smith's conduct. How many of you feel that way?

Often, the juror with the strongest reaction, bias, or prejudice will immediately raise his or her arm, followed by others. Always question the juror with the strongest reaction first, asking:

> Mr. Juror, how strong are your feelings? Do you feel so strongly about this issue that you could not render a verdict for the plaintiff, even if the evidence was overwhelming that Dr. Smith was negligent? Mr. Juror, I want to thank you for being open, candid, and honest about your feelings. Of those of you who also raised your hands, how many of you feel as strongly as Mr. Juror?

Once you have identified the several jurors who have stated that they could not possibly render a fair and impartial verdict, no matter what the evidence, then challenge those jurors for cause, as a group. Never challenge the first juror for cause before questioning the remaining jurors. The remaining jurors could perceive this as a punishment for being honest and candid, and they may withhold their opinions to avoid punishment.

Do not tell the jurors about the evidence that will be introduced to humanize the plaintiff and to explain his lifestyle. Save that for opening statement. Any jurors who did not raise their hands or have a noticeably unfavorable reaction to the plaintiff's lifestyle will be open to later evidence explaining the plaintiff's background and lifestyle. With luck, the defendant will be unfamiliar with favorable evidence regarding the plaintiff and will be pleased with the appearance that you have made a tactical blunder, self-destructing during the first stage of trial.

If defense counsel is alert and aware of the additional evidence the jury will hear, she will request to voir dire the jury in response to the challenge for cause, and she will attempt to rehabilitate those jurors who would favor the defense if selected. More often than not, it is so obvious to everyone in the courtroom that those challenged for cause could not be fair and impartial, the defense does not object to the challenge for fear of losing credibility with the remaining jurors in the courtroom.

There may be some jurors who cannot be challenged because their answers to the above questions have not been adverse to the plaintiff. Once those jurors have been seated, you can deal with the remaining problems and issues in the following manner:

> My client, Frank Sager, was injured when his motorcycle collided with a car, and he was brought to the hospital by ambulance. Dr. Smith came to the hospital from his home in the middle of the night and treated Frank's injuries. We allege that, at a later date, Dr. Smith was negligent in treating Mr. Sager. Now it would be natural for some people to assume that if you are called in the middle of the night to render emergency treatment, you should not be held legally responsible if you later negligently injure that same person. Ms. Juror, how do you feel about that? How many of you other jurors share the feeling that a doctor who gets out of bed in the middle of the night and renders treatment should be legally excused if he is later negligent and, by his negligence, injures the patient?

The answers to these questions and others[4] will assist you in exercising peremptory challenges. At the end of the voir dire and jury selection process, you may not have a friendly jury, but with luck you will not have any hostile jurors. You must then use your opening

---

4 See Chapter Eight, "Voir Dire."

statement to overcome any reservations the jurors may have about you, your client, or the merits of your case.

Opening Statement

Use opening statement as the first major step to overcome the previously identified problems.

Dealing with the Plaintiff's Background

During voir dire, the jurors heard only the unfavorable information about the plaintiff's background and lifestyle. Now use opening statement to humanize the plaintiff and create sympathy for him.

> Ladies and gentlemen, on May 1, 1992, Frank Sager was operating a motorcycle within the speed limit when he was struck at an intersection by a drunken driver who ran a red light. Frank was not at fault, and there will be no dispute about that. He sustained injuries to his left leg, hip, and shoulder, which were not severe and did not require treatment in the intensive care unit. Dr. Smith treated him for those injuries, but instead of rendering proper treatment, he crippled Frank for the remainder of his life.
>
> This was particularly tragic because Frank was finally making progress in overcoming nearly insurmountable problems. His problems started at an early age when his mother died and he ran away from home because of an abusive alcoholic father. He was circulated among relatives until age 16, when he began working and attempting to support himself, often living in the streets. At age 18 he joined the military, observed the tragic death of his best friend, began abusing alcohol and drugs, but received an honorable discharge.
>
> Following his discharge, he continued to abuse alcohol and drugs, joined a motorcycle gang, and was convicted of theft. As a condition of probation, he had the good fortune of meeting Joyce Jones, a counselor who will be here to testify. With the help of Joyce Jones and others, he successfully completed an alcohol recovery program, obtained employment, established new friendships, and left the motorcycle gang.
>
> On the evening he was struck by an automobile, he was on his way home from an Alcoholic's Anonymous meeting. He still had a beard and long hair and he was riding his motorcycle. However, he was not "filthy," "smelly," or unkempt, and he was not wearing a chain. These allegations by the defendant and his nurse will be refuted by the state police who investigated the accident, by the ambulance attendants, and by others.
>
> Frank Sager had a tragic childhood; he had two strikes against him before he was an adult. He suffered through further tragedies as a

> young adult but was finally overcoming the problems that crippled him emotionally and as a member of our society. He was finally on his way to a decent and productive life when he was struck by the automobile. He received injuries from which he would have fully recovered with proper medical care and treatment; instead, he sits here brain damaged and partly paralyzed because of the negligence of Dr. Smith. Now, let me explain how Dr. Smith crippled this young man . . .

Overcoming Jury Sympathy for the Defendant

During voir dire, the jurors received information that could cause them to have sympathy for the defendant. The opening statement should now be used to overcome that sympathy.

> Ladies and gentlemen, Dr. Smith came to the hospital from his home the night that Frank was injured because he was on call and expected to be available for emergencies. All of this was by prearrangement with the hospital. He will testify that he wanted to enter into this contract with the hospital agreeing to be available at night because this arrangement substantially increased his income and he therefore preferred night duty. He was not inconvenienced by this call because he was on duty that night and, in fact, had responded to an earlier call at the hospital and was expecting to receive his customary number of calls that night. However, the plaintiff had no choice in deciding which doctor would be called by the hospital or in selecting the defendant.
>
> In short, the defendant was being paid while sitting at home waiting for emergency calls, when he could have been in the doctors' waiting lounge at the hospital. Had the doctor been in that lounge, Frank Sager would have received an earlier diagnosis and prompt treatment. Instead, his treatment was delayed because Dr. Smith was at home and not at the hospital.

Witnesses

To further humanize your client and to explain the reasons for his problems and lifestyle, call as witnesses the counselor and any friends or members of Alcoholics Anonymous who would make a favorable impression on the jury. These witnesses should describe the plaintiff's good qualities and his efforts to overcome the tragedies he has faced. If your client is able to testify, call him as the last witness, when he will be least vulnerable to cross-examination.[5]

---

5 See Chapter Seven, "Planning the Trial: Theory, Witnesses, and Trial Strategy," for a more detailed discussion of these issues.

Consider calling as your first witnesses all of the people who will create sympathy for the plaintiff by humanizing him and describing his tragic background; then call witnesses who will describe the auto collision and the fact that the plaintiff was not at fault but was again a victim. All of this testimony lends credence to the facts you told the jury in opening statement and enhances your credibility before you cross-examine the defendant and his witnesses.

Next, consider calling liability witnesses, including the defendant, for cross-examination before putting on evidence of damages sustained as a result of the defendant's negligence. The plaintiff should be the last witness to testify in your case-in-chief.

Summation

Use summation to further deal with the problems presented by the plaintiff's background and lifestyle and to mitigate any sympathy for the doctor's position:

> Ladies and gentlemen, I told you in my opening statement that we only wanted justice—a fair and reasonable assessment of damages. Justice requires being fair to both sides. It would not be fair to Dr. Smith if Frank Sager were overcompensated for his losses.
>
> At the beginning of this trial, we candidly and honestly told you about Frank's troubled childhood and young adult years so that you would understand why his future earning capacity, which has been destroyed by Dr. Smith, is not as substantial as one might expect, and so that you could fairly assess damages. However, throughout this trial, defense counsel has unnecessarily overemphasized and dramatized Frank's past—sometimes subtly, sometimes not so subtly. Even Dr. Smith, after he had crippled Frank, exaggerated and highlighted Frank's troubled past in the hospital and office records, and again in his testimony. He even accused Frank of being "filthy" and "smelly" in the emergency room of the hospital.
>
> We now know, after hearing the testimony of police officers, ambulance attendants, and those present at the Alcoholics Anonymous meeting that Frank had just attended, that this was a gross exaggeration. You might ask why defense counsel and Dr. Smith wanted to divert your attention to Frank's past. Why did they want you to focus on matters that have absolutely no bearing on the liability issues in this case—matters that are not being contested and are not in dispute? The answer is simple: Dr. Smith was negligent and cannot offer a satisfactory explanation for his conduct, so they have tried to divert your attention away from liability to matters that could arouse bias and prejudice toward the plaintiff. Why else

would they exaggerate and overemphasize the plaintiff's background?

Folks, the court has instructed you that your verdict cannot be based on sympathy, bias, or prejudice, and I know that you will follow the court's instructions because you told me under oath at the beginning of this trial that you would. When this trial started, I challenged and excused those jurors who stated that they were biased and would not give Frank a fair trial. You were selected because you are fair and impartial people, and I am confident that you will see that justice is served in this case.

Because the defendant and his counsel want to talk about Frank's background, I will accommodate them, but I don't think they really want to hear what I have to say. You see, Frank has already paid in rare coin for his mistakes, for everything that made him socially unacceptable, even though he was not responsible for some of those events. He paid for his alcoholism with the loss of his friends, family, and health. He paid for his theft with a criminal record that will remain with him for the rest of his life. He paid for his mistakes with a loss of self-respect. He went through the humiliation and depression of being turned down for employment because of his troubled past. Yes, he has paid in rare coin for all his mistakes, and now he appears in court seeking justice for Dr. Smith's mistakes.

When Frank Sager and his guardian first came to me with his complaints about Dr. Smith and told me about his troubled background, he questioned whether he would receive a fair trial in Boulder, and I told him that he would. I told him that he was not responsible for the injuries he received in the auto collision, and was not responsible for then receiving additional crippling injuries inflicted on him by Dr. Smith.

Frank Sager once believed that justice was only for the advantaged and the privileged, and not for the weak, oppressed, and disadvantaged. He was wrong. The rich and the poor, the weak and the strong are all treated equally in a court of law in our democracy. Justice is blind and treats everyone equally. By your verdict, you can show Frank Sager that there is justice and that in this case Dr. Smith, not Frank, was wrong and must pay.

Dealing with the Plaintiff's Future Loss of Earning Capacity

The following illustrates a way of persuading the jurors to assess damages for future loss of earning capacity, despite the plaintiff's history of unemployment.

Defense counsel argues that Frank is not entitled to damages for a future loss of earning capacity because he was seldom employed before he was injured, and he could have continued with a lifestyle of sporadic employment throughout the rest of his lifetime. Why would defense counsel make this argument, knowing that Frank had already changed his lifestyle before he was injured? He had stopped abusing alcohol and drugs, he was regularly attending AA meetings, and he was looking for employment and had filed applications in numerous places. He had made new friends and was anxious to put his background behind him and move on to a new life. He was deprived of that opportunity by Dr. Smith's negligence. We will never know what kind of employment or career Frank would have had. We will never know how successful he might have been; he was deprived of these opportunities by the negligence of Dr. Smith. You should therefore give Frank, who was not at fault in this matter, the benefit of any doubt, and should not award Dr. Smith for his negligence by giving Dr. Smith the benefit of any doubt about Frank's future.

Overcoming Jury Sympathy for the Defendant

To minimize any sympathy that the jury might still feel for the doctor, dramatize and emphasize any evidence you have that establishes aggravated conduct or gross misconduct, as opposed to simple negligence or a negligent "mistake." Perhaps the doctor did not return telephone calls, or maybe he spoke harshly to the plaintiff. Perhaps he treated the plaintiff's serious problems in a casual or offhand manner or showed a lack of concern in other ways. If the doctor altered or destroyed relevant records, this should be emphasized.

In the absence of aggravated conduct, you might minimize the sympathy factor by emphasizing that the doctor was paid well for coming to the hospital in the middle of the night; that he had chosen to take night duty for economic reasons, not out of kindness; and that the plaintiff had no choice in deciding which doctor would be called by the hospital or in selecting the defendant. Stress that the plaintiff was a captive at the mercy of the defendant; that he put his life in the defendant's hands; and that he had to totally rely on the skill and expertise of this stranger.

When appropriate, you can debunk a defendant-doctor by comparing him to another type of professional with which the jurors have more familiarity; for example, you can compare an orthopedic surgeon with an auto mechanic,[6] a neurologist or surgeon with an electrician (put in the wrong electrical system and a building burns; cut the

---

6 See Case Example I.

wrong nerve and cause a foot-drop), a urologist with a plumber, or a pharmacist with a dietitian. In short, use analogies to defrock and demystify the magical and ethereal aura that sometimes envelops the medical profession. Who knows—in a proper case you may want to compare a proctologist to a sewer worker.

Case Example II has further illustrated how you must carefully select which segments of the trial are best suited to overcome problems and how to address the issues presented by those problems.

CASE EXAMPLE III

In Case Example III, a medical negligence suit is filed against a popular small-town physician who saved your client's life and then negligently created complications that resulted in additional disability. One of the defenses to the negligence claim is that the defendant used the same procedures and techniques in treating other patients with the same condition in the past without incident; therefore, the unexpected bad result in this case could not have been the result of negligence—it had to be the result of some unforeseeable and unexplained event.

Problems

The problems raised by this case example include the following:

- How do you prevent the defendant from emphasizing that she saved the plaintiff's life?
- How do you prevent the defendant from introducing evidence that she used the same procedures in the past, without incident, and how do you prevent her from suggesting that she was not negligent on previous occasions and therefore was not negligent on this occasion?
- How do you overcome the doctor's reputation and popularity in the community?

To resolve or minimize these issues, again consider the use of each segment of the trial as discussed previously in this chapter.

Motions in Limine

Consider filing a motion in limine to prevent defense counsel from focusing on the non-negligent conduct ("I saved his life"), which is not relevant. Argue that the prejudicial effect outweighs the probative value and that such testimony would only be introduced to gain sympathy for the doctor.

In a similar fashion, file a motion in limine to prevent any reference to the procedures that the physician has performed on other patients in the past. Argue that evidence that the physician was not negligent on previous occasions is not admissible to show that the physician was not negligent on this occasion. Again, the prejudice far outweighs the probative value of such testimony. Encourage the court to force counsel to focus on the issue in this case. Although the defendant may not have been negligent before and although the defendant saved the plaintiff's life, these facts do not excuse her negligence that caused the plaintiff's injury and disability.

Voir Dire

As in the previous case examples presented in this chapter, consider which of the identified problems can be dealt with on voir dire, such as the doctor's reputation and her popularity in the community.

Because this is a small community, many of the jurors will know the defendant-doctor personally or by reputation. It will be important to identify those jurors and to determine the nature of their relationship to the doctor (for example, patient, neighbor, or friend) and determine how that relationship will impact the juror if selected in this case.

Just as important is the juror's social and economic position in a small community. Even a juror who does not know the defendant will be reluctant to render a verdict for the plaintiff if the juror perceives that others in the community who are of importance to the juror might react unfavorably to such a verdict.

A juror's decision can be adversely affected by a concern that the juror's employer or co-workers might react unfavorably to the verdict, or that the juror's relatives or friends might react unfavorably. There may be any number of reasons that a juror would not want to offend certain people in the community who might later learn of the verdict.[7]

In a small town, you should expect to have jurors called who are patients or former patients of the defendant, who have friends who are patients of the defendant, or who are related to the defendant. Some of these jurors may admit that they could not render a verdict against the defendant even if the defendant was negligent, thus allowing you to challenge them for cause.

A juror will often express loyalty and friendship for a doctor who is seated in the courtroom by proudly stating that he is a patient of the doctor and would not render a verdict against her. The juror has little choice but to align with the doctor if the doctor is the only specialist in town or if the juror expects to have a continuing comfortable relationship with the doctor.

---

7 See Chapter Eight, "Voir Dire," for examples of ways to address these types of problems.

Discuss these relationships with the jurors to elicit candid and honest responses to your questions.[8] If you are able to seat a jury of people who are not beholden to the doctor, who are not fearful of anyone's reaction to their verdict if it is for the plaintiff, and who might get some personal satisfaction out of "dethroning" the doctor, you may have a chance of winning in this small-town atmosphere.

Accordingly, select jurors who do not identify with the doctor's social class or position in the community, who do not receive good medical care, who avoid the medical profession because it is too expensive, who resent being treated as second-class citizens by the medical profession, or who may show their resentment in the verdict rendered.

If the court denies your motion in limine, confront the "I saved his life" issue head-on in voir dire.[9] You must identify those jurors who would excuse the doctor's negligence because she saved his life on a previous occasion. Once you have exercised all challenges for cause and before you exercise peremptory challenges, you should further voir dire the remaining jurors to solicit promises under oath that they will be fair.

Do not attempt to rehabilitate jurors or solicit promises of fairness before exercising your challenges for cause. To do so would be counterproductive and could defeat your challenge. Conduct further voir dire to minimize the doctor's conduct in saving your client's life. For example,

> Those of you who indicated that a doctor who saves a person's life should not be held legally responsible for later negligently injuring that same person, let me ask you this: Do you believe that anyone in our society who saves a person's life should then have a legal right to negligently inflict injury on that person? Mr. Juror, do you believe that a police officer who saves a woman whose life is being threatened by an armed intruder should have a legal right to later negligently injure that woman? If the police officer is later driving the woman somewhere for her protection and runs a red light and collides with another vehicle, causing serious injury to the woman, is it your belief that the officer should be protected from suit because he earlier saved her life? Do you understand that police officers, like doctors, are paid to save lives, although doctors may earn considerably more money for doing so?

---

8 See Chapter Eight for specific techniques for discussing this issue.

9 See Chapter Eight for discussion.

If the court should instruct you in this case that the fact that the defendant may have earlier saved our client's life is no defense to her later negligence, would you follow the court's instructions? Would any of you be unable to do so because of the feelings you have expressed?

If no one in our society is excused from negligently injuring someone whose life they had earlier saved, do any of you believe that an exception should be made for doctors and that they should be treated differently? Do any of you believe that doctors are somehow above the law that applies to everyone and that they should be immune from suit simply because they are doctors? Ms. Juror, I am sure that you realize that police officers, fire fighters, and people in many occupations put their own lives in danger when saving the lives of others; is that correct? Now Dr. Margaret Pitt did not put her life in danger in giving the plaintiff a drug called epinephrine, which saved his life when he was having a severe asthma attack, but do you feel that she should be immune from suit if she later negligently injured the plaintiff?

Opening Statement

As demonstrated in previous sections of this chapter, use the opening statement to further deal with the identified problems. Dramatize the acts of negligence involved and minimize the doctor's conduct in saving the plaintiff's life. Capture the jurors' attention and keep them focused on the real issue in the case: the doctor's negligence.[10]

Witnesses

In cross-examining the defendant-doctor, you should be polite and understanding, keeping in mind the defendant's popularity, reputation, and credibility. Also, caution your expert witnesses not to unnecessarily attack the defendant but to be critical in a professional and understanding way. Your expert witnesses will probably be outsiders who are not familiar with the community in which you are trying the case. Members of that community, including the jurors, may not receive unwarranted criticism of the doctor favorably.

Summation

Remind jurors that they swore under oath to render a verdict for the plaintiff if they determined that the defendant negligently injured the plaintiff, and that they would not excuse the defendant's negli-

---

10 See Chapter Nine, "Opening Statement," for techniques.

gence because she saved the plaintiff's life earlier. Also remind the jurors that they swore under oath to follow the court's instructions, and that the court has instructed them that the defendant's earlier conduct is no defense to this claim of negligence.

Likewise, if the judge denied your motion in limine and permitted the defendant to testify that she had performed this same procedure on many people previously without adverse effects, request that the judge instruct the jury that evidence that the defendant was not previously negligent cannot be used as evidence that the defendant was not negligent on this occasion or as a defense. Again, remind the jurors that it is their civic duty and responsibility to follow the law and apply it to the facts of this case, as they swore under oath they would do. In addition, consider using an analogy to further minimize the effect of such testimony:

> With regard to the defendant's testimony that she had previously performed this procedure on many patients without injuring them, I am reminded of the driver of an automobile who was daydreaming on one occasion, ran a red light, and collided with another vehicle. The driver explained that he had driven that route through that intersection hundreds of times on his way to work and had never run a red light. However, he knew that he had on this occasion, and he admitted liability. He knew that his good driving record did not excuse his negligent conduct. In a similar fashion, the court has instructed you that the defendant's success in previous surgeries on other patients is no excuse for her negligence in treating Jim.

By making an analogy that jurors understand, you can often place a frivolous argument into proper perspective.

CASE EXAMPLE IV

Donna White, age 26, complained to Dr. Brown of a tiny lump in her breast. Dr. Brown dismissed her without diagnostic testing after reassuring her that she did not have cancer. He advised her to return if the symptoms progressed. Over the course of the next six months, she did return on two occasions because she thought the lump had increased in size, but each time Dr. Brown assured her that she did not have cancer, and no diagnostic testing was done. Finally, six months after her initial complaint, diagnostic testing revealed cancer that had spread to the lymph nodes.

Ms. White brought suit, alleging that the doctor had failed to timely diagnose and treat her breast cancer. The defense claims no responsibility for damages because the treatment that was later rendered when the cancer was discovered would have been necessary had an earlier diagnosis been made. Further, the defense claims that Ms. White's opportunity to survive and live a full life was not changed by the delay in diagnosis and treatment.

This type of defense is also commonly raised when physicians fail to diagnose and treat heart disease in a timely manner. In such a case, the defendant might argue that heart disease is progressive and that earlier treatment would not have changed the course of the disease.

Problems

The problems raised by the facts in this case example include:

- How do you establish that the plaintiff was injured by a late diagnosis and treatment of breast cancer?
- How do you deal with damages during trial when the injuries are intangible and consist of the loss of a percentage chance of living a full life, coupled with the fear of cancer recurrence?
- In proving damages, how do you distinguish between the kind of fear that would have existed with a timely diagnosis and the kind of fear that exists with a late diagnosis?
- How do you deal with the defense argument that the plaintiff's medical problems result from cancer and not from the doctor's conduct?

The technique of using each segment of the trial to deal with identified problems has been demonstrated at length throughout this chapter. In previous case examples, the use of motions in limine had to be seriously considered. In this breast cancer case, though, it is apparent that the identified problems do not raise evidentiary issues that can be addressed by motions in limine. However, other segments of the trial process can be used to overcome or diffuse these problems and issues, commencing with the voir dire examination of the jury.

Voir Dire

You must use voir dire to identify those jurors who would not react favorably to the plaintiff's claim that she was damaged by a late diagnosis and those jurors who would not be inclined to fault Dr. Brown. To identify them, you must inquire about each juror's experience with cancer and knowledge of cancer.

If a juror has had personal experience with, or an awareness of, a type of cancer that is incurable no matter when the diagnosis is made, it could affect his attitudes in this case. Other jurors may have faced situations in which cancer was detected and treated early but the outcome was unaltered. Jurors with fibrocystic disease of the breast may have received the same type of care that was provided to the plaintiff by Dr. Brown and would be less inclined to blame Dr. Brown for the delayed diagnosis.

Accordingly, ask each juror if he knows anything about cancer from personal experience, from the experiences of their relatives or friends, from literature or studies about cancer, or from any other source. If there are jurors who have had such direct or indirect experience with cancer, you should question each one to determine what type of cancer was involved, what stage it was in when diagnosed and treated, and whether the treatment was successful. Then ask:

> From your own knowledge or experience with cancer, do any of you believe that cancer of the breast is incurable and untreatable? Mr. Juror, what is the basis of that belief? How strong is that belief; that is, is it a belief that is so strong that you could not listen with an open mind to medical testimony to the contrary? Mr. Juror, what if all of the doctors who testify in this case agree that early detection and treatment of breast cancer can make a difference in the outcome? Would you still have any doubt about that proposition?

In addition to detecting juror bias, it is important to establish a theme, at the outset, that early detection and treatment of breast cancer prolongs life and saves lives. When you are dealing with damages, it is also important to explore the juror's reactions to prolonging the life of a terminally ill patient. This gives you valuable information on a juror's attitude about the value of life. Further, you want to detect jurors' attitudes about assessing damages if the injury is intangible and consists of the loss of a percentage chance of living a full life. For example:

> Ladies and gentlemen, in this case you will hear evidence that if the plaintiff's cancer had been detected and treated one year earlier by Dr. Brown, she would have had better than a 50 percent chance of living a full life. However, because it was not detected earlier, she now has less than a 50 percent chance of living five years, and she has only a 5 to 10 percent chance of living a full life.
>
> Do any of you believe that you would be unable to assess damages to the plaintiff if you decided Dr. Brown was negligent solely because no one knows how long the plaintiff will live now and because she still might live a full life? Ms. Juror, why are you troubled by this? Why would you find it difficult to assess damages? Do you all believe that a person should not be deprived of a 100 percent chance of living a full life because of another's negligence? In other words, none of you would have a problem with the proposition that negligently causing the death of another is wrong and the wrongdoer should pay? Is that correct? But what if someone, through their conduct, reduces your chance of living a full life by 90 percent, so that you only have a 10 percent chance of living a full life? Do any of you believe that the wrongdoer should not pay for depriving a person of a 90 percent chance of living a full life?

> If the court should instruct you at the conclusion of this trial that if you find that Dr. Brown was negligent and his negligence has reduced the plaintiff's chance of living a full life, you must assess damages for that loss, would any of you be unable or unwilling to do so? Would any of you do so reluctantly because of a belief that the law is wrong and that damages should not be assessed under those circumstances?
>
> Is there anyone here who believes that anyone with cancer is destined to die because it is God's will, or that the medical profession should not interfere with a disease process like cancer and that nature should take its course unhampered by treatment or medical interference? How many of you believe that treatment of a disease like cancer only prolongs the pain and suffering, and perhaps treatment should not be rendered? Mr. Juror, what is the basis of that belief? Why do you feel that way? Do the rest of you believe that every day of life is precious and that every human being should strive to live a full and complete life? Do you believe it is appropriate for people to seek medical attention to prolong life?
>
> Is there anyone here who has never gone to a doctor for an illness, disease, or injury? For those of you who have gone, did all of you expect the doctor to exercise his best skill and knowledge in caring for you and in treating your condition? Have all of you had the experience of totally relying on a doctor to do so?

In summary, the voir dire examination should be used to detect jurors who have unfavorable attitudes about the problems raised in this case so that you can assess the nature and depth of those attitudes and exercise peremptory challenges to excuse any unfavorable jurors. At the same time, you should introduce the theme you will carry out throughout the trial. Then use opening statement to further overcome or defuse the identified problems.

Opening Statement

Dealing with the Problem of Showing that Early Detection Is Important

You must defuse the defendant's theory that earlier detection and treatment of the cancer would not have made a difference in the outcome. You can do this in a dramatic way by capturing the jury's attention at the outset.[11]

---

11 See Appendix E for a sample opening statement.

Dealing with the Damages Issues

In addition to persuading the jury that the plaintiff was deprived of a percentage chance of living a full life, you must explain to the jury how the delay in treatment resulted in damages that the plaintiff would not have incurred with timely detection and treatment. For example:

> Because Donna's cancer was detected six months late and it had already spread to the nodes, it was necessary that she undergo radiation therapy and chemotherapy. Her oncologist explained to her that this therapy would make her unable to have children and that she should have her tubes tied to prevent pregnancy. She was also told that there was a 60 percent chance she would die within five years. She was engaged to be married at that time and wanted to have children in the future, and upon hearing this news, she and her mother sat in the car outside the medical center and cried.
>
> Donna's oncologist will explain that she should not become pregnant because the chemotherapy causes a hormone imbalance which would endanger her life if she became pregnant, yet she can never take birth control pills or hormonal drugs again because these pills increase the risk of cancer recurrence. Donna had radiation therapy and chemotherapy for 32 weeks, lost her hair, was nauseated after chemotherapy, lost her energy and strength, and changed her diet. All of this would have been unnecessary had the cancer been detected six months earlier by Dr. Brown.
>
> What about damages? You will learn that Donna lives in constant fear of death because she now has a 60 percent chance of recurrence within five years; that she cannot have children because of the probable need for additional chemotherapy and radiation therapy should the cancer recur; and even if she could have children, she would not want to risk the chance of having to orphan them. She is reluctant to now marry her fiance for those same reasons. She does not have the energy to complete her college education and work full-time, and she is struggling to maintain her present employment. She is fearful that if she loses her job, she will be unable to obtain other employment because she is now considered high risk for insurance purposes, yet she can only obtain insurance coverage through employment. She could find herself unemployed with no health insurance. Again, all of this could have been avoided by early detection and treatment.

In addition to addressing the problems raised in this case example during voir dire and in opening statement, you need to ensure that the problems are properly addressed by witnesses.

Witnesses

Use expert testimony to establish that the cancer had probably advanced during the delay in treatment, and that if earlier treatment had been rendered, the patient could have been cured or the cancer could have been placed in early remission. Establish that the delay in treatment makes cure unlikely or difficult, and that it also makes remission less probable. Establish that the longer the delay in diagnosis and treatment, the more the disease will progress, and explain that allowing the disease to progress can result in a shorter life expectancy. Also use expert testimony to show that early diagnosis allows more conservative treatment and less long-term damage or injury.

To help show the increased fear of cancer recurrence or death which results from a late diagnosis, consider calling a psychologist or psychiatrist who has expertise in treating cancer victims. Such experts can testify that most cancer patients with a good prognosis can bounce back and get on with their lives, whereas patients with a poor prognosis are unable to do so because of their expectation of recurrence and their fear of death.

Those anticipating recurrence do not make plans for the future because, for example, they fear having children who will be orphaned. They fear planning a marriage, continuing with education, or working hard for promotions in employment. Patients who have an increased fear of recurrence and who face periodic medical monitoring and examinations fear each examination. The patient may be relieved for awhile if the news is good, but the relief is accompanied by a realization that the longer the patient lives, the closer she may be to recurrence and death.

An expert can emphasize the vicious cycle that a patient may fall into when she knows there is a substantial probability of recurrence and death resulting from the late diagnosis. Then, when the plaintiff testifies, she can emphasize the additional emotional injury resulting from the increased risk of cancer recurrence and from the fear of death resulting from the doctor's failure to timely diagnosis and treat the disease.

The defendant will argue that the plaintiff had a reduced life expectancy because of cancer, regardless of the time of diagnosis; he will argue that the doctor is therefore not responsible for damages for any reduction in life expectancy. To rebut this argument, introduce evidence to the contrary, showing that earlier treatment would have increased the plaintiff's life expectancy over what it is now projected to be because of late treatment, and that the plaintiff's chance of living a full life is also now diminished because of late treatment.[12]

Summation

To further address the identified problems, make the following points in summation.

When there is a possibility of cancer, a failure to diagnose can be a matter of life or death. This places an awesome responsibility on the doctor to heighten his level of awareness of this potential diagnosis and to use his best skills and the best technology available to confirm or rule out cancer. A doctor should not treat patients with symptoms suggestive of breast cancer in an offhand or casual manner; he should not merely instruct the patients to return if the symptoms progress or get worse.

Emphasize the tragedy of the late diagnosis by referring to breast cancer as a "time bomb in her body." Explain that "With every minute of every hour, and with every day of delay, it was bringing her closer to death."

There are some cases in which the patient repeatedly complains of a growing lump in her breast and the doctor finally does diagnostic testing at the patient's urging and discovers cancer. In such cases it can be argued that it was not the doctor who saved the patient's life; it was the patient who saved her own life with her persistence.

If defense counsel argues that because no diagnostic testing was done, the plaintiff cannot now prove with 100 percent certainty the condition of her cancer when she first complained of symptoms, and that she thus cannot prove that a delay in diagnosis and treatment allowed a substantial progression of the cancer, you could rebut his argument with the following:

> Although our expert witnesses could not tell you with 100 percent certainty what the condition of Donna's cancer was when she first complained to Dr. Brown, they have rendered opinions on what her condition probably was at that time and why they believe that it substantially progressed before it was finally diagnosed. Had Dr. Brown acted responsibly, the tumor would have been removed one year earlier, the nodes would have been examined, and we would know with certainty the extent of the cancer. The plaintiff was deprived of that opportunity by the defendant's negligence. Dr. Brown

---

12 See Appendix F.12 for an illustration of how these points can be effectively made during the plaintiff's cross-examination of the defendant's expert witness.

should not be permitted to now say, "I did no diagnostic testing or follow-up care, so you cannot prove what her condition would be today if I had treated her one year ago."

Dramatize the outrageousness of the defendant's conduct:

In this case, when Donna first came to Dr. Brown with her complaints, he considered cancer, but he felt that the chance of her having cancer at her age was remote, and he dismissed her without doing diagnostic testing after reassuring her she did not have cancer. Ladies and gentlemen, he gambled with her life! It was not his life he was gambling with, it was Donna's! It was not his wife's life or his daughter's life—it was a stranger coming to him as a patient. But Donna deserved the same level of care and concern that you would expect him to provide to a loved one. She did not receive that care, and her life is now at stake.

CONCLUSION

It is important to identify issues and problems that you must address at trial. Well before you go to court, you must analyze how to use each segment of the trial to overcome problems that develop. It is only through creativity and hard work that a proper analysis and game plan can be perfected. You must then use your skills as a trial lawyer to implement that game plan and lead the jury to a successful conclusion.

APPENDIX A

GATHERING FACTS AND MATERIALS

A.1 OFFICE INFORMATION BROCHURE

Thank you for consulting us. We would like to provide you with some basic information about our office.

Initial Conference Charge

We do not charge for the first half hour of the initial office conference.

Nature of Law Work

Our professional work is limited to damage claims on behalf of persons who are seeking compensation. Most of our legal work involves injury or death claims caused by auto accidents, negligence, or similar causes. We do not accept general legal work, such as wills, real estate, or divorce cases, but we are happy to recommend lawyers to you for this work. In addition, we do accept a limited amount of general trial work involving disputes of all kinds.

Handicapped Parking and Entry Ramp

For your convenience we have available handicapped parking and an entry ramp on the south side of the office. If you will be using the facility, please call the office and advise the receptionist when you are coming, and she will give you additional information.

Fees Charged

Almost all of our legal work is paid on a contingent fee basis. Under this arrangement, we are paid a fee only if we recover money for our client. Generally the fee charged is one-third of the total recovery, except in negligence or other complex cases, in which the fee is 40 percent of the total recovery. A written fee agreement will be provided to all clients of the office. We will provide a full explanation of all fee arrangements to our clients.

Costs

Costs include those bills received from other people in connection with your case, such as court reporters, expert witnesses, and others. We charge an hourly rate for the services of our investigator, who is employed by this office. We provide copies of all important material to the client and charge for those copies also. (We are to be paid for those costs billed in addition to our fee.)

Billing

Clients receive a bill monthly. We will charge 12 percent interest annually on unpaid costs that we have advanced. No bill will be sent for fees in a contingent fee case until the final recovery is made. The bill is itemized, and you can call the bookkeeper if you have any questions. Normally the bill is not paid until the money is collected.

Paralegal Assistants

This office employs trained legal assistants to work with our clients. These nonlawyers will assist the attorney in processing your claim. Your file will be assigned to one primary paralegal who will be familiar with your file at all times; he or she will work with the attorney in representing you.

Time Limits for Suing

There is a time limit for either filing suit or settling your claim. In some cases, such as disputes involving the government, a written claim must be filed before a lawsuit can be brought. There is a time limit for doing that, too. These "statutes of limitations" setting out the time limit for your case should be discussed with the attorney.

Settlement of Lawsuit

We settle the great majority of cases we handle before trial. Many cases require the filing of a lawsuit before a settlement can be made. The fact that a lawsuit is filed doesn't mean a trial will be necessary. No lawsuit will be filed unless you agree first. No settlement will be made without your consent. Claims on behalf of minor children require court approval before settlement or before a lawsuit can be brought.

Seattle Branch

We have, for your convenience, a Seattle branch office located in Pioneer Square. The telephone number is 203-8000. We work out of the Seattle branch office on an appointment basis only. Should this be a more convenient location for you to meet with us, please make arrangements with the receptionist at our Mount Vernon location.

Miscellaneous Notes

We will keep you informed about your case. While the information you give us is confidential, if a lawsuit is brought, the person sued has the right to obtain information about your claim.

Attorney Biography

Paul Luvera has lectured to lawyers throughout the United States on the subject of trial and damage claims. He is admitted to practice before Washington state courts, as well as federal courts, including the U.S. Supreme Court. He is a fellow of the American College of Trial Lawyers, whose membership is limited to one percent of the trial lawyers of each state who have demonstrated outstanding trial ability in the courtroom. He is also a member of the Inner Circle of Advocates, whose membership is limited to those 100 lawyers throughout the United States who have obtained verdicts of one million dollars or more for injured clients. In addition, he is a charter member of the American Board of Trial Advocates, whose membership is limited to outstanding trial lawyers throughout the world, and of the International Society of Barristers, whose membership is limited to qualified trial lawyers in the United States.

A.2 LETTER TO CLIENT

Dear __________:

Thank you for contacting us regarding your unfortunate potential medical negligence claim.

You should know that in the state of Washington a lawsuit must be filed within three years of the wrongful act or one year from the date it was discovered or reasonably should have been discovered. In no event may an adult bring a lawsuit more than eight years af-

(letter continued next page)

(letter continued from previous page)

ter the negligent act has occurred. A child has until age 21 to bring such a lawsuit. After that time, the law bars the claim forever. Keep in mind, however, that the legislature can change the law at any time. It is also possible to be countersued for filing an unfounded or malicious medical negligence case. Therefore, every case has to be evaluated carefully.

The law requires that you have a qualified physician who is willing to testify that medical negligence has occurred in your case. One of the first steps we take in evaluating a medical negligence case is to have a physician review your medical records to see if he will testify that medical negligence has occurred. Physicians charge us for reviewing records. To cover these charges and the cost of obtaining your medical records, we normally require you to deposit $350 in a trust account. We return to you whatever is left in the account after the physicians' bills and the expenses of obtaining records have been paid. Some of our clients cannot afford to make this deposit, and we are always happy to discuss other options. We do not charge for our time in evaluating your case.

To assist us, please examine the following enclosures with this letter:

- A client questionnaire for you to complete;
- Waivers for you to sign and return;
- A booklet;
- A brochure describing our office; and
- An attorney's fee agreement.

Please sign the various waivers and fee agreement, complete the questionnaire, and return these forms to us with your deposit. After you do this, we will immediately obtain your medical records and have a physician review them. Following this review, we will contact you with our recommendations. Once again, we will not charge you for our evaluation of your case.

Thank you again for consulting us about your potential claim. We will take no further action until you complete the enclosed waivers, fee agreement, and questionnaire and return them to us with your deposit.

(letter continued next page)

(letter continued from previous page)

Sincerely,

Paul N. Luvera, Jr.
PNL:js
Enclosure

A.3 ATTORNEY FEE AGREEMENT

The undersigned, hereinafter called "Clients," hire Paul N. Luvera, Jr. and Associates, hereinafter called "Attorney," to represent Clients as legal counsel for all purposes in connection with claims for damage arising out of an incident which occurred on ___________, 19___, resulting in damages to ______________________. Clients and Attorney agree as follows:

1. Initial Evaluation: Attorney will make an initial investigation and evaluate the merits of this case. Clients shall pay the costs of investigation. However, no attorney fees will be charged for Attorney's work in connection with the evaluation. Clients agree to deposit $_______ in Attorney's trust account to pay the expense of obtaining the medical records and the cost of their evaluation by a medical expert. Attorney reserves the right to terminate this agreement after such investigation, whereupon any balance remaining in the trust account shall be returned to Clients.

2. Attorney Fees: Clients will pay an attorney fee of _____ percent of all money collected from any source on behalf of Clients in excess of the amount already paid and advanced by Clients. Should settlement or payment be made on an annuity or periodic payment basis, then the attorney fees shall be computed on the basis of the present cash value of the total settlement or agreed payments. The attorney fees shall be paid from the initial cash payment, rather than from the future payments as received, at Attorney's discretion. At Attorney's option, the attorney fee percentage shall be calculated on the gross recovery and before deducting the amount of costs or other deductions to be made in addition to fees. Costs advanced shall be reimbursed whether or not a recovery is made.

3. Arbitration: Any dispute between Attorney and Client shall be resolved by arbitration. The arbitrators shall be members of the

Washington State Bar Association. The Attorney shall select one arbitrator. The Client shall select one arbitrator. The two arbitrators shall select a third arbitrator. The arbitrators shall, by majority vote, establish all rules pertaining to the arbitration, including determining how the cost of arbitration shall be paid. If the dispute is not resolved, the rules of the American Arbitration Association in effect at that time shall apply and control.

4. No Promises: The Clients acknowledge that the Attorney has made no promises or guarantees regarding the outcome of this case.

5. Withdrawal: In the event of a withdrawal, all costs advanced by the Attorney shall be reimbursed fully. A reasonable fee shall be paid to the Attorney should a recovery be made for or on behalf of the Clients.

6. Fee Division: Clients are aware of, and do not object to, the division of the fee being charged the Client between the Attorney and Associate Attorney, ________________, at the Attorney's discretion. Clients shall pay no additional fee in the event of such association.

7. Costs Advanced: Clients authorize the Attorney to incur such costs as the Attorney, at his sole discretion, determines necessary in the process of Clients' case. Clients agree that all such expenses and costs shall be reimbursed by Clients. Clients agree that costs may include the Attorney's employed investigator or employed nurse, whose time will be billed at the rate of $35 per hour. Costs also include copies provided Clients of documents related to their case. The Clients will receive a regular accounting of costs advanced. The Clients agree that interest of one percent per month shall be added to the accounting and billing provided to the Client.

8. Appeal: If the Clients authorize an appeal of this case, the Attorney's fees shall be increased by 10 percent more than the fees set forth above to cover the additional work.

9. Probate: An action for damages arising out of death may require the appointment of a personal representative. Should a probate be necessary, Clients agree to authorize the Attorney to retain another attorney to process such probate. All costs and fees associated with same shall be paid as part of the costs of this matter.

10. Legal Advice Given: The Clients acknowledge that they have been fully advised regarding the statute of limitations and the time limit for commencing a lawsuit, after which their legal rights will be

lost forever. The Clients further acknowledge being fully advised regarding the need for the filing of any written claims before the commencement of any lawsuit in this matter. The Clients acknowledge being fully advised regarding their legal rights.

We have read the above, understand the agreement, and hereby agree to its terms. There are no other agreements between the parties.

Dated this ____________day of ________, 19___ .

______________________________	______________________________
Client	Client
______________________________	______________________________
Paul N. Luvera, Jr.	Associate Attorney

Attorney at Law
P.O. Box 427
Mount Vernon, WA 98273
(206) 336-6561

A.4 AUTHORIZATION FOR RELEASE OF MEDICAL INFORMATION

WAIVER

RE: Patient ____

To whom it may concern:

This is to authorize any physician, hospital, laboratory, or healthcare provider of any kind to furnish to and discuss with my attorneys, Paul N. Luvera, Jr., Inc., P.S., P.O. Box 427, Mount Vernon, Washington, 98723, Phone (206) 336-6561, any medical information whatsoever regarding myself or my minor child or children. This release of information is to allow my attorneys or any authorized representative to obtain any and all information or opinions, to see or copy any X rays, hospital records, physician's records, or any other material, and to discuss same with personnel, as needed. I hereby waive any physician-patient privilege in this regard.

1. Duration of Waiver: This authorization shall be valid for a period of three (3) years or until you are advised in writing by me of its revocation before the expiration of three (3) years.

2. Copy in Lieu of Original: A copy of the original authorization for release of medical information shall have the same effect as the signed original.

3. Unlawful Disclosure Prohibited: You are hereby notified that state law prohibits any physician, hospital, or health-care provider from releasing *any* information about a patient to some other person *unless* the patient first consents to the release. The unauthorized release of information about a patient can result in the loss of the patient's legal rights and result in a damage claim for such unauthorized release. Therefore, you are hereby directed not to release any information of any nature whatsoever to insurance adjusters, attorneys or their representatives, or any other persons who may contact you or your office staff about this patient unless written consent has been given by the patient for the release of such information. You are authorized, however, to release medical information to the patient's medical insurance carrier or the Department of Labor and Industries as provided in the next paragraph.

4. Medical Insurance: You are authorized to release medical information to my own medical insurance company (Insurance company name: ______________) or the Department of Labor and Industries to ensure that your bill or treatment is paid or reimbursed.

5. Revocation of Other Waivers: I hereby revoke any other authorization for release of medical information that may have been provided to you by any insurance adjuster or insurance company other than my medical insurance company (Insurance company name: ______________________) or the Department of Labor and Industries.

6. *Caution:* In order to avoid possible legal complications, please alert your staff to the restrictions on release of information of any nature whatsoever regarding this patient to persons unauthorized to receive it.

Dated: ____________________ ______________________________

Patient

____

Patient

A.5 MEDICAL NEGLIGENCE QUESTIONNAIRE

A. General Information

1. Your full name: ______________________________________
   (First) (Middle) (Last)
2. Address: ______________________________________
   ____
3. Home #: ____________ Work #: __________ Other: ___________
4. Birth date: ________ Age: _________ Birthplace: ____________
5. Mother's full name: ______________________________________
6. Father's full name: ______________________________________
7. Social security number: ______________________________________

B. Present Marriage

1. Are you presently married? [ ] YES [ ] NO
   If so, please answer the following:

(a) Date of marriage: _________ Spouse's name: _________________

(b) Place of marriage: ______________________________________

(c) Please furnish names, addresses, and birthdays of all children born as a result of your present marriage:

Full Name   Present Address   Date of Birth   Age

(1) ______________________________________

(2) ______________________________________

(3) ______________________________________

(4) ______________________________________

C. Past Marriage(s)

1. Have you been married before? [ ] YES [ ] NO
   If so, please answer the following:

(questionnaire continued next page)

(questionnaire continued from previous page)

(a) Date of marriage: _______ Spouse's name: ________________

(b) Place of marriage: ________________________________

(c) Did the marriage terminate by divorce or death? ___________

(d) Date of divorce or date of death of former spouse: __________

(e) Please furnish the names, addresses, and birthdays of all children born as a result of your previous marriage(s):

	Full Name	Present Address	Date of Birth	Age
(1)				
(2)				
(3)				
(4)				

2. Are you presently paying or receiving support payments for children of a prior marriage? [ ] YES [ ] NO

   If so, please state amount: $ _____ per __________

   Please check one: [ ] RECEIVING [ ] PAYING

D. Residence

Please list addresses where you have resided for the past 10 years and the length of time at each residence.

	Address	From	To
1.			
2.			
3.			
4.			

E. Employment

1. Are you presently employed? [ ] YES [ ] NO

   If so, please indicate:

(a) Employer: ______________________________

(b) Employer's address: ______________________________

(c) Present job title and duties: ______________________________

____

(d) How long have you been employed at this job? ____________

(e) What is your rate of pay? Gross __________ Net ____________

(f) How many hours per week do you work? ______________

(g) What was your gross income for the last 12 months?

2. If you are not now working, have you in the past worked outside the home? [ ] YES [ ] NO

   If so, please provide the employment information requested below beginning with your most recent employment.

	Employer	Address	Dates of Employment	Nature of Work
(a)				
(b)				
(c)				
(d)				

3. Is your spouse presently employed? [ ] YES [ ] NO

   If so, please indicate the following:

(a) Employer: ______________________________

(b) Employer's address: ______________________________

(c) Present job title and duties: ______________________________

____

(d) How long has your spouse been employed at this job? ________

F. Military Service

1. Have you ever been in the military? [ ] YES [ ] NO

   If so, please give dates: ______________________________

(questionnaire continued next page)

(questionnaire continued from previous page)

2. What type of discharge did you receive? ________________

3. Are you now receiving or have you ever received any payments from the Veterans Administration, Social Security, or other sources? [ ] YES [ ] NO

   If so, please give details: ________________

   ____

   ____

4. What is your Veterans Administration number? ________________

G. Police Record

1. Other than minor traffic offenses, have you ever been convicted of a crime? [ ] YES [ ] NO

   If so, please give the following:

	Criminal Charge	Date	Place
(a)			
(b)			
(c)			

2. Is there or has there ever been a restriction on your driver's license? [ ] YES [ ] NO

   If so, please give details: ________________

   ____

   ____

3. Have you ever received any traffic tickets? [ ] YES [ ] NO

   If so, please furnish the following information:

	Nature of Traffic Ticket	Date	What Was Done About It
(a)			
(b)			
(c)			
(d)			

H. Claims and Court Cases

1. Have you ever sued anyone or been sued yourself for anything, including divorce? [ ] YES [ ] NO

2. Have you ever filed any kind of a claim against any insurance company for industrial insurance, for veterans' benefits, or for any other reason? [ ] YES [ ] NO

If you have, please furnish full details regarding such claims:

	Nature of Claim	Date	Result
(a)			
(b)			
(c)			
(d)			

I. Education

Please provide your educational background:

	Name and Location	Number of Years Attended	Year Left	Graduated [Y/N]	Degree
High School					
College/Univ.					
Business School					
Tech. Training					
Other					

(questionnaire continued next page)

(questionnaire continued from previous page)

J. Religious and Fraternal Affiliations

1. Please list the fraternal organizations to which you now belong:

(a) ____________________

(b) ____________________

(c) ____________________

(d) ____________________

2. What is your religious affiliation, if any? Please provide the name of your priest, pastor, or rabbi if applicable.

K. Insurance

1. Do you have any medical, health, or other accident insurance?

[ ] YES [ ] NO

If so, please provide the following information:

	Insurance Company	Address of Company	Agent	Address of Agent
(a)				
(b)				
(c)				
(d)				

Have you made any claim against your insurance?

[ ] YES [ ] NO

2. Do you have any other insurance that would pay any of your medical bills for the accident associated with this case?

[ ] YES [ ] NO

If so, please complete the following:

	Hospital	Length of Stay	Date	Reason for Hospitalization
(a)				
(b)				
(c)				
(d)				

3. Had you ever been ill before the accident associated with this case other than with colds and minor illnesses?

[ ] YES [ ] NO

If so, please complete the following:

Nature of Illness	Date	Name of Doctor

(a) ____________________

(b) ____________________

(c) ____________________

(d) ____________________

4. Did you ever have any accidents or injuries before this accident that required medical attention? [ ] YES [ ] NO

If so, please furnish the following information:

Nature of Accident or Injury	Date	Name of Doctor

(a) ____________________

(b) ____________________

(c) ____________________

(d) ____________________

5. Before this accident, who was the family doctor you consulted when you needed medical attention? If you used more than one doctor, osteopath, chiropractor, or other physician, please indicate:

Name of Physician or Doctor	Date(s) Seen	Reasons Seen

(a) ____________________

(b) ____________________

(c) ____________________

(d) ____________________

6. Other than the doctors involved in this case, what doctors, osteopaths, chiropractors, or other physicians have you consulted in the past five years?

(a) ____________________

(questionnaire continued next page)

(questionnaire continued from previous page)

(b) ______________________________

(c) ______________________________

(d) ______________________________

7. Have you ever had any prolonged or chronic health problems other than those associated with this case? [ ] YES [ ] NO

   If so, please describe fully: ______________________________

   ____

   ____

8. Did you use any drugs or medication regularly before your treatment in this case? [ ] YES [ ] NO

   If so, please describe the drug or medication and its purpose:

   ____

   ____

   ____

9. Have you ever had any auto, life, or health insurance declined or cancelled? [ ] YES [ ] NO

   If so, please give the date and reason: ______________________________

   ____

L. Medical Care in This Case

We need the names of all doctors, osteopaths, chiropractors, or others who treated you or saw you in connection with the problems you are now having. Please answer the following questions very carefully.

1. What is the name of the personal family doctor you saw at the time of the accident in this case?

(a) Name: ______________________________

(b) Address: ______________________________

(c) Phone number: ______________________________

2. What other physicians or doctors have seen you or treated you in connection with your medical problems in this case?

Name and Address of Doctor	Phone Number	What did the doctor do for you?

(a) ______________________________

(b) ______________________________

(c) ______________________________

(d) ______________________________

3. Were you admitted to any hospital in connection with the problem in this case? [ ] YES [ ] NO

If so, please indicate:

Hospital	Length of Stay	Date	Reason for Hospitalization

(a) ______________________________

(b) ______________________________

(c) ______________________________

4. Did you have any operations in connection with your medical problems in this case? [ ] YES [ ] NO

If so, please indicate:

Name of doctor performing surgery: ______________

Names of Doctors Assisting During Surgery

(a) ______________________________

(b) ______________________________

(c) ______________________________

5. If you had an operation in connection with your medical problems in this case, please indicate:

(a) The date of surgery: ______________

(b) The person who recommended the surgeon to do the surgery:

____

(c) Why the surgery was recommended: ______________

____

M. Facts of Injury

It is essential that you prepare a chronological factual statement of what happened to you, starting with the ailment or condition for which you consulted the doctor. This statement should include com-

(questionnaire continued next page)

(questionnaire continued from previous page)

plete details of everything you can remember happening, with dates, names of people present, and summaries of conversations you had with doctors or others about it. If you cannot recall the particular event clearly, ask others in your family to help you fill in the details. If there is not enough room, please continue on separate sheets of paper. Dates, names of doctors and others, descriptions of conversations with the doctors, and accurate statements of what took place are essential to your case. [ALLOW WHOLE PAGE FOR REPLY]

This is what happened to me: ____________________

____

____

____

N. Present Medical Treatment

1. Are you now seeing any doctor, osteopath, chiropractor, or physical therapist as a result of your problems? [ ] YES [ ] NO

If so, please furnish the following information:

	Name of Physician or Doctor	Date(s) Seen
(a)		
(b)		
(c)		
(d)		

2. As a result of your medical problems, are you now taking any aspirin or other medication on the advice of a doctor?

[ ] YES [ ] NO

If so, please give the following information:

	Drug or Medication	Pharmacy Where Purchased	Dates Taken
(a)			
(b)			
(c)			
(d)			

3. Do you now have, or have you had in the past, any special nurses, friends, or others acting as nurses in connection with your medical problem(s)? [ ] YES [ ] NO

If so, please furnish the following information:

Person	Date(s)	Nature of Care

(a) ______________________________

(b) ______________________________

(c) ______________________________

(d) ______________________________

4. Have you used any of the following in connection with treatment?

	YES	NO	From	To
Back or neck brace?	[ ]	[ ]	Dates: ______	
Crutches?	[ ]	[ ]	Dates: ______	
Traction?	[ ]	[ ]	Dates: ______	
Physiotherapy?	[ ]	[ ]	Dates: ______	
Other? (specify) ______			Dates: ______	

O. Lost Wages

As a result of your medical problems in this case, did you lose any time from work? [ ] YES [ ] NO

If so, please furnish the following information:

1. Name of employer: ______________________________
2. Address of employer: ______________________________
3. Net salary per month: $ ______________________________
4. Dates you were unable to work: ______________________________

____

P. Witnesses

1. Please furnish the name of anyone who may have overheard conversations with doctors or nurses about your injuries:

(a) Name: ______________________________

Address: ______________________________

(questionnaire continued next page)

(questionnaire continued from previous page)

Phone number: __________ Age: _____ Job: ______________

What does he/she know? ______________________

(b) Name: ______________________________

Address: ______________________________

Phone number: __________ Age: _____ Job: ______________

What does he/she know? ______________________

2. Please furnish the name of anyone who may know about the effect of the injuries on you, your hobbies and activities, or your physical condition in general.

(a) Name: ______________________________

Address: ______________________________

Phone number: __________ Age: _____ Job: ______________

What does he/she know? ______________________

(b) Name: ______________________________

Address: ______________________________

Phone Number: __________ Age: _____ Job: ______________

What does he/she know? ______________________

3. Please furnish the name of anyone you have not listed previously who may be a witness in your case.

(a) Name: ______________________________

Address: ______________________________

Phone number: __________ Age: _____ Job: ______________

What does he/she know? ______________________

(b) Name: ______________________________

Address: ______________________________

Phone number: __________ Age: _____ Job: ______________

What does he/she know? ______________________

Q. Hardships Resulting from the Injuries in This Case

1. Please describe how the problems you have had in this case have affected you in your normal activities around the home, in your employment, and in your physical health:

[USE ADDITIONAL PAGES IF NECESSARY]

2. Were you ever confined in bed at home as the result of your medical problems in this case? [ ] YES [ ] NO

   If so, please give the dates and the reason: ____________________

   ____

3. Please describe in detail any pain that you have experienced because of your injuries in this case. Include the frequency and nature of the pain. ____________________________

   ____

4. Are there any other difficulties not previously listed that you have experienced because your injuries? [ ] YES [ ] NO

   If so, please describe in detail.

   [USE ADDITIONAL PAGES IF NECESSARY]

5. Please describe how you are getting along and how you feel now:

   [USE ADDITIONAL PAGES IF NECESSARY]

R. Statements by Doctors

1. Do you know of anything any doctor or physician said that might indicate what happened in your case or whose fault it was?

   [ ] YES [ ] NO

   If so, please indicate the name and address of the person making the statement, the date, the names of all persons present, and exactly what was said:

   [USE ADDITIONAL PAGES IF NECESSARY]

2. What have you been told by the doctor(s) about your current physical condition?

   [USE ADDITIONAL PAGES IF NECESSARY]

(questionnaire continued next page)

(questionnaire continued from previous page)

3. Describe your injuries in detail.

[USE ADDITIONAL PAGES IF NECESSARY]

S. Out-of-Pocket Expenses

Please attach to this questionnaire and summarize in detail all the bills you have received because of your injuries in this case.

1. Physicians and Surgeons:

Name	Address	Amount of Bill	Paid?
(a)			
(b)			
(c)			
(d)			
(e)			

2. Ambulance:

Name	Address	Amount of Bill	Paid?
(a)			
(b)			

3. Hospitals:

Name	Address	Amount of Bill	Paid?
(a)			
(b)			

4. Special Nurses:

Name	Address	Amount of Bill	Paid?
(a)			
(b)			

5. Domestic Help:

Name	Address	Amount of Bill	Paid?
(a)			

(b) ____

(c) ____

(d) ____

6. <u>Drugs, Medications:</u>

Drug	Pharmacy	Amount of Bill	Paid?

(a) ____

(b) ____

(c) ____

(d) ____

7. <u>Crutches, Braces, Traction, or Other Devices:</u>

Type	Name of Store	Amount of Bill	Paid?

____

____

8. <u>X Rays:</u>

Name of Doctor	Address	Amount of Bill	Paid?

(a) ____

(b) ____

(c) ____

9. <u>Wages Lost</u>:

(a) Dates of work missed because of accident: ________________

____

(b) Number of hours missed from work because of accident: ______

(c) Amount per hour lost because of accident: ________________

(d) Total amount of wage loss: ______________________________

(questionnaire continued next page)

(questionnaire continued from previous page)

10. <u>Other Expenses:</u>

	Nature of Expense	Amount of Bill	Paid?
(a)			
(b)			
(c)			
(d)			
(e)			

11. Please summarize your total out-of-pocket expenses:

(a) Physicians and surgeons $ __________
(b) Ambulance $ __________
(c) Hospital $ __________
(d) Domestic help $ __________
(e) Nurses $ __________
(f) Drugs $ __________
(g) Crutches, braces, etc. $ __________
(h) X rays $ __________
(i) Lost wages $ __________
(j) Other $ __________

T. Miscellaneous

1. Who do you think is at fault in this case and why?

[USE ADDITIONAL PAGES IF NECESSARY]

2. Can you think of anything that you have not told us that may have some bearing on your case? If so, please indicate this on the following lines.

[USE ADDITIONAL PAGES IF NECESSARY]

3. In completing this interview outline, have you thought of any information we may not have asked you that may be of some assis-

tance to us in evaluating your medical negligence claim? If so, please indicate this in the following space.

[USE ADDITIONAL PAGES IF NECESSARY]

Dated this ______ day of ____________, 19___.

I have read the statement above, and it is true and correct.

____
Client

A.6 LETTER TO HOSPITAL ASKING FOR MEDICAL RECORDS

ATTENTION: Medical Records Department

We represent the patient whose name appears below. We are advised that this patient was hospitalized in your hospital, and we are in need of the hospital records for our client.

We enclose a waiver giving us authority to obtain these records. We request that we be given <u>complete</u> records, including nurse's notes, laboratory records, and all other records relating to this patient.

We acknowledge our obligation to pay you for these records upon receipt of billing information from you. Thank you for your assistance.

Sincerely,

Paul N. Luvera, Jr.

By ___________________________
Legal Assistant

(letter continued next page)

(letter continued from previous page)

Information Requested

Patient Name: ______________________________

Patient #: ______________________________

Address: ______________________________

____

We request: [ ] All records of every hospitalization at any time.

[ ] Records only for (fill in dates):

REMARKS: ______________________________

____

____

____

A.7 LETTER TO CLIENT'S DOCTOR

Re: Your Patient

Dear Dr. ____________:

We are in the process of evaluating a potential claim involving your patient and need medical information in order to complete our evaluation. I understand you have provided medical care for this patient. I enclose a medical waiver authorizing the release of information.

I would appreciate a letter from you outlining generally the patient's medical history leading to your treatment, your diagnosis, a description of any treatment you gave, and your prognosis. I would also appreciate a copy of your billing for all treatment given to this patient and a copy of any clinic notes regarding this patient.

Please bill me for your time in preparing this information. I have provided a form at the bottom of this page for this purpose.

If you have any questions, please let me know.

Sincerely,

Paul N. Luvera, Jr.

PNL/

Enclosures: Medical waiver and self-addressed return envelope.

• •

RE: ________________________ DATE: ____________

My fee for the enclosed report is the sum of $ __________

____

Physician

A.8 INDEX OF MEDICAL RECORDS

The following is an example of how clinic and hospital records may be summarized and indexed for use in a medical negligence case.

Summary Index to the Medical Records of John Q. Smith

Kaiser (Dr. Martin), 2/13/89–5/15/90		Page
	(Records in italics were supplemented during depositions)	
05/20/88	*Application for Kaiser Membership*	*A–D*
02/13/89	Treatment for asthma flare-up	1
02/14/89	Treatment by Dr. Martin	2
02/14/89	Copy of BCH ER records	3–4
02/17/89	*Phone message from Smith to Martin*	*4.1*
02/17/89	Treatment by Dr. Watson	5
02/22/89	Treatment by Dr. Paul	6
02/22/89	Theophylline level check	7
02/23/89	*Phone message from Smith*	*7.1*
02/23/89	*Seen for IV removal, chest X ray & Rx*	*7.2*
02/23/89	Nurse's note re: IV removal	8
02/23/89	Chest X ray report by Dr. Zimmerman	9
02/28/89	*Phone message from Smith to Paul*	*9.1*
03/04/89	Seen by Paul for asthma attack	10
03/04/89	Copy of BCH ER records	11–12
03/06/89	Seen by Paul for asthma	13
04/14/89	*Phone message from Smith to Paul*	*13.1*
04/21/89	*Prescription refill/Albuterol inhaler*	*13.2*
04/27/89	*Prescription refill/Theo-dur tablets*	*13.3*
05/02/89	Seen by Martin for asthma	14
05/02/89	Theophylline level check	15
05/05/89	*Prescription refill/Beclovent inhaler*	*15.1*
05/11/89	*Patient notified of Theoph level*	*15.2*
05/11/89	*Patient notified of Theoph level*	*15.3*
09/05/89	*Phone message from Smith to Martin*	*15.4*
09/26/89	Seen by Martin for asthma	16

09/26/89	Theophylline level check	17
10/09/89	*Phone message from Smith to Martin*	*17.1*
10/12/89	Seen by Dr. Adams for chest pains	18
10/12/89	EKG	19–20
11/02/89	Treatment for pulled muscle	21
12/04/89	*Phone message from Smith to Martin*	*21.1*
12/20/89	Seen by Martin for asthma	22
12/20/89	Pulmonary function report	22
12/20/89	*Referral for outside medical services*	*22.1*
01/09/90	*Allergy Questionnaire*	*22.2–22.5*
01/09/90	Seen by Maxwell for Martin	23–25
01/09/90	Chest X ray, sinus series, pulmonary function	26–28
01/23/90	Seen by Maxwell	29–30
02/06/90	Allergy testing by Maxwell	31–33
02/07/90	Seen by Maxwell	34
03/14/90	Allergy testing by Maxwell	35–36
03/15/90	*Allergy Patient Kardex*	*36.1*
03/15/90	Follow-up by Martin from Maxwell	37
04/06/90	*Spectacle Rx*	*37.1*
04/25/90	*Prescription refill/Albuterol inhaler*	*37.2*
05/10/90	*Prescription refill/Proventil solution*	*37.3*
05/15/90	Seen by Martin for asthma	38
08/14/90	*Prescription refill/Theo-dur tablets*	*38.1*
10/01/90	*Prescription refill/Prednisone tablets*	*38.2*
11/26/90	*Prescription refill/Theo-dur tablets*	*38.3*
12/26/90	*Phone message from Smith to Paul*	*38.4*

Boulder Health Center (Drs. Greer and Henry)

02/26/80	Cover sheet with Dr. Whitfield's name	39
03/05/80	Allergy evaluation by Whitfield	40–44

(records continued next page)

(records continued from previous page)

Summary Index to the Medical Records of John Q. Smith

Boulder Health Center (Drs. Greer and Henry)		**Page**
02/10/86	Chest X ray	45
02/05/87	Seen by Dr. Harvey for cough, congestion	46
09/24/87	Seen by Dr. Carson for wart check	46
11/21/87	Cholesterol/coronary risk panels	47–48
03/25/88	Seen by Dr. Henry for lower epigastric pain	49
12/05/90	Seen by Dr. Greer for severe asthma	50–51
12/05/90	Spirometry & theophylline level check	52–54
12/13/90	Follow-up by Greer for asthma	55
02/12/91	Seen by Greer for asthma	56
04/11/91	Copy of BCH ER report	57–59
04/12/91	Obituary in newspaper	60
Steven Maxwell, MD (Allergist)		
09/27/90	Pulmonary function report	61
09/27/90	Progress note	62
10/11/90	Progress note	63
11/07/90	Progress note	64
04/11/91	Note	64
	Allergy treatment record (9/90–3/91)	65–66
Boulder Municipal Hospital ER Records		
	Treatment of Asthma, 2/14/89	
	Dictated ER report by ABC	67
	Chest (PA and Lateral)	68
	Treatment of Asthma, 3/4/89	
	Cover sheet	69
	Dictated ER report by DRB (Dr. Bailey)	70
	Handwritten (nurses') progress notes	71–72
	Physicians' orders & progress notes	73
	Chest, PA, and left lateral	74
	Theophylline level check	75
	Consent forms	76–77

Treatment of Cardiopulmonary Arrest, 4/11/91

Cover Sheet & Record of Death	78–79
ER handwritten notes	80
Dictated ER report by Dr. Bailey	81–82
ER flowsheet	83
ABGs	84–85
Portable chest	86
EKGs	87

Best Ambulance Service

Boulder County Patient Report	88
Incident Report	89

Rural Fire Protection District

Medical Report by D. Fletcher	90–91
Incident Report by D. Fletcher	92–93

County Coroner's Office

Report of Death	94–96
Autopsy Report	97–102

A.9 SUMMARY OF GENERAL HOSPITAL RECORDS

The following is a summary of hospital records in a medical negligence case. The hospital records were first numbered so that the summary could provide easy reference to the records. The records are summarized in chronological order and divided within that chronology into such topics as case records, doctors' orders, and tests. This type of summary and organization is useful in most cases, because it gathers all of the relevant information from lengthy hospital records into a chronology that you can then use as a reference during the taking of depositions, in preparing witnesses for trial, and in assisting expert witnesses in reviewing the records. Also, you will usually want to relay relevant information to the jury in chronological order. A chronological outline of voluminous records, in this case over 600 pages, is especially helpful in a case that involves negligence over a period of time, as opposed to one dramatic negligent act. In the records that follow, the patient languished for days before receiving the care he should have received immediately following his brain surgery. The patient was hospitalized for surgery to clip an aneurysm in the brain. Following the surgery, there was a negligent failure to timely diagnose and treat vasospasm that resulted in ischemic brain injury.

MEMORANDUM

TO: Jones File

FROM: Kathe Zaslow

RE: Medical Records Summary

Presbyterian Medical Center

12/14/81

Mr. Jones presented at the emergency room around 11:00 p.m. complaining of severe headache and aching eyes and neck. Pain had begun that morning. He had seen Dr. C in the emergency clinic in the morning and received a prescription for Darvocet. Mr. Jones reported no trauma or exertion prior to the headache. Dr. P's exam at Presbyterian revealed marked distress. Neurological signs were negative; fundi were negative. The neck was markedly stiff. Dr. P performed a lumbar puncture. Opening pressure was 240 mm (normal pressure is 70 to 180 mm H_20). The cerebrospinal fluid was grossly bloody. Mr. Jones's blood pressure was 130/70, later reduced to 100/78. The diagnosis was subarachnoid hemorrhage (SAH).

University of Colorado Health Sciences Center

12/15/81

1. *Case Record*. The case record by Dr. K reports that the lumbar puncture at Presbyterian found the cerebrospinal fluid packed with red blood cells; the white blood count was 333; S = 297; L (lymphocytes) = 36. The patient was alert and oriented with flat, sharp optic discs; neurological signs intact; no sensory deficits. He continued to complain of headache. (68-69)

2. *Doctor's Orders*. Dr. K ordered complete lab tests, including platelet count and blood clotting times, electrolytes, ABGs, EKG, and angiogram. Dr. M ordered urine for electrolytes. On 12/17, by Dr. M's order, complete blood count was done daily, platelets and clotting times every four hours. (535-539)

3. *Tests*.

   (A) *Cerebral CAT Scan*. This showed normal-sized ventricles and high-density collection of blood within the left suprasellar cistern extending into the left silvian fissure "without definite parenchymal [referring to the functioning, as opposed to supporting, tissues of an organ] hemorrhage." There was a question of minimal blood in the fourth ventricle. (257)

(B) *Cerebral Angiogram.* The angiogram was performed at the VA Hospital and reported by Dr. S. It showed a 5-mm aneurysm at the bifurcation of the internal carotid artery into the anterior and middle cerebral arteries on the left. (256) There was "minimal proximal spasm of the middle cerebral but no evidence of distal spasm," ventricular enlargement, or mass effect. There was a question of a second aneurysm, 3 mm in size, at the origin of the right posterior communicating artery. Dr. S noted that following the angiogram Mr. Jones's femoral pulses were normal and "neuro intact." (71)

4. *Medications.* At 0210, Dr. K ordered phenobarbital. The patient had four doses before Dr. M ordered Demerol with Vistaril at 6:00 p.m. At 6:30 p.m. Dr. M ordered Amicar, 1.5 grams per hour intravenously, and he discontinued the orders for phenobarbital (Amicar, aminocaprioc acid, is an antifibrinolytic agent used to prevent rebleeding during the preoperative stabilization period). At 9:22 p.m., Dr. M ordered Decadron 10 mg IV push maintained with 4 mg every four hours. (536–538)

5. *IV Therapy.* Dr. K ordered an IV of D5-¼ normal saline with 20 mEq/L of potassium chloride at 100 cc per hour and "nothing by mouth with sips." (535) Dr. S, who would perform the angiogram, ordered "push fluids" and increased the IV to 125 cc per hour until the angiogram (time of day not noted). (535–537) Following the angiogram, Dr. M ordered the IV decreased to 100 cc per hour. (71, 538) The IV administration is charted in the intensive care therapy record. (414)

<u>12/16/81</u>

1. *Case Record.* Dr. M's entry at 0034 reported that the patient was complaining of diffuse headache. He recorded intake of 1200 cc (900 IV and 250 by mouth) and output of 550 cc. Neuro signs were stable at 25. He recorded lab results, all within normal limits except white blood count elevated to 15.2 [normal is 4.5 to 11.0]. Dr. M ordered Decadron 10 mg and 4 mg every four hours. (71)

   Nurse's entries in the case record noted that the patient constantly asked for cigarettes but was not allowed to smoke until further orders. Later, the patient complained of "terrible" pain. "If I can't have a cigarette, I'll leave." The patient was allowed to smoke every four hours. (72,74)

   Dr. K's entry (following a nurse's at 2300) stated that the patient was "feeling better" and the headache lessened. The patient was apprehensive. Dr. K reported white blood count of 8.1. (74) Surgery was to be performed by Monday, 12/21/81. (75)

2. Intensive Therapy Record and ICU Flow Sheets for 12/16 are missing from the record.

12/17/81

1. *Case Record.* Dr. M recorded white blood count of 16.6, "Will recheck white blood count in a.m. Patient has no fever or signs of infection." (77) The nurse's entry states that the patient was taking fluids well, voiding well. Headache continued but relief could be obtained with medication. "Patient needs frequent reminders of SAH precautions." (75) It was noted that the patient wheezed after smoking. (76)
2. *Doctor's Orders.* Dr. M wrote orders for daily complete blood count, and for PT (Prothrombin time) and PTT (Partial Thromboplastin time) every other day. He ordered phenobarbital and at 10:00 p.m. he ordered the IV rate decreased to a level adequate to maintain an open line. (540)
3. *Medications.* By Dr. M's order, the patient had phenobarbital 30 mg by mouth three times a day, from 12/18 to 12/20. (539, 581) Nurse's notes indicated that the patient was very agitated and anxious. (75,76)
4. *Intensive Therapy Record.* There are no intensive therapy records and no ICU flow sheets for 12/17.

12/18/81

Case Record. The patient complained of intermittent, severe headache and that medication did not help very much. Neuro status continued unchanged. Nurse Chat informed the patient of increased danger from smoking and another nurse noted "Discourage smoking." The patient was worried about the surgery and his hospital bill. He continued to receive Amicar at the rate of 1.5 g per hour. Dr. M recorded that the patient was afebrile with white blood count reduced to 13.6. Surgery was scheduled for Monday, December 21. (78–80)

12/19/81

1. *Case Record.* The white blood count was 12.0. The patient complained of sinus tension and throbbing of the pulse in his head. He continued to be neurologically stable. (81, 82)
2. *Doctor's Orders.* Dr. K ordered complete blood count, PT/PTT, platelet count, BUN, creatinine, glucose, and electrolytes, and he

ordered 10 units whole blood for Monday's surgery. (His order looks as if it might be "6" overwritten as "10".) (87, 540) The lab results, reported on 12/20, were within normal limits. (85)

<u>12/20/81</u>

1. *Case Record.* Neuro and vital signs were stable; the patient was anxious and complained of headache, which was relieved with medication. "H.O. notified of sinus pressure without neuro change." The nursing plan was to continue to monitor closely the neuro status. Nurse Cot noted that the patient "seems anxious—wife staying in hospital the majority of the time." (83, 84)
2. *Doctor's Orders.* Preoperative medication orders were for Demerol 100 mg, Vistaril 50 mg, Robinul 0.2 mg, and continued medication with Decadron. (540)
3. *Preoperative Anesthesia Note.* Dr. D reported "no increased ICP" and he planned general anesthesia. (850)

<u>12/21/81</u>

1. *Case Record.* The last preoperative entry is by C. Cot, R.N., who stated that the patient was extremely anxious. Neuro signs were unchanged and the urinary output was adequate. She gave Valium and pain medication and the patient slept for about five hours. (87) The last neuro sign recorded in the intensive therapy record is 25, at 4:00 a.m. Preanesthetic injections were given at 6:30 a.m., probably by C. Cot. (579)
2. *Operative Records.*

   (A) *Operative Report.* Report lists Dr. Star, responsible staff surgeon; assistants Dr. V and Dr. K; and anesthetists Dr. E and Dr. D. Dr. Star described the surgery as a "left frontotemporal craniotomy with clipping of carotid bifurcation aneurysm." He stated "The brain was moderately tight before we began." He opened the chiasmatic cistern with a bayonet and "as it came forth, we had better brain retraction." He could see clearly the left optic nerve and the left third cranial nerve. The aneurysm projected up and slightly backward at the bifurcation. After the clipping he did not observe "any aneurysmal bleeding or apparently any into it," and no bleed from small vessels behind the aneurysm. "There was a little bit of retractor bleeding on the undersurface of the frontal lobe"; he patched it with Gelfoam and irrigated the area thoroughly. Dr. Star stated that blood loss was less than 250 cc. He used a microscope from the time of reaching the optic nerve until the aneurysm clipping. (633–634)

(B) *Anesthesia Record.* Premedications were administered at 6:30 a.m. (579) According to the Nurses' Procedure Record, anesthesia started at 7:50 a.m. and the operation started at 9:40 a.m. (617) On the Anesthesia Record, Remark #1 indicates that throughout the procedure the anesthetists monitored blood pressure, heart rhythm and rate, temperature, and direct arterial pressure. The surgeons ordered 20 mg of Lasix at about 10:15. The anesthetist notes that he increased ventilation for two periods between 10:30 and 11:00, following which he checked ABGs. He increased ventilation again for a 14-minute period, and during the same period administered Nipride drip. There is no indication that he rechecked ABGs. (There is no remark on the anesthesia record that blood pressure was increased while the clip placement was checked.) Postoperative vital pulse was noted at 76, respirations (illegible), temperature (blank). Following surgery the patient was placed on a warming blanket with ace wraps on both legs. The anesthesiologist administered Regonal 20 mg and Robinul 0.8 mg and suctioned and extubated the patient in the operating room before sending him to the recovery room at 1:40 p.m. (616)

(C) *Fluid Replacement.* According to the Anesthesia Record, estimated blood loss was 400 cc and urinary output was 1030 cc. (616) Replacement was by D5RL, 800 cc; Ringer's Lactate, 900 cc; Albumin 500 cc. Dr. K's postoperative note and the Intensive Care Record of 12/21 give the same amounts. (88, 421)

3. *Postoperative Records.*

(A) *Case Record.* Dr. K's postoperative note says that there were no surgical complications and that the patient went to the recovery room in stable condition. (88)

(B) *Doctor's Orders.* Dr. K wrote postoperative orders at 10:30 p.m. He ordered an IV of D5-¼ normal saline with potassium chloride at 100 cc per hour. He ordered immediate blood and electrolyte tests, with repeat tests at 6:00 p.m. Medications were to be Decadron, 4 mg IV every four hours, and Dilantin 100 mg IV every eight hours. He left orders to call the house officer in case of abnormal heart rate, blood pressure, or temperature. (542)

When the patient did not awaken and his pupils were observed to be unequal and reacting poorly, Dr. E, anesthesiologist, ordered 0.4 mg Narcan (naloxone) at 3:00 p.m. There is apparently a second order for Narcan 0.4 mg at 3:40 p.m. and a third order at 4:00 p.m. for Narcan 0.2 mg. (421) Dr. E signed an order (date and time not recorded) for D5.2 NS with potassium chloride and

4 mg naloxone to run at 25 cc per hour until 7:00 a.m. on 12/22. (543) Dr. E gave orders to transfer the patient to ICU at 4:00 p.m. (421) At 9:30 p.m. Dr. M gave oral orders for a chest X ray to be done the next morning. (543)

(C) *Intensive Care Record.* At 1:45 p.m., the patient's blood pressure ranged from 136/76 to 165/73; pulse 60 to 135. His left pupil was larger than the right, and both reacted very slightly to light. The Intensive Care Record records his temperature once at 2:05 p.m., at 37 degrees Celsius. Following the first dose of Narcan at 3:00 p.m., the nurse noted "much more active after Narcan—deeper respirations. Does not respond to voice commands." (421)

(D) *Tests.*

(1) *CAT Scan.* Dr. K ordered a stat CAT head scan to rule out intracranial hemorrhage and subdural hematoma. Dr. S's report says that this noncontrast study was performed approximately three hours after the patient left the operating room. He compared it to the preoperative CAT scan, and noted some changes: the ventricles were enlarging; there was a "moderate" amount of blood in the right ventricle (on the first study there was only minimal blood in the fourth ventricle). There was a "large area of density" in the region of the ventral hypothalamus, probably representing either parenchymal hemorrhage or blood-soaked Gelfoam. Subarachnoid blood was still visible but had not increased. (260–261)

(2) *Chest X rays.* Dr. K ordered X rays twice, apparently to check placement of the central venous pressure line. (428) Both reports stated "No acute infiltrates seen." (259, 263) "Cerebral hemorrhage" is the diagnosis on Dr. K's 12/22 request for X ray. (263)

4. *Case Record.* Nurse G received the patient from the recovery room at 7:30 p.m. Pupils were unequal and nonreactive and the patient responded only to deep pain. The patient was on a respirator and he was febrile and placed on a cooling blanket. The nurse noted "A-line infiltrated." Neuro score was 11 out of 25. Dr. M made a report of the patient's neurological and vital signs which begins "N.O.S." (not on staff) "CAT of head postoperative without acute changes except normal postoperative." (89, 91)

<u>12/22/81</u>

1. *Case Record.* The patient was febrile and unresponsive to commands. The left pupil was dilated and nonreactive; the right pupil reacted. The patient was restless and seemed somewhat more purposeful in movement than previously. Tracheal suctionings were

bloody. The patient had blood in his urine from pulling on his catheter. Nurses placed him in soft restraints and continued to monitor his neurological signs. (92–93)

Dr. Co saw the patient for pulmonary therapy and recommended treatment for pneumonia. Following his pulmonary notes, he wrote "Addendum—now less responsive, dilated poorly reactive right pupil and increased general extensor tone. Suspect intracerebral hemorrhage—will assume not hypoxic." (95)

2. *Doctor's Orders.* There are no doctor's orders on 12/22 except Dr. M's order for Tylenol. (543)

3. *Tests.*

   (A) *Laboratory.* The blood lab results at 4:00 a.m. show sodium and chloride outside the normal ranges. (365) These are charted in the Intensive Care Therapy Record. There are no further electrolyte reports after 4:00 a.m.; the next laboratory report is for 12/23 at 1:26 a.m. (Dr. K's order was for daily electrolytes.) Apparently the intake-to-input ratio on 12/22 was 2250/2615. (424, 425) The respiratory care lab reported hypoxia. (311, 312)

   (B) *Chest X Rays.* Chest X ray showed infiltrates in the upper lobes, suggestive of aspiration pneumonia. (264)

4. *Intensive Care Flow Sheet.* The nursing record shows the patient was intubated and ventilated. The neuro score was 13. (428)

<u>12/23/81</u>

1. *Case Record.* Nurse K's note reports difficulty in maintaining adequate ventilation. "Patient is agitated most of the time—on Apnea alarm though has not had any apneic periods." (96)

   The nurse's entry at 7:30 a.m. says that at 1:30 a.m. both the left and right pupils were fixed and dilated. (97) At 2:00 a.m., following hyperventilation and administration of Mannitol and Urea, the right pupil was still dilated but now reactive to light. Nurse K's intensive care flow sheet shows that the neuro score remained 13 during the morning of 12/23, and improved to 17 at 1800. (430, 432) The patient was taken for a CAT scan at 3:00 a.m. (97) Pulmonary notes said that the patient continued to be on 60 percent oxygen and Apnea alarm. Breath sounds were clear. (97, 98)

2. *Doctor's Orders.* Dr. K ordered penicillin and daily chest X rays. At 2:00 a.m. he ordered Mannitol followed by Urea and changed the IV order to 3 percent sodium chloride at 50 cc per hour. (544) He ordered a stat CAT scan which was completed at approximately 3:45 a.m. At 4:00 a.m. he ordered Decadron increased to 8 mg every six hours, and at 4:30 he ordered type and cross for two

units of whole blood. (Unable to locate corresponding lab slip or a record of transfusion.) At 7:30 a.m. Dr. K ordered 20 mg Lasix IV and "replace urine output cc/cc with 3 percent sodium chloride—not to exceed 100 cc per hour." (546)

3. *Case Record.* At 7:00 p.m. Nurse W reported that following Lasix at 6:00 p.m. the patient diuresed 1150 cc, his left pupil reacted sluggishly to light, he showed simple withdrawal from pain, some purposeful movement, his neuro score was 17, and he became more agitated with increased posturing. She questioned seizure activity; her assessment was "fluid overloaded for postoperative neuro patient." She gave phenobarbital to control agitation. (99) The patient had 20 mg Lasix again at midnight. (432)

4. *Doctor's Orders.* On the evening of 12/23, Dr. M wrote an order to discontinue 3 percent normal saline solution and replace it with D5-½ normal saline with potassium chloride at 75 cc per hour. (547) By 7:00 p.m. on 12/23, blood electrolytes had returned to the normal range, with glucose and chloride elevated. (367) The intake:output ratio on 12/23 was 1825/3965. (431)

5. *Tests.*

   (A) *CAT Scan.* Dr. K ordered a CAT scan of the head at 2:00 a.m. on 12/23, and it was performed at 3:00 a.m. (430) On 12/30 Dr. S dictated his reports of both the 12/21 and the 12/23 studies. The 12/23 CAT scan was without contrast. The ventricles had further enlarged. Slight herniation, present on 12/21, was still apparent. There was probable "infarction in the bilateral lenticulostriate distribution." "There is more clotted blood along the left silvian fissure. . . . and probably represents parenchymal hemorrhage. . . . This is an extension of the blood previously noted to be in the ventral hypothalamus." In summary, Dr. S stated that the two postoperative films showed progressive and at least moderate obstructive hydrocephalus, apparent hypothalamic hematoma, enlarged on the second study, bilateral infarction, and diffuse cerebral edema. (260–262)

   (B) *Chest X Ray.* Following the CAT scan the patient had a chest X ray at 9:46 a.m. Dr. K's radiology order gives the diagnosis of "cerebral hemorrhage." The X ray showed persistent infiltrates, right subcutaneous air, and possibly air in the mediastinum. (265)

12/24/81

Case Record. Urinary output continued to fluctuate and "H.O. aware of urinary output," according to the nurse's note at 5:00

a.m. (101) The patient had one more IV of 20 mg Lasix at noon. (435) Dr. M noted that the hyponatremia had been corrected by Lasix and 3 percent saline. Patient remained unconscious, exhibiting "decorticate posture bilaterally" according to Dr. M. (100) Dr. M reported that the patient was unresponsive to verbal stimuli. Following his notes are Nurse W's at 1900, stating that the patient made delayed response to commands. (100–105) Neuro status for 12/24 was 17. (436) The patient remained febrile. (101)

Dr. Mar reported that chest X rays showed subcutaneous emphysema (pathological accumulation of air in tissue) in the right supraclavicular region, possibly caused by the central venous pressure catheter or by traumatic intubation. The upper lobes continued to show infiltrates, and Dr. Mar expected further difficulties and continued need for ventilation. (102)

12/25/81

Case Record. The patient was febrile. Pulmonary physician suggested that the fever and the "paradoxic breathing pattern" might be a central nervous system process; he thought that a lumbar puncture was indicated. Dr. M reported lab results. The white blood count was 13.6. (108–109) Dr. M's diagnosis on his request for a chest X ray was "cerebral hematoma." (268) Nurses checked the neurological status every two hours and during most of 12/25 the score was 16-17. (439)

12/26/81

Case Record. Dr. Moon noted at 8:00 p.m. that "ventilation required to reduce FIO_2 (fraction of inspired oxygen) by adding PEEP (positive end expiratory pressure). Clearly needs bronchodilation. . . ." He recommended aggressive respiratory therapy, Bronchosal, and Aminophylline drip. (116) The patient had frequent PVCs (preventricular contractions), and his neuro score deteriorated from 15 to 12. (442)

12/27/81

Case Record. Further observations seemed to rule out pulmonary complications as the source of fever. Dr. Mar questioned meningitis. An infectious disease consult noted stiff neck, white blood count equal to 14.5, and continuing problems with hypoxia.

Dr. M performed a lumbar puncture and reported the results. He noted that the cerebrospinal fluid was xanthochromic (indication, earlier SAH). The nurse's report describes the fluid as "essentially clear." (118–120) The patient remained febrile. (123) The cerebrospinal fluid lab report showed normal protein and cytology. Culture results after two days were negative; the sample taken on 1/18 was cultured with negative results. (327, 358). Dr. Mar still could not determine the cause of hypoxic incidents. White blood count was 18. Dr. K noted that he could not use anticoagulants in treatment of the lung problems because there was a possibility of intracerebral hemorrhage; however, he did start mini-Heparin. (125–127) The patient's neurological score was 12.

<u>12/28/81</u>

Case Record. A nurse reported "patient seems to be going downhill. Neuro score 10. Responds to only deep pain—left pupil still dilated and nonreactive—urinary output good—patient very stiff." She noted that his wife seemed very depressed. The nurse suggested in her note that "doctors talk with patient's wife especially after angiogram to try and let her know just how he really is." (129)

On 12/28, patient's wife consented to an angiogram, having been advised that the benefits might be "diagnosis of reason for slow recovery." For patient not to undergo the procedure would mean "not know diagnosis; continued or worsened condition." (618)

<u>12/29/81</u>

1. *Case Record.* An extensive note (by the radiologist?) appears in the case record following angiogram. The angiogram demonstrated incomplete clipping of the aneurysm, no vessel occlusion, although the lenticulostriate was not well seen, and severe spasm of the distal internal carotid, proximal anterior carotid, and middle carotid. (131)

   The angiogram report in the medical records was dictated by Dr. S on 11/3/83. The hospital cannot find the original dictation. According to Dr. S's interpretation, the vessels in spasm are patent. Circulation is slowed and perhaps there are secondary intravascular changes. There is no obvious collateral flow in the area of the middle cerebral artery.

   A nurse's entry reported that the patient did not follow commands; he was having cardiac arrhythmias; he was febrile. (133) The patient's neuro score ranged from 14 to 11. (449)

2. *Doctor's Orders.* There were no new orders following angiogram.

<u>12/30/81</u>

Case Record. Dr. K wrote an extensive Neurosurgical Progress Note. The patient was comatose, with "probable cerebral ischemia secondary to vasospasm." (135) He made another extensive note at 9:30 p.m. Neuro scores were 13 (later overwritten with 12) and 11. (447)

12/31/81

Case Record. Neuro scores were 13 to 17. (451) A nurse made a note to check on the possibility of weaning from the ventilator. Dr. Mar planned no extubation. He queried whether nitroprusside would be of value in treating the vasospasm. (143)

K's entry reported that the patient was still comatose and febrile, and he ordered physical therapy. (145)

A nurse noted later that the neuro status was improving. The right pupil showed good response to light; the left remained fixed and dilated. The patient responded to his name and occasionally to commands. The patient was started on nasogastric tube feeding. (147, 555) Dr. K gave an order to decrease the IV rate to 50 cc per hour. (556)

1/1/82

Case Record. The patient had an elevated temperature of unknown cause. Nurse D reported that he was "neurologically improved especially when family present." Dr. K noted, "Remains comatose" and "unchanged neurologically." The patient remained febrile with white blood count of 10.2. (150) Nurse Coy's note followed K's: "Difficult to assess if patient follows commands; does squeeze hand when instructed and when not instructed." (148–151) Neuro scores were 16.5 to 17.5. (454) Dr. K ordered Decadron decreased to 3 mg IV every six hours. (556)

1/3/82

1. *Case Record.* The patient's neuro score was 14. His temperature was elevated and the white blood count was 16.7. Dr. K's note discusses the results of the 12/29 angiogram: "Angiogram showed marked left cerebral vasospasm—probably present since operation (13 days). Dr. Kin feels that hypervolemic/hypertensive treatment is not helpful unless instituted immediately (i.e., intra or immediately postoperative) and that vasospasm should resolve within the next week (usually two to three weeks for resolution). The patient has probably suffered ischemic brain damage, however, most of which will probably be irreversible." (159) Dr. K planned to discuss tracheostomy with the attending doctor. (157–160)
2. *Doctor's Orders.* Dr. K ordered Lasix, IV of sodium chloride with potassium chloride, input/output monitoring, and electrolyte testing. (558)

1/4/82

Case Record. Dr. G made a neurological exam. "Neuro status has apparently not changed significantly in past two weeks. Patient continues to be a problem with pulmonary toilet. ENT recommends tracheostomy as does pulmonary. Will discuss with Dr. Kin and schedule for tracheostomy ASAP." (164)

1/5/82

Tests.

CAT head scan. Dr. S interpreted the film. Hydrocephalus had progressed from Grade 2.5 of 4 to 3 of 4; it was almost certainly obstructive. "There remains low density [blood?] related to the surgery." Bilateral lenticulostriate infarction was evident, and possibly additional infarction in the left frontal and parietal areas. Hemorrhage in the hypothalamus had resolved. (282)

1/6/82

Case Record. Dr. C noted that "further SAB is a definite possibility." (173) He did not make reference to the CAT scan of 1/5. The neurosurgery progress note planned a tracheostomy for 1/8. (176)

1/7/82

Case Record. Infectious Disease still had no explanation for the fever. They questioned sinus and drug fever. (176) The patient's neuro score remained at 16 to 18. Dr. Z's neurosurgery note commented that the CAT had shown dilated ventricles "slowly improving." "Tracheostomy and possible ventriculoperitoneal ventishunt on Monday."(179)

1/8/82 to 1/10/82

Case Record. Ensuing entries continued to refer to the planned ventriculoperitoneal (V/P) shunt. (183, 185–87). On 1/7, Dr. Z and patient's wife signed a consent for tracheostomy and possible shunt to be performed by Drs. Kin and Z. (619) Another consent form for the same procedure was begun but not completed, and is undated. (610) A third consent, dated 1/10, authorizes Dr. Star to perform the surgery, described as "V/P shunt, possible tracheostomy." (620)

1/11/82

Operative Report. Drs. Star and H performed a tracheostomy. Dr. Star's report and his discharge summary do not mention consideration of the shunt procedure. Dr. Star's indications for the surgery were that following SAH "the patient had a very clean operation, but postoperatively he developed arterial spasm and needed prolonged intubation." (635, 641) Dr. H's postoperative note stated that the shunt procedure was planned for next week if the patient's fever could be eradicated. (193)

<u>1/13/82</u>

Case Record. Dr. Z wrote a preoperative note planning a V/P shunt "as long as patient remains afebrile." (197)

<u>1/14/82</u>

Case Record. Nurse Arm reported that "family concerned about news that 'parts of brain are dead'—feel they receive mixed messages." (198) Dr. H entered a note that Dr. Star had postponed the shunt. "Family advised." (22) The neuro score was 13 to 14. (481)

<u>1/18/82</u>

1. *Operative Report.* Dr. Star, assisted by Dr. Z, performed a ventriculoperitoneal shunt. Dr. Star stated that the procedure was indicated because patient "has had some progressive hydrocephalus and we thought that the patient would wake up better with ventriculoperitoneal shunt." Dr. Star found "about 5 cm of CSF" which was under pressure and squirted out. He removed 5 cc of fluid "for cells and culture and protein and sugar." (636) The single CSF lab report for 1/21/82 describes the fluid as clear with culture negative at two days; it does not report on protein and cytology. (358) Dr. Star tunnelled tubing from the ventricles to an abdominal incision into the peritoneum. He observed that "fluid flowed readily through the shunt" before closing the head and abdominal incisions. (636)
2. *Case Record.* The patient was afebrile; white blood count was 9.2. (206) Postoperative notes by a doctor and Nurse D reported no change in neuro status, patient stable, afebrile. "Patient is arousable but does not follow commands." Neuro score was 19 to 20. At 11:00 p.m. the patient had a grand mal seizure of approximately one-and-a-half minutes' duration. "Left pupil dilated but reacting slowly (even after seizure)." The nurse questioned if the shunt was working properly. (208–209)

<u>1/19/82 to 1/20/82</u>

Case Record. The patient was on phenobarbital. He had no further seizure activity. Temperature was slightly elevated. (210–212)

1/21/82

Case Record. Dr. G's neurosurgery note reported "No apparent improvement after shunt placement. Awaiting CAT scan to rule out subdural or any complicated factors in recovery." (216)

1/22/82

Tests. Dr. G requested the CAT to rule out subdural hematoma or residual hydrocephalus. Dr. S dictated his report on 3/1/82; "This is read after the fact and in fact after the CAT of 2/22/82. This will, therefore, be a summary." There was "diffuse right frontoparietal subdural effusion" that was 4 mm thick on 1/22 and 11 mm thick on 2/22. "This right-sided lesion is slightly indenting the brain and is probably under tension." (295)

1/25/83

Doctor's Orders. Dr. H noted no change after the V/P. He reduced Dilantin and phenobarbital to rule out stupor secondary to oversedation. (226)

1/27/82

Case Record. Dr. H's note reported "No response to commands. Plan feeding gastrostomy." (231) A speech-language note says that the patient followed short commands consistently for about ten minutes. (231–232)

1/29/82

Case Record. Dr. H performed the gastrostomy tube placement. (638, 639)

2/11/82

Case Record. Patient was discharged to Garden Manor Nursing Home. Drs. Star and G wrote the Discharge Summary, dictated and transcribed on 2/9/82. (640–642)

The Discharge Summary states that surgery took place "without any initial complications. However, when the patient was returned to the 5 North ICU he was found to have a dilation of the left pupil with no response." The postoperative CAT "showed no acute changes except no evidence of blood clot." The Summary states that from the fourth to the fourteenth postoperative day the patient was treated with antibiotics. Over the ten-day period pneumonia resolved and "The patient became afebrile." (641) (Dr. Star's summary does not report on fever of 38 to 38.5 Celsius for 1/8 through 1/11 as noted in the Case Record (189–191), and does not say that fever was the reason for postponing the shunt procedure.)

The Discharge Summary notes that on 12/29 the patient had "repeat cerebral angiography which was reported to show the surgical clip in the correct area although there was evidence of a residual aneurysm beneath it." (641)

"As his neurologic status remained unchanged over the preceding two weeks and repeat computerized tomography of the head showed no focal lesions to account for his mental status," the doctors performed a tracheostomy on 1/11/82; and "on 1/18/82 a ventriculoperitoneal shunt was placed with the thought that postoperative hydrocephalus may account for his decreased mental status." (641)

A.10 SUMMARY OF ICU RECORDS AND FLUID THERAPY

The following is a detailed summary of the ICU records and fluid therapy from the same case and hospital records described in Appendix A.9. However, this appendix is more detailed because the information on fluid intake and output was critical in establishing the delayed diagnosis and treatment of the vasospasm. The treatment being rendered would only aggravate the vasospasm because proper treatment required substantially increasing fluid intake, which was not done. The detailed records of fluid intake and output were therefore important for expert witness review and for use in cross-examining the defendant's witnesses.

In the following summary, the calculations in the left-hand column show the net fluids based on intake and output. There is also reference to a missing therapy record and to the doctor's orders relevant to intake and output. The vital signs and changes in the patient's condition based on intake and output are also summarized.

MEMORANDUM

TO: Jones File

FROM: Kathe Zaslow

RE: Summary of Intensive Care Unit Records and Fluid Therapy

<u>12/15/81</u>

Intake	3380	Dr. K ordered an IV of D5-¼ normal saline with 20 mEq/L of potassium chloride at 100 cc/hr and "nothing by mouth with sips." Dr. S, radiologist, ordered "push fluids" and increased the IV to 125 cc/hr until the time of angiogram. (535–537) Following angiography, Dr. M ordered IV rate decreased to 100 cc/hr. (71, 538)
Output	1100	
	+2280	

(Drs. P and Kin make one reference that suggests that it is important to prevent dehydration and hypovolemia before angiogram. (Neurosurgery 3(3) 1978, p. 367).)

The urinary output total of 550 cc (3/10) does not match with the record, which indicates 600 cc + 600 cc + 550 cc. The output total (10–6) shows HNV (has not voided), but the chart shows 850 cc. Specific gravity was 1.020 (normal is 1.0–1.03). (414)

12/16/81

Intensive Therapy Record Missing

Blood electrolytes were within normal limits, with sodium and chloride in the upper range. (415) Urine electrolytes were: sodium, 39; chloride, 72; therapy potassium, 30.6. (364)

12/17/81

Intake 3629
Output 2350
+1279

By Dr. M's report. "Intake 3629 p.o." (77) (This appears to be a 24-hour total. His note says 3629 by mouth, but the patient was on an IV at 100 cc/hr until 2000, when the rate was lowered to keep a line open. Amicar was being administered continuously.) The nurse's entry states that the patient was taking fluids well and voiding well. (75)

12/18/81

Intake 4049
Output 2925
+1124

The patient was getting an IV of D5-¼ normal Output saline with 20 mEq/L potassium. Amicar was infusing at 37 cc/hr, about 300 cc over an eight-hour period. (418)

12/19/81

Intake 5412
Output 4825
+ 587

The patient's oral intake was 4490 cc. He had D5–¼ NS with potassium chloride to keep a line open, and Amicar at 1.5 gm/hr. Blood pressure was stable. Specific gravity was 1.005. (419)

12/21/81

Intake 5644
Output 4600
+1044

The patient was receiving Amicar drip of about 300 cc over each eight-hour shift. The 24-hour oral intake was 4620 cc. (422)

In the operating room for the 5.5-hour period 0750–1300:

Intake	D5RL	800 cc	(7:45–11:15)
	RL	900 cc	(7:45–11:30)
	Albumin	500 cc	(11:30–)
Intake Total		2200 cc	
Output	EBL		400 cc
	Urinary Output		1030 cc
Output Total			1430 cc

The difference between intake and output was +770 cc.

Intake	1212
Output	2650
	– 1438

The 16-hour period, 1400 on 12/21 to 0600 on 12/22. The intensive therapy record for 2:00 to 10:00 p.m. on 12/21 shows administration of 1112 cc crystalloid. This appears to be the total of 150 cc for delivery of Dilantin, another 300 cc NS for Dilantin, 500 cc D5.2 with 20 mEq/L potassium, and 162 cc and for delivery of a drug. (To be consistent with doctor's orders, the drug should be Narcan, but the record appears to read "Amicar." (424) Dr. K's postoperative order (542) was for Dextrose and normal saline with potassium chloride, and the Medication Record (582) reflects the same order, but the Intensive Care Record (421) indicates that potassium, rather than potassium chloride, was administered.)

Dr. K's postoperative order was for IV at 100 cc/hr "total IV fluids," plus Decadron, Dilantin, and Cimetadine by IV at intervals. (542) The Medication Record indicates that Decadron and Dilantin were given by "IV push," Cimentadine by IV piggyback. (583)

According to entries in the Recovery Room Record, Narcan was given three times intravenously. How much, if any, additional IV fluid was given for Narcan delivery? A fourth Narcan order was for 4 mg in crystalloid at 25 cc/hr. Fourteen hours of this IV at

25 cc/hr would total 350 cc, close to the total of 362 cc shown in the record. (424)

The total intake of 1912 cc over the 16-hour period is consistent with 350 cc for delivery of Narcan (?), 1400 cc of D5.2 with potassium, and 200 cc for Dilantin delivery.

Blood pressure readings during this time appear to be adequate to high, 130s-160s/50s–80s, pulse rapid, especially after Narcan. Venous pressure was recorded once, at 2:00 p.m. on 2/21, as 8. (421) An A-line reading is recorded once, at 1630 on 12/21, as 136/90. (424)

The patient was febrile (39.3–38.3) and was treated with alcohol bath and Tylenol. (424)

12/22/81

Intake	2250
Output	2615
	– 365

The patient was being suctioned, and he was febrile. Nurse K (430) says that the patient was suctioned for large amounts of bloody fluid, and the Case Record reports suctioning for thick, bloody secretions. (92) (The Intake/Output Records do not include suction fluids in the output totals.) The patient's IVs were normal saline for Dilantin and D5.2 with potassium. Blood pressure was 140–150/70–80, pulse 70s–90s. (427)

Blood electrolytes as charted on 12/22 at 4:00 a.m. show sodium and chloride below normal. Specific gravity was 1.022 (WNL). (424) It appears that the laboratory did not report blood electrolytes again until 1:26 a.m. on 12/23; sodium was 123 (normal 134–141) and chloride 87 (normal 95–106). (364) However, these same results appear charted at 2445. (427) Specific gravity was 1.028 (WNL) at 1:00 a.m. on 12/23. (310) Pulse was 110. (427)

12/23/81

Intake	1825
Output	3965
	–2140

The patient was intubated at 0030, and he continued to be suctioned for "copious" secretions. (96) Pulse and temperature were elevated. (429) Between 1:30 and 2:00 a.m.,

Dr. K called for a CAT scan. (427, 544) Nurse K, in the Case Record, gives this sequence of events: The patient was intubated at 2400; until 0230 the left pupil was fixed and dilated; at 0130 the right pupil was also fixed and dilated. With hyperventilation, Manitol and Urea, the right pupil was still dilated but reactive to light at 0200. The patient went to CAT scan at 0300. (97) Nurse B noted that on return from CAT scan the patient was suctioned for "thick" secretions. (96) With his order for Manitol and Urea, Dr. K changed the IV order to 3 percent sodium chloride at 50 cc/hr. Nurse K took Dr. K's oral orders at 0430 for type and cross of two units whole blood. At 7:30 a.m. on 12/23 Nurse K took Dr. K's verbal orders for Lasix and replacement of urine output 4 cc with 3 percent sodium chloride, not to exceed 100 cc/hr. (544–546)

The patient continued to receive Lasix during the day of 12/23. At 7:00 p.m., Nurse W reported that, following Lasix at 6:00 p.m., the patient diuresed at 1150 cc and his left pupil reacted sluggishly to light. His neuro score improved from 13 to 17 between 1500 and 1800. Nurse W reported "vigorous pulmonary care given for last 12 hours, suctioning every hour for initially large amounts thick tan blood-streaked sputum—most recently thinner, lighter tan—smaller amounts; breath sounds clear after suctioning." She assessed the patient as "fluid overloaded." (99)

12/24/81

Intake	1975
Output	2027
	– 52

The neuro signs remained constant at 17. Eight-hour intake/output totals were: 825/1195; 700/414; 50/415. (435) Nurse B wrote in the Case Record that the patient was "suctioned every one to two hours for large amounts of thick, old blood-tinged mucus sputum. Large amounts of secretions suctioned from above ET cuff through mouth, also blood-tinged." (102) The patient had 20 mg Lasix at noon. (436)

A.11 SUMMARY OF PULMONARY CARE RECORDS

The following is a detailed summary of the pulmonary care extracted from the entirety of the voluminous hospital records that are summarized in Appendix A.9. Since pulmonary monitoring and care are not customarily kept as separate records but are found intermittently throughout the entire hospital record, it is important to separately summarize the pulmonary care chronologically when the pulmonary condition is relevant to the issues in the case. In this case, to focus on changes in the patient's respiratory status it was important to summarize from all record entries the references to the patient's pulmonary monitoring. The changes in respiratory status further reflected that the wrong treatment was being rendered following surgery and should have alerted the doctors to the necessity of making a correct diagnosis and changing the treatment protocol. Accordingly, reviewing the entirety of the records for all references to the patient's pulmonary monitoring, with easy reference to hospital page numbers, permitted the plaintiff's expert witnesses to focus on the changes in respiratory status. It also provided a summary that could then be used to cross-examine the defendant-doctor and the defendant's expert witnesses.

MEMORANDUM

TO: Jones file

FROM: Kathe Zaslow

RE: Medical Records Outline of Pulmonary Care

1. *Preoperative Records.*
   Preoperative ABGs showed "metabolic alkalosis" on 12/17 (303) and "metabolic alkalemia" on 12/21. (306)

   Two preoperative chest X rays were normal. (255,258)

   The patient was anxious and wanted to smoke. (72) He was allowed to smoke every four hours. (74) A nurse noted that his breath sounds were clear, with occasional wheezing after smoking. (72–76)

2. *Surgery (Anesthesia Record), 12/21/81.*
   The anesthetist increased ventilation for two periods between 10:30 and 11:00, following which he checked ABGs. He increased venti-

lation again for a 14-minute period and, during the same period, administered Nipride drip (hypotensive). There is no indication that he rechecked ABGs. At the conclusion of surgery, the anesthetist administered Regonal 20 mg and Robinul 0.8 mg, and suctioned and extubated the patient in the operating room before sending him to the recovery room. (616) (Regonal is given to reverse the action of muscle relaxant drugs. Robinul is used to diminish tracheal and bronchial secretions.) The anesthetist recorded postoperative vital signs: blood pressure 120, pulse 76, respirations 28 (?). (616)

3. *Postoperative Records.*

   Recovery Room. Patient arrived in the recovery room at 1:45 p.m. There is no note of any complications until 2:25 p.m., when the nurse noted "left pupil greater than right. Both react very sluggishly to light." At 3:00, Dr. E, anesthesiologist, ordered 0.4 mg Narcan (naloxone). (Narcan is used to reverse the effects of anesthesia.) There is apparently a second order for Narcan 0.4 mg at 3:40 p.m. and a third order at 4:00 p.m. for Narcan 0.2 mg. Following the first administration of Narcan, a nurse noted "much more active after Narcan, deeper respirations. Does not respond to voice commands." Dr. E signed an order (date and time not recorded) for D5.2NS with potassium chloride and 4 mg naloxone to run at 25 cc per hour until 7:00 a.m. on 12/22. (543) Dr. E gave orders to transfer the patient to ICU at 4:00 p.m. (421)

4. *Recovery Room ABGs.* ABGs ordered by Dr. K in the Recovery Room were reported normal. The report indicates that the patient was on 4 liters of oxygen and breathing spontaneously at 20 respirations per minute. Temperature was 37 degrees Celsius. The interpretation of ABGs at 1500 on 12/21 was "metabolic alkalosis and hyperoxia with supplemental oxygen therapy." (307–308) A nurse noted in charting ABGs that the patient was on 4 liters of oxygen. (421)

<u>12/21/81</u>

At 1730, the ABGs indicated "normal pH with compensated metabolic alkalosis and severe hypoxia (for age) with supplemental oxygen therapy." (307) At 1930, Nurse G (?) noted "ABGs adequate on 4 liters" (89) At 9:30 p.m., Dr. M gave oral orders for a chest X ray to be done the next morning. (543) At 2000 hours, a nurse noted "oral airway in." (425)

<u>12/22/81</u>

ABGs at 1:30 a.m. showed severe hypoxia. (311) (Our nurse expert said that the ABGs reported at 4:30 a.m. showed improvement at acceptable oxygenation. (312) She thought this was probably a result of orders for oxygen therapy, but she could not locate the orders.) At 6:00 a.m. a nurse noted that the patient was on 4 liters of oxygen and "mist mask on." (92) The patient was being suctioned every one to two hours for thick, brown-yellow secretions. (92, 93) At 2000 Nurse K noted coarse bronchi bilaterally throughout. "Nasal airway removed. Oral airway inserted. Suctioned nasotracheal for large amounts of bloody secretions. Orally suctioned large amounts bloody white." Further notes at 2330 indicate that the patient was continuing to be suctioned for bloody secretions and had loud bronchi bilaterally. (428) ABGs sent at 2330 showed severe hypoxia. (312) At 2400, the patient was intubated and ventilated. (428)

Dr. Co (pulmonary) examined the patient that night. (There does not appear to be a written doctor's order for consultation.) Dr. Co noted that the chest X rays showed right upper lobe and left upper lobe infiltrates, and his impression was aspiration pneumonia. He noted results of gram stain for nasotracheal and endotracheal suctionings. Dr. Co suggested "intubate to control secretions and, if necessary, ventilation." He recommended penicillin and repeat cultures. Dr. Mar apparently reviewed Dr. Co's entry in the Case Record. (94–95)

Chest X Rays. Initial X ray showed no infiltrates. X ray at 11:46 p.m. on 12/22 showed the development of bilateral infiltrates in the upper lobe.

<u>12/23/81</u>

Dr. K ordered 60 percent oxygen and T-piece at 2:00 a.m. At 11:30 a.m., Dr. K ordered Gentamicin (antibiotic). (545–546)

Chest X Rays. X ray in the morning showed persistent infiltrates. "Subcutaneous emphysema is now identified, more prominent in the right cervical soft tissues. A pneumomediastinum is suspected, but cannot be confirmed." (259, 263–265)

The Respiratory Nurse noted at 6:30 a.m. "will ventilate if necessary to hyperventilate, but will need sedation (e.g., Pavulon) to control patient on ventilator." (96). (Pavulon is a muscle relaxant used in conjunction with mechanical ventilation.) Nurse K noted that the patient was restless and agitated, and that he had been medicated with Pavulon. Following CAT scan, he was placed back on a T-piece at 60 percent oxygen, by Dr. K's order. (545) The respiratory therapist noted that the patient was on the apnea alarm, but had not had any apneic episodes. (98)

Nurse W observed at 1900 that the patient had received vigorous pulmonary care over the last 12 hours, with hourly suctioning. Breath sounds were clear after suctioning.

<u>12/24/81</u>

The patient continued on the T-piece with 60 percent oxygen through the day, when the second entry by pulmonary physicians appears in the Case Record. (102) Dr. Mar and apparently another doctor signed the entry stating that the lungs were clear. "Review of X rays shows subcutaneous air in the right supraclavicular region—? CVP? Traumatic intubation??" Lung infiltrates had increased. "Expect ABGs to deteriorate and need for ventilation." Later that day, Dr. M recorded the impression "probable aspiration pneumonia vs. chemical pneumonitis." (104)

<u>12/25/81</u>

ABGs at 9:00 a.m. showed mild hypoxia. (320) Dr. Mar noted that the patient was febrile and thought fever might be due to abscess around the larynx secondary to traumatic intubation, or to central nervous system infection. He suggested a lumbar puncture. He observed that the patient exhibited a "paradoxic breathing pattern." He doubted the cause was diaphragmatic fatigue and suggested that it was a central nervous system process. At 1915 Dr. Co ordered the oxygen through the T-piece reduced to 50 percent. (548)

Chest X Rays. X rays of 12/25 and 12/26 continued to show subcutaneous emphysema, with no mention of pneumomediastinum.

<u>12/26/81</u>

At 0045 ABGs showed moderate hypoxia. Dr. Mar and Dr. Co (?) noted that the lungs were clear and that X rays showed clearing of infiltrates. (111)

At 1515 ABGs showed severe hypoxia. (323) A nurse's entry at 1800 said that the patient was experiencing preventricular contractions. She noted that there was no change in blood pressure, heart rate, respiratory rate, or color during the hypoxic episode. She questioned pulmonary embolus and ARDS (acute respiratory distress). The patient's white blood count and temperature were elevated. Dr. M's working diagnosis was ARDS. Lung scan had shown low probability of pulmonary embolus. Dr. M planned to treat the patient with a change of antibiotics and PEEP. (112–114) Dr. Moon's impression was early ARDS. He recommended PEEP, aminophylline drip for bronchodilation, and full cultures. (116)

12/27/81

The patient was treated with 5 cm PEEP and FIO_2, 50 percent. ABGs showed moderate hypoxia. (324) The patient had a repeat lung scan, which was negative for pulmonary embolus. The cause of the hypoxic episode the previous day remained unexplained. Dr. Mar questioned meningitis as the cause of the patient's continuing fever. (118)

An infectious disease specialist saw the patient and noted that blood and urine cultures to date had been negative. Sputum gram stain showed heavy polymorphonuclear cells with heavy gram rods and some diptheroids. This doctor felt that CSF culture might suggest the source of infection. (Culture of the CSF was later returned negative.) The next infectious disease entry into the Case Record is on 12/30. (137)

Dr. M noted that the patient had almost returned to baseline ABGs, that the picture looked less like sepsis and ARDS, and more like atelectasis of the left lung base, as a cause of the hypoxic incident. (122, 123) Dr. Co discontinued PEEP. (549)

Chest X Rays. X rays of 12/27 and 12/28 refer to mediastinal emphysema and mediastinal air. (271-272)

12/28/81

Dr. Mar initialed an entry into the Case Record that noted that the patient was off PEEP. "Will add Bronkosol." Dr. Mar noted that even though the lung scan showed a low probability of pulmonary embolus, it was still a likely cause of the patient's hypoxemia. (125)

12/29/81

An ENT specialist recommended a CAT evaluation of the patient's neck. (132) Dr. K reported the assessment, "probable peripharyngeal abscess secondary to trauma during intubation last week." (135) Neck CAT scan showed the presence of a large soft-tissue mass that was deviating the endotracheal tube and the trachea to the right. This scan did not reveal any abnormal fluid collections or drainable abscess. There were small collections of air within the subcutaneous tissues consistent with subcutaneous emphysema. (274) The fever, increased white blood count, and retropharyngeal abscess appeared to be resolving, and no surgical treatment was planned. (136)

Chest X Rays. The X ray report of 12/29 notes "resolving pneumomediastinum." (273)

12/30/81

The infectious disease specialist did not refer to CSF culture results, but recommended a new antibiotic to treat retropharyngeal abscess caused by anaerobic bacteria. "Would follow chest X rays closely—mediastinitis is not an infrequent complication with these infections." (137)

After 12/29/81

The patient continued to have elevated temperature and white blood count. He remained intubated with T-piece, and on 1/3, Dr. C recommended tracheostomy. (160) Tracheostomy was eventually performed on 1/11/82, by Drs. Star and H. (635, 641)

On 1/7/82, a doctor on infectious disease service suggested that drug fever or "erosion of the nasogastric tube into the ethmoid sinus" might be causing the fever. (176) But apparently doctors never made definitive diagnoses of the patient's pulmonary problems.

APPENDIX B

DISCOVERY IN A MEDICAL NEGLIGENCE CASE

B.1 INTERROGATORIES TO INDIVIDUAL DOCTORS

The following interrogatories were drafted in *Smith v. Denver Medical Center,* an obstetrical case involving medical and hospital negligence arising out of the birth of an asphyxiated, brain-damaged baby. The interrogatories demonstrate how medical and hospital records can be clarified in advance of depositions. Further, the doctors' reasons for rendering specific care and treatment can be obtained. The doctors are also asked for their opinions about the care and treatment rendered and the cause of the infant's brain damage.

PLAINTIFF'S FIRST SET OF WRITTEN INTERROGATORIES TO DEFENDANTS

DR. A, DR. D, DR. M, DR. W, DR. WAL

Each of the defendants, Dr. A, Dr. D, Dr. M, Dr. W, and Dr. Wal, is requested individually to answer each of the following interrogatories and individually to file a set of answers to them.

These interrogatories are ongoing and the answers to them should be supplemented if additional information becomes available to the defendants.

[Curriculum Vitae]

1. Set forth a detailed summary of your education, experience, and training in your profession, and attach a copy of your curriculum vitae.

[Position at Medical Center]

2. State what your title or position was and describe your duties at the Denver Medical Center Ob-Gyn Clinic from November 3, 1982, through April 6, 1983; if your position and/or responsibilities varied or changed during that time, please describe any such changes.

[Relationship with Other Physicians]

3. With regard to the care and treatment of Jeannie Smith from November 3, 1982, through April 6, 1983, were you working under the supervision of any other physician? If so, state:
   A. The name of the physician(s) who supervised your care and treatment of Jeannie Smith.
   B. The nature of the supervision, instruction, or direction.
   C. When and why you worked under the direction of each physician named.

[Questions about Prenatal Records]

4. Regarding the Denver Medical Center Ob-Gyn Clinic Admission Form (60–02109), state:
   A. The name and position of the person who completed the portions of Jeannie Smith's chart labeled "previous pregnancies," "medical history," and "present pregnancy."
   B. The name of the person who placed the "?" in front of "SGA" under the section labeled "previous pregnancies."
   C. When you became aware of the following information contained under "previous pregnancies": that Jeannie Smith had a previous pregnancy resulting in birth in June of 1979 after three-and-a-half hours of labor; that her baby had had a birth weight of 2 pounds ¼ ounces; and that there was a question whether the infant was small for gestational age with meconium stain present.
   D. Whether you ever became aware of the previous pregnancy history described in paragraph 4.C. above. If you did, state:
      (1) When and how you first became aware of it.
      (2) What significance you attached to the pregnancy history when you learned of it, and what medical significance you now attach to it.
      (3) Whether that pregnancy history places Jeannie Smith in a medium- or high-risk category with regard to the prenatal and perinatal care and treatment she received from November 3, 1982, to April 6, 1983.
      (4) Whether those historical data suggest a medium- or high-risk pregnancy.

E. The name of the person who filled out the lower portion of the Admission Form containing the date of April 6, 1982, and the signatures of defendants Dr. A and Dr. Wal. Also state:

(1) Your interpretation of the information contained in the section titled "Medical HX Update," and what significance, if any, you attach to it.

(2) The precise time the information was placed on the Admission Form. If the precise time is not known, state when in the sequence of events this information was obtained and the form completed.

(3) Who determined on 4/6 that Jeannie Smith's pregnancy and delivery were "low risk."

5. With regard to the Denver Memorial Ob-Gyn Clinic prenatal record for Jeannie Smith, reflecting on the upper left-hand portion an LM date of June 27, 1982, and EDC date of April 3, 1983, please provide the following information:

A. Identify by name, current address or last known address, and official title or position, those persons whose initials appear at the bottom of the prenatal record for each of the following dates that Jeannie Smith was examined at the clinic:

(1) November 3, 1982

(2) December 1, 1982

(3) December 29, 1982

(4) January 5, 1982

(5) February 2, 1983

(6) March 2, 1983

(7) March 16, 1983

(8) March 23, 1983

(9) March 29, 1983

(10) March 30, 1983

B. The prenatal chart on each of the dates listed above describes Jeannie Smith's pregnancy as "low risk." If you examined or evaluated the patient on any of those dates, state the date that your evaluation or examination occurred and, for each such date, explain how you arrived at the opinion that the patient was in a low-risk category. Also state:

(1) Whether you considered Jeannie Smith's previous pregnancy and delivery history as described in question 4.

(2) What factors you considered in arriving at your opinion that Jeannie Smith's pregnancy was low risk.

C. If you examined or evaluated Jeannie Smith during any of the prenatal visits listed under A of question 5, state:

(1) What significance, if any, you attached to her history of fundal height measurements as well as the fundal height measurement that you took.

(2) Whether you have any explanation for her fundal height measurement remaining the same (37 cm) on March 16, 1983, and March 23, 1983, and decreasing to 32 on March 30, 1983. If you do have an explanation, what is it?

D. If you performed the examination on March 30, 1983, or made any observations of Jeannie Smith on that date, state:

(1) Who placed the arrow on her chart for fetal movement on March 30, 1983.

(2) If there was a decrease in fetal movement or no fetal movement on March 30, 1983, whether you have any explanation for that finding. If you do have an explanation, what is it?

E. Regarding Jeannie Smith's weight recorded on her prenatal chart, do you have any explanation for the decrease in weight which occurred between March 23, 1983, (162 pounds) and March 30, 1983 (161 pounds)? If you do, what is your explanation?

F. Do you have any explanation for the estimated fetal weight of 3,200 grams remaining the same from March 16, 1983, through March 30, 1983? If so, state your explanation.

G. Regarding Jeannie Smith's prenatal charts, do you have any explanation for the following combination of entries made between March 16, 1983, and March 30, 1983: no change in estimated fetal weight, a drop in fundal height from 37 to 32 cm, and a decrease in Jeannie Smith's weight from 162 to 161 pounds? If you do, state your explanation.

H. Describe how you estimated fetal weight and how you measured fundal height for each occasion you did so during Jeannie Smith's prenatal care.

I. Describe how you detected fetal heart tones and movements on each occasion you did so during Jeannie Smith's prenatal care.

J. Describe how you determined fetal presentation and gestational date on each occasion you did so during Jeannie Smith's prenatal care.

K. Did you order or review an ultrasound examination of Jeannie Smith during her prenatal care? If you did, state:

(1) When you reviewed the ultrasound films and what they showed.

(2) Who ordered the ultrasound films, where they were taken, and where the films are currently located.

6. With reference to the Ob-Gyn Clinic Progress Notes and clinical records regarding the patient, if you examined or observed the patient on any of the dates reflected in the Progress Notes or in other records reflecting clinic visits, state for each such examination and for each such date:

A. What examination you performed, what your examination consisted of, and what the results of your examination were.

B. If you made an entry in the chart, state the date of the entry and set forth verbatim the content of your handwritten chart notes.

C. State conclusions you reached as a result of your examination and of any history you or the nurse obtained.

D. State what treatment, if any, was rendered and why it was rendered.

E. State the full name and present address or last known address of the author of the nutrition entry dated December 1, 1982.

F. With regard to the entry signed by Dr. A on March 31 at 1630 hours, state:

(1) What significance, if any, Dr. A attached to the complaint of contractions every five minutes.

(2) If an external fetal monitor was placed at that time, what the tapes revealed.

(3) How the fetal heart tone was determined to be 140.

(4) Whether Dr. A clinically evaluated the "moderately palpable contractions" which are charted.

(5) Who determined that the cervix had dilated to 1 cm with 50 percent effacement in the minus-2 stage of labor.

(6) Who decided to have the patient walk for a period of time and report back.

(7) Whether Dr. A concurred in the assessment noted in the entry for 1630 hours. If not, please state what Dr. A's assessment of the patient was at that time.

G. State the full name, address or last known address, and official title or position of the author of the entry made on March 31, 1983, at 1800 hours. Further state:

(1) Who was the supervisor of the author of that entry.

(2) Whether the information contained in that entry was reported to Dr. A.

(3) What is meant by the entry "OFM FHT 140."

(4) Whether an external fetal monitor was placed on the infant to determine fetal heart tones. If so, where the fetal monitor tape is now.

(5) Precisely what information was conveyed to the patient about the notation that she was sent home with labor precautions and about why the precautions were given.

(6) Whether you recommended and/or ordered the Seconal 20 mg which was given to the patient to take at home. If not, state who did.

(7) What instructions that patient was given about when to take the Seconal and in what amounts.

H. With regard to the entry dated March 22, 1983, state: The name of each person whose signature appears after the entry; the present or last known address of each such person; and the official title or position of each such person at the clinic. Further state:

(1) The name of the person who made the alteration or change in the entry by adding the word "told" above that portion which is obliterated.

(2) Why Jeannie Smith was told to spend at least four hours a day in bed lying on the left side as much as possible.

(3) What is meant by "toxemic precautions" and what toxemic precautions were taken or ordered.

(4) What signs, symptoms, or evidence was suggestive of toxemia.

I. With regard to the entry date March 29 for 0600 hours, identify the author of that entry and state that person's last known or present address and official title or position at the clinic.

Also state:

(1) Precisely how the fetal weight was determined to be 2,700.

(2) Your interpretation of the entire entry and your explanation of the findings and information in the entry.

(3) What impressions or conclusions were reached as a result of the examination performed at that time.

(4) Whether a fetal monitor was used to determine fetal heart tone. If so, where the fetal monitor tape is now.

7. With reference to the Prenatal Record, if you attached any significance to the 8½-pound weight gain by Jeannie Smith and the increase in fundal height from 31 to 35 between the February 2 and March 2, 1983, visits, compared to the fundal height of 37 cm and weight gain of only 1½ pounds between the March 2 and March 16, 1983, visits, state:

   A. What significance you attached to those findings.

   B. Whether you attached any significance to those findings compared with all other prenatal charting during the same time frame. If so, state what significance you attached to the combined charting.

8. The prenatal charting for March 22, 1983, indicates that Jeannie Smith had mild basal hypertension; blood pressure of 130/88 and baseline 110/70; 1+ edema; and trace proteinuria. Explain:

   A. What significance can be attached to those observations.

   B. Why on March 22, 1983, the patient was prescribed bed rest on the left lateral side as much as possible.

   C. Whether bed rest on the left side is a recognized method of intervention when there is possible fetal distress.

   D. Whether there was any evidence of possible fetal distress on March 22, 1983. If so, describe in detail any suggestions of fetal distress.

9. Jeannie Smith's prenatal records for March 23, 1983, show a weight loss of 2 pounds in the previous week; the week of gestation is listed as 38 cm by date, but only 37 cm by fetal size, with no change in the estimated weight of 3,200 g. State:

   A. What significance can be attached to those findings.

   B. Whether these findings are suggestive of a high-risk or moderately high-risk pregnancy, and, if so, in what way they are so suggestive.

C. Whether those findings are suggestive of possible fetal distress and, if so, in what way are they so suggestive.

D. Whether these findings are customary and normal. If so, state what in the customary and normal course of pregnancy causes such findings to occur.

E. For the March 22, 1983, blood pressure entry of 130/58 that shows the "58" circled on the chart in ink, who placed the circle around the 58 and why.

F. The significance of the blood pressure reading of 130/58 and whether the reading is normal or abnormal.

[Questions about Emergency Visit to Clinic and Missing or Destroyed Records]

10. In the early morning of April 6, 1983, Jeannie Smith appeared at the Denver Memorial Ob-Gyn Clinic with contractions and intense pain, and she was examined by a physician. State:

A. Who examined her, what the examination consisted of, and what the findings or results of the examination were.

B. Whether the patient's admission to the clinic was recorded in any way at the clinic.

(1) If it was, describe the documents in which it was recorded in detail and state what happened to the original copy of each document and where either the original or a copy is currently located.

(2) If it was not, please explain why no record was made of her admission, her examination, and the findings of that examination.

(3) If the chart for that visit and examination was lost or destroyed, state when you first became aware this had occurred.

(4) If you at any time reviewed any documents or charts related to that visit and examination, state when you last reviewed such charts or records.

C. The name, address or last known address, and official title or position of each nurse or nonphysician employee on duty at the Denver Memorial Ob-Gyn Clinic on April 6, 1983, between 5 a.m. and 12:00 noon, and state the time that each such person was on duty. Also state:

(1) The name of the person responsible for recording a patient visit and a description of the document or record reflecting the visit.

(2) The name of the person responsible for completing forms or documents to secure payment for a patient visit and a description of the documents used for that purpose.

(3) Whether records were made of Jeannie Smith's early morning visit on April 6, 1983, for purposes of billing or securing payment. If so, describe such records.

(4) State the name and present or last known address of any nurse or nonphysician employee who spoke with Jeannie Smith when she first arrived at the clinic in the early morning on April 6, 1983, and the name of any nurse who assisted in securing a history or in performing an examination.

D. Whether the physician who examined Jeannie Smith in the early morning of April 6, 1983, consulted with any other physician(s) or person(s) before Jeannie Smith was permitted to return to her home that morning. If so, also state:

(1) The name of each person consulted and the substance of the consultation.

(2) Any recommendations that were made by the consultant, and whether the consultation was reduced to writing.

E. Why Jeannie Smith was permitted to return home from the clinic on the morning of April 6, 1983.

F. Whether during her examination on the morning of April 6, 1983, any instruments or equipment was used to determine fetal heart tone and/or fetal distress. If so:

(1) Describe precisely what equipment or instruments were used for that purpose.

(2) State the results of such diagnostic testing.

(3) State whether the results of such diagnostic testing were recorded anywhere.

(4) If the results were not recorded, explain why.

G. Whether, when Jeannie Smith appeared at the clinic in the early morning of April 6, 1983, any examination was performed in an effort to determine whether there was fetal distress. If so:

(1) Describe in detail precisely what was done to detect fetal distress and by whom.

(2) State the results of any such efforts, whether they were recorded or charted. If so, state where the results were recorded and charted. If not, explain why not.

(3) State whether such records or charts are still available. If so, state where they are. If such records or charts are missing or lost or were destroyed, explain when they disappeared and why.

11. The April 8, 1983, Denver Memorial Hospital Discharge Summary for Jeannie Smith dictated by Dr. A and signed by Dr. Wal, states that Jeannie Smith was seen "in the a.m. on the day of her admission and again was checked, and [it] was found that her cervix was not changed and was having irregular contractions. The patient returned home, and after several hours at home had called and was again having irregular contractions. At that time [she] was instructed to take one of the Seconal tablets previously prescribed for her...."

A. Name any charts or records Dr. A reviewed to refresh his memory about the results of an examination of Jeannie Smith performed on the morning of April 6.

B. If no charts or records were referred to, explain how Dr. A refreshed his memory or otherwise recalled those events.

C. If Dr. A received information from any other person concerning the events on the morning of April 6, 1983, state the name, address, and official title or position of each such person.

D. After which examination did Dr. A note that Jeannie Smith's "cervix was not changed"?

E. State precisely what the condition of her cervix was on the morning of April 6, 1983, and the times of any examinations performed.

F. With regard to the "irregular contractions" on the morning of April 6, 1983, state when she was having contractions, how often, how irregular they were, how strong they were, and how long they lasted.

G. State who received the telephone call with regard to the patient returning home and then phoning to inform the clinic that "she was again having irregular contractions."

(1) Explain how Dr. A learned of that telephone call.

(2) State who instructed Jeannie Smith to take one of the Seconal tablets and why the patient was so instructed.

(3) State whether a Seconal tablet is contraindicated if a fetus is in distress. If it is, explain why.

(4) State by history how many Seconal tablets the patient used between March 28, 1983, and the time she was advised to take the tablet.

(5) With regard to the answer to subparagraph (4), state who obtained the history and when the history was obtained.

12. State the name of each physician responsible for the care and treatment of Jeannie Smith on the morning of April 6, 1983, and the name of each physician who monitored her during labor.
13. State whether Dr. A was under the supervision or direction of any other physician with respect to the care of Jeannie Smith on the morning of April 6, 1983. If so, state the name of the supervising physician.
14. State when Dr. Wal first become aware of Jeannie Smith's visit to the clinic on the morning of April 6, 1983. Also, describe in detail any information, input, or advice Dr. Wal gave to any other physician, any nurse, or Jeannie Smith herself on the morning of April 6, 1983, about the care and treatment of Jeannie Smith.
15. In the Discharge Summary described in question 11, Dr. A states that Jeannie Smith was advised to take one of her Seconal tablets on April 6, 1983, and that "shortly thereafter, patient started having an irregular pattern of contractions every four to five minutes and was returned to the hospital at that time and was found to be in active labor and was dilated to 5 cm." With regard to this point:

    A. State whether you discussed Jeannie Smith's condition with her on the telephone, and, if you did not, who did.

    B. State how you learned of this telephone call.

    C. State whether Jeannie Smith was asked to "return to the hospital" or to return to the Denver Clinic.

    D. State who examined Jeannie Smith and found her to be "in active labor and dilated to 5 cm," and where this examination took place.

    E. State whether the results of this examination were charted or recorded and, if so, on which charts or records they were noted. If they were not recorded, explain why not.

    F. State whether there are any records at the clinic showing the patient's return to the clinic for examination. If there are, describe those records. If no record was made, explain why not.

    G. State whether any records of her return to the clinic were made for the purpose of billing or receiving payment. If they were, describe those records and explain what happened to the original and any copies.

H. If the charts or records were lost or destroyed, state when you first discovered that they had been lost or destroyed.

I. Describe in detail the examination that resulted in Jeannie Smith's being found "...to be in active labor and dilated to 5 cm. The patient was taken to the labor and delivery area."

(1) Were any instruments or equipment, including an external fetal monitor or a fetuscope, used to determine or detect fetal distress during the course of that examination? If so, describe what testing was done and the results of those tests.

(2) Describe in detail any suggestion of fetal distress during, or as a result of, that examination.

(3) Was there any suggestion that Jeannie Smith's was a high-risk pregnancy during, or as a result of, that examination?

(4) Was Jeannie Smith's designated pediatrician, Dr. K, informed by Dr. A or anyone in the clinic that Jeannie Smith was being admitted to labor and delivery? If so, state the name of the person who informed Dr. K or Dr. K's office of this fact. If not, explain why not.

(5) Did you instruct anyone to inform Dr. K's office or to inform Dr. K of Jeannie Smith's admission to the hospital?

[Questions about Labor Records and Fetal Distress]

J. What time did Jeannie Smith arrive at the clinic on April 6, 1983, when she was found to be in active labor and dilated to 5 cm, and what time did she leave the clinic to be taken to the labor and delivery area?

K. What time did Jeannie Smith arrive at the clinic on her first visit there in the early morning of April 6, 1983, and what time did she leave to return home?

L. When Jeannie Smith was delivered by wheelchair from the clinic to labor and delivery on April 6, 1983, did she have a portable external fetal monitor on?

16. Referring to Part 1 of the April 6, 1983, Labor Record and Progress Notes of the Denver Medical Center hospital records for Jeannie Smith, please state the name of the person who completed the top portion of the form above "Comments," indicating 40 3/7 weeks' gestation with onset of labor at 12:30 a.m. on April 3, 1983,

and reflecting spontaneous rupture of membranes occurring at 1400 hours on April 3, 1983, and showing a 2+ meconium stain on admission to the labor ward. Also state:

A. Whether the spontaneous rupture of membranes occurred in the clinic at 1400 hours, before Jeannie Smith was admitted to the labor and delivery ward of the hospital and examined in that ward at 1425 hours.

B. Whether the patient's membranes ruptured during a vaginal examination in the clinic, as opposed to in the labor and delivery area.

C. Who performed the vaginal examination resulting in the patient's membranes rupturing.

D. Whether during the vaginal examination, when the patient's membranes ruptured, the meconium stain was determined to be 4+ meconium stain or a 2+ meconium stain.

E. The medical significance of a 4+ meconium stain and of a 2+ meconium stain.

F. Whether "cervix: 5 cm with spontaneous rupture of membranes," indicated at the bottom of the record paragraph of the April 8, 1983, Discharge Summary dictated by Dr. A occurred during the physical examination described in that paragraph.

G. Whether the top portion of the Labor Record and Progress Notes, Part 1, was completed on the patient's admission to labor and delivery at approximately 1420 to 1425 hours on April 6, 1983. If not, state when that part of the form was completed.

17. Was any portion of the first page of the Labor Record and Progress Notes, Part 1, completed by Dr. A? If so, state which portion.

18. With regard to the entry at 1435 hours to the April 6, 1983, Labor Record and Progress Notes, Part 1, in the Denver Medical Hospital records for Jeannie Smith, that states "external monitor on": Was the external monitor on at that time?

19. On the Labor Record for the hour 1440 there is a notation that Jeannie Smith was dilated 7–8 cm, and a notation is made of the spontaneous rupture of membranes with 4+ meconium stain. State:

    A. The name of the person who performed the examination at 1440 and measure the dilation at 7–8 cm.

B. When the internal fetal heart monitor was started (at 1441 hours it is noted that the internal scalp electrode is "on").

C. What significance you attached to the entry made at 1440 hours.

20. Was there any evidence by external fetal heart monitor of fetal distress at 1425 hours or at 1435 hours? If so, describe in detail precisely what evidence of possible fetal distress existed at those times.

21. Was there any evidence of fetal distress by fetal monitor at 1440 hours? If so, describe in detail precisely what evidence existed by fetal monitor tape of fetal distress.

22. Was there any evidence of fetal distress when the internal fetal monitor was on at 1441 hours? If so, describe in detail precisely what evidence of fetal distress existed on the fetal monitor tape at that time.

23. At 1441 hours and before, was any portion of the internal or external fetal monitor tapes abnormal? If so, describe precisely what abnormalities were reflected on the tapes and when.

24. With regard to the entry at 1445 hours on the Labor Record and Progress Notes, Part 1, indicating the administration of Nisentil, state:

    A. Who made that particular entry, and why Nisentil was administered in that dosage at that time.

    B. Whether Nisentil is contraindicated when there is fetal distress.

    C. When and under what circumstances Nisentil is contraindicated during pregnancy.

    D. Whether the combination of Nisentil and Seconal is contraindicated with fetal distress.

    E. What effect Nisentil has, and what effect Seconal has, on the fetus.

25. With regard to the entry 1450 hours on the Labor Record and Progress Notes, Part 1:

    A. Identify the person who made the entry.

    B. State who examined the patient and concluded that there was 5-cm dilation.

    C. State whether, when the entry was made at 1450, consideration was given to the 7-8 cm dilation recorded at 1440 hours. If so, explain what consideration was given to the earlier entry.

    D. State whether you have any explanation for the inconsistent entries on dilation at 1440 and 1450 hours. If so, set forth the explanation.

26. With regard to the entry at 1459 hours on the Labor Record and Progress Notes, Part 1:
    A. State the name of the person who made the entry noting "Nisentil."
    B. Explain why Nisentil, and that dosage of Nisentil, was administered at that time.
    C. State whether there was any evidence of fetal distress between 1425 hours and 1459 hours. If there was, describe in detail any suggestions or evidence of fetal distress.
27. Please interpret and explain the entry made at 1500 hours on the Labor Record and Progress Notes, Part 1, and state:
    A. Your opinion of what caused the fetal heart tones to drop suddenly to 60 or below.
    B. Whether the combination of the use of Nisentil at 1445 hours and 1459 hours contributed to the sudden drop in fetal heart tones. If so, explain how it contributed.
    C. How you were alerted to the findings recorded at 1500 hours.
28. With regard to the entry at 1501 hours on the Labor Record and Progress Notes, Part 1, indicating that the patient was being taken to the delivery room for emergency delivery and "Dr. A here," state:
    A. Who made the initial decision, and why the decision was made, to transfer the patient to the delivery room for emergency delivery.
    B. How Dr. A was notified of the emergency and when he arrived at the hospital.
    C. Who made the entry at 1501 hours, and whether the same person also made the entry of "FHT's monitored" at 1510 hours. If it was not the same person, identify the person who made that entry.
29. With regard to the handwritten last paragraph on the Labor Record and Progress Notes, Part 1, which commences "course reviewed as per Dr. A," state:
    A. The time and date that the entry was made, the name of the person who made it, and why it was made.
    B. In detail, what conversation the author of the entry had with Dr. A before making the entry.

30. Set forth verbatim the content of the entire note contained on the second page of the Labor Record and Progress Notes, Part 1, which is signed by Dr. A. Further state:

    A. The time and date that the note was entered in the hospital records.

    B. Precisely when Dr. A first observed beat-to-beat variability and/or late decelerations on the fetal monitor tapes and whether this was first observed on the external monitor tapes or on the internal monitor tapes.

    C. Precisely when Dr. A first reviewed any fetal monitor tapes related to Jeannie Smith and where that review took place.

    D. Whether Dr. A, on first reviewing any portion of the fetal monitor tapes, reviewed all of each tape from the commencement of the tape to the end of where it was then recording. If the entire tape was not reviewed, describe which portion of the tape was reviewed when Dr. A first looked at it.

[Questions about Interpretation and Destruction of Fetal Monitor Tapes]

31. With regard to the fetal monitor equipment and tapes used on Jeannie Smith and her fetus:

    A. State the name of the person or persons who first applied the external fetal monitor equipment to Jeannie Smith and, with regard to both the external and internal fetal monitors, state:

        (1) The name of each person who, to your knowledge, supervised the use of each monitor on Jeannie Smith and her fetus.

        (2) The name of each person who, to your knowledge, checked the fetal heart tones with respect to each monitor used, and the methods each used to check the fetal heart tones.

        (3) With regard to each person, how often, or with what frequency, the fetal heart tones were checked.

    B. State whether you reviewed any portion or all of the external fetal monitor tape before the internal fetal monitor was applied. If so, describe what portion of the external fetal monitor tape was observed, what observation you made, and what conclusions you reached.

C. State whether you concluded that any portion of the external fetal monitor tape was abnormal in any way. If you did, describe the abnormalities.

D. State whether you determined that the external fetal monitor tape was suggestive of fetal distress. If you did, describe what portion of the fetal monitor tape was suggestive of fetal distress.

E. State whether you observed any beat-to-beat variability or late decelerations on the external fetal monitor tape. If you did, describe the nature and extent of them.

F. If you did not observe any portion of the external fetal monitor tape *before* the internal fetal monitor tape was commenced, state whether at any time previously you observed or studied the external fetal monitor tape. If you did, state:

(1) When you last saw the external fetal monitor tapes and where they then were located.

(2) Why you later studied them.

(3) Where you later studied them.

(4) Who was present when you studied them.

(5) What observations or conclusions you reached as a result of your study of them.

(6) Whether you put your observations in writing. If you did, describe the written document and where it is now located.

(7) Whether you reported your observations or findings to any other person. If so, state the names of all such persons.

(8) Whether any other physician or person reported to you that he or she had reviewed, studied, or read the tapes. If so, state the name of any such person and state precisely what information was given to you by such person regarding observations or study of the tapes.

G. State whether you reviewed, observed, or studied any portion of the internal fetal monitor tapes between the time they were applied on April 6, 1983, and the time they were removed for the emergency delivery. If you did, state:

(1) When you last saw the internal fetal monitor tapes and where they were then located.

(2) Why you later studied them.

(3) Where you later studied them.

(4) Who was present when you studied them.

(5) What observations or conclusions you reached as a result of your study of them.

(6) Whether you put your observations in writing. If you did, describe the written document and where it is now located.

(7) Whether you reported your observations or findings to any other person(s) and, if you did, the names of all such persons.

(8) Whether any other physician or person reported or read the tapes. If anyone did, state the names of all such persons and state precisely what information was given to you by them regarding their observations or study of the tapes.

H. State whether you at any time studied the internal fetal monitor tapes used for Jeannie Smith and her fetus on April 6, 1983. If so, state:

(1) Why you later studied them.

(2) Where you later studied them.

(3) Who was present when you studied them.

(4) What observations or conclusions you reached as a result of your study of them.

(5) Whether you put your observations in writing. If so, describe the written document and state where it is now located.

(6) Whether you reported your observations or findings to any other person(s). If so, state the names of all such persons.

(7) Whether any other physician or person reported to you that he or she had reviewed, studied, or read the tapes. If so, state the names of all such persons and state precisely what information was given to you by them regarding their observations or study of the tapes.

(8) Whether you concluded that any portion of the tapes was abnormal in any manner. If so, describe the abnormalities.

(9) Whether you determined that the tapes were suggestive of fetal distress. If so, describe what portion of them was suggestive of fetal distress.

(10) Whether you observed any beat-to-beat variability or late decelerations on the tapes. If you did, describe the nature and extent of such beat-to-beat variability and late decelerations.

I. State whether you learned at any point in time that the external and internal fetal monitor tapes used for Jeannie Smith on April 6, 1983, were lost or disappeared and now cannot be found. If you did, state:

(1) When you first heard or understood that the tapes were lost or had disappeared, and from whom you received this information.

(2) Whether you made an attempt at any time to find or locate the fetal monitor tapes. If you made such an attempt, state when you made the attempt, what the effort or attempt consisted of, and what you discovered or learned.

J. State whether you at any time checked out or removed the fetal monitor tapes from the place where they are customarily kept or stored. If so, state when and where this occurred.

K. State whether you have heard, from any source, where the fetal monitor tapes can be located at the present time. If so, set forth the information available to you.

L. State whether you have been informed by any person that the fetal monitor tapes were lost or destroyed. If so, state the name of the person who gave you this information and state precisely what information was conveyed to you.

M. State whether you participated, directly or indirectly, in the loss or destruction of the fetal monitor tapes or of any portion of the fetal monitor tapes.

32. Have you at any time been a member of any formal or informal committee of the defendant-corporation (hospital or clinic) at which the subject of internal hospital or clinic rules, regulations, or guidelines related to the preservation or destruction of fetal monitor tapes was discussed or was a topic on the agenda? If so, state:

A. The name of the committee, staff committee, or group, and the names of the persons on the committee.

B. When and where any meetings took place.

C. Whether minutes or other written memoranda or documentation was made of the proceedings, the name of the custodian of such documents, where the documents are kept, and whether you have in your possession a copy of any such documents.

D. Whether the committee at any time recommended to the hospital that the hospital enact internal rules and regulations, or formulate policies, regarding the preservation or destruction of fetal monitor tapes. If so, describe in detail, or attach to your answers, copies of the recommendations.

33. Are you a member of the defendant-corporation's ob-gyn hospital staff committee, or have you ever been a member? If so, state:

    A. The dates or time frame of your membership.

    B. Whether you have held a designated official position on the staff committee and, if so, what your official title or position was and the years in which you held that position.

    C. Whether the ob-gyn staff committee at any time recommended or reviewed proposed internal rules, regulations, procedures, or policies to be enacted by the hospital or others regarding the preservation or destruction of fetal monitor tapes. If so:

        (1) Describe in detail any recommendations made and when they were made, and attach to your description copies of the recommendations.

        (2) State when such matters were reviewed by the committee, what the review consisted of, and the results of that review.

    D. Whether you at any time recommended to the defendant-corporation that internal rules, regulations, or policies be enacted or enforced with respect to the preservation or destruction of fetal monitor tapes. If so, describe any recommendations you made, state when you made them, and state what action was taken on your recommendations.

34. Are you aware, directly or indirectly, of the loss or destruction of fetal monitor tapes at the defendant's hospital or the defendant's ob-gyn clinic regarding any patient other than the plaintiff? If so, state:

    A. Approximately how many such incidents have been called to your attention and how you learned of them.

    B. What recommendations or action you took on learning of such incident(s).

    C. Whether any or all such incidents were a topic of discussion at any hospital staff or administrative committee meeting so far as you know. If so, describe the administrative committee or staff committee and state when such discussions took place.

D. Whether fetal monitor tapes with regard to any patient you have treated or in whose treatment you assisted have disappeared or been lost or destroyed from the defendant's hospital or ob-gyn clinic. If they did, state how many such patients this applies to.

35. To your knowledge, has the defendant-corporation at any time enacted an internal rule, regulation, administrative order, or administration or staff policy regarding the preservation or destruction of fetal monitor tapes? If so:

A. State when you first became aware of any such rule, regulation, or policy.

B. State your understanding of the content of that rule, regulation, or policy when you first became aware of it. If convenient, attach a copy of that policy, rule, or regulation.

C. If the policy, rule, or regulation was altered, amended, or changed after you first became aware of its existence, describe any such amendment, alteration, or change and state when it was made. If convenient, attach a copy of the amended document to your answers.

D. Describe what you understood the rule, regulation, or policy to be in April 1983. If convenient, attach a copy of the rule, regulation, or policy to your answer.

36. To your knowledge, has the defendant-corporation or any member of its staff received criticism or complaint from any source with respect to the failure to preserve fetal monitor tapes or for the loss or destruction of fetal monitor tapes? If so, state:

A. The nature of the criticism or complaint.

B. When each criticism or complaint was received or occurred, and the number of such criticisms or complaints of which you are aware.

C. What action, if any, was taken by the ob-gyn staff at the hospital in response to such criticisms or complaints.

37. Are you familiar with the guidelines and recommendations of the American College of Obstetricians and Gynecologists (ACOG) with respect to the storage and preservation of fetal monitor tapes and records? If so:

A. Did you at any time become familiar with the guidelines and recommendations as contained in *Standards for Obstetric-Gynecologic Services* (ACOG, 5th Edition, 1982)? If so, when did you first become aware of the guidelines and recommendations contained therein?

B. Did you at any time recommend or request that the defendant-corporation adopt or enact the guidelines and recommendations of ACOG with respect to the storage and preservation of fetal monitor tapes and records? If so, when did you make such recommendations and to whom?

38. In April 1983, were either internal or external fetal monitor tapes considered by the Denver Memorial Ob-Gyn Clinic to be a part of the mother's official clinic or hospital records, and/or a part of the infant's official clinic or hospital records after birth? State:

A. Whether your answer was based on any known clinic or hospital policy, rule, or regulation: if so, set forth the rule, regulation, or policy that was the basis for your answer.

B. Whether your answer was based on general procedures or custom and habit. If it was, set forth the general procedures, custom, or habit.

39. In or before April 1983, were you familiar with any hospital accreditation standards regarding the storage and preservation of fetal monitor tapes? If so, state:

A. What accreditation standards you were familiar with and when and how you first became familiar with them.

B. Whether, to your knowledge, the defendant-hospital at any time violated such standards. If you believe it did, state when and under what circumstances.

40. Did you at any time complain to the administration of Denver Memorial Hospital about the failure to preserve fetal monitor tapes or copies of fetal monitor tapes, or complain about or call attention to the loss, destruction, or failure to preserve fetal monitor tapes? If so, state:

A. Approximately how often, when, and to whom you made such statements or such complaints.

B. Whether any of the statements or complaints were made in writing. If so, and if you have copies of such documents, state where they are stored, and, if convenient, attach copies; if you do not attach copies, set forth the substance of any such complaints or statements.

C. What communication, if any, you received from the hospital in response to your statements or complaints.

[Questions about Disappearance of Records]

41. In April 1983, what was the practice or custom of the Denver Memorial Ob-Gyn Clinic with regard to making records of or charting information about a patient's visit to the ob-gyn clinic and any examinations performed there? State:
    A. Whether such charts and records were customarily kept by the clinic. If they were and if they were kept pursuant to any rule, regulation, or guideline adopted by the defendant-corporation or ob-gyn clinic, describe the regulation, rule, policy, or guideline in effect in April 1983. If convenient, attach a copy of any such guideline, rule, or regulation.
    B. What your custom and practice was in April 1983 with respect to:
        (1) Documenting in writing a patient's visit to the ob-gyn clinic.
        (2) Charting any history taken from the patient or the patient's family.
        (3) Charting any physical examination performed on the patient.
        (4) Charting any findings or signs or symptoms found or observed as a result of the patient's examination.
        (5) Charting any diagnostic tests performed and the results of those tests.
        (6) Charting any medical plan devised for treatment, any treatment rendered, and any medication prescribed.
        (7) Charting any diagnosis, preliminary impression, or differential diagnosis made.
        (8) Charting any plan for follow-up care.

42. With respect to Jeannie Smith's appearance at the Denver Memorial Ob-Gyn Clinic on the morning of April 6, 1983, or to the telephone calls that Jeannie Smith made to the clinic during the morning of April 6, 1983, or to Jeannie Smith's appearance at the clinic a second time in the late morning of April 6, 1983, all as described in her April 8, 1983, Discharge Summary dictated by Dr. A, state:
    A. Whether you have any explanation for the fact that neither Denver Medical Center Hospital nor Denver Memorial Ob-Gyn Clinic has any records of the visits, examinations, and telephone calls.

B. Whether, based on internal rules, regulations, and guidelines, or on custom, habit, or informal policy, records should have been made of Jeannie Smith's visits and examinations at the clinic on April 6, 1983.

C. Whether, to your knowledge, records were made of her visits and examinations on April 6, 1983. If you believe they were, state the name or names of those persons who charted or made records of her visits and examinations.

D. Whether you have any explanation why there is currently no copy of those records and why there are no charts of those examinations.

E. Whether, at any time, you reviewed charts and records of those visits and examinations. If you did, state when and where.

F. Whether such records were lost or destroyed. If they were, state on what formal data you base your knowledge or opinion.

[Questions about Use of Fetal Monitor Equipment at the Clinic]

43. In April 1983, did the Ob-Gyn Clinic at Denver Medical Center have fetal monitoring equipment available independent of the hospital for use in the clinic? If so, describe the type (internal, external, or both) and nature of that equipment, giving the name of the manufacturer, the trademark, and other appropriate information. Also state:

    A. What the custom and habit of the clinic was with reference to any tapes made on the fetal monitoring equipment in the clinic.

    B. What your practice was with regard to the preservation, storage, loss, or destruction of fetal monitor tapes made in the clinic.

    C. Whether the clinic had any rules, regulations, or policies regarding the storage, preservation, loss, or destruction of tapes.

    D. Whether to your knowledge the hospital had any rules, regulations, or guidelines with respect to the preservation, storage, loss, or destruction of such tapes.

[Questions about Rupture of Membranes, Abnormal Labor, and Fetal Distress]

44. With regard to the April 8, 1982, Discharge Summary dictated by Dr. A and signed by Dr. Wal as attending physician, state:

A. Who examined Jeannie Smith "in the a.m. on the day of her admission," when she was "checked and found that her cervix was not changed and was having irregular contractions." State also:

(1) The condition of her cervix.

(2) How often she was having irregular contractions (including a description of the irregularity, and nature and strength of those contractions).

(3) Whether she was first examined by a nurse before she was examined by an M.D. If she was, name the nurse.

(4) Whether an effort was made to determine fetal distress at that time. If it was, state what that effort consisted of and what the results were.

B. With regard to the notation, "Shortly thereafter, patient started having an irregular pattern of contractions every four or five minutes and was returned to the hospital at that time and was found to be in active labor and was dilated to 5 cm," state:

(1) Who received the information above from the patient and when it was received.

(2) The time the patient returned to the hospital.

(3) Who found the patient to be in active labor and how frequent the contractions were at that time.

(4) Whether any evaluation was made of possible fetal distress when the patient was found to be in active labor and, if it was, who made the evaluation, what it consisted of, and what the findings were.

(5) The nature of the contractions Jeannie Smith was having at that time.

(6) Whether the patient was in severe pain at that time.

(7) Whether the patient arrived in the clinic by wheelchair because of the severity of her pain.

(8) How long the patient was in the clinic before she "was taken to the labor and delivery area" as charted in the Discharge Summary.

(9) Whether the patient was a high-risk pregnancy patient when she returned to the clinic. If she was, describe those signs, symptoms, or characteristics that made her a high-risk pregnancy patient. If not, state how you would

characterize her condition (e.g., low risk, moderate risk) and on what you would base your evaluation of risk.

C. With regard to the notation, "During a vaginal check the patient's membranes ruptured and was found to be 4+ meconium," state:

(1) The appearance in detail, of the meconium that caused you to rate it as 4+.

(2) The type of scale on which a meconium rating of 4+ is based.

(3) What the significance is of a 4+ meconium finding when the membranes rupture.

D. With regard to the notation, "The patient was having decreased variability in her baseline but otherwise there were no decelerations noted initially," state:

(1) Whether the decreased variability in the baseline appeared as soon as the external monitor tape began functioning. If it did not, where on the tape did it first occur?

(2) When the decelerations were first noted and where they were first noted on the external monitor tape.

E. With regard to the notation, "Shortly thereafter, though, the patient was having considerable variable decelerations with each contraction and continued to have decreased beat-to-beat," state:

(1) The time Jeannie Smith had "considerable variable decelerations" and when the decelerations first appeared on the external monitor tape.

(2) Who first noted the variable decelerations.

(3) Who first noted that the tapes "continued to have decreased beat-to-beat" variability, and when that person first noted it happening.

(4) Whether the decreased beat-to-beat variability was first recognized on the external or the internal monitor tapes.

F. With regard to the notation that "the patient was very active with contractions every two to three minutes," state:

(1) When the contractions every two to three minutes were first noted and by whom.

(2) What the quality of the every two to three minute contractions was.

(3) What the condition of Jeannie Smith's cervix was when the contractions were first noted every two to three minutes.

G. With regard to the Discharge Summary notation that "after a brief period of ten to fifteen minutes, cervix was checked again and was found to be complete and pushing and because of the great concern for the fetal heart tones which were continuing to have decreased variability as well as considerable variable decelerations down to 6, 15, +60," state:

(1) Who checked the cervix again.

(2) What is meant by the language "found to be complete and pushing."

(3) Whether Dr. A reviewed the fetal monitor tapes during his dictation on April 4, 1983, stating that there were "considerable variable decelerations down to 6, 15, +60." If he did, state where the dictation took place and where the fetal monitor tapes were reviewed on April 8, 1983.

(4) If Dr. A did not review the tapes during his dictation, whether he reviewed any other charts or records summarizing the variable decelerations to dictate the Discharge Summary. If he did, name the documents he reviewed.

[Questions about Delivery and Condition of Infant at Birth]

H. With regard to the Discharge Summary notation that "initially, the position was R-O-T, but rapidly rotated to O-A with descent to the perineum," state:

(1) Who first observed that the position was R-O-T, and what significance you attached to the R-O-T position.

(2) How the position was "rotated to O-A" and by whom.

(3) What procedures were required to deliver the infant's head in the "O-A position."

I. With regard to the Discharge Summary notation that a "second degree midline episiotomy" was used and that "the infant was suctioned with a DeLeed of the perineum," state:

(1) Why a second-degree midline episiotomy was performed, and describe in detail the size and place of the second-degree midline episiotomy.

(2) Why the infant was suctioned with a DeLeed.

(3) Whether a nurse, physician, or any other person was instructed to apply pressure to Jeannie Smith's abdomen during the DeLeed suctioning and, if so, why. If anyone applied pressure to the patient's abdomen during the DeLeed suctioning, state the name of each person who did so.

J. With regard to the Discharge Summary notation that "there was considerable staining of meconium noted at that time. The infant was delivered spontaneously," state:

(1) The nature and extent, in detail, of the meconium staining and what significance you attached to it.

(2) Whether the infant was choking on meconium or whether the meconium appeared in any way to interfere with the infant's ability to breathe. If it did, describe in detail exactly what was observed in that regard.

(3) Whether a pediatrician was alerted to the fact that the birth might occur with meconium aspiration and, if so, when the pediatrician was so notified.

K. With regard to the Discharge Summary notation that "the cord was clamped rapidly and the infant was passed to the pediatrician," state:

(1) Precisely where the cord was located at time of delivery.

(2) Whether the cord was wrapped around the infant's neck or head, or whether it was found in a position otherwise considered to be abnormal. If it was, state precisely the abnormal position.

(3) Your observation of the length of the cord and its condition.

(4) Whether the cord was delivered to pathology for analysis and, if not, why not.

(5) The name of the pediatrician whom the infant "was passed to" and when that pediatrician first arrived in the delivery room.

(6) Whether that pediatrician was in the delivery room before the cord was clamped.

(7) When that pediatrician was first contacted and requested to be present, and by whom.

L. With regard to the Discharge Summary notation that "cords were visualized and suctioned, Narcan was given for the reversal of any narcotics still on board. The infant had difficulty initiating a respiratory effort, was bagged for a considerable amount of time, was intubated briefly for suctioning of meconium below the cord," state:

(1) By whom the cords were visualized and suctioned, and where and when these actions took place.

(2) By whom the infant was bagged.

(3) What is meant by "a considerable amount of time." State approximately for what period of time the infant was bagged.

(4) Who "briefly" intubated the infant by suctioning of meconium below the cord, and how much meconium was suctioned below the cord.

(5) Whether any records were made of the amount of meconium suctioned.

(6) Whether the meconium was suctioned below the cord when the infant's head was delivered and before the rest of delivery occurred.

(7) Whether the meconium was suctioned below the cord after delivery of the infant was complete and, if so, how soon after delivery.

M. With regard to the Discharge Summary notation that "Apgars at 1 minute was 1, at 5 minutes were 2 and at 1 minutes were 4," state whether Dr. A was aware of the Apgar scoring when it occurred. If not, when he first became aware of the Apgar scoring and how he was informed of the Apgar rating or scores made.

N. With regard to the final diagnosis on the Discharge Summary, "2) hospital intrauterine meconium aspiration of the infant, 4+ meconium was noted at the time of delivery," state:

(1) Whether you attribute the infant's asphyxia to intrauterine meconium aspiration. If not, precisely what do you believe was the cause of asphyxia?

(2) When you believe the infant, as a fetus, was first in fetal distress, and how you arrived at that conclusion.

45. Did you or did anyone else to your knowledge at any time dictate a summary of the delivery room operation, delivery, or procedure? If so, state:

A. Who dictated the hospital record and when.

B. Whether that dictation was typed and placed in the hospital records at any time.

C. Why the dictated summary is no longer in the hospital records.

46. With regard to the delivery of the infant on April 6, 1983, state:

A. The name and present or last known address of every person who was present during the delivery, and precisely what function or role each person performed during the delivery.

B. With regard to each person present, whether that person is still an employee of the defendant-corporation.

C. For each such person not currently employed by the defendant-corporation, any information available about where that person is now employed or located.

47. Did you, at any time before spontaneous delivery of the infant, consider the possibility of performing a c-section on Jeannie Smith? If so, state:

A. When and why you first considered that possibility.

B. Whether you had any discussion with Jeannie Smith or her husband about a possible c-section and, if so, where and when that conversation took place and what was said.

48. Referring to the Denver Medical Center Delivery and Nursery Data Chart (Form 60–04204) dated April 6, 1983, and showing the time of delivery as 1510 hours, state:

A. The name of the person or persons who completed and filled out that form and, if more than one person participated in filling out the form, which portion of the form was filled out by each person.

B. Who determined the "stages of labor," and how they determined them.

C. Who completed that portion of the chart listing "newborn medications."

D. The name of the "assistant doctor" appearing on that chart and the role he played in the delivery or care and treatment of Jeannie Smith.

E. The name of the person who filled out that portion of the chart opposite the words, "cords visualized," and the chart entry that is after "cords visualized".

49. With regard to the hospital Progress Report in Jeannie Smith's hospital records for April 7, 1983, commencing with the entry at 630 hours and the handwritten statement "infant at Children's intubated; meconium aspiration, will check condition today," state:
    A. Who made that entry.
    B. How that information was received from Children's Hospital and who at Children's Hospital reported on the infant's condition.

[Questions about the Cause of Baby's Condition at Birth]

50. On the top of the next page of the Progress Report for April 7, 1983, with regard to the statement "reassure patient baby's condition not due to anything she did," state:
    A. The name of the author of that entry.
    B. What the author's understanding was of the cause of the baby's condition.
    C. Where the author received information on what had caused the baby's condition.
51. In the Progress Report for April 8, 1983, after the entry at 1220 hours, there is a notation, "discharge summary dictated 4/8." With regard to this notation, state:
    A. The name of the author of that statement.
    B. Why that statement was placed in the Progress Report notes.
    C. Whether the patient was discharged on April 9, 1983.
    D. Why the Discharge Summary was dictated on April 8, before the patient was discharged on April 9.
    E. Why the Discharge Summary states that "she was discharged on the Narcan in excellent condition."
    F. Whether the Discharge Summary was dictated after the patient was discharged from the hospital and, if so, why the hospital records reflect that it was dictated on April 8.
52. With regard to when Dr. Wal signed the Discharge Summary, state:
    A. Whether Dr. Wal first carefully read and reviewed the Discharge Summary before signing it.
    B. Whether Dr. Wal discussed the content of the Discharge Summary with Dr. A before it was dictated by Dr. A.

C. Whether Dr. Wal assisted Dr. A in the delivery on April 6, 1983, and, if so, what assistance was rendered, and what, precisely, Dr. Wal did during the delivery.

53. When did Dr. A and when did Dr. Wal first learn that the baby's EEG at Children's Hospital was abnormal?

54. Did Dr. A dictate the Discharge Summary after learning that the baby's EEG was abnormal?

55. Did either Dr. A or Dr. Wal inform Nurse S. Lang that the baby's EEG came back abnormal?

56. Were copies of the EEG or a summary of the findings on the EEG delivered to Denver Memorial Hospital or to Dr. A or Dr. Wal on April 8, 1983?

57. State precisely what the duties and responsibilities of Chief Resident Dr. D were with respect to the supervision of Resident Dr. A as they relate to the care and treatment of Jeannie Smith. Also state:

    A. Why Dr. D was not present during the delivery of the Smith baby on April 6, 1983.

    B. When Dr. D first became aware that the Smith baby had been delivered.

    C. How Dr. D was so informed and by whom.

    D. When Dr. D first discussed with Dr. A the delivery of the Smith baby.

    E. What information was conveyed to Dr. D by Dr. A regarding the delivery of the Smith baby in that first conversation.

58. The Neonatal Intensive Care Flow Sheet for the Smith baby reflects that the baby was delivered to the Neonatal Intensive Care Unit and, at 1645 hours on April 6, 1983, it was charted that "entire facial area and head severely bruised with dependent edema." In that regard, state:

    A. The cause of this condition.

    B. Whether birth trauma caused the condition.

    C. Whether this was, in fact, the condition of the baby's face and head when the baby left the delivery area.

59. Following delivery of the baby on April 6, 1983, did Dr. A meet with Jeannie Smith in her room at the hospital to explain what had occurred during or before delivery with respect to the condition of her infant? If so, state:

A. Who was present during the meeting when the explanation was made and precisely what explanation was given to Jeannie Smith by Dr. A.

B. Whether Dr. A or anyone in his presence showed Jeannie Smith portions of the fetal monitor tape and explained the tape to her.

C. What explanation was given to Jeannie Smith with reference to the fetal monitor tape.

60. To the best of your recollection, state exactly what statements were made to Jeannie Smith and what her response was, or state the substance of the statements made to Jeannie Smith and her response.

61. To your knowledge, did Dr. A or anyone else meet again with Jeannie Smith, her husband, or both to explain what had occurred at the hospital or why their infant was transferred to Children's Hospital? If so, state:

A. When and where any meetings took place.

B. What information was given to Jeannie Smith or her husband.

C. What explanation was made about their infant's condition.

D. Who was present at each of the meetings.

62. Is the passage of meconium in utero a sign of intrauterine asphyxia? With regard to this question, state:

A. When you first considered the possibility that there could be intrauterine asphyxia.

B. What first caused you to consider that possibility.

C. What abnormalities on the fetal monitor tapes were consistent with intrauterine asphyxia.

63. Did you at any time before delivery of the infant take or order fetal blood sampling to assess the acid-base status of the fetus?

A. If so, state precisely when the fetal blood sampling occurred and what the results of the blood tests were.

B. If not, state why fetal blood sampling was not done to assess the acid-base status of the fetus.

64. In your present view, did any of the medications administered to the mother before the birth contribute to fetal distress? If so, state:

A. Which of the medications contributed to fetal distress.

B. Whether there was any indication from the fetal monitor tapes that the medications administered contributed to fetal distress. If there was, explain how this was demonstrated on the fetal monitor tapes.

65. In your opinion, is it possible that any medications administered to Jeannie Smith before the delivery of her infant contributed to fetal distress? If so:

A. State which of the medications administered could have contributed to fetal distress.

B. Explain how such medications could have contributed to fetal distress.

66. Is there a correlation between the occurrence of late decelerations and alterations in fetal acid-base status secondary to fetal hypoxia? If so, state:

A. The correlation between the two.

B. Whether there was any correlation discovered or observed with reference to the Jeannie Smith pregnancy.

67. Is the combination of late decelerations and loss of beat-to-beat variability particularly ominous as a sign of fetal distress? Was there prenatal evidence of late decelerations accompanied by loss of beat-to-beat variability in the prenatal period during Jeannie Smith's hospitalization on April 6, 1983?

68. Can variable decelerations, if severe or prolonged, result in fetal hypoxia and acidosis?

69. When variable decelerations are accompanied by or evolve into late decelerations, or when beat-to-beat variability is diminished or lost, is the likelihood of significant fetal hypoxia markedly enhanced?

70. What fetal heart rate patterns are indicative or productive of fetal hypoxia? Were any of the fetal heart rate patterns indicative of or productive of fetal hypoxia present in the prenatal period during Jeannie Smith's hospitalization on April 6, 1983?

71. With regard to the cord blood sample taken at the time of the birth on April 6, 1983, state:

A. The purpose of taking a cord blood sample at the time of the birth.

B. Whether the cord blood sample taken at the time of delivery was analyzed for acidosis. If it was not, do you have any explanation why it was not?

C. Whether the blood sample taken from the cord showed any evidence of acidosis. If it did, state the amount or degree of fetal acidosis present, and whether that amount was consistent with prenatal hypoxia.

72. In addition to the use of an electronic fetal monitor and fetal scalp blood samples to monitor acidosis, list the other techniques and equipment available to detect fetal distress at Denver Memorial Hospital in April, 1983, and state:

A. Whether, at that time, continuous assessment of fetal pH by scalp electrode was available and in use at the hospital.

B. Whether fetal PO_2 by transcutaneous oxygen electrode could be used at the hospital at that time.

C. Whether there was equipment available at the hospital at that time to detect and determine the nature and extent of fetal breathing. If so, state what the equipment was.

73. Was ultrasonic equipment used at the hospital on April 6, 1983, to help assess the condition of the fetus before the delivery of Jeannie Smith's baby?

A. If it was available, was the equipment used? If not, why not?

B. If ultrasonic films were done, state precisely when this occurred, why films were ordered, and what findings were made in studying the films.

74. Was it your understanding, in April, 1983, that use of Nisentil during labor could result in fetal heart rate beat-to-beat variability? State:

A. Whether Nisentil was contraindicated in 1983 if there was any evidence of fetal distress. If it was, explain why.

B. Whether Nisentil was withdrawn from the market in October 1980, because it could cause respiratory arrest or fetal distress if given during a mother's labor. If it was, state when you became aware that it was.

75. For each occasion that Nisentil was administered to Jeannie Smith on April 6, 1983, state:

A. How the Nisentil was administered. If it was administered by IV, state why.

B. Whether there is a synergistic effect when a combination of Seconal and Nisentil is administered to the mother during labor, and what the effect is on either the mother or the fetus.

76. Was there any evidence or indication of possible meconium aspiration before the birth with regard to Jeannie Smith's pregnancy? If so, state:

   A. Precisely and in detail what evidence existed of meconium aspiration before birth.

   B. Whether the pediatrician who was present after the delivery of the Smith infant was informed before delivery of possible meconium aspiration. If so, state which pediatrician was so informed and how and by whom he was informed.

77. In April 1983, did you consider thick meconium to be evidence of fresh meconium, indicating a recent passage due to actual fetal distress? If you did not, state whether you were aware of any medical literature or opinions to the contrary.

78. With regard to fetal scalp pH, state:

   A. What significance you attach to the fetal scalp pH lab results.

   B. What the fetal scalp pH lab results were, and when you first became aware of them.

79. Immediately after delivery of the infant plaintiff, was any endotracheal intubation performed, based on your observations or knowledge? If so, state:

   A. When it was first performed, by whom, and where it was performed.

   B. Whether any record was made of the endotracheal intubation and, if so, where the record was made.

   C. Whether there was any breathing assistance rendered to the infant immediately following delivery and, if so, how it was rendered, what equipment was used, when it was used, and who used it. Also state whether any equipment used was functional or whether any problem using it was noted. Describe any problem that was noted.

   D. Whether any improvement was noted in the baby's condition as a result of intubation or any breathing assistance rendered.

[Questions about Insurance Coverage]

80. Do you have liability insurance coverage for the matters alleged and set forth in the Complaint on file herein? If so, state:

   A. The name of each insurance company providing coverage and the insurance policy limits.

B. For each insurance policy, whether you have primary coverage or excess or umbrella coverage, and whether it requires you to pay coinsurance or a deductible.

C. The policy time frame or period covered by each insurance policy, and the nature and type of insurance coverage each provides.

B.2 INTERROGATORIES TO DEFENDANT-HOSPITAL

The following interrogatories show how information can be obtained from the hospital and nursing staff in advance of depositions by asking questions about entries in the hospital records. The interrogatories also seek important information about the identity of witnesses, the destruction of fetal monitor tapes and records, the defendant-doctors' hospital privileges, and the hospital's internal rules, regulations and policies.

PLAINTIFF'S FIRST SET OF WRITTEN INTERROGATORIES TO DEFENDANT DENVER MEDICAL CENTER

Plaintiffs hereby request that defendant Denver Medical Center, by and through its duly authorized agents, officers, and directors, answer in writing and under oath all of the below-listed interrogatories, pursuant to the Colorado Rules of Civil Procedure, and that said defendant base its answers to interrogatories on the collective knowledge of all persons having any affiliation with said defendant.

Please note that these interrogatories are ongoing and therefore the answers to them should be supplemented if additional information or knowledge becomes available to the defendant Denver Medical Center.

[Questions Seeking the Identification and Location of Witnesses]

1. With regard to each nurse or corporate defendant employee who filled out, signed, or initialed the documents listed below, state the name of the nurse or employee, the nurse or employee's official title or position in the hospital or clinic at the time the documents were filled out, signed, or initialed and whether that nurse or employee is still employed by the hospital or clinic. If any such employee is not still employed by the hospital or clinic, then set forth the person's last known address and present place of employment, if known.

   A. The prenatal records, including the Prenatal Flow Chart and Prenatal Progress Notes and Reports for Jeannie Smith from November 1982 through April 1983.

B. The Ante-Partum Record for Jeannie Smith, and the "Pregnancy History," which states, in part, "?SGA mec. st. FLD."

C. The "Interview Sheet OB Clinic" (Form 600-290).

D. Jeannie Smith's inpatient hospital records at defendant's hospital from April 6, 1983, through April 9, 1983. For this document, state also the name of the person or service that typed the discharge summary dictated by Dr. A and signed by Dr. Wal, M.D.

E. The Labor Record and Progress Notes for April 6, 1983.

F. The Denver Medical Center form 60-02109, which contains categories for "previous pregnancies," "medical history," and "present pregnancy," and lists as "intern" Dr. A and Dr. Wal.

G. The Denver Medical Center "Delivery and Nursery Data" (Form 60-04204).

H. The Recovery Room record for Jeannie Smith dated April 6, 1983.

I. The Denver Medical Center "Medication Orders Sheet" (Form 60-0000-4).

J. The hospital "Progress Report" charts on Jeannie Smith commencing April 6, 1983.

2. For each nurse or corporate defendant employee who filled out any portion of, signed, or initialed the hospital records listed below for Baby Smith on April 6, 1983, state the person's full name and address, the official title and position, and whether the person is still employed by the hospital. If that person is not presently employed by the hospital, state that person's last known address and present place of employment, if known.

   A. The "Physicians Orders" (Form 60-0000-4).

   B. The "Department of Radiology—Consultation Request and Report" dated April 6, 1983. For this document, also state the above information for:

      (1) Each person whose handwriting appears on the form requesting the chest X rays taken at 4:40 p.m.

      (2) The person who obliterated that part of the record following the language "chest X ray" under "examination requested" for the X rays taken at 4:40 p.m.

   C. The "Department of Radiology Consultation Request and Report" indicating that the X rays were taken at 7:40 p.m.

D. The Neonatal Intensive Care Flow Sheet commencing at 1530 hours and ending at 2040 hours.

E. The chart for Baby Smith containing "output," "ventilation," and "gases."

F. The "Delivery and Nursery Data" sheet.

[Questions about Hospital's Internal Rules, Policies, and Regulations]

3. Describe and set forth with particularity all standing orders and nursing guidelines, rules, and regulations applicable to or governing the nursing staff working in the Neonatal Intensive Care Unit at the defendant's hospital on April 6, 1983. Describe these by title, content, and date enacted. If convenient, attach copies of them to your answers to these interrogatories.

4. Describe and set forth with particularity all internal rules and regulations of the hospital applicable to or governing the storage and preservation of fetal monitor tapes. Describe these by title, content, and date enacted. Also:

   A. State when such guidelines, rules, or regulations were first enacted; their content at that time; any amendments, alterations, or changes subsequently made to them; and the date of any such alterations, amendments, or changes.

   B. State which rules or regulations were applicable in April 1983.

   C. Describe precisely and in detail any alterations, amendments, or changes to the April 1983 internal rules, regulations, guidelines, or protocols and when any amendments or changes were made after April 1983.

   D. Attach copies of all such rules, regulations, protocol, and procedures, including all subsequent amendments or changes.

[Questions about Patient Census]

5. State how many patients were in the labor and delivery rooms of the hospital between 1400 hours and 1520 hours on April 6, 1983. State also:

   A. How many deliveries occurred during that time period.

   B. How many of the deliveries were done by c-section and how many were done vaginally.

6. With respect to the hospital facilities on April 6, 1983, state:

   A. How many patients the labor area or rooms accommodated.

B. How many patients the delivery area of labor and delivery accommodated.

C. How many fetal monitor units were available for use in labor and delivery and, of those, how many were external fetal monitor units and how many were internal fetal monitor units.

D. Describe the units available by make, model, and name of manufacturer.

[Questions about Fetal Monitor Equipment]

7. Identify by name, model, manufacturer's title, or other descriptive language the external and internal fetal monitors used on Jeannie Smith and on her fetus in the labor room on April 6, 1983.

8. State whether the defendant-corporation's ob-gyn clinic at Denver Medical Center had the possession or use of fetal monitor units in the clinic in March and April 1983, and if so:

   A. State the number of internal units and the number of external units available in the clinic for use by clinic personnel.

   B. Describe any internal rules, regulations, protocols, guidelines, or policies governing or regulating the storage or preservation of fetal monitor tapes in the ob-gyn clinic in March and April 1983 and thereafter.

[Questions about Preservation and Destruction of Patient Records]

9. Describe any internal rules, regulations, policies, procedures, or protocols which regulated or governed the storage or preservation of patient charts or records resulting from patient care in the defendant-corporation's ob-gyn clinic in March and April 1983 and thereafter.

[Questions about Defendant-Doctors' Hospital Privileges]

10. With regard to each physician named as a defendant in this lawsuit, state:

   A. The nature, type, and class of surgical or other privileges that the physician had at the defendant's hospital in March and April 1983.

   B. Whether any of the defendants were employees of the defendant-corporation; if any were, list their names and official titles or positions, and state whether they received a salary.

   C. The names of all staff committees or administrative committees on which each defendant served as a member or chaired, and the time frame during which each defendant served on such committee or committees.

D. When each defendant applied for staff privileges, what privileges were applied for, and when the privileges were granted or received.

E. Whether any of the defendants has lost staff privileges at the defendant-hospital and, if so, when the staff privileges were terminated, and why.

F. Each defendant's official title or position, if any, at the defendant's hospital or ob-gyn clinic in March and April 1983.

[Questions about Delivery]

11. With regard to the delivery of Baby Smith on April 6, 1983:

A. State the name of every hospital employee who assisted in or was present during the delivery, and the official title or position of that person.

B. State the name of any anesthesiologist, pediatrician, ob-gyn, or other physician present and whether that physician was an employee of the hospital or of the ob-gyn clinic.

C. State whether the umbilical cord or fetal blood from the cord was delivered to the hospital laboratory for analysis and diagnosis. If it was not, state why not.

D. State whether charts and records were kept of the pediatric care rendered in the delivery room and whether those records were completed and charted in the delivery room. If not, state whether such failure violates any internal rules, regulations, or protocol of the hospital.

E. If the failure to chart and record the pediatric care rendered in the delivery room does violate any hospital rules, regulations, or protocol, describe in detail precisely which rules, regulations, or protocols were violated.

[Questions about Prenatal Records]

12. Were ob-gyn clinic records of the defendant-corporation made and charted for Jeannie Smith's early morning visit to the clinic on April 6, 1983, for her subsequent visit later that morning before she was admitted to the defendant-hospital, and for the examinations performed at those times? State:

A. Where those charts and records are currently located, and name their custodian.

B. Precisely what happened to charts and records that were made but no longer exist.

C. Whether if charts and records were not made or no longer exist, any internal rules, regulations, or protocols of the hospital were violated by the failure to chart and record the visits and examinations on the morning of April 6, 1983. State also whether internal rules, regulations, or protocols were violated if such charts and records were not stored and preserved.

D. Precisely which, if any, rules, regulations, or protocols of the defendant-corporation were violated; identify these rules, regulations, or protocols by title, name, and date of enactment.

[Questions about Defendant-Doctors' Privileges]

13. Have the staff privileges of any of the defendant-doctors at any time been revoked or temporarily suspended? If so, state which privileges were revoked or suspended and when and for whom they were revoked or suspended.
14. Did defendant Dr. A have c-section and/or forceps and/or DeLeed suctioning delivery privileges on April 6, 1983?
15. Did the defendant-corporation at any time undertake a case review of deliveries performed or treatment rendered by any of the defendant-physicians? If so, state which defendant-physicians.

[Questions about Fetal Monitor Tapes and Fetal Distress]

16. With regard to application and use of an external or an internal fetal monitor in the labor room on Jeannie Smith and her fetus on April 6, 1983, at the defendant-hospital, state:

A. The name of each nurse or person who first applied the external or the internal electronic fetal monitor and the time that it was applied.

B. The name of each nurse or person who watched, observed, periodically checked, or monitored the information being secured on the external or the internal fetal monitor tape.

C. The observation of each hospital employee who observed the external or the internal fetal monitor tape, the times that each person first observed any abnormalities on the tape, and the abnormalities observed.

D. Whether any abnormal readings observed on the external or the internal fetal monitor tapes were charted anywhere in the nurses' charts and notes or in the hospital records.

(1) If so, state precisely where each abnormality is recorded or charted in such records.

(2) If all abnormalities observed were not noted or charted in the hospital records by the person observing them, state whether the failure to chart violates any internal rule, regulation, guideline, or policy of the hospital. If it does, set forth the number, title, and description of each such rule, regulation, guideline, or policy. If convenient, attach copies of the relevant rule, regulation, guideline, or policy.

17. Following the birth of Baby Smith, were the internal or external fetal monitor tapes or any portion of them reviewed or studied for any purpose by any hospital staff or administrative committee, person, or group of persons? If so, state:

A. The name of each person who participated in the review or study, and the official title or position of each.

B. When the tapes were reviewed or studied and why.

C. Whether any conclusions were reached and, if so, precisely what they were.

D. Whether any written memoranda or notes were made of the observations or review. If they were, describe the written memoranda or notes with sufficient particularity that they can be the subject of a Notice to Produce.

E. Who the custodian is of any such written memoranda or notes and where such memoranda or notes are located.

F. When any person employed by the hospital last saw the external fetal monitor tapes and where the tapes were then located.

G. Whether, based on the defendant-corporation's composite knowledge, any physician or other person reported—independently of the content of the patient's hospital record—that he or she had reviewed, studied, or read the internal or external fetal monitor tapes. If so, state the names of all such persons and precisely what information was given by such persons regarding their observations or study of the fetal monitor tapes.

H. Whether any employee of the defendant-corporation determined that the internal or external fetal monitor tapes were suggestive of fetal distress. If so, state the name of each corporate employee who did so, and for each such employee describe what portion of the fetal monitor tapes he determined to be suggestive of fetal distress.

I. Whether any corporate employee observed any beat-to-beat variability or late decelerations on the external or the internal fetal monitor tape. If any did, describe the nature and extent of any beat-to-beat variability and late decelerations observed.

[Questions about Disappearance of Fetal Monitor Tapes]

18. Did the defendant-corporation, through its officers, agents, and employees, at some point learn that the Jeannie Smith fetal monitor tapes, both external and internal, made on April 6, 1983, were lost or had disappeared and could not be found? If so, state:

    A. When you first heard or understood, and from whom, that the tape's whereabouts were unknown and that the tapes could not be located.

    B. Whether at any time you made an attempt to find or locate the fetal monitor tapes and, if so, what the effort or attempt consisted of, when you made the attempt, and what you discovered or learned. Describe the incident in detail.

    C. Whether at any time you permitted the fetal monitor tapes to be checked out or removed from their place of storage or from the place where they are customarily kept or stored. If you did, state when and where and give the name of the person to whom you gave permission to check out or remove the tapes.

    D. Whether you have heard from any source where the fetal monitor tapes can be located at the present time. If so, set forth the information available to you.

    E. Whether you have been informed by any person that the fetal monitor tapes were lost or destroyed. If so, state the name of the person who gave you this information and state precisely what information was conveyed to you.

    F. Whether you participated, directly or indirectly, in the loss or destruction of the fetal monitor tapes or any portion of the fetal monitor tapes. If so, explain how you participated.

19. Has any committee of the defendant-corporation formally or informally reviewed the subject of hospital or clinic internal rules, regulations, or guidelines related to the preservation or destruction of fetal monitor tapes? Has the preservation or destruction of fetal

monitor tapes been discussed at or been on the agenda for any such committee or group? If so, state:

A. The name of the committee or group, and the names of the persons on the committee or in the group.

B. When and where such meeting or meetings took place.

C. Whether minutes or other written memoranda or documentation was made of the committee proceedings and, if so, the name of the custodian of the minutes or documents, and where the minutes or documents are maintained.

D. Whether you have in your possession a copy of any such minutes or documents.

E. Whether the committee at any time recommended to the hospital that the hospital enact internal rules and regulations or formulate policies regarding the preservation or destruction of fetal monitor tapes. If so, describe the recommendations in detail or attach copies of the recommendations to your answers.

20. In April 1983, did the defendant-corporation have an active ob-gyn hospital staff committee? If so, state:

A. The names of each person on the committee and those who chaired the committee for the five years immediately before April 1983.

B. Whether the ob-gyn staff committee at any time recommended that internal rules, regulations, procedures, or policies be enacted by the hospital regarding the preservation or destruction of fetal monitor tapes. If it did, describe in detail the recommendations it made and when it made them. Attach copies of the recommendations to your answers.

C. Whether the ob-gyn staff committee at any time reviewed preservation or destruction of fetal monitor tapes. If so, state when such matters were reviewed by the committee, what the review consisted of, and the results of that review.

D. Whether the ob-gyn staff committee at any time recommended to the defendant-corporation that internal rules, regulations, or policies be enacted and enforced with respect to the preservation or destruction of fetal monitor tapes. If so, what recommendations were made, when were they made, and what action was taken by the defendant-corporation?

21. Are you aware, directly or indirectly, of the loss or destruction at your hospital or ob-gyn clinic of the fetal monitor tapes of any patient other than Jeannie Smith? If so, state:
    A. Approximately how many such incidents have been called to your attention, how you learned of such incidents, and what recommendations or action, if any, you took on learning about them.
    B. Whether any or all of such incidents were a topic of discussion at any hospital staff or administrative committee meeting as far as you know. If they were, name the administrative committee or staff committee and describe when such discussions took place.
22. To your knowledge, has the defendant-corporation or any member of its staff received criticism or complaints from any source with respect to the failure to preserve fetal monitor tapes or the loss or destruction of fetal monitor tapes? If so, state:
    A. The nature of the criticism or complaints, when they occurred or were received, and how many you are aware of.
    B. What action, if any, was taken by the ob-gyn staff at the hospital, by the hospital administration, or by the defendant-corporation with reference to such criticism or complaints.
23. Are you familiar with the guidelines and recommendations of the American College of Obstetricians and Gynecologists (ACOG) with respect to the storage and preservation of fetal monitor tapes and records? If so:
    A. When did you first become aware of the guidelines and recommendations?
    B. Did you at any time become familiar with those guidelines and recommendations as contained in *Standards for Obstetric-Gynecologic Services* (ACOG, 5th Edition, 1982)? If so, when did you first become aware of them?
    C. Did you at any time consider enacting as hospital policy the guidelines and recommendations of ACOG with respect to the storage and preservation of fetal monitor tapes and records? If so, state when and the name of each person who participated in such consideration.
24. In April 1983, were external fetal monitor tapes or internal fetal monitor tapes considered by the Denver Memorial Ob-Gyn Clinic to be a part of the mother's clinic or hospital official records, or a

part of the infant's clinic or hospital official records after birth, or both? Also state:

A. Whether your opinion or impression was based on any known clinic or hospital policy, internal rule, or regulation. If so, set forth the internal rule, regulation, or policy.

B. Whether your opinion or impression was based on general procedures or custom or habit. If so, set forth the general procedures, custom, or habit at that time.

25. In April 1983 and before, were you familiar with any hospital accreditation standards regarding the storage and preservation of fetal monitor tapes? If so, state:

A. Any accreditation standards you were familiar with, and when and how you first became familiar with them.

B. Whether, to your knowledge, the defendant-hospital at any time violated such standards. If so, state when and under what circumstances.

26. Has the hospital administration, through its officers, agents, and employees, at any time received a complaint from any physician with respect to the failure to preserve fetal monitor tapes or microfilm copies or to make other copies of fetal monitor tapes to preserve their content? If so:

A. On approximately how many occasions has the hospital received such criticism or complaints?

B. When was each such criticism or complaint made?

C. Who received the criticism or complaints?

D. Were any of the criticisms, complaints, or statements made in writing? If so, do you have copies?

E. If you have copies of any complaints or documents, where are they stored? If convenient, attach copies.

F. If you do not attach copies, then set forth the substance of any complaints or statements made.

G. What response did you make to each statement or complaint? Are those responses in writing? If so, where are they stored?

[Questions about Disappearance of Clinic Records]

27. State precisely and in detail what system and what mechanical equipment was used by the defendant-corporation for the dictation of patient hospital records in April 1983. In that regard:

A. Was a central system used?

B. Were any "stat" lines used within that system? If so, what documents were to be dictated by staff physicians or other persons on the "stat" lines?

C. How and when was a physician informed by the hospital that a patient's records were incomplete?

D. What privileges were temporarily cancelled if a physician failed to complete hospital charts and records after being informed by the hospital that a patient's hospital charts and records were incomplete?

E. Identify any hospital rule, regulation, guideline, policy, or procedure which governed when and under what circumstances hospital records had to be complete after a patient's discharge from the hospital.

F. On April 6, 1983, was there any mechanical failure in the dictation and recording systems used at the hospital for the dictation of hospital records? If so, describe the mechanical failure or breakdown in detail, and state when and by whom the repairs were made.

G. Between March 25 and April 15, 1983, was all dictation from the hospital system or systems typed in-house? If not, state:

(1) What independent service was used and on what dates.

(2) Why an independent service was used during that time, and whether it was used in conjunction with in-house typists.

28. Were ob-gyn clinic records of the defendant-corporation made and charted for Jeannie Smith's telephone calls to the clinic on April 6, 1983, and during the week before?

A. If so, where are the charts or records currently located, and who is their custodian?

B. If charts or records were made, but no longer exist, precisely what happened to the charts or records?

C. Were internal rules, regulations, or protocols violated if charts or records were not made or no longer exist?

D. If any internal rules, regulations, or protocols of the defendant-corporation were violated, precisely which rules, regulations, or protocols were violated? Please list them by title, name, and date of enactment.

[Questions about Insurance Coverage]

29. State the name(s) of the insurance company or companies which insured the Denver Memorial Hospital and/or the Denver Memorial Ob-Gyn clinic for the matters set forth in the complaint and, for each such company, state the name of the company, the type of coverage it provided (e.g., primary, co-insurance, excess, or umbrella coverage), the policy limits, and any deductible.

B.3 OUTLINE OF DEPOSITION TESTIMONY GIVEN BY A DEFENSE EXPERT

The following is an outline of a deposition taken by plaintiff's counsel in an obstetrical negligence case. The deponent, Dr. Black, was the defendant's expert witness on causation.

Background Information

Dr. Black is a child neurologist at Babies Hospital in Brinkton and is not a neonatologist (p. 3). His experience and training in perinatology consists of what he received in medical school, his internship, and his residency (pp. 3–4). He is board certified as a pediatric neurologist, does not have a subspecialty, and spends the largest portion of his time in general child neurology (p. 4). His vitae is marked Exhibit 1 (p. 4).

He received a letter from defense counsel's paralegal dated 6/13/89, which is marked Exhibit 2. He then talked about the case on the telephone with defense counsel, whom he did not know (p. 5). He also received the enclosures listed in the letter of 6/13/89 (pp. 6–7).

His assignment was to look at causation. Upon reviewing the information enclosed with Exhibit 2, he arrived at preliminary opinions (p. 8).

Opinions

He concluded that the patient had a placenta abruptio, which caused the bleeding that prompted her to go to the hospital. He further concluded that the intrauterine asphyxial event was related to the placenta abruptio "as part of the whole constellation of findings" (p. 8).

There were other things that could have contributed to the intrauterine hypoxia, but there was no evidence of those things in the record (p. 9).

He was unable to conclude when the hypoxic event occurred (p. 9). He then received the depositions of Dr. G, Dr. E, and Dr. R, and his review of those depositions did not change his preliminary conclusions (p. 10).

When asked for his present opinion regarding the most probable cause of Cassie's condition as discovered at birth and thereafter, he stated, "I don't think I can come up with a probable cause," and explained, "The child's prematurity and the complications associated with prematurity, the asphyxia and the problems that attend asphyxia, and then whatever may have occurred at some point where we don't have any clear information about, or a genetic illness—any of these could be the cause" (p. 11).

When asked which of Cassie's problems he would relate solely to prematurity that would be unrelated to asphyxia, he stated, "I can't make that distinction" (p. 11).

When asked if Cassie had any problems he would relate to asphyxia as opposed to prematurity, he stated, "Only the measures that we do on a young infant shortly after birth. But in terms of long-term effects, I can't make a distinction there either" (p. 11).

He found no evidence or history of genetic illness that caused or contributed to her problems (p. 11).

He found no indication of a causal relationship between Cassie's problems and any other events, by history or medical records, other than prematurity, asphyxia, or both (pp. 11–12).

Gestational Age

He has no reason to question or dispute the maturity rating of 31 weeks at birth (p. 12), and he does not know what the margin of error is on that particular maturity rating. But Cassie was average for gestational age and weight and height (p. 12).

He was asked, "In 1984, in the absence of intrauterine asphyxia, would you expect a 31-weeks gestational age newborn to have the problems that Cassie had at birth?" (p. 12), and he stated that a child of this age and weight generally does well and that a majority of them are normal children "with perhaps some minor abnormalities that may or may not show up until they get to school age" but that a significant minority can have severe problems like Cassie's (p. 13).

He stated that for the minority born with Cassie's problems at that age, there are a number of things that can be the cause, including infection of the uterus or the placenta, or simply prematurity (p. 14). He also stated that trauma to the uterus or uterine ischemia can result in some degree of asphyxia to the fetus, "but not necessarily." For example, cocaine can cause uterine ischemia resulting in an early onset of labor (p. 15). When asked how he distinguishes between uterine ischemia and uterine hypoxia, he stated, "I think the net effect is very similar" (p. 15).

He stated that an onset of seizures at age 7 hours in a 31-weeker of average size and weight would generally not occur in the absence of intrauterine hypoxia because "seizures are not a sole manifestation of prematurity" (p. 16). But then he stated that what Cassie evidenced at 7 hours of age may not necessarily have been seizures and that sometimes what looks clinically like a seizure is not supported by EEG (p. 16), particularly if it is a singular event, as it was in this case (p. 16). But he could not say with a reasonable degree of medical probability that she did not have seizure activity. He said, "I just don't know" (p. 17).

Infections

When asked if an infected placenta was a cause of Cassie's newborn problems or condition, he stated that the path report showed chorioamnionitis, but that with no cultures, he doesn't know whether the condition was caused by an infection (p. 17). The records show no evidence that the newborn suffered from a fetal infection; furthermore, the newborn showed no signs of infection (p. 18).

Rupture of Membranes

Based on the information he reviewed, he doesn't believe that the rupture of membranes occurred at any time before the mother was taken to the operating room for a c-section (p. 18).

Fetal Alcohol Syndrome

He saw nothing in the charts or records that would suggest that the child had fetal alcohol syndrome (pp. 18–19).

Premature Labor

He does not know what caused the mother to go into premature labor and does not relate the mother's use of alcohol during pregnancy to any of the newborn's problems (p. 19). Nor does he relate her use of tobacco during pregnancy to any of the newborn's problems (p. 19).

Heparin

When asked if he could relate the mother's subcutaneous heparin therapy during pregnancy to any of the newborn's problems, he stated that he could not answer questions concerning the effect of heparin in an obstetrical situation, that he didn't know whether heparin therapy during pregnancy increases the risk of placenta abruptio (p. 19), and that he didn't know whether that therapy could interfere with clot formation or spontaneous healing of a placenta abruptio (pp. 19–20).

Fetal Distress

From the charts and records there is no indication of fetal distress on the 16th. He did not look at the fetal monitor strips, and he is not an expert on interpreting strips (p. 20).

Hypothetically, if the fetal heart rate baseline was approximately 130 on the morning of the 16th with good reactivity and good variability, that would be an indication that the fetus was not under stress or distress at that time (pp. 20–1).

Maternal Blood Pressure

He believes the mother's blood pressure remained pretty constant through the 16th and the morning hours of the 17th (p. 21). He looked at the prenatal blood pressures, which remained pretty constant with an average of 110/60, which is normal for a prenatal patient (p. 22).

A slight decrease in the mother's hemoglobin and hematocrit would not trouble him if she started off at her normal value (p. 23).

If she had a decrease in temperature to 97 degrees accompanied by some slight decrease in hemoglobin, hematocrit and blood pressure, that combination would trouble him if she showed some physiologic response that suggested she was hypovolemic and anemic. "Then I think that is a potential source for a problem," he said (pp. 23–4).

Tachycardia

He doesn't know how to interpret the increase in heart rate the morning of the 17th; nor does he know whether that indicates that the child was stressed (p. 24).

He doesn't know if a change in fetal heart rate baseline from 130 to 165 plus for a sustained period of time is consistent with placenta abruptio (pp. 24–5).

He can relate bradycardia and perhaps the variable decelerations to a stressed infant, but he doesn't know whether the infant's stress is also related directly to the placenta abruptio in contrast to anything else (p. 25).

Aspiration of Amniotic Fluid

He understands the amniotic fluid was bloody at the time of delivery (pp. 25–6), and he is not sure whether the records showed evidence that the fetus had aspirated amniotic fluid containing blood in utero, "but normal respiratory movements would move amniotic fluid in and out of the child's lungs early on" (p. 26).

If the newborn passed bloody stools, that would be consistent with swallowing blood but not necessarily with aspirating blood (p. 26).

The fact that Dr. Whitting removed blood with a DeLee catheter only indicates there was blood in the oral pharynx; it does not necessarily indicate there was blood in the lungs (p. 27). But that does raise a question as to whether blood was also in the lungs, and the records show that blood was obtained from suctioning the trachea (p. 27).

When asked "If the newborn was not breathing at the time of birth and had no respirations, would you expect the aspiration of blood to have occurred by the infant's gasping in utero as opposed to having occurred after birth?", he stated, "It could occur at either time," explaining that if they put a mask over the nose and mouth during resuscitation, blood in the oral pharynx could have been forced into the lungs (p. 28), but there is no evidence that they did or did not bag the child, and the very first note on 5/17 at 1630 hours was that the baby was intubated at 30–40 seconds of age by Dr. Whitting (p. 28).

Dr. Black understands that a potential problem with intrauterine hypoxia is that it can result in the infant gasping in uterine and hence aspirating amniotic fluid, "but infants under normal circumstances can also have respiratory efforts in utero" (p. 28). He stated that such respiratory efforts in utero are normal (pp. 28–9).

When asked if it is true that aspirating amniotic fluid in utero is considered to be an abnormal condition as opposed to a normal one, he stated that it produces problems "if there is meconium and the child aspirates that" (p. 29). You shouldn't see meconium in the lungs of a newborn. "Most of the meconium occurs just before delivery or as a sign of the child being stressed" (p. 29).

When asked if there was an indication of fetal stress or distress at any time before delivery, he stated, "not clearly" (p. 29), and he stated that he didn't know how to interpret the tachycardia (p. 30).

He was asked to assume that the FHR baseline on the morning of the 16th was 130, and that it increased so that it was above 160 by the morning of the 17th and remained above 160, gradually increasing to 170–180 for a period of at least 3 hours before the mother was taken to the delivery room. He was asked to assume that at least 15 minutes before delivery, the tachycardia changed to severe variable decelerations just before the fetal monitor tape was removed 14 or 15 minutes before delivery, that a spinal anesthetic was administered, and that the FHR baseline dropped to the 70–80 range, where it remained until the time of delivery. He was asked if that painted a picture of fetal distress (pp. 30–1), and he stated that he didn't know what the tachycardia represented, but that when there were variable decelerations and a heart rate of 70, that "certainly would raise the flag that the child was under stress at that point" (p. 31).

He doesn't know whether a decrease in the beat-to-beat variability when the severe variable decelerations are taking place is further evidence of fetal distress (pp. 31–2).

He doesn't know what the possible causes of fetal tachycardia are other than anemia (p. 32).

Intrauterine Asphyxia

He stated that the blood gas following birth of 6.9 with a base excess of –23 was "probably a manifestation of the child's asphyxia" and that early pH's would correlate with intrauterine asphyxia (p. 32).

He relates the newborn's neurological status to prematurity and asphyxia (p. 33).

When asked if he would expect a 31-weeker of average size and weight to have pupils fixed and dilated with poor response to light at the time of birth in the absence of asphyxia, he stated, "There may be other causes for it, but certainly asphyxia would be one of the considerations" (p. 33).

The newborn's hypotonic condition at birth could be a manifestation of prematurity, or it could be related to asphyxia; all prematurely born infants have some degree of hypotonia (pp. 33–4).

He relates the intracranial hemorrhage to prematurity, but when asked if he would expect a 31-weeker of average size and weight to have an intracranial hemorrhage in the absence of hypoxia or asphyxia, he states statistically that it could happen but it is less likely to happen with a 31-weeker than with a younger, smaller infant" (p. 34). But it was "an uncommon phenomenon" for a 31-weeker of average size and weight to have an intracranial hemorrhage in the absence of intrauterine hypoxia (p. 34).

When he was asked, "In the absence of intrauterine hypoxia or asphyxia, what are the possible causes of intracranial hemorrhage in a 31-weeker of average size and weight?", he stated, "Just prematurity in and of itself, respiratory distress, changes in the child's blood pressure, changes in the child's blood volume, and changes in the child's acid base balance." He said that conceivably there could be vascular malformations, but that would be highly unlikely (p. 35). He doesn't know whether Cassie had respiratory distress at birth that was unrelated to asphyxia, he doesn't know what caused Cassie's persistent fetal circulation, and he doesn't know whether intrauterine aspiration of blood can cause persistent fetal circulation (p. 35).

He doesn't know whether Cassie had hydrocephalus following birth (p. 36).

He doesn't know what caused her heart murmur, but children who are premature with respiratory problems will have patent ductus, which can cause a heart murmur (p. 36).

He would not expect an infant who aspirated blood in utero to develop respiratory problems although meconium could cause such problems (p. 36). There was no meconium in the amniotic fluid noted at the time of delivery (p. 36).

Apgar Scores

When asked if the Apgar scores of 1 and 3 are consistent with intrauterine asphyxia, he stated that they are in a term child, but in a premature child it is more difficult to correlate the two (p. 37). When asked what he would expect the Apgar scores to be in a 31-weeker severely asphyxiated, he stated, "They certainly could be 1 and 3" (p. 37).

Maternal vs. Fetal Blood

He doesn't know whether the blood found in the amniotic fluid at birth was maternal, fetal, or a combination of the two (p. 37).

Causation

In the absence of intrauterine asphyxia or hypoxia in this case, he would have expected Cassie to be a normal, healthy, 31-weeker at the time of birth (p. 38).

Onset of Labor

He doesn't know whether the bleeding resulting from the placenta abruptio caused the onset of pain and contractions—that is an obstetrical question (pp. 38–9).

In his experience, an irritable uterus can result from placenta abruptio, but that is still more of an obstetrical question (p. 39).

Prognosis

He has no opinion on Cassie's life expectancy other than that children who are this severely injured often have a shortened life-expectancy, and that theoretically, children of this age can live into their 40s and 50s with good medical care (pp. 39–40). He does not have enough information about the child's course to the present day to give a prognosis on life expectancy with a reasonable degree of medical probability (p. 40).

He is not critical of the pediatric care rendered following delivery and is not going to offer opinions on the pediatric care (p. 40).

Likewise, he will not be offering opinions on the standard of care of Dr. Hubert (pp. 40–1).

Causation

He believes the fetal bradycardia can be in part attributed to the spinal anesthetic. When asked, "If the placental blood flow has already been impaired by placenta abruptio, can a spinal anesthetic further impair that blood flow?", he stated that that is an obstetric-anesthetic type of question that he cannot answer (p. 41).

When he states that he believes the spinal anesthetic can contribute to the fetal bradycardia, that's just based on knowledge he's acquired over the years. He doesn't know how that comes about; that is beyond his field of expertise (pp. 41–2). He cannot isolate Cassie's problems at birth to a single cause. The two most likely causes are related to prematurity and to asphyxia (p. 43). He found nothing in the records or in the general medical history that would permit him to state that there was some other likely cause in addition to prematurity and asphyxia. He says that this is "more a reflection of [his] ignorance" (p. 43).

Hydrocephalus

There were ultrasound changes, but the CAT scans did not describe evidence of hydrocephalus. He would prefer to rely on a CAT scan and would be very suspicious of an ultrasound (p. 44).

Causation

Defense counsel tries to rehabilitate the witness on his earlier testimony that in the absence of hypoxia or asphyxia he would expect Cassie to be a normal, healthy child (pp. 44–5). Dr. Black adds that there is a distinct minority of children born prematurely who do not suffer from asphyxia and who are neurologically abnormal (p. 45).

B.4 DEPOSITION OUTLINE FOR DEFENSE EXPERT WITNESSES

This is an outline prepared by the authors, which they have used as a guide when deposing defense expert witnesses in obstetrical negligence cases. Not every question needs to be asked in every case; rather, this outline should serve as a loose checklist. The structure departs from the basic outline format in that some items are posed as questions or complete sentences, while other items are denoted only by key words. The outline encompasses a wide scope of inquiries and can be used as a guide to obtain thorough information in your depositions.

A. Introduction
   1. Identify the attorney and her client.
   2. If the witness doesn't understand a question or wishes to explain an answer at any time, please advise.
   3. Has the witness had a chance to discuss this with the defense attorney?
   4. Does the witness understand the importance of this deposition?

B. Information Reviewed for Deposition
   1. Have you had the opportunity to review:
      a. Hospital records?
      b. X rays?
      c. Clinic records?
   2. Please identify or provide copies of all articles, papers, books, treatises, or journals that you reviewed before this deposition.
      a. Mark as exhibits all documents produced, and ask the reporter to please make sure a copy of the deposition containing the same is provided to your office.

C. Implied Bias Questions
   1. Have you ever been asked to evaluate a potential medical negligence case on behalf of a defense law firm?
      a. Dates
      b. Number of cases
      c. For defense or plaintiff
      d. Opinions regarding the presence or absence of negligence in those cases
   2. Have you ever been asked to evaluate a potential medical negligence case on behalf of any insurance company?
      a. Dates
      b. Number of cases
      c. For defense or plaintiff
      d. Opinions regarding the presence or absence of negligence in those cases
   3. Before today, have you ever testified in a deposition in a medical negligence case of any kind?

   a. Do you have a copy of the deposition? If so, please provide it.
   b. How many times
   c. For plaintiff or defense
   d. Opinions regarding the presence or absence of negligence in those cases
4. Have you ever testified in a court of law or arbitration in connection with a medical negligence case?
   a. Do you have a copy of the testimony? If so, please provide it.
   b. How many times
   c. For plaintiff or defense
   d. Opinions regarding the presence or absence of negligence in those cases
5. Have you ever been involved politically in medical negligence legislation or other activity regarding medical negligence matters?
   a. Please explain the circumstances.
6. Have you, or has any professional group to which you belong, ever been sued for medical negligence?
   a. Dates
   b. Nature of cases
   c. Claims of negligence
   d. Defending attorneys
   e. Outcomes of cases
7. Apart from medical negligence, have you ever given your deposition in any kind of personal injury case?
   a. How many times?
   b. For the defense or the plaintiff? Please specify percentages.
8. Apart from medical negligence, have you ever testified in a court of law in any personal injury case?
   a. How many times?
   b. For the defense or the plaintiff? Please specify percentages.
9. Have you ever served on a morbidity, mortality, or surgical committee or any other peer review committee charged with the duty of evaluating medical care by a physician?
   a. If so, please provide full details.

10. Has (defense lawyer and firm) ever acted as your lawyer?
    a. Dates and names of attorneys
    b. Nature and outcome of case
    c. Have copy available of deposition taken

D. Answers to Interrogatories
1. Review answers to interrogatories
    a. Qualifications and training
    b. Medical license and hospital privileges
    c. Special incident hearings
    d. Clinic or other records—changes or alterations
    e. Causation or opinions

E. General Qualifications
1. Get curriculum vitae.
2. Where did you do your residency? Who was the chief of the residency program?
    a. What texts were used at that time?

F. Experts
1. Relationship to other defendants or hospital involved
2. Regarding any defense or plaintiff expert:
    a. Do you know any of them?
    b. If so, what is your relationship with them?
    c. Have you discussed this particular case with them?
    d. Have you seen any reports or letters from them regarding this case?
3. Who do you consider to be experts who are highly qualified regarding this matter?
    a. Have you contacted any of these people or asked a lawyer to do so?

G. Medical Literature
1. What professional journals do you receive in the medical area involved in this case?
    a. Have you read these before this deposition?
2. Are you aware of any statistical study, article, paper, research document, textbook, or treatise containing information that you would regard as being reasonably reliable concerning the general subject of this case?

a. Has there been any review of the above in connection with this case that you have not previously identified?

3. What books do you have in your office on this subject?

a. Have you read or examined any of them in regard to this case or deposition?

H. Prenatal Care Given Patient

1. Start with the first entry in the clinic record and review up to the relevant date.
2. Review all medical background before the relevant date.
3. Read all handwritten entries.
4. Review mother evaluation
   a. Height
   b. Weight
   c. Blood pressure
   d. Risk assessment and reason for same
5. Review fetal evaluation
   a. Fundal height
   b. Fetal weight
   c. FHR
   d. Station
   e. Effacement
   f. Dilatation
   g. Vertex
   h. Fetal assessment test—amniocentesis, ultrasound, estriols, Rh titer, etc.
6. Discuss expected problems or special instructions

I. Labor

1. Admission assessment
   a. Time of onset of labor
   b. Observation and evaluation of fetal status—medical or obstetric complications
   c. Contraction on admission—time of onset, frequency, duration, and quality
   d. Membranes on admission—time of rupture and condition of fluid

e. Maternal assessment

f. Fetal assessment and evaluation

2. General labor record

a. Onset of first stage of labor

b. Onset of second stage of labor

c. Onset of third stage of labor

d. Fetal heart rate monitoring

e. Cervical dilation

f. Stations

g. Effacement

h. Contractions—frequency, duration, and quality

J. Delivery

1. Time when patient was moved to the delivery room

a. Cervical dilation

b. Contractions—frequency, duration, and quality

c. Fetal heart rate

d. Station

2. Vacuum extraction, forceps, or cesarean

3. Complications with delivery

K. Newborn Care

1. Apgar scoring

a. Who did the scoring?

b. Was it reviewed by anyone else?

2. Resuscitation, bag, suction, intubation

3. Weight at birth

4. Times of events

5. At what time was the infant moved to the nursery or the intensive care nursery?

L. Informed Consent

1. Advice given patient

a. Nature of proposed treatment

b. Anticipated results

c. Risks of same

d. Chance of success or complication

e. Anticipated benefits if successful

2. Patient's response or reaction to the advice

3. Any memorandum, signed consent forms or the like, or entries in clinic records regarding the advice and the patient's response to the advice

4. Total time spent in advising the patient on informed consent issues

a. Who was present?

5. Miscellaneous

a. Was the patient surprised with the results?

b. Rare occurrence situation

M. Negligence Claims

1. Review claims of negligence with the witness

2. What is your explanation?

3. Are there other possible explanations that you considered but rejected? Are there some possibilities that you did not consider?

a. Describe them fully.

b. Give reasons for your rejections.

4. In your opinion was there a failure to exercise reasonable care in this case?

a. *Harris v. Groth,* 663 P.2d 113, 116 (Wash. 1983), holds that a health-care provider must exercise the degree of "care, skill, and learning expected of a reasonably prudent health-care provider." Further, under *May v. Zorman,* 487 P.2d 270, 272 (Wash. Ct. App. 1971), defendant-doctors must answer questions regarding "findings and actual cause of treatments, their diagnoses, and their opinions" regarding negligence.

5. Are you aware of different approaches used by other competent physicians under similar circumstances?

6. Do you claim that the doctor's conduct was just a "judgment call" and not negligence? Are there physicians who would disagree?

7. Have you discussed your findings, opinions, or conclusions with any other physicians before today?

a. What were your full reasons and circumstances for doing so?

8. Did you discuss this case with any other physicians before arriving at your findings, opinions, or conclusions?

    a. What were your full reasons and circumstances for doing so?

9. Are you aware of any other physicians who may have reviewed this case?

    a. What were their full reasons and circumstances for doing so? Please list the physicians' names.

N. Diagnosis and Prognosis of Infant

1. Do you have any opinions based on reasonable medical certainty regarding the life expectancy of the infant?

    a. Please state all opinions.

    b. State the basis for those opinions.

    c. Identify all articles, books, papers, etc., utilized or relied on, and mark them as exhibits.

2. Do you have any opinions based on reasonable medical certainty regarding the prognosis for this infant?

    a. Please state all opinions.

    b. State the basis for those opinions.

    c. Identify all articles, books, papers, etc., utilized or relied on, and mark them as exhibits.

3. Do you have any opinions based on reasonable medical certainty regarding the future treatment required for this infant?

    a. Please state all opinions.

    b. State the basis for those opinions.

    c. Identify all articles, books, papers, etc., utilized or relied on, and mark them as exhibits.

4. Do you have any opinions based on reasonable medical certainty regarding the future cost of care for this infant?

    a. Please state all opinions.

    b. State the basis for those opinions.

    c. Identify all articles, books, papers, etc., utilized or relied on, and mark them as exhibits.

5. Do you have any opinions based on reasonable medical certainty regarding any additional diagnostic or other studies that you feel should be done or might be done to help medical professionals more accurately arrive at opinions in this case?
   a. Please state all opinions.
   b. State the basis for those opinions.
   c. Identify all articles, books, papers, etc., utilized or relied on, and mark them as exhibits.
6. When did you last examine the infant? What was the result of that examination?
7. When did you last examine the mother? What was the result of that examination?

O. Miscellaneous Questions
Note: Kipling once wrote

> I keep six honest serving men
> (They taught me all I knew);
> Their names are What and Why and When
> And How and Where and Who.[1]

In a similar light, one could say that the four honest serving men for doctors are Inspection, Palpation, Percussion, and Auscultation.

1. Do you have any information or any reason to suspect or believe that the records of this mother or infant may have contained erroneous entries or misstatements of facts? If so, please specifically identify and explain the circumstances.
2. Do you have any information or any reason to suspect or believe that the records of this mother or infant may have contained altered or changed entries? If so, please specifically identify and explain the circumstances.
3. Do you have any opinion as to whether some other physician, nurse, or health-care provider who was not a named defendant in this lawsuit may have been negligent in caring for the mother or infant and may have contributed to the injuries in this case? If so, please identify such person and state the full circumstances.

---

1 RUDYARD KIPLING, JUST SO STORIES 57 (1974).

4. Are you aware of any special investigation, special incident, or other inquiry made by the hospital or its staff regarding this incident not found in hospital records?

5. Are you aware of any personal notes or diary entries of any kind regarding a nurse or doctor who might have been involved with this patient that are not found in the hospital records?

6. Res Ipsa Loquitur: Would this result be expected normally in the absence of negligence?

   a. How common is this occurrence?

   b. How many times in your personal experience have you observed it? Over how many years?

APPENDIX C

PREPARING FOR DEPOSITIONS

C.1 PREPARING FOR DEFENSE QUESTIONING OF PARENTS IN A BIRTH-INJURY CASE

In preparing your clients for their depositions, it is helpful to have a checklist of questions commonly asked by defense counsel. You can refer to the list when instructing the clients on how to properly respond to any questions that they might be asked during the deposition.

For example, in medical and hospital negligence cases involving birth injuries, there are some standard questions that are usually asked of the involved parents. The defense asks questions in an attempt to discover anything besides health-care negligence that might explain the birth injuries. The defense also asks questions that might show that the parents, rather than the health-care providers, are somehow responsible for the birth injuries.

The parents must be prepared to accurately respond to such questions. If the parents are not prepared and they inadvertently provide inaccurate information, it could harm their case. The following is an outline of the areas of inquiry parents may be subject to during deposition in a birth-injury case.

1. Birth date
2. Marital status (i.e., living together, divorced)
3. Employment
4. Education
5. Pregnancy information
    a. How the mother learned she was pregnant
    b. Whether pregnancy was planned
    c. Whether contraception was used before the pregnancy

(1) Type of contraception

(2) Length of time used

(3) Details associated with the use of any contraceptive device involved

d. Date of first consultation, name of physician

e. Whether the mother became aware of any problems she was having with the pregnancy

f. Use of marijuana or recreational drugs of any kind during pregnancy

g. Use of alcohol during pregnancy, frequency of use

h. Urinary tract infection problems during pregnancy

i. Problems of vaginal discharge during pregnancy

j. Problems of nausea and vomiting during pregnancy

k. Whether the mother suffered from edema during pregnancy

l. Whether the mother developed any problems during her pregnancy that may have indicated a possibility that the baby might be born prematurely

m. Whether the mother remembers anything abnormal occurring during pregnancy

6. Any family history of anyone born with mental retardation, cerebral palsy, or other birth defects, including full details (cause, severity, extent of problem, identification of relatives involved, age, marital history, etc.)

   a. Complete review of all brothers and sisters in parents' families as well as their marriages and children. This will involve marital history, ages of children, and whether children have any health problems of any nature

   b. Whether the mother ever took birth-control pills

   c. Prior abortions or voluntary terminations of pregnancies

   d. Whether parents had a birth plan, and if so, where it is presently located, what it provided, and records of full discussions with doctor regarding it (Of particular interest would be the parents' attitude about monitoring during labor.)

7. Details of the birth and events following the birth

   a. Whether the mother complained of monitoring devices during labor and asked that they not be used

b. Whether the mother wanted a "nonintervention" type labor and delivery

c. Whether the obstetrician ever said anything to the mother about anything unusual during the prenatal course

d. Whether the parents have any pamphlets, books, handouts, or printed material from any prenatal class, and if so, where they are presently located

e. Whether the mother read any books or pamphlets during pregnancy about labor and delivery, and if so, the titles of books and other materials she read

f. How labor started

g. What was done after labor started

h. What the mother recalls about contractions becoming intense, and what happened at that point

i. What the mother remembers happening throughout labor, including anything anybody said, what monitoring there was, and other details (Of interest would be the parents' knowledge of the time when anything occurred, whether the parents checked a clock or had some other way of knowing when any event occurred. This will be tied into the hospital record entries.)

j. What was said by any nurse or doctor during labor or delivery

k. What nurses or doctors did in the way of listening to heart rate or monitoring

l. What time the mother was taken to the delivery room

m. What time the obstetrician, anesthesiologist, or other doctor arrived

n. What occurred in connection with delivery

o. Whether the parent knows the time of delivery by looking at a watch or a clock or from what was said

p. What the doctors or nurses said after delivery

q. When and how the parents learned of a problem, and how long after the delivery the parents began to ask questions

r. When the parents first saw the infant

s. What observations the parents had of the infant after that time, including whether they saw any problems

t. Discussion with any doctors or nurses after the birth about the cause of the problem, and the exact circumstances surrounding such discussions

u. Discussions or comments by the doctor about vaginal delivery as opposed to c-section delivery or other types of delivery while mother was in labor

8. Whether the parents have talked with any physician who has been critical of the hospital or the doctors in their care of the mother during her pregnancy, labor or delivery
   a. Describe all conversations
   b. Identify the persons who made the statements
9. Whether parents have talked to any nurse who has been critical of the hospital or the doctors in their care of the mother in her pregnancy, labor, or delivery
   a. Describe all conversations
   b. Identify the persons who made the statements
10. Whether the parents have reviewed the medical records themselves
11. Whether the parents have any criticism of the doctor's or hospital's care of the baby after the baby was born
12. The baby's condition and the requirements of the parents' care for the baby at the time of deposition
    a. How the parents feed him, whether he can chew, description of his eating ability
    b. Amount of time required
    c. Whether the child goes to day care or special ed, and if so, when he arrives and when he is picked up
    d. Amount of time the parents spend with the child on weekends (The purpose of question 12.d. is to show that for a large part of the time, the baby is with somebody else, and therefore the parents don't have the responsibility of taking care of the infant.)
13. The health of the baby up to the present time, the baby's present doctor, the present status of the baby's condition, a description of any seizure disorder and the type of medications being taken
14. Whether the parents are aware that the baby has any physical abnormalities, heart problems, liver problems, kidney problems, or any other problems

15. How frequently the baby sleeps through the night and how frequently he does not, and a description of what happens and what has to be done
16. Whether the doctors have told the parents whether there is any hope that the baby will be able to talk
17. The kinds of movements the baby makes
18. Whether parents have made any plans about the baby's future; whether they have decided what they are going to do in the long run (The purpose of this question is to determine whether or not the parents plan to have the child institutionalized.)
19. Whether parents have help in the home with the baby at the present time
20. Whether parents make their own baby food or use canned baby food
21. Whether either parent has ever been under the care of a psychologist or psychiatrist
22. How the situation has affected each parent's life with his or her spouse
23. Whether parents plan to have other children
24. Whether there is anything else about this baby's birth that has affected the parents in any way
25. Previous marriages and past marital history
26. Occupation of each parent (and present spouse if applicable)
27. Whether either parent has had any serious problems, such as any major physical disabilities or mental problems of any kind
28. Whether either parent has been under the care of a psychologist or psychiatrist because of the birth injuries to the child
29. Whether parents plan to see a psychiatrist or psychologist
30. Whether either parent has consulted anyone regarding own mental health, spouse's mental health, or marital problems
31. Whether either parent has ever been hospitalized for any major illness
32. Whether either parent is aware of any problems with the child's birth that also occurred with the parent's own birth
33. Whether either parent spent an extended period of time in the hospital at his or her own birth
34. Whether either parent's mother suffered from any major disease
35. Each parent's state of health

36. In the father's own words, what he remembers of the mother's pregnancy, including problems or anything significant, such as abnormal weight gain
37. Whether the mother suffered any traumas, such as falls, automobile accidents, or anything of that nature
38. Whether the mother complained to the father of vaginal discharge or cramping during pregnancy
39. Whether the mother suffered any contractions in a period of a month or so before labor
40. What the father remembers about how active the baby was during pregnancy
41. Whether the mother smoked cigarettes or drank alcohol during the first three months of pregnancy
42. Whether the mother used sleeping pills during the first three months of pregnancy
43. Whether the mother took any medication of any kind at the time she became pregnant
44. Whether the mother used drugs of any nature before or during her pregnancy
45. What the father recalls about any classes taken regarding prenatal matters
46. Whether or not the parents planned to have a natural childbirth
47. What the father knew about or was advised about monitoring
48. Whether either parent observed any labor or delivery or took any tours of any hospital labor or delivery rooms before the birth of their own child
49. How long it took from the time the doctors decided to deliver to the time of actual delivery
50. Whether the parents had faith in the obstetrician and felt he was a good obstetrician
51. How the parents feel about doctors in general and felt about doctors in general at the time of the birth, especially whether they trusted the doctor's judgment or not
52. Whether the parents thought there was an emergency situation at the time of delivery
53. Opinions expressed by any doctor as to the cause of injuries or problems

54. All out-of-pocket expenses incurred in connection with the matter
55. A description in the parents' own words of their criticisms of the doctors or hospitals
56. The names and addresses of all people who have had significant contact with the baby, including nurses, teachers, and others
57. Anything the baby particularly likes to do or likes parents to do for him or with him
58. Questions relating to the baby's future needs that an expert may have projected, such as dental care, travel-safety chairs, or wheelchairs, and whether any agency is paying or willing to pay for the same
59. Whether any changes, such as widening doorways for wheelchairs, have been made to the house in order to accommodate the child
60. What kind of additional assistance the parents want in order to take care of the child; what they would do with the child on weekends and how much time they would spend with the child if they had assistance
61. Whether either parent intends to work
62. Whether the parents have any firm plans as to what they are going to do when their baby reaches age 21; whether that is something the parents have discussed with counselors; whether placing the child in a group home or an institutional care facility is a possibility; what personal experience the parents have had with institutions or group homes
63. The health and condition of any other child born to the same parents
64. In cases involving problems with a statute of limitations, questions will frequently be asked of the parents regarding their awareness of a potential lawsuit. Those questions would deal with:
    a. When they first became aware of the problem
    b. When they first consulted lawyers or asked doctors about the cause of the problem or about other issues regarding parental awareness of a cause of action

C.2 DEPOSITION OF A REGISTERED NURSE

Attached are excerpts from the deposition of a registered nurse testifying for the plaintiff as an expert witness in a medical and nursing case. The witness testified that the nursing staff at the hospital was negligent in its care and treatment of an obstetrics patient in her third trimester of pregnancy who was hospitalized with complications and gave birth to a severely brain-injured child. The selected portions of this deposition illustrate many of the items discussed in the text. When defense counsel attempts to unfairly cross-examine the nurse, plaintiff's counsel intervenes at appropriate times to protect her. Once the ambiguities in defense counsel's questions are clarified, the witness gives direct responsive testimony that the hospital nursing staff was negligent. The examination is by defense counsel.

Mrs. Green is the plaintiff. Mrs. Morgan is the deponent. Nurse Alexander, Nurse Witt, and Nurse Howe took care of the plaintiff during separate nursing shifts at the hospital. Dr. Burt is the attending physician.

Q: Have you been called upon as an expert in the past to judge the conduct of nursing personnel in relation to the hospital accreditation manual published by the Joint Commission?

A: No.

Q: This is the first time?

A: Yes.

Q: Have you ever practiced nursing in the state of Wyoming?

A: No.

Q: Do you have knowledge of the standards of practice for nurses in labor and delivery at Grand Hospital in Cheyenne, Wyoming?

A: No.

Q: What effort, if any, up to this moment, have you made to ascertain what the standards of practice were for nurses in labor and delivery in Wyoming in 1979?

A: I referred earlier to the material that I have read: the policies and procedures of the hospital itself.

Q: Exhibit 11?

A: Yes. The practices as described by the nurses who gave their depositions and the depositions of the physicians regarding the functions and duties of the nurses.

Q: Specifically, do you know what the standards of practice were in January 1979 concerning the reading and interpreting of fetal monitor tapes by nursing personnel at the hospitals in Cheyenne, Wyoming?

A: According to the policy and procedure manual, the nurses were given instructions for the application of the monitors. In their depositions, the nurses also said that they had attended seminars on reading monitors. Having worked with Corametric monitors and similar types of equipment in other hospitals, I feel that I have some knowledge as to what the nurses should have been looking for and what their level of knowledge should have been.

Q: Will you agree that the reading and interpretation of fetal monitors can be extremely sophisticated?

A: Oh, yes.

Q: And would you agree that the level of sophistication of nursing personnel—let's just take the metropolitan Denver area—varies from hospital to hospital in terms of reading and interpreting fetal monitors?

A: I'm sure that it does. My experience from hospital to hospital has been that the hospitals that have fetal monitors generally have nurses who have received training in reading, interpreting, and understanding decelerations and what is involved with decelerations.

Q: What was the standard of practice for labor and delivery nurses in reading fetal monitors in Cheyenne, Wyoming, in January of 1979?

A: The standard was that nurses be able to read the equipment and the printout and interpret the results. They were expected to be able to recognize decelerations and to know the different types of decelerations and their possible causes. I am referring specifically to Nurse Alexander's testimony, I believe.

Q: In your opinion, was Nurse Alexander's interpretation of the fetal monitor tape appropriate? Did it meet that requisite standard?

Comment: When Nurse Alexander looked at the fetal monitor strip during the care of the patient, there was only one deceleration, and the fetus was not yet in distress. Thereafter, the fetal monitor tape showed decelerations combined with a loss of beat-to-beat variability, which evidenced fetal distress.

However, Nurse Alexander did not again review the fetal monitor tape or, if she did, she negligently failed to chart the abnormalities and possible fetal distress. During her deposition, she could not remember whether she had again looked at the fetal monitor tape and recognized the fetal distress. In this question, and in the ones that follow, defense counsel is attempting to elicit an opinion that Nurse

Alexander was not negligent based on her interpretation of the tape. It was the plaintiff's position that Nurse Alexander was negligent in failing to later review the tape and properly interpret it, or if she did later review the tape and did not chart the abnormalities, she was negligent in failing to do so. Because Nurse Alexander had no memory of whether she again looked at the tape and noted the abnormalities, and the abnormalities were not charted, a jury could determine that she did again review the tape because it was her custom and habit to do so, and that she either negligently interpreted the tape or negligently failed to chart abnormalities. The above question was therefore ambiguous and misleading, and plaintiff's counsel begins a series of objections to protect the witness.

Plaintiff's Counsel: Objection, at what point in time?

Defense Counsel: When she read it.

Q: Based upon your review of the records and the deposition?

A: Her initial assessment of the fetal monitor tape, within 10 minutes after she came on duty, was that there were late decelerations.

Q: All right. In your opinion, based on everything you know, did the conduct of Nurse Alexander meet the requisite standard of nurses reading and interpreting fetal monitor tapes? Your answer a minute ago was yes, before you were interrupted. Is that still your answer?

Plaintiff's Counsel: No, my objection was at what point in time. I guess you are limiting it to the time that Nurse Alexander testified she looked at the tape.

A: Nurse Alexander didn't make any subsequent remarks following the one deceleration on the chart as to any continuing deceleration, any change in the beat-to-beat variability. So, if we are limiting it to that period in time, yes, I think she made an appropriate assessment.

Plaintiff's Counsel: When you say "that period of time," do you mean when she made the notation on the chart that there may have been a late deceleration?

A: Yes.

Q: Based on what you know about this case, throughout the period of time that she was involved in the reading and interpretation of the fetal monitor tape, do you have an opinion as to whether or not her conduct fell within the requisite standards for nurses under the same or similar circumstances in Cheyenne, Wyoming, in 1979?

Plaintiff's Counsel: Now he is asking you about the time period between 7 o'clock and the time the monitor was taken off for the c-section.

Defense Counsel: No, I'm not. Because Nurse Alexander didn't see Mrs. Green at that time.

Q: Do you have an opinion in that regard?

Plaintiff's Counsel: Well, she was responsible for the patient as the R.N. during that entire period of time. Whether or not she saw her during that entire period of time, I suppose depends on what her testimony is.

Q: Do you have an opinion as to whether or not Nurse Alexander's conduct in reading and interpreting the fetal monitor tape during the period of time she was involved in the care and treatment of Mrs. Green fell within the acceptable standards of nursing care under the same or similar circumstances in Cheyenne, Wyoming in 1979?

A: There is information in the policy and procedure manual—also in the booklet put out by the Joint Commission on Accreditation of Hospitals—that alludes to the fact that nurses are supposed to maintain charts. Nurse Alexander never made any reference to the fetal heart rate pattern after she made the initial assessment of possible late deceleration.

Q: That's not what I asked you.

Plaintiff's Counsel: Yes, it was.

Q: Listen carefully to my question.

Plaintiff's Counsel: She is answering; let her finish.

Defense Counsel: Excuse me, counsel.

Plaintiff's Counsel: I object.

Q: My question is: Do you have an opinion as to whether or not Nurse Alexander's conduct in reading and interpreting the fetal monitor tapes as it relates to the care and treatment of Mrs. Green in January 1979 in Cheyenne met the acceptable standards for nurses under the same or similar circumstances?

Plaintiff's Counsel: I object to that, because if she can't refer to the charting, she has no way of knowing what Nurse Alexander did in interpreting those tapes.

Q: If you don't have enough data to express an opinion in that regard, just tell me.

Plaintiff's Counsel: You are not allowing her to have the data. You said she can't refer to the charts.

Defense Counsel: Excuse me counsel, you don't need to educate your witness; she is a professional.

Q: We will get to the chart in a second. Let's just talk about her conduct in reading and interpreting the tapes.

A: Standards of practice require that nurses chart. And there is nothing on the chart that says anything about her interpretation. So I have to assume that she did not follow the standards of practice that were explicitly explained in the hospital policies and procedures because she did not chart anything additional. There is no indication that she made any further assessment.

(Whereupon, there was a recess.)

Q: Mrs. Morgan, you had occasion to review a series of depositions and hospital records before you were called upon to express an opinion. Is that correct?

A: Yes.

Q: I want you to take into consideration the totality of that information. Taking that into consideration, whether it was charted or not by Nurse Alexander, do you have enough data to express an opinion as to whether her reading and interpretation of the fetal monitor tapes fell within the acceptable standards of nursing care? If you don't have enough data, tell me. If you do, let me know that.

A: You are referring specifically to Nurse Alexander?

Q: Right.

Plaintiff's Counsel: She came on at seven, I believe.

A: In view of the fact that she did not chart additional material, there is no way that I can determine what her actions were.

Q: In other words, you don't have enough data to express an expert opinion concerning the acceptability of her reading and interpreting the fetal monitor tapes?

A: The only additional data that I have is the fact that nothing occurred as far as Mrs. Green's condition was concerned.

Q: Am I correct that you do not have enough data to express an expert opinion concerning Nurse Alexander's reading and interpretation of the fetal monitor tapes?

Plaintiff's Counsel: I want to object to this because I think it is unfair and misleading.

Defense Counsel: No.

Plaintiff's Counsel: Yes, it is misleading, because a lack of data enables her to express an opinion because if it is not charted, it didn't happen. Therefore, it is a misleading question because of the way you are phrasing it.

Defense Counsel: In her deposition she testified to reading and interpreting the fetal monitor tape, and I am asking this witness to take the same data into consideration that she did in formulating this written report for you. Just tell me whether she had an expert opinion as to whether Nurse Alexander's conduct met the acceptable standards for nurses in reading and interpreting the fetal monitor tapes.

Comment: Here the defense counsel either is mistaken or is misleading the witness; Nurse Alexander testified by deposition that she could not recall again reviewing the fetal monitor strip that contained evidence of fetal distress. Plaintiff's counsel reminds the witness of this, and defense counsel does not pursue the matter further.

Plaintiff's Counsel: I think that you ought to call to her attention specifically what information you are referring to.

Defense Counsel: No, I am asking her to use the wealth of knowledge supplied through the information you gave her. All right?

Plaintiff's Counsel: In all fairness to the witness—and correct me if I'm wrong—Nurse Alexander's testimony was that she can't now remember when she looked at the tapes or, if she did, what she then noticed on those tapes except for the one record that she made.

Q: The one thing that is very clear to me, Mrs. Morgan, is that you are critical of the lack of charting by nursing personnel. That's one area of criticism. Is that right?

A: Correct.

Q: Now, I'm asking you simply whether you have enough data, taking into consideration the depositions and everything else, to express an expert opinion as to whether Nurse Alexander's conduct fell within acceptable standards or outside of acceptable standards in reading and interpreting the fetal monitor tapes as they relate to Mrs. Green.

Comment: In the remaining portion of the deposition, the witness demonstrates confidence in answering questions. She is confident because she has conducted a thorough review of depositions and records, and her preparation permits her to give direct answers to the questions, express appropriate opinions, and give the basis for those opinions.

A: Yes, I believe I have.

Q: Okay. And what is your opinion in that regard?

A: My opinion is that she apparently did not make a proper assessment of the continuing decelerations and the loss of beat-to-beat variability.

Q: What is that opinion based on?

A: The fact that they continued to the time of Mrs. Green's cesarean section, yet no notation was made that the doctor had been notified or that any kind of nursing procedure had been initiated to try to obtain a better readout that might indicate that the infant was in a better state of health.

Q: So your opinion is based on the absence of charting to show that anything was recognized or that any effort was made to resolve something that may have been recognized?

A: I mentioned also the fact that the fetal monitor tapes continued to show the same pattern until there was a loss of beat-to-beat variability, and at that time the deceleration stopped. But there was also a loss of beat-to-beat variability, and that continued.

Q: When did the patient start active labor, based upon your review of the fetal monitor tapes?

A: The patient was having contractions when she was admitted to the hospital.

Q: That's not my question. My question was: When was she in active labor?

A: It is difficult to determine active labor unless you do a vaginal exam and determine the dilation of the cervix. You can have contractions that show on the fetal monitor, and you can palpate, yet if the patient is not dilating, she is not in active labor by definition.

Q: Can you express an opinion as an expert, based on the materials you have reviewed, as to when Mrs. Green first went into active labor?

A: Based on the material, I would assume that she was in active labor when she was admitted to the hospital.

Q: What are Braxton Hicks?

A: Braxton Hicks are contractions that are generally not felt by a patient but that are palpable and recognizable as contractions.

Q: Are they active labor in your opinion?

A: No, they are defined as inactive. They do not result in the delivery of the infant.

Q: Do you have an opinion as to whether or not Mrs. Green was experiencing Braxton Hicks contractions during the period of time she was on the monitor?

A: Yes.

Q: What is your opinion in that regard?

A: That she was not experiencing Braxton Hicks.

Q: Uterine irritability—is that something different from active labor?

A: Yes.

Q: And is that reflected on the monitor strips in Mrs. Green's case?

A: Yes, it is.

Q: So it is your opinion that she was experiencing, in addition to active labor contractions, uterine irritability?

A: Yes.

Q: What do you do as a nurse to rule out Braxton Hicks contractions?

A: Generally, you observe the patient for a period of time, assessing the type of contractions that she is having and whether or not she is progressing in labor and dilating.

Q: But when you can't do a vaginal exam, what do you do to rule out Braxton Hicks?

A: Reasons for not doing a vaginal exam would include that the patient had ruptured membranes or that the patient was bleeding. If the patient had ruptured membranes, you would go ahead and deliver the infant and there wouldn't be any question of Braxton Hicks. If the patient were bleeding, you would not be concerned with the Braxton Hicks; you would be concerned with the bleeding.

Q: You are saying that if a patient gives a history of bleeding or shows evidence of bleeding on admission, you would not be concerned with determining whether uterine responses on the monitor strip were Braxton Hicks versus active labor; is that what you are saying?

A: You wouldn't be concerned about whether or not she was having Braxton Hicks, no. If she were showing a pattern of uterine irritability you would be very concerned, particularly in conjunction with an episode of bleeding.

Q: Based on your review of the records and your review of the deposition of Nurse Witt, do you have an opinion as to whether or not her conduct in reading and interpreting the fetal monitor tapes fell within the acceptable standards of nursing care?

A: Yes.

Q: What is your opinion?

A: That it did not.

Q: And specifically why?

A: Well, there was a period of time from the time she was put on the indirect monitor until the time that she went off duty that the patient was experiencing late decelerations, and according to Dr. Burt's testimony, this was never brought to his attention. A chart entry was not made of the late decelerations. There is no notation on the chart that there was an episode of bleeding, and Dr. Burt denies that the nurses told him about an episode of bleeding.

Also, no notation was made of the patient's pain in connection with uterine irritability, nor was any such pain or irritability brought to Dr. Burt's attention. There is no evidence that any attempt was made to reposition the patient to obtain a different type of readout or to alleviate any of the symptoms that showed on the fetal heart tracing.

Q: If you assume that Nurse Witt told the truth in her deposition, based on that which is contained in the chart, do you have an opinion whether or not her conduct in reading and interpreting the fetal monitor tape met the acceptable standards for nursing care?

A: Yes, I feel that they did not meet the standards.

Q: Specifically why?

A: You will have to be specific in your question then.

Plaintiff's Counsel: He is now asking you only about the fetal monitor tapes and her reading and interpreting the fetal monitor tapes, as opposed to other things such as the onset of bright red bleeding and the failure to chart.

A: All right. I will state again that there was a period of time from 2:55—about 3 o'clock—until 7 o'clock, that late decelerations continued on the tape. There are apparently four hours of late decelerations during that period with no nursing intervention or assessment of the same.

Q: Do you recall Nurse Witt testifying in her deposition that she did see late decelerations and that she did report them? Do you recall that?

A: No.

Comment: Plaintiff's counsel now reassures the witness that she is correct so that she will not back down or concede this point if defense counsel pursues it further.

Plaintiff's Counsel: I will object to that because I don't believe that was her testimony.

Q: In your opinion, other than Nurse Witt and Nurse Alexander, did any other person in labor and delivery have responsibility for reading and interpreting fetal monitor tapes other than the physicians?

A: There was a period of time during the period that Mrs. Green was admitted that Nurse Howe was covering labor and delivery and was responsible. The policy and procedures manual says that, ideally, the patient is to be on the fetal monitor throughout labor. The fetal monitor was not applied until Nurse Witt came back from the operating room; Nurse Howe was in charge of labor and delivery at that period of time, and I assume she could have applied the fetal monitor.

Q: Are you saying, then, that Nurse Howe fell below the acceptable standards in not putting the fetal monitor on shortly after the patient was admitted?

A: According to the standards at the hospital, it is to be on the patient during her course of labor and delivery, and she did not put it on.

Q: During active labor, is that right?

A: What does it say specifically?

Comment: In the following section, plaintiff's counsel assists the witness in making a crucial point.

Plaintiff's Counsel: Here. (referring to document)

A: "Each patient in labor is to have a fetal monitor attached."

Q: So you are critical of her for not putting on the monitor prior to the time it was actually done by someone else at roughly 2:55; is that right?

A: 2:25.

Q: Or 2:25?

A: The standards state it is to be applied, and it is my understanding that she did not apply it.

Defense Counsel: Okay. Thank you.

APPENDIX D

VOIR DIRE

D.1 ANONYMOUS PLANNED PARENTHOOD SURVEY

1. Is it morally right for a married woman to use birth-control measures such as the IUD (intrauterine device), birth-control pills, a diaphragm, foam, etc.?

   a) Certainly

   b) It depends on the circumstances

   c) Don't know

   d) No

   e) Absolutely not

   Why? ____

   ____

   ____

2. A drug company markets an IUD and claims that it is safe. The company knows the IUD will eventually cause an infection, but the company's officials do not tell doctors or the public because they want to sell as much of their product as they can. A doctor inserts the IUD in a woman, and she gets an infection that results in a hysterectomy. The woman is not married and has been sexually active with a total of six men over her lifetime. She had an abortion before the IUD was inserted. What percentage of fault, if any, do the doctor, the woman, or the drug company bear?

   The drug company?_______ %

   Why? ____

   ____

   ____

The woman? ______ %

Why? ____

____

____

The doctor? ______ %

Why? ____

____

____

3. Is it morally right for an unmarried woman to use birth-control measures such as the IUD, birth-control pills, a diaphragm, foam, etc.?
   a) Certainly
   b) It depends on the circumstances
   c) Don't know
   d) No
   e) Absolutely not

   Why or why not? ____

   ____

   ____

4. What is your religious preference? ____________________
5. Please circle your marital status:
   a) Single
   b) Married
   c) Divorced
   d) Separated
   e) Widowed
6. Please circle your age group:
   a) 18–25
   b) 26–35
   c) 36–45
   d) 46–55
   e) 56 or older
7. What is your occupation? ________________________________

8. If you are retired, what was your occupation before you retired?

____

9. What is your education level?
   a) Lower than high school graduate
   b) High school graduate
   c) High school graduate with vocational/technical training
   d) Some college
   e) College graduate
10. Are you a registered voter?

    [ ] YES [ ] NO If so, where? ____________________
11. What is your ethnic origin?
    a) Caucasian
    b) African American
    c) Asian or Pacific Islander
    d) Hispanic
    e) Native American
    f) Other (Please specify)
12. Please check one: [ ] MALE [ ] FEMALE

D.2 JUROR QUESTIONNAIRE

Juror Questionnaire Instructions

1. Please complete each of the questions, taking care to write your juror number on each page where indicated. Press firmly with your pen, as you are making two additional copies.
2. Sign the questionnaire on the last page.
3. Separate the three-part forms and clip your pages together by color. Leave the divider sheets clipped to the clipboard.
4. Return the clipboard and the three sets of questions and answers to the bailiff.
5. If you have any questions, please direct them to the bailiff.

JUROR QUESTIONNAIRE

This questionnaire is designed to save time in jury selection. Please complete the form in blue or black ink, and answer the questions completely and accurately. You have a right not to answer any question about therapy or medical treatment. This Court and the lawyers involved in this case will keep confidential all answers you provide.

1. Name ________________ Juror number ________________
2. Home address ________________________________
3. Where were you born and raised? ______________ Age ______
4. Occupation and employer ________________________________
____
5. Marital status ________________________________
6. Spouse's occupation and employer ________________________
____
7. How long have you worked for your present employer? ______
8. Number of children (specify sex and age) ________________
9. Children's occupations and employers ____________________
____
10. Your level of education/degrees ________________________
11. Prior military service (specify branch and rank) ____________
____
12. Close friends or relatives in medicine ____________________
____
13. Close friends or relatives who are attorneys ______________
____
14. Have you been convicted of a crime other than a traffic violation in the past ten years? ________ When? ________________
Where? ____________________ What? ____________________
____
15. Have you ever been a witness in court? ____ When? __________
What type of case? ________________________________
16. Have you or any of your family members ever had a particularly good or bad experience with a doctor? If so, please briefly describe:
____
____
____
____

17. Have you seen or heard any advertisements in the last six months criticizing persons who use the judicial system to get money as compensation for personal injuries or damages caused by another? If so, what have you heard or seen?

____

____

____

____

18. Does anything concern you about medical negligence lawsuits in which money damages are being sought? If so, what is your concern? ____

____

____

19. What are your feelings about people who file lawsuits for money damages for personal injuries? ______________________

____

20. Do you feel that lawsuits are filed too frequently? If so, please state why: ____

____

____

21. What concerns, if any, do you have about awarding money as damages to an injured person? ______________________

____

____

22. Without having heard any of the evidence or law in this case, do you have a limit of the amount of money you could award as damages to an injured person? If so, what is the limit? ________

____

23. This is a medical negligence case. If the jury in this case were to award money damages, would you feel that it would have some economic effect on you personally?

[ ] YES [ ] NO [ ] MAYBE

If so, in what way? ____

____

____

____

24. Do you believe a person should be allowed to sue his or her medical doctor? Why or why not? ______________________

____

25. Based on what you have heard or read about the court system, do you believe that jury verdicts overcompensate, undercompensate, or adequately compensate medical negligence claimants? Please explain the basis of your belief.

____

____

____

26. Please look at the attached list of witnesses and set forth the names of those whom you recognize or think you might know.

____

____

____

____

27. Add any other comments you feel are important to your possible service as a juror in this trial of a medical negligence lawsuit for money damages.

____

____

____

I SWEAR OR AFFIRM THAT THE ANSWERS ABOVE ARE TRUE AND CORRECT.

____

SIGNATURE

D.3 SUMMARY OF RESPONSES TO SELECT QUESTIONS FROM THE JUROR QUESTIONNAIRE

18. Does anything concern you about medical negligence lawsuits in which money damages are being sought? If so, what is your concern?

    YES: 7

    NO: 21

    Remarks: "People doing it just for the money"
    "Increased insurance rates"
    "Medical care costs to rise"
    "Driving doctors out of practice"

20. Do you think lawsuits are filed too frequently? If so, please state why.

    YES: 11

    NO: 11

    SOMETIMES: 5

    N/A: 1

    Remarks: "People view it as an easy way to get money"
    "It has become very easy to receive huge monetary awards"
    "Too many people want money"
    "Too quick to sue for minor matters"

22. Without having heard any of the evidence or law in this case, do you have a limit of the amount of money you could award as damages to an injured person?

    YES: 0

    NO: 2

    DEPENDS: 23

    N/A: 3

    Remarks: "Damages done"
    "The age of the victim"
    "Depends on injury"
    "Depends on circumstances"

23. This is a medical negligence case. If the jury in this case were to award money damages, would you feel that it would have some economic effect on you personally?

    [ ] YES [ ] NO [ ] MAYBE

    If so, in what way?

    YES: 3

    NO: 21

    MAYBE: 3

    N/A: 1

    Remarks: "Higher malpractice insurance for doctors raises people's insurance in general"

    "All cause the cost of medical care to rise"

    "Less doctors are practicing"

    "Insurance goes up for doctors and then fees increase accordingly"

    "Because of the cost of malpractice insurance, the consumer ends up paying higher doctor bills"

24. Do you believe a person should be allowed to sue his or her medical doctor? Why or why not?

    YES: 20

    NO: 5

    MAYBE: 3

    Remarks: "Yes, some violate confidence and are negligent in their care of patients"

    "Yes, incompetence and negligence should not be allowed to happen"

    "Yes, if an obvious mistake has been made because of a lack of care and concern"

    "No, if the doctor does his best and to the best of his knowledge"

Responses to Questions Calling for Comments

19. What are your feelings about people who file lawsuits for money damages for personal injuries?

    "I believe if the person filing the lawsuit is suffering from malpractice, they should be compensated"

"I think people who file lawsuits are encouraged by disreputable, unprofessional attorneys"

"I feel they should get just compensation for their injuries if proved"

"Too many people try to get something for nothing"

"Not very good"

20. What concerns, if any, do you have about awarding money as damages to an injured person?

"That the amount awarded is fair and not too exorbitant"

"They get what they deserve—no more, no less"

"Too large awards because of percentage arrangement with attorneys"

"Sometimes the awards are too high"

"That the person would not use the money properly"

25. Based on what you have heard or read about the court system, do you believe that jury verdicts overcompensate, undercompensate, or adequately compensate medical negligence claimants? Please explain the basis of your belief.

"I have no idea; I have never been involved before or stopped to think what would be adequate compensation"

"The news often reports those cases that are extreme and I am sure we do not hear much about the under or adequately compensated claimants; I guess I am concerned about the overcompensated amounts that some juries have awarded"

"I have nothing to base a belief on"

"Overcompensate; no amount of money can repay grief for an accidental death"

"Jury verdicts can and do all of the above at times. Depends on individual cases and particular juries"

"Adequately compensate—although the highly publicized cases where large amounts for damages are awarded stay in a person's mind"

"I think that each case should be handled on an individual basis, but some are ridiculously overcompensated"

27. Add any other comments you feel are important to your possible service as a juror in this trial of a medical negligence lawsuit for money damages.

"The majority of doctors do their professional best and do not deliberately do harm to their patients"

D.4 VOIR DIRE OUTLINE

This outline was used by plaintiff's counsel to voir dire the jury in a medical negligence case in which it was alleged that the plaintiff became a quadriplegic as a result of improper and untimely treatment following injuries sustained in an automobile collision. This outline illustrates the manner in which specific questions can be posed to accomplish some of the goals described in Chapter Eight, "Voir Dire."

Lara v. Dr. G and Dr. B

Trial commencing February 24, 1986

Dates: 12/17/83—Auto accident, admission to Lutheran Hospital

12/23/83—Improper surgery by Dr. G

12/29/83—Transfer to Swedish Hospital

12/31/83—Proper surgery by Dr. S, who attempted to correct the problem

03/07/84—Transfer to Craig Hospital

A. Introductions:

1. William T for the plaintiffs, Leonard and Carolyn Lara
2. Peter P and Kathy M for the defendant, Dr. B
3. Marjorie M and Jim O for the defendant, Dr. G
4. The Honorable Raymond Dean Jones, Judge, presiding

B. Summary of Case: In this lawsuit, it is claimed that Leonard Lara was partly paralyzed as a result of an auto accident. He was taken to Lutheran Hospital, where he came under the care of Dr. G, who consulted with Dr. B. It is claimed that Dr. G was negligent in his treatment or in his failure to treat the patient in a timely manner. It is also claimed that Dr. B was negligent in his consultation, which resulted in further paralysis to Mr. Lara's hands, arms, and upper body.

C. Voir Dire of Individual Jurors: Request the jurors' background information, including where they were born and raised; their marital status; their present occupation; the occupation of their spouse; their educational background; the number of children they have; and the employment history of each member of their family. Then question each juror as follows:

1. Do you know any of the other jurors?
2. Do you have jury experience?

3. Do you have courtroom experience as a witness, party, or other participant in a trial?
4. Do you have experience in equating injuries with money damages—as a claim adjuster, or as an employee of an industrial commission, for example?
5. Are you now or have you ever been employed by a stockholder or policyholder? Do you have any experience as a stockholder or policyholder? Do you have a direct or indirect interest in the Hudson Insurance Group or in any insurance company? (This is the liability insurance carrier for the defendants.)
6. Do you have training or experience in law or medicine?
7. Are you or is any member of your immediate family employed by any health-care facility? Are you or is any member of your immediate family in the health-care industry? Do you have a financial interest in any aspect of the health-care industry?
8. Are you familiar with the incident involved in this trial, or have you heard about it from any source?
9. Do you know, professionally or socially, the defendant-doctors, the doctors with whom they share office space, or anyone on their staffs?
10. Do you have experience with neurosurgery, paraplegia, quadriplegia, or paralysis of any kind? Do you have any experience with cerebral palsy, polio, or Craig Hospital rehabilitation?
11. Do you have experience with major surgery? Abdominal surgery? Do you have an opinion about whether family practice doctors can perform with the same competence as medical specialists?
12. Do you have any disability, medical condition, disease, or personal problem that would prevent your sitting as a juror for several days?
13. Do you have friends or neighbors who are physicians?
14. Have you or has any member of your immediate family had complications or problems as a result of any medical or surgical treatment, particularly problems with the use of the limbs or problems involving partial paralysis following surgery?
15. Do you know any nurses or other personnel at Lutheran Hospital, Swedish Hospital, or Craig Hospital? Have you or has anyone in your family been hospitalized there?

16. How do you feel about suing physicians for negligence?
17. Are you or is any member of your family currently under medical care or treatment of any kind?
18. Do you know, professionally or socially, the defense attorneys or any secretary, lawyer, or other person you believe to be employed by them? Are you a client of any of the people mentioned above?
19. Do you have any knowledge of the law with respect to suits against doctors?

D. Voir Dire of the Entire Panel: Present the following categories of questions and instructions to the prospective jurors as a group:

1. Relationship to witnesses:

   Do any of you know any of the following persons who may be called as witnesses? (Attach list of prospective witnesses.)

2. Relationship with Health-Care Providers:

   a. Have any of you or have any of your relatives or close friends ever been employed in any capacity by any physician, chiropractor, osteopath, dentist, hospital, nursing home, clinic, physician's office, dental office, or any other institution or practitioner of the healing arts?

   b. Do any of you or do any of your relatives or close friends suffer from any chronic or disabling illness that requires regular or periodic medical care, examination, treatment, or therapy of any kind? Do any of you engage in any business that depends in whole or in part on the sale of goods or services to any health-care provider? Do any of you do business directly or indirectly with any health-care provider or institution?

   c. Have any of you ever been engaged in a business or occupation related to the sale of medical devices, medical services, medical equipment or machines, or drugs?

   d. Are any of your children or other dependents currently pursuing a course of study in any of the medical or healing arts, nursing, paramedical services, or similar vocations?

   e. Do any of you own stock in or have any other proprietary interest in any hospital, medical supply company, drug company, or other business concerned in whole or in part with selling goods or services to any aspect of the medical profession or any related healing arts profession?

f. Have any of you or any of your relatives been hospitalized or operated on within the last five years? Have any of you or any of your relatives made arrangements for or received counseling to have surgery or to have hospital care or treatment in the immediate future?

g. Do you raise funds for or donate time to Lutheran Hospital, Swedish Hospital, Craig Hospital, or any other hospital?

3. Bias:

a. This lawsuit involves a claim by Mr. and Mrs. Lara that Dr. G used the wrong traction and treatment for Mr. Lara's injury and waited too long to perform surgery; that he then consulted with Dr. B, and the two together decided on the wrong surgery, which Dr. G performed and which was unsuccessful. Mr. Lara became paralyzed in his hands, arms, and upper body because of the negligence of both Dr. G and Dr. B. The law does permit suits against professional people—doctors, lawyers, dentists, CPAs, and others—in cases in which the professional people are simply negligent. Is there anyone here who feels that the law should not permit lawsuits against physicians in cases in which they are not being accused of a criminal or reckless act but are being accused of simple negligence?

b. The doctors' reputations are not an issue in this case. There will be no evidence that a lawsuit like this has any effect on reputation, and you must follow the Court's instructions on the law because it would be improper for you to render a verdict based on reputation.

c. This is not a lawsuit requesting that the physicians lose their licenses to practice medicine; it is a lawsuit involving simple negligence.

d. Mrs. Juror, if you went to a mechanic and he told you what was wrong with your car, made the repairs and charged you for them, but made the wrong diagnosis and the wrong repairs, would you be upset about that? Do you feel there's anything different about a physician who performs the wrong surgery and doesn't correct the problem? Mr. Juror, would you hold the driver of a car responsible if the driver ran a red light and struck your car? If a physician were negligent and ran a medical red light and caused harm, would you hold that physician responsible if an expert testified that the physician was negligent?

e. Is there anyone here who feels that a doctor is above the law and can do no wrong? Or that, if a doctor is wrong, he should not be sued? Do you all believe that the law should apply equally to all people, whether laypeople, business people, or professional people?

4. Sympathy:

There will be testimony that may cause you to feel sympathy toward Leonard Lara and his family, but it would be improper for you to base your verdict on sympathy for them. By the same token, it would be improper for you to render a verdict for Dr. B and Dr. G because you feel that such a verdict is necessary to protect their reputations or their licenses to practice medicine.

5. Personal Relationships with Physicians:

a. Do any of you personally know a doctor or have a close personal friend, neighbor, social club member, or relative who is a physician of any kind?

b. Are any of you personally acquainted with any physician?

c. Is there any panel member who does not go to physicians as a matter of personal preference?

6. Alcohol:

On Friday afternoon, December 17, 1983, Mr. Lara was calling on Allway customers. He has no present memory of what occurred between his 4 p.m. appointment and the time of the accident. He had a glass of wine around 2 or 3 o'clock in the afternoon, and he doesn't remember having anything to drink after that. Yet his blood alcohol test following the accident showed that he had been drinking very recently. The automobile he was driving left the roadway and rolled, resulting in damage to his spinal cord and vertebrae.

Some of you may wonder how, after drinking and driving and becoming involved in an auto accident because of his own negligence, he now has the audacity to bring a lawsuit against physicians who were probably trying to help him and may have even saved his life.

How many of you get upset when you read about drunk drivers injuring themselves or other people? Do you, or does anyone in your family, belong to organizations that oppose drinking and driving--groups like Mothers Against Drunk Driving? Do any of you feel that the doctors' negligence should be excused because Mr. Lara was injured through his own fault? If the law were to the contrary, would you follow the law?

7. Consultations and Second Opinions among Physicians:
   a. Do any of you know anything about why doctors sometimes consult with other physicians before performing surgery or rendering medical treatment?
   b. Have any of you ever had any personal experience with second opinions? Have you requested that a physician get a second opinion, or have you personally secured a second opinion before undergoing any surgery or medical treatment?
8. Questioning Medical Information:
   a. How many of you have ever questioned a doctor in detail about a surgical procedure that was being recommended? Do you feel it was appropriate to do so? Did you believe that the doctor fairly and completely answered all questions?
   b. How would you describe your relationship with your family doctor or any other treating doctor?
   c. Do you believe in the proposition that a patient should be able to rely on the information supplied by a physician?
   d. If any of you have sought a second opinion from a physician before undergoing surgery or medical treatment, did you do this on your own, or were you asked to do so by the treating physician? Is there anyone here who feels that it is inappropriate to get another opinion before undergoing surgery?
   e. Has anyone here had complications from surgery or medical treatment? Did you blame the doctor for them? Did you feel anyone was at fault? Had the doctor told you in advance that a bad result was possible?
9. Personal Interest in Medicine:
   a. Do any of your relatives or close friends have any knowledge of nursing, medicine, or related fields from any source?
   b. Has anyone in your family taken medical or medically related courses, or does anyone read articles or stories dealing with medicine or doctors?

c. Is anyone here fascinated with medicine or surgery? Do you watch television programs in which they perform surgery and explain it as they go along?

d. Is anyone involved with an animal hospital, or does anyone work for a veterinarian?

10. Religion:

a. Do any of you have a religious belief that would make you uncomfortable filing a lawsuit if you felt someone was at fault?

b. Does anyone believe that it is essentially God's will if there is a bad result in surgery and that the doctor should not be blamed?

11. Damages:

Mr. and Mrs. Lara seek damages for Mr. Lara's inability to be independent because his arms and hands are now paralyzed, whereas his paralysis would have only been in the lower extremities if the doctors had not been negligent. If you find liability in this case, you must follow the Court's instructions and award damages for the additional injury caused by the physicians, and not for the paralysis that Mr. Lara already had when he came to the hospital. If the physicians were negligent and their negligence caused additional damages to Mr. Lara, it would be unfair to Mr. Lara not to compensate him adequately for the additional paralysis.

E. Ideal Jurors: The following types of people would make desirable jury members:

- People who are in good health and have never had a bad result from surgery or people who have filed a claim or suit because of a bad result (people with bad results will not identify with the Lara family if they did not file suit);
- People who would not identify with the medical community through social strata, economics, politics, or other areas;
- People who are distrustful of physicians or who fall into a socioeconomic class that does not receive good medical care;
- People who appear to be warm and caring and who show some sympathy to the plaintiffs; and
- People who go to chiropractors or other nonphysician medical specialists because they do not trust medical doctors.

F. Undesirable Jurors: The following types of people would be best avoided for the selection of this jury.

- People who provide attendant care to a disabled family member, receive no compensation, and believe it is a duty to provide such care without compensation;
- People who identify with the medical profession or the health-care industry and believe that plaintiffs use the courts as a lottery; and
- People who own small businesses or have been directly affected by substantial increases in insurance premiums as a result of what they perceive to be an increase in unnecessary litigation.

APPENDIX E

OPENING STATEMENT

SANCHEZ v. PLANNED PARENTHOOD

One of every 10 or 11 women in the United States of childbearing age will develop cancer of the breast. You will learn in this case that the early detection and treatment of a cancerous lump in the breast can be the difference between life and death. You will learn that a very large percentage of the women whose cancers are detected early will survive and that a six-month delay in detection and treatment can result in a young woman having only a 40 percent chance of surviving five years instead of an 85 percent chance that she will survive five years and a 30 percent chance that she will be cured and live a full life. You will learn in this case that Donna Sanchez now lives with the fear of death because her cancer was not detected and treated by the defendants when she went to them for help in 1987.

You will learn that Donna Sanchez knew about cancer of the breast before 1987, regularly performed self-breast-examinations, and was a knowledgeable and educated person who had completed high school and attended college. She worked full-time in the computer field while going to college to obtain a bachelor's degree in computer science. In June 1987, at age 26, while doing a regular breast examination several days after her menstrual period, she discovered a small lump in her left breast. This had never happened before and she became concerned and called a friend, Roberta Romero, and then decided to go to Planned Parenthood (PP) for an examination. Donna had paid Planned Parenthood $150, which entitled her to one year of office calls.

On June 23, 1987, Lucy Smith, a physician assistant (PA) at Planned Parenthood, examined Donna's breast and said that she could feel the lump, but that it was nothing to worry about. Based on what the PA told her, Donna left with the impression that all women eventually develop lumpiness in the breast that is normal, and it was not painful.

The PA will testify that she thought she was feeling a ridge where the edge of the breast is connected to the chest tissue and muscle, and that she explained to Donna that this is what Donna was feeling, not a lump in the breast. The PA had completed her university training in 1986 and became a part-time employee of Planned Parenthood in February 1987. She had received no specific training at PP in breast examinations, but had been observed for two weeks by a nurse as she conducted general pelvic and physical exams.

After the exam, Donna was greatly relieved and told her friend, Roberta Romero, about the examination.

Donna continued her monthly breast examinations and could still feel the lump, which seemed the same. She was not alarmed until August 1987, when she noticed a twinge in lifting her arms over her head. By the end of September, the lump seemed larger. She was again worried, and again called Roberta Romero, who advised her not to return to PP. In early October, Donna called the Women's Center at Humana Hospital, was referred to Dr. H, and made an appointment for 10/30/87.Donna completed a form in Dr. H's office and said: "have lump on left breast which is getting larger; it has been present for four months. Saw health-care provider who `said it was just muscle' and did nothing."

After reading the form, Dr. H felt the lump, but told Donna that it was nothing to worry about. She came away from that meeting thinking it was a cyst that was growing. She could now see the lump in looking in a mirror and thought it was growing quite large. She told Dr. H that she might want it removed for cosmetic reasons. Dr. H gave her a piece of paper on which he wrote: "Dear Dr. R: Could you please examine Ms. Sanchez and remove her breast lump. Thanks." Dr. H charted "nontender cystic mass 1 by 1.5 cm, lymph node or breast cyst." He drew a diagram in his charts that shows an upper outer quadrant left breast lump, ¾ inch in diameter. Donna asked Dr. H when she should see Dr. R to have it removed, and he explained there was no hurry; she could wait until after the holidays.

Again, Donna was greatly relieved and assumed it was a cyst that was growing and becoming unsightly. She had just started a new job, and she decided to wait and have the lump removed later for cosmetic reasons.

Donna met her boyfriend, Robert B, on October 31, 1987, at a Halloween party, and they began going together and became serious. He first noticed the lump in December; Donna had never mentioned it to him. When he mentioned it to her, she seemed embarrassed.

Donna telephoned Dr. R for an appointment, which was scheduled for January 11, 1988. He felt the same lump or mass and charted that Donna had first noticed it six months ago and it "has progressed in size and is now 1 inch in diameter." He told her it could be cancer and should be removed; he ordered a mammogram and scheduled Donna for surgery on January 15, 1988, to remove the lump and axillary lymph nodes.

Dr. R's charts state that Donna had discovered the lump six months ago, that she was seen at PP and told it was "nothing to worry about," and that she then saw Dr. H, who referred her to Dr. R. Before surgery on January 15, 1988, Dr. R charted that he could feel two swollen lymph nodes in addition to the lump in the breast. The PA and Dr. H did not feel the swollen lymph nodes, which indicates that the cancer might have spread to Donna's lymph nodes since Dr. H had examined Donna in October.

Dr. R performed a lumpectomy, not a mastectomy, and told Donna that she had cancer; that of the 12 lymph nodes that had been removed, she had cancer in 11; that the cancer had spread from her breast to the nodes; that the mammogram showed a mass of 2.3 by 2 cm (1 inch = 2½ cm); and that during the operation he removed the lump, which was approximately 1½ inches in diameter. The lump was just beneath the skin and attached to it; the tumor was not deep in the breast.

Donna was told she must have chemotherapy and radiation therapy and was referred to Dr. O, an oncologist.

On January 21, 1988, Dr. O met with Donna and her mother, Rose Sanchez, and explained what radiation therapy and chemotherapy would consist of. He seemed cold and uncaring, and Donna wanted a doctor that she could work with in fighting cancer. She left his office in tears.

Donna looked for another oncologist and was referred to Dr. P. Dr. P was the first doctor who explained to Donna that without radiation therapy and chemotherapy she would die. Even with treatment, there was a 50 percent chance that she would die within five years. He recommended that she not have children and that she have her tubes tied to prevent pregnancy. Donna's mother was with her during this appointment with Dr. P, and after receiving this information, Donna and her mother sat in the car and cried. Donna did not want her tubes tied. She had a serious relationship with Robert B and wanted children in the future.

Donna sought another opinion from Dr. F on February 1, 1988. Dr. F advised her that she could not become pregnant for the next five years because chemotherapy would cause a hormone imbalance. He also told her that she could not take birth control pills or other hormonal drugs again because they would increase the risk of cancer recurrence. She underwent radiation therapy five days a week and chemotherapy every week for eight weeks and then every other week for the next 32 weeks. She continued working, but lost her hair, was nauseated after chemotherapy, and lost her energy and strength. She tried to reduce the risk of cancer recurrence by going on a wholesome low-fat diet and taking vitamins.

Donna began going to a wellness community called QuaLife in April 1988 to address her emotional and mental needs. She felt anguish and anger knowing that the early detection of cancer can result in a cure, but because of her late detection, she only had a 50 percent chance of surviving five years.

Donna must have frequent examinations with blood tests and mammograms for the first five years following her cancer treatment. Thus far those examinations have been normal and have shown no evidence of cancer. However, Donna worries constantly about recurrence.

Donna has always worked full-time since high school, and she was going to college to obtain a degree when her cancer was diagnosed. She has continued to work through her treatment, but she no longer has the energy to attend college at night or on the weekends and has stopped attending. She is still employed full-time.

Dr. William A. Robinson is an oncologist, a professor of medicine, and head of the Division of Oncology at the University of Colorado. He is a specialist in breast cancer and Chairman of the National Scientific Advisory Board for the American Cancer Society. He will tell you that Donna had cancer in June 1987; that it was Stage I and localized; that it had probably not yet spread to the lymph nodes; that it could have been diagnosed at that time and successfully treated; and that the overall survival rate for Stage I breast cancer is 85 to 90 percent. He will make some assumptions in favor of the defendants that Donna was already receptor negative by June 1987 and the cancer was poorly differentiated and somewhat fast growing. Even giving the defendants all of that benefit of the doubt, he will testify that had Donna been treated in June 1987, she still would have had a 60 to 65 percent chance of surviving and living a full life.

Dr. Robinson will testify that it takes an average of seven to ten years before a lump is 1 cm in diameter; that you cannot feel a lump until it is almost 1 cm in diameter; that Donna's description of the lump as feeling smaller than a marble and larger than a pea indicates that it was under 1 cm in diameter. Donna detected it at an ideal stage for treatment, and a mammogram at that time would have shown a lump smaller than 1 cm in diameter. Ninety to 95 percent of breast cancers of that size can be detected, particularly if the lump is near the surface just beneath the skin.

The lump detected in June was the same lump removed in January, but it had grown considerably and spread into the lymph nodes, which placed Donna at a Stage II cancer and gave her only a 50 to 60 percent chance of surviving the next five years.

Dr. Robinson will further testify that the delay of two and one-half months caused by Dr. H decreased Donna's chances for survival because the longer you wait to remove a lump, the greater the chance it will spread into the lymph nodes and become a Stage II cancer.

Dr. Robinson will explain that Donna has the type of breast cancer that is most commonly diagnosed and that most breast cancers are poorly differentiated, estrogen negative, and somewhat fast growing, like Donna's. If this type of breast cancer is detected when the lump is under 2 cm in diameter, as Donna's was when she first discovered it, and before it spreads to the lymph nodes, statistics show that 65 to 95 percent of patients with these cancers are cured. Had Donna's cancer been treated in July 1987, she probably would have been cured of it.

Dr. Robinson will explain that there is no palpable "edge of breast tissue," and no ridge where the breast connects to the chest, and that the PA, Ms. Smith, was therefore feeling a cancerous lump and not the edge of the breast tissue. Further, Ms. Smith felt the lump in the upper outer quadrant of the breast where cancer is most frequently found. Dr. Robinson will tell you that a woman who does her own breast exam is a more reliable examiner than practitioners, and that most cancerous lumps are first detected by the women experiencing them and not by health practitioners. He will also tell you that you cannot and must not rule out cancer by feeling the lump, because cancer can be a life-threatening condition. Therefore, you must do diagnostic testing to determine whether a lump is a cyst, a swollen lymph gland, or cancer.

Dr. Robinson will testify that although no one can say with certainty when Donna's cancer spread to her lymph nodes, statistically there is only a 25 percent chance it had spread in June 1987 because it was then less than 2 cm in diameter, and her lymph nodes were not swollen. Dr. H could not feel the lymph nodes in October 1987, but Dr. R felt enlarged lymph nodes in January 1988.

It takes a billion cells to make a mass of 1 cm or about 25 doublings of cells. A 1 cm mass is required before cancer can be diagnosed, and thus all breast cancer exists for years before it is diagnosed. Nevertheless, breast cancer can be cured if it is less than 2 cm in diameter when it is discovered. All of the breast cancer survival studies and statistics are based on the detection of lumps that are at least 1 cm in diameter and large enough to feel or see by mammogram. However, Donna's cancer was not diagnosed at 1 cm, and it doubled several times between June and January until it was larger than 2 cm and had spread into her lymph nodes.

If the PA, Ms. Smith, could not feel the lump, she should have referred Donna to a physician for examination and diagnostic testing or for another appointment three or four days after her menstrual period.

Ernestine K is a certified nurse practitioner who is familiar with the expected standards of practice of physician assistants and the entrance requirements and state regulations applicable to PAs. She teaches nurses and works with PAs. She will testify that Planned Parenthood was negligent in not having appropriate written guidelines for PA Smith and other nurses and PAs to follow in examining patients, making referrals, and recording the patient's medical history, examination results, assessment, and treatment.

Ernestine K will testify that Smith should have referred Donna to a physician for examination and diagnostic testing, or at the very least should have scheduled Donna for another examination three days after Donna's next menstrual period; that a patient is a more reliable examiner because she has the advantage of knowing her own body and having feelings and nerve endings within it that permit her to detect a lump. Like Dr. Robinson, Ernestine K will testify that you cannot feel the edge of the breast where it connects to the chest wall because there is no edge or well-defined connection, and that the PA apparently could feel the lump but did not recognize it as a lump.

Ernestine K will also testify that under state regulations, a PA must be supervised by a physician, and that PP's own internal rules require that a resident physician supervise the PA. However, Donna's PA was not supervised. A resident was at Planned Parenthood that afternoon but did not review or sign the chart. This lack of supervision violated both state regulations and PP policy. No resident at any time supervised PA Smith or knew how she was examining breasts. Smith did not consult with any other person or ask any other person to examine Donna; she simply decided that Donna was mistaken and did not feel a lump, only the edge of her breast. Ernestine K will testify that these procedures and this conduct were negligent.

Dr. V is a board-certified ob-gyn who will testify that PP was negligent in not enforcing state regulations and requiring residents to supervise PAs, and that PA Smith was negligent in not referring Donna to her supervising physician. This physician was only at the clinic one afternoon a week, but would have been there at one o'clock the afternoon of Donna's visit. PA Smith was negligent in not consulting and not referring Donna to a physician for diagnostic testing or at the very least in not scheduling Donna for another breast exam. Even if PA Smith told Donna that she should return to the clinic in the future if she continued to feel the lump, Dr. V will testify that this would have been inadequate advice because the PA had already assured Donna that there was no lump in her breast. She would have had no reason to return.

Dr. V will testify that Dr. H was negligent in not telling Donna that she needed diagnostic testing to rule out cancer and in failing to enter a differential diagnosis of possible cancer on Donna's chart. He was negligent in deciding that Donna's lump was either a cyst or lymph node after Donna told him that it had been there for four months and had started growing again in the last two months. If Dr. H had intended to refer Donna to Dr. R for further diagnostic testing to rule out cancer, he certainly did not make that clear; however, it will be apparent from Donna's testimony and Dr. H's charting that Dr. H did not refer Donna to Dr. R to rule out cancer.

Dr. V will testify that Dr. H's failure to immediately arrange for diagnostic testing and treatment caused an additional delay of two and one-half months, and increased Donna's chance of having her cancer recur by 10 to 20 percent. Dr. Robinson will likewise testify that this two and one-half month delay in treatment increased the chance of Donna's cancer recurring.

Dr. V will testify that Donna's cancer was probably Stage I in June, and if it had been treated at that time it could have been removed and probably cured; that it continued to grow to Stage II cancer by January 1988 and increased from about 1 cm to 2½ cm in diameter with node involvement by January. By January the cancer was Stage II, and Donna now has only a 50 percent chance of living for five years after the lump's removal.

In short, there will be testimony that because of Planned Parenthood's negligence followed by the negligence of Dr. H, Donna's breast cancer was not detected and treated until January 1988, and the six months' difference between the time that Donna first sought treatment and the time she got it may be the difference between life and death.

You are going to hear conflicting testimony in this case about the conversations between Donna and Ms. Smith at PP in June 1987 and about the conversation between Donna and Dr. H in October 1987.

We understand that PA Smith may testify that she told Donna to return to PP if the lump remained and continued to worry her. Donna can only remember that PA Smith told her the lump was nothing to worry about. However, the expert witnesses will testify that even if Smith gave this advice, she was negligent in not referring Donna to a physician or scheduling another appointment for further examination and testing.

We understand that Dr. H will testify that he referred Donna to Dr. R because of the possibility of cancer but did not mention cancer to Donna because he did not want to frighten her. He claims that he did not tell Donna that the lump was not cancer and did not tell her it was nothing to worry about. Dr. H's office charts will be introduced to show that he did not believe that Donna had cancer, but believed that her lump was just a cyst or lymph node.

Although you will be called on as fact finders to resolve the conflicting testimony, our experts will testify that even assuming PA Smith and Dr. H's versions are correct, they were both negligent.

You will hear testimony from physicians selected by PP to testify as expert witnesses on PP's behalf. We believe they will testify that Donna's cancerous lump was growing so rapidly that it was too tiny to be felt in June, and Donna was therefore mistaken in her belief that she felt a lump at that time and felt the edge of her breast instead. PP's experts will also testify that Donna's lump was so tiny in June that even a mammogram would not have detected it.

Those same experts will then testify that had Donna's lump been detected at PP in June, it had probably already spread to her lymph nodes and it was therefore too late to cure the cancer and save Donna's life.

Likewise, physicians selected by Dr. H as his expert witnesses will testify that Donna's cancer had to be growing so rapidly that it was already at Stage II, had already spread into the lymph nodes, and was too advanced to cure when Dr. H examined her. They will argue that if Dr. H did anything wrong, it doesn't matter. They will testify that he was not negligent and did nothing wrong.

However, our expert witnesses will testify that 75 percent of all cancers of the breast are cancers like Donna's and that most of these cancers are fast-growing. Donna's cancer is therefore not unusual, and the success rate for its treatment is high if it is detected and treated early. Early detection of all fast-growing cancers is the key to curing them and can be a matter of life and death.

In short, we understand that both defendants will be calling expert witnesses to render opinions that the defendants were not negligent, or that even if they were negligent, so what? It would not have made any difference to Donna anyway because her cancer could not be successfully treated. Any delay in its treatment was not important.

What about damages? You will learn that Donna lives in constant fear of death because she now has a 50 to 60 percent chance of cancer recurrence within five years of her treatment. She cannot have children because of the probable need for additional chemotherapy and radiation therapy. Even if she could have children, she fears that she would die of cancer and leave them motherless, and she is now reluctant to marry Robert B, with whom she is living. You will learn that she does not have the energy to complete her college education and work full-time; she cannot advance in her job; she is fearful of being turned down for employment because she is an insurance risk; she can only get insurance through her employment; and she may become unemployed and have no health insurance.

You will hear substantial additional testimony about other items of damage that I will not mention at this time. However, at the conclusion of trial, we will ask you to render a verdict for Donna in an amount that you consider to be a reasonable and fair assessment of her damages. Thank you.

APPENDIX F

EXAMINING WITNESSES

F.1 CASE SUMMARY, THEMES, AND CLAIMS OF NEGLIGENCE

Cox Case Summary

This is a case of a specialist failing to take routine precautions against allergic reactions in his patient and prescribing morphine in the face of a known allergy to codeine.

This is also a case about hospital nurses not paying attention to a recovering surgical patient, finding the patient in a coma but not knowing how to do CPR correctly, and then waiting 15 minutes before calling for help.

Themes

1. When a patient is at risk for drug reactions the physician should take routine precautions to avoid that risk.
2. Surgical patients have the right to expect that nurses will monitor their conditions carefully and know what to do in an emergency.

Claims of Negligence

Hospital Fault

1. *Did not question morphine order.* The nurses did not question the use of morphine, even though they had recorded an allergy to an opiate narcotic in the patient's hospital records.
2. *Did not watch for drug reactions.* The nurses were not prepared for possible drug reaction problems, even though such reactions are a known risk in postoperative patients.
3. *Waited 15 minutes.* The nurses waited fifteen minutes while the patient was in a coma before calling for help.

4. *Called doctor at home.* When the nurses finally sought help, they phoned a doctor who was at home rather than notifying the emergency doctor in the hospital.
5. *Did not call for code emergency.* The nurses violated hospital policy in not calling for a code emergency.
6. *Did not know CPR.* The nurses did not know how to perform CPR correctly even though they were responsible for a surgical patient.
7. *Did not record events.* When the nurses recorded the events in the patient's hospital chart they did not do it according to hospital policy. Instead, they wrote an account the next day with the help of their supervisors and put it in the patient's chart.

Neurosurgeon Fault

1. *Did not take patient's history.* He did not take the time to obtain the patient's admitting history but instead had somebody else take the history.
2. *Ignored allergy information.* He ignored the abundant evidence of the patient's allergy to opiate narcotics:
    a. The patient told him she was allergic to codeine;
    b. He recorded her allergy history in his records;
    c. Allergy history was recorded in her past hospital charts; and
    d. Allergy history was recorded in her past medical records.
3. *Ordered opiate in spite of allergy to codeine.* He then ordered morphine, an opiate, in the face of a known allergy to codeine and in spite of the risk involved.
4. *Ordered doses that caused cumulative buildup.* He ordered doses that involved the risk of cumulative buildup and created narcotic overdose with allergic reaction.
5. *Switched to an opiate from the synthetic he'd prescribed the year before.* When he did surgery on the patient in 1987, he chose a non-opiate synthetic drug, Buprenex. The patient experienced no problems from medications received in 1987. But in 1988 the neurosurgeon switched to an opiate narcotic, and the patient had an allergic reaction, causing brain damage.
6. *Disregarded anesthesiologist's orders for non-opiate.* He disregarded the fact that a specialist in drug use, the anesthesiologist, had ordered non-opiate synthetic drugs for the patient. The neurosurgeon was the only physician who ordered any opiate drug for the patient.

7. *Combined Phenergan with a high morphine dosage.* The neurosurgeon further compounded the problems by improperly combining Phenergan with a high dosage of morphine, resulting in over-sedation and helplessness.
8. *Immediately discontinued morphine after learning of coma.* As soon as he learned of the patient's coma he ordered the morphine discontinued because it was the cause of the coma. But the damage had already been done.

F.2 TRIAL AND WITNESS SCHEDULE

The following is a sample outline of a trial schedule that describes the order of events, the schedule for witnesses, and the anticipated time allotted for each event and witness. A parenthetical remark is sometimes made under a witness's name to remind the lawyer of the nature of that witness's testimony. A double question mark is sometimes placed after a witness's name as a reminder that the time and date has not yet been confirmed with the witness, or the lawyer is still undecided about calling the witness at that time and date. In this tentative trial schedule, time has been allotted for a lay witness, not yet named, because the lawyer has not yet decided which lay witness to call. Often, a tentative trial schedule is altered several times before it is finalized. Then, adjustments during trial are often necessary as emergencies arise and unexpected events occur which necessitate rearrangement and rescheduling.

Cox Witness Schedule

(Trial Date: May 4, 1992)

Monday, May 4th (1st Day)

9:30–10:30	Pretrial Motions	(1 hr)
10:30–12:00	Jury Selection	
1:30–4:30		(4.5 hr)

Tuesday, May 5th (2nd Day)

9:30–10:30	Jury Selection, cont.	(1 hr)
10:30–11:30	Plaintiff's Opening Statement	(1 hr)
11:30–12:30	1st Defendant's Opening Statement	(1 hr)
2:00–3:00	2nd Defendant's Opening Statement	(1 hr)

Plaintiff's Witnesses

1.	Beth Cox (Plaintiff)	3:00–3:30	(.5 hr)
2.	(Lay Witness) (Damages)	3:30–4:00	(.5 hr)

Wednesday, May 6th (3rd Day)

3.	Dr. Sally Powers?? (Treating neurologist—diagnosis and prognosis)	9:30–11:00	(1.5 hr)
4.	Nurse Diane Brothers?? (Adverse) (Responsible nurse)	11:00–12:00 1:30–3:00	(2.5 hr)
5.	Nurse Patty Wilson?? (Nurse expert v. hospital)	3:00–4:00	(1 hr)

Thursday, May 7th (4th Day)

5a.	Nurse Patty Wilson, cont.	9:30–12:00	(2.5 hr)
6.	Dr. Paul Drake?? (Adverse) (Defendant-doctor)	1:30–4:30	(3 hr)

Friday, May 8th (5th Day)

7.	Dr. Alan Teller (Expert v. doctor)	9:30–12:00 1:30–3:00	(4 hr)
8.	Nurse Florence Balew?? (Nurse expert v. hospital)	3:00–4:30	(1.5 hr)

Monday, May 11th (6th Day)

8a.	Nurse Florence Balew, cont.	9:30–11:00	(1.5 hr)
9.	Dr. Lana Gillis, Ph.D. (Expert re: pharmacology)	11:00–12:00 1:30–4:30	(4 hr)

Tuesday, May 12th (7th Day)

10.	Dr. Ely Trump (Expert neuropathologist—drugs caused it)	9:30–12:00 1:30–2:30	(3.5 hr)
11.	Dr. Fred Port, Ph.D. (Expert re: pharmacology)	2:30–4:30	(2 hr)

(schedule continued next page)

(schedule continued from previous page)

Wednesday, May 13th (8th Day)

11a.	Dr. Fred Port, cont.	9:30–10:30	(1 hr)
12.	Dr. Lee South (Neuroradiologist—brain stem not injured)	10:30–12:00	(1.5 hr)
13.	Dr. Benjamin Kosar (Neurologist v. doctor)	1:30–4:30	(3 hr)

Thursday, May 14th (9th Day)

13a.	Dr. Benjamin Kosar, cont.	9:30–10:30	(1 hr)
14.	Mike Cox (Plaintiff's husband—narrates day-in-the-life video)	10:30–12:00	(1.5 hr)
15.	Maria Wolfe (Lay damages witness)	1:30–2:15	(.75 hr)
16.	James Cox (Lay damages witness)	2:15–3:00	(.75 hr)
17.	(Lay witness) (Damages)	3:00–3:45	(.75 hr)

Friday, May 15th (10th Day)

18.	Arnold Lund (Expert on costs of care)	9:30–12:00 1:30–2:30	(3.5 hr)
19.	Dr. Lee South (Expert economist)	2:30–4:30	(2 hr)

F.3 EXHIBIT LIST

The following is a sample of an exhibit list to remind the lawyer of the exhibits available for use in the examination and cross-examination of the defendant-doctor and expert witnesses. This exhibit list is intended for use in helping to establish that the neurosurgeon knew, or should have known, that the use of an opiate narcotic could result in an allergic reaction causing brain damage.

Exhibits

Medical World News magazine (advertisement)
Dr. Dorsey's copies of Key 'Dear Doctor' letters

Books

DSM-III
Goodman and Gilman
Wineberger

Transparencies

Key

Key Physician Desk Reference documents
Key admissions
Key promotional
Key organization chart
Key 10-Ks
Key letter to FDA re: placement of warning

FDA

FDA regulations re: warnings
FDA guidelines
PDR 1979

Witnesses

Hendele's letters
Golub memos
Wineberger memos

Other

Joel's 'Dear Doctor' letter
Code for pharmaceutical companies
Damage elements
Marketing defined
Opening statement
Settlement agreement
Warning examples

F.4 OUTLINE OF DIRECT EXAMINATION OF A TREATING PHYSICIAN

This outline and those that follow in this appendix were created for a lawyer's personal use. The outlines were never intended to be followed slavishly or read from. Accordingly, although some questions are written out in full, others are often simply denoted by key words.

A. *Qualifications*
   1. Name and professional address
   2. Profession
   3. Where licensed
   4. Educational background
      a. Years of pre-medical college
      b. Years of medical school—where
      c. Internship—where
      d. Years of residency
         (1) Where
         (2) What field—explain
      e. Honors
      f. Board certification
         (1) Explain process of certification
         (2) What field
   5. Length of medical practice
   6. Special qualifications
      a. Articles published
      b. Books written or contributed to
      c. Papers delivered
      d. Memberships
      e. Experience in this area
         (1) Importance of practical experience

B. *First Contact with Plaintiff*
   1. Have you examined the plaintiff?
   2. Where and under what circumstances did you first examine the plaintiff?
   3. When did you first treat the plaintiff?

C. *History*

1. What is a history?
2. Why did you take a history?
3. What history did you obtain in this case?
4. How was the history obtained (from the patient or from other sources)?

D. *Physical Examination*

1. What was the nature of the physical examination you made?
2. What general observations did you make during the physical examination?
   a. Limitation of motion
   b. Bleeding
   c. Shock
   d. Complaints of pain
   e. Fractures
   f. Obvious injuries

E. *Diagnosis*

1. Did you take any X rays or have them taken?
   a. Were they taken under your direction, supervision, and control?
   b. Do the X rays reasonably and accurately represent the anatomy shown?
2. Did you arrive at a treating diagnosis in this case?
3. State your diagnosis, and explain it to the jury
4. Medical illustration
   a. Do you recognize this? What is it?
   b. Is it a reasonable, accurate diagram?
   c. Will this illustration assist you in explaining your diagnosis?
5. Use the illustration, and explain your diagnosis to the jury. Interpret the X rays for the jury.

F. *Hospitalization*

1. Did the treatment require hospitalization?
2. How long was the patient hospitalized?
3. What was done for the patient while the patient was in the hospital?

G. *Hospital Records*

1. Do you recognize these? What are they?
2. Indicate generally what topics the records cover.
3. How were these records prepared?
4. Read the following significant portions of the records:
    a. Admitting diagnosis
    b. Physicians' orders
    c. Progress records

H. *Surgery*

1. Was surgery required?
2. When was the surgery performed?
3. What was the nature of the surgery?
4. Was there subsequent surgery? (If so, when and of what nature?)

I. *Drugs or Therapy*

1. Did you prescribe drugs? For what purpose?
2. Did you prescribe physical therapy? For what purpose?

J. *Mechanical Devices*

1. Did you prescribe any mechanical devices?
    a. Neck collar
    b. Brace—cast—splint—traction
    c. Wheelchair
    d. Walker
    e. Cane
2. Why?
3. How long were the devices used?

K. *Other Treatment*

1. Did you prescribe any other treatment?
    a. Bed rest
    b. Home exercises
    c. Hot baths
    d. Avoidance of activity
2. Why?
3. How long did the patient undergo these treatments?

L. *Most Recent Examination*

1. When did you last examine the patient?
2. Is the patient still under your care?
3. When is your next appointment with the patient scheduled?

M. *Locality Rule*

1. From training and experience, are you generally familiar with the standards of care to which medical practitioners are held for problems such as those in this case?
    a. Is the standard of care for problems such as those in this case relatively uniform throughout the United States?
    b. From your training and experience, are you generally familiar with what is regarded as appropriate and reasonable medical care for the type of medical problem involved here?
2. Have you made an effort to investigate the standard of care practiced by physicians in this locality at the time of this case? If so, how? Have you
    a. Talked with physicians?
    b. Toured the hospital?
    c. Practiced in similar hospitals/clinics/communities?
    d. Read depositions in this case of doctors familiar with this locality?
    e. Seen hospital manual/rules, etc.?
    f. Had experience with a similar nursing situation?
    g. Trained nurses regarding this kind of problem?

N. *Negligence Claims*

(See claims of negligence in Appendix F.1. Ask the doctors for opinions and explanations regarding each of these claims. Then ask the following questions.)

1. In your opinion did the conduct of Dr. Smith in this case fall below the standards of practice exercised by a reasonably careful and prudent physician?
2. Please explain why you have this opinion and the basis for your opinion.
3. Are you aware of different approaches used by other competent physicians under similar circumstances?
4. "Matter of judgment"—Was Dr. Smith's exercise of judgment

in this case reasonable under the circumstances? Do you feel that his exercise of medical judgment fell below the standards of practice of reasonably careful and prudent physicians?

5. Have you discussed your findings, opinions, or conclusions with any other physicians before today? If so, give full reasons and circumstances for doing so, and the names of the physicians.
6. Have you discussed this case with any other physicians before arriving at your findings, opinions, or conclusions? If so, give full reasons and circumstances for doing so, and the names of the physicians.
7. Are you aware of any other physicians who may have reviewed this case? If so, give physicians' names and their reasons and circumstances for reviewing the case.

O. *Miscellaneous Questions*

1. Do you have any opinion as to whether some other physician, nurse, or health-care provider who was not named as a defendant in this lawsuit may have been negligent in the care of the patient and contributed to the injuries in this case? If so, please identify such person and state the full circumstances of the person's negligence.
2. Res ipsa loquitur: would this result be expected normally in the absence of negligence?
   a. How common is this occurrence and result?
   b. How many times have you observed such an occurrence and result? Over how many years?

P. *Causation*

1. What in your opinion were the contributing and proximate causes of the injuries sustained in this case?

Q. *Prognosis*

1. Permanent injury
   a. What is a permanent injury?
   b. Does the patient have any injuries that are considered permanent?
   c. Describe each one.
2. Effect of injuries in future (generally)
   a. Disability (temporary—permanent—partial)

(1) walking
(2) jumping
(3) running
(4) climbing
(5) crawling
(6) standing
(7) turning
(8) stooping
(9) crouching
(10) kneeling
(11) sitting
(12) reaching
(13) lifting
(14) carrying
(15) throwing
(16) pushing
(17) pulling
(18) fingering
(19) feeling
(20) talking
(21) hearing
(22) seeing

3. Impairment of the patient's earning ability
   a. Has the patient's capacity to work and earn money been affected by injuries? Describe.
   b. Does the patient tire or become fatigued more quickly as result of injuries?
   c. What is the patient's future in the labor market with a history of injury like this?
4. Family life generally
   a. Will the patient's daily routine at home be affected by the injury? Describe.
   b. What will be the effect of the injuries on the patient's family life with the spouse and children?
5. Future pain and discomfort
   a. What is your opinion about whether the patient will have pain or discomfort in the future as a result of injuries?
   b. Nature of pain and discomfort
      (1) Future hospitalization
      (2) Future drugs
      (3) Future physical therapy
      (4) Future injections
   c. Length of time that will be required for each of the above
   d. The expense that will necessarily be incurred for each of the above
6. Life expectancy

R. *Bills*

1. Do you recognize these bills?
    a. What are they?
    b. Do these bills represent reasonable and necessary expenses for treatment of the patient?

S. *Conclusion*

1. Is there anything further you can tell us about the patient's condition that I failed to ask about?

F.5 OUTLINE OF DIRECT EXAMINATION OF A PLAINTIFF'S EXPERT WITNESS ON MEDICAL CAUSATION AND INJURIES

Direct Examination of Dr. Cloud

A. *Background*

1. Dr. Cloud will explain the medical aspects of brain injury
2. Qualifications
3. Date of examination of the plaintiff

B. *Records Reviewed*

1. What reviewed
    a. Dr. Folger (clinical neuropsychologist)—examination of 2/7/91
    b. Dr. Bean—testimony/report (Under evidentiary rules, Dr. Cloud can describe Dr. Bean's testimony and report if it is the type of information that is reasonably relied on by experts in his field in forming opinions on the subject.)

C. *Dr. Cloud's Report*

1. Review the contents of the report
    a. Life expectancy
    b. Causation—areas of brain damage
    c. Permanence of injury (Use brain illustration and model)

D. *Dr. Bean's Report*

1. Review the contents of the summary and report
    a. Life expectancy
    b. Causation—areas of brain damage
    c. Recommendations
    d. Is the plaintiff at risk for mental illness?

E. *Dr. Folger's Report*

1. Review the contents of the summary and report
    a. Mt. Fuji example
    b. Cripe findings
    c. Summary and impressions
    d. Practical implications

F. *Economic and Noneconomic Damages*

Use transparencies that describe and itemize the economic and noneconomic damages.

F.6 OUTLINE OF DIRECT EXAMINATION OF PLAINTIFF

The following is a sample outline of the direct examination of a client in a medical negligence case.

A. *Identification*

1. Name, address
2. Marital status
    a. Are you currently married?
    b. How long have you been married?
    c. Were you married previously?
3. Children
    a. Prior marriage
        (1) Ages
        (2) Living at home
    b. Current marriage
        (1) Ages
        (2) Living at home
4. Occupation—length of time

B. *Activities and Health before Injury*

1. Health
    a. Shoulder
    b. Back
2. Normal recreational activities
3. Mental attitude
4. Motivation

5. Ability to handle stress/problems
6. Achievements
7. Employment history and any past injuries arising out of employment
8. Any health problems before injuries sustained in this case

C. *Beginning of Problems*

1. Memory of first awareness of problems, including any medical attention received

D. *Dr. Stanley's Care*

1. Memory generally of how client got along under Dr. Stanley's care and what Dr. Stanley did. (See summary of Dr. Stanley's deposition for reminders of areas of inquiry.)
2. Weight
3. Medication
4. Back problems

E. *Dr. Bloom's Care*

1. Memory regarding Dr. Bloom's care
   a. Weight
   b. Medication
   c. Back complaints
   d. Shoulder complaints
2. Memory regarding decision about first manipulation
   a. Information received from Dr. Bloom regarding risks/benefits of manipulation
   b. Pain and discomfort following first manipulation
3. Same regarding second manipulation
   a. Information received from Dr. Bloom regarding risks/benefits of manipulation
   b. Pain and discomfort following second manipulation

F. *Hope University and Dr. Rugg*

1. Referral to Hope University
   a. Mental attitude
   b. Motivation
   c. Weight

d. Medications
e. Back complaints
f. Shoulder complaints

2. Memory of circumstances and care at pain clinic
    a. Situation afterwards—how got along, etc.
3. Circumstances of first surgery performed by Dr. Rugg
4. Decision about fusion
    a. Considerations
    b. Mental attitude
    c. Motivation
    d. Back complaints
    e. Shoulder complaints
5. How client got along following the fusion

G. *Back—Dr. Snell*

1. Circumstances regarding statements client made to Dr. Snell that could be considered admissions.
    a. See notes concerning statements made by Dr. Snell that are inconsistent with her recollection and have her explain the inconsistencies.
2. When did back pain start?

H. *Present Situation*

1. Family activity
2. General health
    a. Shoulder—limitations
    b. Employment—attempts to work
    c. Weight
    d. Back
    e. Motivation
    f. Mental attitude
3. Changes in life
    a. Life
    b. Relationships with family members
    c. Recreation
    d. Personality

4. Consortium change
    a. Assistance around house—chores
    b. Assistance with money contribution
    c. Effect on children
    d. Change in closeness/personality
    e. Change in communication
    f. Effect on happiness

F.7 OUTLINE OF POINTS TO MAKE REGARDING DAMAGES WHEN QUESTIONING WITNESSES

Often, there are a number of points that you want to emphasize when questioning damages witnesses, and the following outline illustrates some of these points in the case of a brain-injured plaintiff who works part-time washing dishes.

A. *How Will Money Help Michael?*
    1. Are there any programs?
    2. Does he need an aide?

B. *Possible Phrases*
    1. "Michael is a shell of the person he was or could be."
    2. Michael is a small child in a man's body.
    3. Michael cries sometimes because he knows he's different and people make fun of him.

C. *Areas of Concern*
    1. Michael will never have the ability to safely care for a child of his own.
    2. If Michael ever has a child, he will not be able to teach the child new tasks, take the child to the zoo, teach the child to play baseball, etc.
    3. He will never be able to do the things he wants to do in life.
    4. Ms. Moody used an analogy of a sign "Slippery When Wet." That's why Michael will never be able to drive a car on his own: he would never understand the meaning of such a sign.
    5. Michael will miss out on most of the joys of life:
        a. He is able to marry, but who would marry him?
        b. (Note: Some jurors may feel washing dishes is a good job) Michael's able only to do menial jobs. There is nothing

wrong with that if it's his choice, but his chance to do anything else has been taken from him.

6. The issue is what was taken away from him rather than what he is left with.
7. If asked to go to the basement and get a box of soap, he would forget why he went to the basement.

Probable Defense Questions to Michael

Note: Michael is easily led by questions. He wants to please.

1. Are you happy?
2. Do you like your job?
3. Do you want to get married?
4. Do you like to sail, swim, ride a bike?

F.8 OUTLINE OF DAMAGES

A generic outline of damages for trial purposes and for use in examining witnesses is often helpful. The following is a sample of an outline in a brain-injury case.

Damages Elements

Noneconomic Damages

1. Nature and extent of injury
   a. Permanent brain damage
   b. Extent of effect on
      (1) Employability
      (2) Independence
      (3) Relationships
      (4) Daily living
      (5) Mental health
2. Mental disability
   a. Memory
   b. Verbal skills
   c. Abstract reason
   d. Reason/common sense
   e. Academic skills
3. Mental suffering
   a. Lack of self esteem
   b. Lack of confidence
   c. Fear of future
   d. Frustration
   e. Worry
   f. Embarrassment
4. Loss of enjoyment of life
   a. Loss of pride in work
   b. Loss of freedom
   c. Loss of independence
   d. Loss of marital goals
   e. Risk to mental health
   f. Altered view of future
   g. Altered view of self
   h. Altered view of world
   i. Loss of intellect
   j. His knowledge that he is brain damaged

Economic Damages

1. Annual physical
2. Daily supervision
3. Counseling
4. Special magazines
5. Case manager
6. Vocational counsel
7. Job coach

One-Time Costs

1. Good Sam program
2. Housing for live-in

Future Losses

1. Loss of wages

F.9 OUTLINE OF CROSS-EXAMINATION OF HOSPITAL NURSES

It is helpful to have an outline of the points to be established in cross-examining hospital nurses when the hospital is named as a defendant. The following is a sample outline from a case involving negligent nursing care that contributed to a bad outcome.

Theme: When a child is admitted to a hospital in a life-threatening condition, the staff should be particularly watchful and cautious.

A. *Doctor's Orders Concerning 40-Percent Oxygen Were Disobeyed*

1. Child taken from oxygen tent
    a. Oxygen was as essential for this baby as for a deep sea diver
    b. Without oxygen the baby would suffocate
    c. Show Dr. Henderson's orders
        (1) "Nurses clearly understood" doctor's orders to keep in oxygen tent
        (2) In view of doctor's orders, it violated nursing standards to "intermittently" give oxygen
        (3) Use of a blow-by was not within the "spirit and intent" of the doctor's orders
        (4) Doctor learned that nurses had the baby outside the oxygen tent for one hour and probably more, violating nursing standards
        (5) Removing the baby from the oxygen tent is only appropriate for short periods

B. *Doctor's Orders Concerning the Heart Monitor Were Disobeyed*

1. Heart alarm on the monitor disconnected for this at-risk child
    a. No problems with "artifacts" were recorded while the heart monitor was on before catheter
    b. No recorded problems in hospital chart with monitor accuracy or artifacts after catheter and until arrest
    c. No record of nurse removing monitor or reason for removing it in original hospital chart
    d. Monitor was immediately reattached by nurse when the baby's heart stopped
    e. When asked by hospital investigator three days later why the monitor had been removed, Nurse Smith said "be-

cause of continual alarm due to high heart rate." She did not state it was disconnected because of "false alarms", "not working right", or "artifacts."

f. The word "artifacts" was never recorded by any nurse in the hospital record—even in a late entry note

g. It was the established standard of practice to reattach the heart monitor before use of the catheter and as soon as the infant was placed back in the oxygen tent

h. School fire alarm: you can't assume it's a fire drill and ignore it

i. Dr. Henderson

(1) Learned from nurses that the heart monitor had been disconnected

(2) Gave a verbal order to connect the monitor as before

(3) Believes that had Brandon been on monitor, the alarm would have alerted nurses of Brandon's deterioration sooner

(4) Had no reason to believe that the care would be any different after the catheter than before, but the care turned out to be "substantially different" after the catheter up to the arrest

C. *Abnormal Vital Signs Were Ignored*

1. Inconsolable crying and hyper-irritability

a. The only way an infant can verbally communicate a problem is by crying

b. Crying is a child's warning system to let others know there's a problem

c. Common sense—if you can't make a child stop crying, something is wrong

2. Very abnormal respiration

3. High heart rate caused alarm to continuously go off

D. *Hospital Rules and Nursing Policy Were Violated*

1. Doctor was not notified of a hospital rule requiring the attendant nurse to inform the doctor of changes in patient condition

a. Hospital rules dictate that any calls to a doctor out of concern for an infant are to be recorded by the nurse

b. There is no record of any call registering concern to any doctor by any nurse after the catheter

c. If calls are made to a doctor who does not respond, hospital rules say that the nurse must do something

d. See Langley testimony

(1) If a call was made after each vital sign and the nurse is to record calls to the doctor, why weren't the calls recorded? She had time:

Hrs.—Time	Hospital Records
1320—1:20	Page 38.3
1420—2:20	Page 38.6
1520—3:20	Arrest (between first recorded vital sign at 1:20 p.m. and the arrest at 3:30, the nurse had two hours to record phone calls.)

e. Dr. Henderson

(1) His clinic note

(2) "Still unclear why nurses did not ask any physicians for help or advice"

(3) Nurse August admitted to him that the nurses had not contacted any doctor during the two hours before the arrest

(4) Nurse August's statement to the investigator that she called Dr. Langley twice is inconsistent with what she told Dr. Langley the next day

2. No corrective action by the nurses

a. If you call the fire department and they don't show up, you've got to call back or do something—you don't let the house burn down

3. The baby was not closely observed—a hospital rule requires special attention to changes in patient during oxygen therapy

a. The nurse was "quite distressed" and admitted to the doctor that she had gotten busy and left the baby with a student nurse just before the arrest

4. Medical records were deficient

a. Missing patient care plan

(1) Rule went into effect June 1984

(2) If the patient care plan is not a permanent record, why does the hospital rule indicate that the plan should be kept on file?

E. *Excuses, Denials, and Blaming Others*

1. Excuses

   a. Not an oxygen problem—the arrest was caused by sudden choking on food

      (1) See cause material

         (a) Blood-gas studies

         (b) Ease of ventilation

         (c) X ray report

         (d) Documented last feeding at 1:30

         (e) Dr. Henderson interview of mom plus nurses

      (2) Occam's Razor—when there are several possible explanations, the simplest is usually the most likely one

         (a) When you hear hoofbeats, you're usually hearing horses and not zebras

   b. "Dr. Langley is not our resident"

   c. Mother sued too late—she should have known

2. Denial

   a. Dr. Henderson did not give an order concerning the monitor—it was left to nursing judgment to remove it

3. Blaming others

   a. Mom's fault

      (1) Oxygen was removed so she could feed the baby, and it was okay; she didn't feed or use blow-by correctly

      (2) Alarm was disconnected because mom complained

   b. Nurses called Dr. Langley twice, and he didn't come

F. *General Points*

1. Commonsense medical negligence case

   a. Health-care providers knew from the beginning that the baby was obviously at risk

2. Both sides agree that the child has irreversible brain damage

   a. Did the brain damage happen while the patient was in the hospital under the care of hospital nurses?

3. Nurses are the eyes and ears of the doctor—if they have any question, they must notify the doctor

4. Accountability and responsibility
   a. Improves quality of health care
   b. Reason for quality control in hospital
5. Nurses are expected to be able to recognize significant abnormal changes in an infant like Brandon
6. In medicine, it is important to promptly react to any significant abnormal condition before it becomes life threatening
   a. That's why ambulances and fire trucks have red lights and sirens—get there fast
   b. Easier to put out campfire than forest fire
   c. Better to be safe than sorry
7. Would it be a failure to exercise reasonable nursing prudence for a nurse to see a significant abnormal sign in Brandon and not act on it?
   a. Red warning light on instrument panel of 747

F.10 GENERAL OUTLINE OF CROSS-EXAMINATION OF DEFENDANT AND DEFENSE EXPERTS

The "collateral attack" portion of the following outline raises issues that may show bias by the witness or otherwise attack the credibility of expert witnesses. The questions raised do not constitute a direct attack on the substance of the witness's opinions. Following the collateral attack is a section containing general medical principles that most doctors will concede and that are helpful in obtaining concessions from the defendant-doctor and the defense expert witnesses. Obtaining concessions on general medical principles applicable to a particular case then forces the witness to make further concessions on the facts and substance of the case at issue.

A. *Collateral Attack*

Note: First review the deposition outline of the witness for information on how the witness will respond to the areas of inquiry.

1. Fees
   a. How many hours to date
   b. Hourly rate
      (1) Preparation
      (2) Trial
   c. How much did the witness bill plaintiff's counsel for deposition testimony?

2. How much time did the witness spend on the case yesterday and today, and what are the total fees to date?
3. Refer to deposition notes regarding the witness's deposition testimony:
   a. Number of times the witness testified for plaintiffs compared to defendants
   b. Relationship to defendants or their expert witnesses
   c. Prior testimony against a doctor, nurse, or hospital in a medical negligence case
   d. Any bias caused by being sued in the past
4. Lack of information
   a. Lacks records or documents to base opinion on

B. *General Principles*

Note: Select one or more principles as a theme.

1. Do you agree that when any risk of life is involved, the doctor should always follow the rule "It is better to be safe than sorry"?
2. Do you agree that any risk of serious bodily injury or death is unacceptable if reasonable means could have been used to minimize or eliminate the risk?
3. Do you agree with the following general principle of medical care?

   > The greater the risk of injury, the greater the duty to a patient to provide good care and treatment.

4. Do you believe that the first priority of medicine should be the safety of the patient?
5. The public has a big stake in safe medical care, doesn't it?
6. Would you agree with me that if a doctor is not prepared to know how to diagnose and treat people with the problems the plaintiff had, the doctor shouldn't accept the case?
7. When doctors accept patients, aren't they saying, "Don't worry. I am trained and qualified to take care of you"?
   a. Do you agree that if a doctor, clinic, or hospital is not prepared to treat you right, you should not be accepted or admitted as a patient and your money should not be taken?

8. Do you agree that the plaintiff had the right to expect to receive good quality medical care for professional services that were paid for?
9. The defendant-doctor billed the plaintiff for professional services, didn't she?
10. Isn't a doctor someone people go to to get better?
11. Would you agree that if there is ever a time when a person should be able to relax and trust somebody else, it is when you put your life in the hands of a doctor?
    a. When a patient puts his or her life in the hands of a doctor, don't you agree that the patient has a right to assume that he or she will receive safe and competent care?

C. *Principles of Patient Care*

1. When a patient puts his or her life in the hands of a doctor, the patient has a right to trust and rely on getting the best care. Once a physician agrees to undertake care of a patient, a duty of reasonable prudence is owed in professional care
2. When any question of safety is involved, the policy ought to be "If there is any doubt, don't take a chance"—safety first
    a. Utilize all diagnostic testing
    b. A fence at the top of a cliff is better than an ambulance waiting in the valley below
    c. It's better to be safe than sorry
    d. An ounce of prevention is worth a pound of cure
3. Are doctors trained to perform careful examinations and do appropriate testing to rule out possible problems and to arrive at a diagnosis?
    a. Trained to make differential diagnoses
    b. Importance of using differential diagnoses to rule out possible causes of symptoms, making a correct diagnosis, and ruling out more serious causes
    c. Treating symptoms without discovering their cause is bad medicine
    d. Not good medicine to:
        (1) Fail to do appropriate testing to rule out serious underlying causes of symptoms
            (a) The doctor undertaking treatment is obligated to order appropriate tests

(2) Assume the cause of a condition without doing any testing to discover the cause

e. A careful, competent doctor would want to rule out a more serious condition's being the cause of the problem

f. Physicians are taught to treat the whole person, not just symptoms, aren't they?

4. Would you agree that it is a general principle of medicine that the risk of serious medical harm should always be eliminated when there are reasonable means available to do so?

5. Would you agree that in deciding whether to perform diagnostic testing, you must weigh the cost of that testing against the potential risk of harm to the patient if the tests are not conducted?

   a. Would you agree that if the potential risk of harm to the patient is serious injury or death, the cost of diagnostic testing is warranted and the tests should be performed?

   b. Would you agree that a patient has a right to make the choice about such gambles with the patient's life?

D. *Right to Trust the Doctor's Judgment*

1. Didn't the patient have the right to trust and rely on the doctor's medical advice?

2. Don't people believe that if they don't follow their doctor's advice, they won't get better?

   a. Wouldn't you agree that even the president of the United States should follow and rely upon his doctor's advice?

3. Do you agree that once a doctor agrees to undertake treatment of a patient, the doctor has a duty to give good medical care?

E. *Better to Be Safe Than Sorry*

1. When human life is involved, the policy ought to be "If there is any doubt, don't take a chance"; "better to be safe than sorry"

2. One of the very important obligations of a competent emergency room doctor is to recognize the presence of life-threatening conditions in a patient

   a. That's a fundamental principle of medicine

3. If a doctor or nurse is going to accept "life and death" responsibilities in a hospital emergency room, that person has the obligation to carry out duties carefully

4. In medicine, it is important to take care of problems before they get out of hand and become life threatening
    a. A stitch in time saves nine
    b. It is easier to put out a campfire than a forest fire

F. *Importance of Finding the Cause of Problems*
1. Doctors are trained about the importance of finding the cause of a patient's problems—especially when a life-threatening cause could be involved
    a. People can die if their symptoms are treated but the underlying cause of the symptoms is not

G. *Importance of Signs*
1. If a red warning light on the dash board of an airplane began flashing, a careful, competent pilot would be expected to find out why
    a. Medicine treats vital signs the same way
    b. Would it be poor practice for the pilot to put a piece of black tape over the warning light and keep flying?
    c. Medicine is no different

H. *Correct Testing Was Never Done*
1. There were abnormal signs that were ignored
2. Correct diagnostic testing was never done
3. Regarding testing that should have been done,
    a. How would the test be done?
    b. How long would the test take?
    c. How much pain would the test cause?
    d. How much would the test cost?
    e. How much risk would the test involve?
    f. How much benefit would be derived from the test?
    g. How long has this test been available to the medical establishment?
    h. Do nurses know about this test?

I. *Patient's Right to Expect Safe and Proper Treatment*
1. Doesn't a patient have a right to expect that proper and safe medical care will be provided by the doctor?

2. Doesn't a patient have a right to assume that if the doctor sees signs of problems, the doctor will take appropriate action?

J. *Doctor Is in the Best Position to Know*

1. Doctors and hospitals have control of patient's care

a. They have a corresponding duty to exercise care for the patient's safety

b. It is hard for us to get them to listen, but the medical establishment will be out of control unless we require it to be responsible and accountable

(1) Responsibility: if you have control over the life of a patient, you are responsible for the patient's safety

(2) Accountability: if you fail to fulfill your obligations, you are accountable for the consequences

K. *Doctors Must Accept Their Responsibility*

1. If a pilot ejects from a plane and the parachute doesn't open, the parachute's manufacturer will not be permitted to say "Too bad, it's your fault, not ours. If you had flown safely you would never have needed the safety parachute."

L. *Doctors Must Use Common Sense When It Comes to Patient Care*

1. Doctors must use common sense regarding what is reasonably safe under the conditions

2. Reasonable safety and common sense mean

a. We are better off as a society if patients receive reasonable and safe care

b. Common sense begins with the obvious, inexpensive things:

(1) Reacting to abnormal signs

(2) Making careful observations and monitoring

F.11 CROSS-EXAMINATION OF VOCATIONAL EXPERT

There are some standard areas of inquiry that can be used in any case. The following is a sample outline of areas for cross-examination of the defendant's vocational expert.

Cross-Examination of Vocational Expert

A. *Not Hired by the Plaintiff to Help Him Find Work*
   1. Where did you examine the plaintiff?
   2. Were you hired by state to examine the plaintiff and testify at trial?
   3. Are you being paid for examination and testimony?
      a. What is your hourly rate? What is your amount of billing?
   4. You knew that you were not to help the plaintiff find work
      a. The plaintiff was not your client
      b. You knew that whatever your opinions were, the plaintiff wasn't your responsibility, so you were not going to actually find work for him

B. *Saw the Plaintiff Only Once*
   1. You saw him only one time, ________ years after the auto accident and surgery
      a. At your office
      b. During normal working hours
      c. You saw other clients the same day; you didn't set the day aside for the plaintiff
   2. How long did you meet personally with the plaintiff?
   3. How long did you spend taking the plaintiff's history?
   4. How long did you take for testing?

C. *No Personal Information about Work Ability Obtained*
   1. Never discussed work ability with plaintiff's personal physicians
   2. Never discussed work ability with plaintiff's family
   3. Never discussed work ability with plaintiff's fellow workers
   4. Never discussed work ability with plaintiff's employers

D. *Affirmative History in Your Report*
   1. Question on affirmative and favorable facts in report

F.12 EXAMINATION AND CROSS-EXAMINATION OF A DEFENSE MEDICAL EXPERT

The following is a direct and cross-examination in a wrongful death action for failure to timely diagnose and treat breast cancer. The action was brought by the mother of Theresa Garcia against the Lovelace Medical Center and four of its employees: Dr. F, who saw her on July 27, 1982; Dr. S, who saw her on July 30, 1982; Nurse D, who saw her in September 1982; and Dr. J, who saw her on December 14, 1982. Ms. Garcia was complaining of a painful lump in the breast, and Dr. F diagnosed it as a subcutaneous nodule that was not cancerous, and was probably fibrocystic disease or an adenoma (a benign tumor). Dr. S, Nurse D, and Dr. J detected no abnormality in their examinations. The examiners could detect no lymph node enlargement during this time. Ms. Garcia moved from Colorado to New Mexico where cancer was diagnosed by Dr. T and Dr. Mc in April 1983. When detected, it was pathologically a Stage IV cancer that had spread to three lymph nodes. The patient was treated by lumpectomy and chemotherapy but later died.

The following direct examination of the defense medical expert, an oncologist (Dr. G), is used to impeach the plaintiff's oncologist, Dr. R, who has already testified. Dr. G renders opinions that the cancer could not have been detected at the Lovelace Medical Center; that had it been detected by defendants, early treatment would not have made a difference in the outcome; that it was a fast-growing cancer, which explains why it became detectable just nine months after the patient first appeared at the Lovelace Medical Center; that the treatment rendered in New Mexico was the same treatment that would have been rendered in Colorado had the cancer been detected earlier; and that plaintiff's chances of survival were not decreased by the failure to detect the cancer earlier in Colorado.

On cross-examination, William Trine establishes that the witness has relied on erroneous information in arriving at his opinions and that when the correct information is used as the basis for opinions, the defendants were probably negligent. He establishes that the doctor's views are not supported by medical literature and that his opinions are not supported by the prevailing view of his peers or by the American Cancer Society. Mr. Trine also demonstrates how medical literature and the expert's written report and deposition can be effectively used to impeach the witness, and how bias can be demonstrated and effectively used to impeach the witness's credibility.

Direct Examination

By Ms. Smith (defense counsel):

Q: Dr. G, would you give the jury a summary of your educational background?

A: I took my premedical education at Northwestern University in Evanston, Illinois. After three years, I went to the medical school at University of Illinois in Chicago, following which I interned and took on a year's residency at the University of Cincinnati. After two years in the military, I took two more years of internal medicine residency at the University of Minnesota, followed then by two years of a medical oncology fellowship at the University of Minnesota.

Q: What is a medical oncology fellowship?

A: It consists of training in the medical management of malignancies, but in so doing we need to learn about other specialties, such as surgical oncology, pathology, radiation therapy, and the fields that are allied with cancer.

Q: What has been your continuing association with the University of Colorado Medical School?

A: I am now an associate clinical professor, and I have worked with a number of members of the faculty of the University in various projects related to cancer.

Q: And at what hospital are you on staff?

A: I am the chief of staff at St. Luke's Hospital, and I am also on the active staff of St. Joseph.

Q: Do you hold any consultant position?

A: I am the permanent medical oncology consultant to Fitzsimons Army Hospital.

Comment: With the following questions, counsel demonstrates that the witness may have better qualifications than the plaintiff's expert, Dr. R.

Q: Doctor, were you a member of the search committee for the head of the section of medical oncology at the University of Colorado Medical Center?

A: That's correct.

Q: And what did that mean, to be on the search committee?

A: The university had been looking to upgrade its medical oncology department, and so embarked on a national study, search study, to find a head of the proposed department. And I was a member of that search committee.

Q: And when was there a head chosen for the oncology department?

A: I guess it was about a year and a half ago.

Q: Who was chosen?

A: Dr. Paul B.

Q: Not Dr. R?

A: No.

Q: Do you know Dr. R?

A: Yes, I do.

Q: In what context do you know Dr. R?

A: Well, we worked together, beginning in 1972, when I came to Denver, at the university for two years.

Q: Are you familiar with his various specialties within the field of oncology?

A: I am.

Q: What are they?

A: The study and treatment of leukemias and lymphomas.

Q: Doctor, do you have an area of specialty within the field of oncology?

A: Per se, no, but I would have to say that of the cancers that I am involved with, the most frequent cancer is breast cancer.

Q: Doctor, do you have any association with the American Cancer Society?

A: Yes, I was chair two years ago of the Professional Education Committee. And I ran the Vail Midwinter Cancer Conference for about five years.

Q: Do you belong to professional societies, Doctor?

A: Yes. I am a member of the American Society of Clinical Oncologists. I am a member of the Denver Clinical and Pathologic Society, and the American Medical Society, the Denver Medical Society.

Q: Have you written in the area of medical oncology?

A: Yes, I have a bibliography that includes about seven papers, one of which deals with the treatment of breast cancer.

Q: Doctor, could you explain to the jury what your experience is with the treatment of breast cancer, and by that I mean the extent of your practice in that area?

A: I can be involved with a patient with breast cancer at any point along the way—when a breast cancer is first suspected or when it is detected—to have my input as to what kind of treatment should be done; I can be involved after the diagnosis has been made; and I am involved with determining what kind if any further therapy is needed, such as chemotherapy, hormonal therapy, further radiation therapy, or further surgery, and then I will manage that patient permanently from that point on.

Q: What percentage of your practice would you estimate deals with breast cancer as opposed to other cancers?

A: I would guess that maybe 20 to 25 percent of my practice is breast cancer.

Q: Doctor, are you a member of the American Society of Clinical Oncology?

A: Yes, I am.

Q: What is your position with that organization?

A: I have been a member for close to 15 years. I have no particular position.

Q: Do you know Dr. S?

A: I do.

Q: And what is your knowledge of Dr. S; in what context do you know him?

A: We worked together on the American Cancer Society some years ago for a number of years. I also see him at St. Joe when I am there, and have seen him at tumor conferences.

Q: And that work with the American Cancer Society, that's volunteer work?

A: That's correct.

Q: Did you at my request review medical records of Theresa Garcia from Lovelace Medical Clinic?

A: I did.

Comment: In the following testimony, the witness concludes that the cancer found in New Mexico was not the lump that was felt by Dr. S when Ms. Garcia was first examined at Lovelace.

Q: And based on your review of the medical records, Doctor, do you have an opinion to a reasonable degree of medical probability whether Theresa Garcia had breast cancer on July 30, 1982, when she was seen by Dr. S?

A: I think she probably did.

Q: Doctor, if you will just answer whether you have an opinion, and then I will ask you what is that opinion.

A: I'm sorry. Yes, I have an opinion.

Q: What is the basis for that opinion?

A: The basis for that opinion is that breast cancer does not occur in a body when somebody first detects it. It takes time to progress from the first cell to billions of cells when it is first able to be detected. What we consider to be a small cancer may in fact contain many billions of cells. Nobody knows what that length of time is, but we have a scientific idea what it is. It can probably be anywhere from one to 15 years, depending upon how quickly that particular breast cancer is growing.

Q: Is there any way to determine what the rate of growth is in any individual person, other than to say statistically it can be one to 15 years?

A: The only way we have, and it's really not a very good way, is to see the cancer at two points in time, and then to extrapolate to see when the first cell must have begun. But even that is fraught with difficulties and dangers, because breast cancers may vary in their rates of growth.

Q: Doctor, you have reviewed Dr. F's notes regarding the location of the subcutaneous nodule in the inner aspect of the left breast near the nipple, have you not?

A: On the outer aspect of the left breast?

Q: The inner aspect of the left breast, near the nipple on Dr. F's notes.

A: Yes, I have.

Q: And also reviewed the location of the cancerous lesion found in New Mexico between five and seven o'clock under the nipple at the edge of the areola?

A: Yes.

Q: Do you have an opinion to a reasonable degree of medical probability whether the nodule felt by Dr. F was the same as the cancer that was found under the nipple in New Mexico, even though it was in the same quadrant of the breast?

A: I do have an opinion.

Q: What is that?

A: That they are probably not one and the same.

Q: And can you tell us what is the basis of the opinion?

A: The nodule that Dr. F felt he described as being subcutaneous. Subcutaneous means underneath the skin, but distinct from the breast tissue, which is beneath the subcutaneous tissue.

I have never run into a cancer that has been feelable, what we call palpable, that's been less than one centimeter. We simply cannot feel a cancer in breast tissue that is less than one centimeter, and this was described as being subcutaneous, which means to me not in breast tissue, and less than one centimeter, and I would not regard that as being a cancer.

Q: Doctor, there has been a question regarding fibrocystic disease, and intermittent pain that can be associated with fibrocystic disease. Do you have an opinion whether intermittent pain is related with other disease processes as well?

A: I do.

Q: And what is that?

A: Pain can be related to mastitis, which is an inflammation of the breast due to many possible causes. Pain in the breast can be related to women's periods, in that they can be painful at a certain point in her period. Fibrocystic disease is such a common disease that many people don't consider it a disease anymore, but simply a disorder. Occasionally, pain can be associated with a cancer.

Q: Doctor, what were the findings of the four individuals who saw Theresa Garcia at Lovelace, and by that I mean Dr. F, who saw her on July 27, 1982; Dr. S, who saw her on July 30, 1982; Nurse D, who saw her in September of 1982; and Dr. J, who saw her December 14, 1982, regarding the status of Theresa Garcia's breast and axilla area?

A: The axilla was felt to be normal or negative by all four examiners. Dr. F felt what I described before, a subcutaneous nodule that was quite small. Shortly thereafter, Dr. S was able to detect nothing, no abnormality in the breast. Nurse D detected no abnormality and Dr. J detected no abnormality.

Q: Doctor, can you describe to us what the physical findings were of Dr. T and Dr. Mc, who examined Theresa Garcia in New Mexico in April of 1983, and would you like the record, Doctor? Would that assist you?

A: Yes.

Ms. Smith: Could we hand the witness Defendant's Exhibit B?

Q: Doctor, do you have before you the progress notes from Lovelace Medical Clinic?

A: Yes, I do.

Q: And let me ask the question again, Doctor. What were the physical findings of Dr. T and Dr. Mc when they examined the axilla area in April of 1983?

A: I see no comment about the axilla from Dr. Mc, and Dr. T says that axilla is normal.

Q: Dr. Mc's notes I think appear on April 4, 1983, on the next page. What is Dr. Mc's opinion regarding the feel of the axilla?

A: Both axillae are unremarkable.

Q: Doctor, do you have an opinion whether the palpable finding of these physicians both at Lovelace in 1982 and in New Mexico in 1983 give you any indication as to the true status of the nodes within the axilla?

A: I do have an opinion.

Q: And what is that, Doctor?

A: That there is no relationship between what they can feel and what is actually in the axilla.

Q: And why is that, Doctor? What is the basis?

A: We usually go on the rule of thirds, and that is that a third of the time, with breast cancer, if we feel lymph nodes in the axilla, these lymph nodes do not contain cancer. They are probably just a reaction set up by the patient because of the presence of cancer. Also, a third of the time, if we feel no nodes in the axilla, and there is a breast cancer, that when we look at those lymph nodes under the microscope, there is cancer in those lymph nodes.

Q: That means then the nonpalpability doesn't have any significance?

A: It's of no moment.

Comment: Counsel next elicits opinions that it is impossible to determine what stage the cancer was in when the defendants examined Ms. Garcia at Lovelace, but that it was a fast-growing cancer.

Q: Based on what you found as the physical findings in April of 1983 of Dr. T when he noticed a small thickened area and normal breast tissue and normal axilla area, does this give you a reason to state to a reasonable degree of medical probability what the extent of the cancer was in April of 1983 based only on that physical examination?

A: No, it does not.

Q: What about July of 1982? Does the information from that physical exam in 1982 give you any information regarding the cancer in July of 1982, simply physically?

A: None whatsoever.

Q: What other things do you need before you are able to discuss the extent or true status of a cancerous lesion?

A: I need to know what its actual size is. That is, not how large or small it feels within the breast, because there is often inflammation around the cancer which just adds to the size of what we are dealing with. What I need to know is, under the microscope, exactly what the extent of the cancer is. I also need to know what it looks like under the microscope. Is there evidence of invasion of vessels that suggests that the cancer has already spread throughout the body, whether it be venous channels or lymphatic channels? I need to know whether or not there is necrosis, which is death of cancer cells. When there is necrosis, it suggests that the cancer is growing so quickly that it's outgrowing its blood supply. Just as an army advances faster than its food supply, necrosis suggests a very aggressive cancer.

Q: Did you review the pathology reports from the biopsy and lumpectomy done at Lovelace in April of 1983?

A: I did.

Q: Would you refer to those? I think that's Exhibit D in the notebook you have.

A: It says here, and I quote, "Many regions have central necrosis."

Q: What other information does that pathology report contain that is significant with respect to this cancer in Theresa Garcia?

A: It says here, "Lymphatic and small vessels also contain tumor," and then it describes infiltrating out into the surrounding breast tissue.

Q: Does this pathology report indicate to you what kind of cancer Theresa Garcia had?

A: This to me strongly suggests an aggressive kind of breast cancer with a less than adequate response to being contained.

Q: And does it have a pathological classification?

A: It's an infiltrating duct cancer.

Q: We have heard some testimony, Doctor, that that kind of cancer is considered a garden-variety cancer. Can you tell me in what percentage of women with breast cancer infiltrating duct carcinoma or cancer appears?

A: That comprises about 75 percent of all breast cancers.

Q: So even though 75 percent of women with breast cancer will have this kind, that doesn't mean that it is a better kind of cancer in terms of survival rates?

A. That's correct.

Q: Doctor, what were the results of the estrogen and progesterone or hormonal receptor studies that were done in New Mexico?

A: They were both negative.

Q: What significance does that have?

A: That implies that this cancer was not under the regulation of hormones, which means that it tended to be a more aggressive kind of cancer than if it were regulated by hormones.

Q: Dr. R spoke about the benefits of adjuvant chemotherapy for premenopausal women who had negative hormone receptivity. Does the fact that there seems to be some benefit from adjuvant chemotherapy change the underlying premise you just referred to?

A: There is perhaps a 10 or 15 percent improvement in survival if you compare women who get adjuvant chemotherapy with positive nodes versus those who don't get adjuvant chemotherapy. But there is no distinction between those women, whether they have estrogen receptors or not.

Q: So the prognostic indication of estrogen receptors is not changed by adjuvant chemotherapy?

A: The receptors are irrelevant when it comes to the benefits of adjuvant chemotherapy.

Q: Dr. R spoke at length about clinical staging. Can you tell us if there are a number of staging systems and how and when they are used, Doctor?

A: The staging systems are a rather old form of describing the extent of breast cancers. Their main value was in allowing one doctor to speak about a breast cancer as being a certain stage; he could relay this information to another doctor by saying, "This is that stage or that stage."

The clinical stage is unimportant, because that is only half of the information. The clinical stage is what the lump feels like, what the surrounding tissue looks like, and what the armpit and the axilla feel like. But that's only preliminary data. What's important is what we call the pathologic staging—what it looks like under the microscope, that is, the breast, and the cancer within the breast, and what is actually in the lymph nodes in the armpit—not whether we feel them or not.

Q: Based on what you know from reviewing the Lovelace records, and also based on your information and your opinion that cancer was present in July of 1982, are you able to make any predictions, or do you have any opinions regarding the staging of the cancer at that time?

A: I do have a prediction, and that is that it was impossible to determine the size of that cancer nine months before.

Q: If Dr. R assumed this was a Stage I cancer, based simply on the clinical exam, does that assume then that there are no axillary nodes involved, or there are no positive axillary nodes?

A: Stage I by definition means it has not gone to the nodes.

Q: Is there any other information in this case that you have regarding this patient in July of 1982 that would give you an indication of what stage she might have been?

A: It's impossible to know what stage she was at that time.

Q: Are you able to say to any degree of medical probability what the status of the axillary nodes was in July of 1982?

A: I would say that the lymph nodes probably contained cancer at that time.

Q: Why do you say that? Doctor, what is the basis of that opinion?

A: The aggressiveness of this cancer, which I think we have established by looking at the material from March of 1983, suggests that from its inception this was a rapidly spreading cancer.

Q: Doctor, if you assume axillary node involvement, in other words, positive axillary nodes in July of 1982, do you have an opinion as to what Theresa Garcia's chances of survival were in July of 1982?

A: They were quite poor.

Q: And what's the basis for that, Doctor?

A: The lymph nodes were already involved, and because we have seen what an aggressive cancer this was in March, there is no reason to suspect it was any less aggressive nine months before.

Comment: In the following testimony, the witness impeaches Dr. R's opinion that early detection and treatment would have substantially increased Ms. Garcia's chance of survival.

Q: Are you able to assign it a statistical figure, in terms of five-year, 10-year, or 15-year survival rate? Can you talk about that statistically?

A: In what situation?

Q: Assume, Doctor, as you have, that there are positive axillary nodes in July of 1982.

A: It would depend upon, first, how many axillary nodes were involved then. We have no idea how many lymph nodes were involved with cancer in March of 1983. All we know is that three were involved, but only three were sampled. It's entirely conceivable that if we had taken out 20, all 20 would be involved. The number of nodes involved determines how good or bad the survival is. Naturally, it's better to have one positive node than it is to have 10 or 20 positive nodes, so I simply cannot estimate her chances of survival in July, because I don't know how many nodes she had even nine months later.

Q: Dr. R implied that if Theresa had lived five years, she would have had a normal life expectancy. Do you have an opinion, Doctor, as to the survival curves and whether they stop at five years, as Dr. R implied?

A: If a woman lives for five years after a mastectomy, without a recurrence, she still stands a risk of developing a recurrence at seven years, or at 10 years, or at 20 years, or at 30 years for that matter. At no point does she reach a probability of living as long as a woman who has not had breast cancer.

Q: Are you able to quantify the survival statistics on the board behind you? Perhaps we could pull that forward for you, Doctor.

A: I am going to draw what we consider a survival curve, and this is "T," which is time based in years. This is zero years, and let's say this is 10 years, and this would be five years, and this is the percentage of patients alive.

This is not exact. It depends upon what set of patients you are dealing with, but just for this discussion, let us say that most if not all of Stage IV patients are dead within five years.

At Stage I, you can see how many are alive. Then at Stage II, which is when the lymph nodes, the axilla, are involved, fewer are alive. At Stage III, even fewer are alive. The whole point is that in time, beginning with Stage I, women continue to die of their breast cancer, because a prevalent theory is that surgery or any kind of treatment doesn't affect the survival of what's going to happen to a woman with breast cancer.

Her survival depends upon the inherent activity or inactivity of her cancer. All this tells us is that women with Stage I cancer tend to have inactive cancer. Patients with Stage IV tend to have active cancer. Stage II is somewhere in the middle.

If one group were to live a normal life, we would see a curve that went up at first, but that at five years began to flatten out. Whenever we see a flat survival curve, that group of patients has been cured. For patients with other kinds of cancer, we do in fact see survival curves that flatten out, but as long as we have been studying breast cancer, for more than a hundred years, we have seen this continual slope. It slopes downward because women are continually, whether they are at Stage I or II or III, developing evidence of recurrence somewhere else in the body, and are continually dying of breast cancer.

That is why we can never use the words "five-year cure" with breast cancer. We may use it with other cancers, but never with breast cancer. We may talk about a five-year survival, but never five-year cure. I have seen women who have had a recurrence of breast cancer 35 years after their mastectomy. The point is that they are never cured. Upon the diagnosis of breast cancer, we must assume that it's already in the system. That's not true for other cancers. It's not true, for instance, with colon cancer. If you find a colon cancer, you can cure it because it's localized, but this does not pertain to breast cancer. We never see this.

Comment: Counsel next elicits opinions based on the assumption that the lump felt in Colorado was the same cancer that was later diagnosed in New Mexico.

Q: Thank you, Doctor. Dr. R made another assumption, and that was he assumed that the nodule felt by Dr. F was in fact the same cancer that was diagnosed subsequently in New Mexico. Now, we know that's not your opinion, Doctor, but assuming for a moment that this is correct, can you determine the extensiveness of this cancer in July of 1982?

A: No, because that nodule may have just been the tip of the iceberg, and it may have in fact been larger than 0.8 or 0.9 centimeters.

Q: Doctor, in New Mexico, was what Dr. T and Dr. Mc initially felt also the tip of the iceberg?

A: Yes, it was.

Q: Even if we call it Stage I, can you make statistical projections such as Dr. R did, assuming estrogen-receptor negativity, that the five-year survival rate was 65 percent?

A: If you look at all patients with Stage I, at five years about two-thirds of them will be alive. Then you have to ask yourself: Who are the one-third that have died of their disease? They are the patients who have negative estrogen binding, negative progesterone binding, evidence of vessel invasion, and tumor necrosis.

Comment: The witness next testifies that the treatment rendered in New Mexico was no more extensive than the treatment would have been had the cancer been detected and treated in Colorado. Counsel is attempting to show that no additional damages resulted from late detection.

Q: Doctor, I would like to talk about treatment choices for just a moment. In New Mexico, Theresa Garcia was given a choice between mastectomy and lumpectomy with radiation therapy. What was the basis on which the doctors gave her that option, if you can tell us, from your review of the record?

A: I would think that they gave her that option because they considered the tumor to be resectable, that is, they could get the whole tumor out, and then apply radiation therapy. But I do not think her situation lent itself to a lumpectomy and radiation therapy.

Q: Does lumpectomy always go together with radiation therapy, or do you separate those?

A: If you do a lumpectomy, you must do radiation therapy because of the risk that there is either a second tumor in that breast that you will not get with just a lumpectomy, or that the tumor has extended beyond what you thought was the lump.

Q: So in choosing lumpectomy, Theresa Garcia was in fact choosing lumpectomy with radiation therapy, is that right, Doctor?

A: Yes.

Q: Based on the discovery, the surprising discovery, that Dr. T made during the lumpectomy regarding the extensiveness of Theresa Garcia's cancer, was the decision regarding lumpectomy the best method of treating the extensiveness of her cancer?

A: I do not think so because after part of the tumor was removed, they could see from the pathologic slides that tumor was left behind, because it extended beyond the margins of the lumpectomy. We know that when we leave cancer behind in the breast the radiation therapy cannot sterilize it. So the breast should have been removed.

Q: But the fact that the breast was not removed in this instance, that they did not do a mastectomy, did that make any difference in your opinion, Doctor, as to the ultimate outcome?

A: It did not.

Q: And why is that?

A: Because we already know that it had gone to at least three lymph nodes and I suspect many, many more. It had already invaded blood vessels, and I suspect it was already in many places in her body.

Q: Now, I would like you to assume for a moment, Doctor, that if the cancer had been diagnosed in July of 1982, and had been found to be Stage I with estrogen-receptor negativity, what then would the treatment choices have been in July of 1982?

A: If her tumor were small enough to be removed with just a lumpectomy—by convention that's about two to three centimeters, depending, of course, on the size of the breast—then she could have had a lumpectomy followed by radiation therapy. However, my understanding is that she had rather small breasts, so that even if the tumor were fairly small, it still comprised a significant proportion of the breast, and the lumpectomy would have been so mutilating that there would have been no gain from just a lumpectomy and the radiation therapy in terms of cosmetics.

Q: And the fact that she was estrogen negative, as Dr. R postulated, would that have any effect on the treatment plan? Would that involve chemotherapy or not?

A: Even if her lymph nodes were negative, at that point, if her estrogen receptors were negative, I would have given her chemotherapy.

Q: And, Doctor, if she had had positive axillary nodes, what impact would that have had on her treatment plan, had she been diagnosed in July of 1982?

A: The therapy would have been the same. That is, chemotherapy. But we would have known that her prognosis would have been poor.

Q: What are the side effects of chemotherapy?

A: The side effects, depending upon the drugs that she gets, could be hair loss, nausea, vomiting, diarrhea, sores in the mouth, and numb fingers.

Q: Had there been positive axillary nodes and estrogen-receptor negativity in July of 1982, as you postulate, then she would have been given chemotherapy at that time, is that correct?

A: That's correct.

Comment: The witness next testifies that the cancer was not clinically detectible in July 1982, and if it had been treated at that time, the outcome would have been the same.

Q: Based on your review of the records, Doctor, do you have an opinion to a reasonable degree of medical probability whether Theresa Garcia's cancer was clinically detectable in July of 1982?

A: Yes, I do.

Q: And what is that opinion?

A: I believe it was not detectable.

Q: And what is the basis for that?

A: Because an experienced observer, namely Dr. S, could feel no mass.

Q: Do you have an opinion, Doctor, to a reasonable degree of medical probability, what Theresa Garcia's ultimate outcome would have been had she been diagnosed in July of 1982?

A: I do.

Q: And what is that?

A: The same as had she been diagnosed nine months later.

Q: And what is the basis for that opinion? Why do you say that?

A: I say that because when we detect breast cancer, we are not detecting it early. Nobody ever talks about early breast cancer. We may talk about minimal breast cancer. But we never talk about early breast cancer, because we know that by the time a breast cancer is detectable, it has been present for a long time, often many, many years, and so we are finding it at the end of what we call its natural history. So, in fact, early is really late.

Q: And does that hold true also, Doctor, if it's a rapidly growing cancer, and has been present for only two or three years, as you indicated it may have been?

A: If it's rapidly growing breast cancer, or even, as we call it, acute breast cancer, then it spreads out of the breast past nodes, probably at an even earlier stage in its natural history.

Q: Is the growth rate of cancer detectable by staging, by analysis, or by classification?

A: There is no relationship between the stage and how rapid it's growing.

Q: Doctor, do you have an opinion as to whether the clinical staging or the knowledge regarding growth rate affects prognosis?

A: They both determine prognosis.

Q: How does the growth rate affect the prognosis?

A: The more rapid the growth, the more concerned we are that the resistance of the host or the patient has broken down, and the cancer cells are through the lymph nodes and out into the system. That's growth rate. If the cancer has already gotten to the lymph nodes, that also tells us that the resistance of the host or the patient has broken down. It has gotten past the breast and now is in the next station, which is the lymph nodes.

When we find it in the lymph nodes, we worry that it's even beyond the lymph nodes, which means the rest of the system.

Q: Doctor, based on your review of the pathology report before you, and on the medical records that describe Theresa Garcia's course, do you have an opinion as to the growth rate of her cancer?

A: I do.

Q: And what is that?

A: It would appear to be a rapidly progressing, fast-growing breast cancer.

Q: That doesn't mean that it wasn't present in July of 1982, does it?

A: No.

Ms. Smith: Thank you, Doctor. I have no further questions.

Cross-Examination

By Mr. Brown (defense counsel):

Comment: Counsel next elicits testimony that breast pain is generally not associated with cancer of the breast. This supports the expert's opinion that the lump felt at Lovelace was not the cancer later discovered in New Mexico.

Q: Doctor, you testified a few minutes ago that there are other diseases that may cause breast pain. You mentioned mastitis, problems affiliated with menses, fibrocystic disease, and occasionally cancer.

In your experience as an oncologist, what is the most common cause of breast pain, from the list you have given us?

A: Probably menses, menstrual periods.

Q: What would be the next most common cause?

A: Mastitis.

Q: Doctor, could you tell us how often cancer is a cause of breast pain?

A: My own experience would be it's less than 10 percent, perhaps less than 5 percent. In other words, fewer than one out of 10, or maybe even one out of 20 women.

Q: There has been some testimony by plaintiff's experts regarding pain fibers, and that a nodule or lesion near the surface of the skin of the breast would somehow pull down on the skin and cause pain. Do you have an opinion as to whether that's the case?

A: I have never heard that, nor seen it in writing.

Q: Do you know if there are any articles on the subject?

A: I have never seen it in writing.

Q: You are referring to the medical literature, is that correct?

A: Yes.

Comment: The witness further explains why the lump felt at Lovelacewas not the cancer later discovered in New Mexico.

Q: Now, with respect to a nodule that is small, subcutaneous, movable, and very close to the skin surface, as Dr. F testified. Given your knowledge of the pathology report of Theresa Garcia's breast cancer, would that type of nodule represent the type of cancer that was later diagnosed?

A: I do not think so.

Q: What is the basis for your opinion?

A: She had the kind of cancer that infiltrates the breast; an analogy might be putting sand in a sponge. It insinuates itself like fingers throughout the breast, and there is never an actual mass. If there is a mass, or nodules, that suggests that the host has done something or the patient has done something to keep it localized. Once it starts to infiltrate, it shows that the resistance of the host is not good, but the cancer in those situations is not palpable. You just can't feel a nodule under those circumstances, and I suspect that that was the situation in July of 1982.

Q: Doctor, in terms of how the breast tissue feels when it has this type of infiltrating cancer cells within it, as the pathology reports demonstrated in Theresa Garcia's cancer, how does that feel to the clinician examining the breast?

A: The breast may feel normal.

Q: Now, when a cancer is a solid mass, could you please describe to the jury what type of extensions of cancer cells may radiate from that mass? Are they radiating typically from the breast tissue? Do you want to draw them?

A: Yes.

Comment: The witness makes a drawing that resembles a daddy longlegs spider.

Q: Why don't you flip over to the next page.

A: In the usual situation, there is a nodule, which is usually irregular, because that's the nature of breast cancer. There may be slight protrusions from it that we can see only under the microscope, but we can't feel those. They are too fine and too thin. But in Theresa Garcia's case, I think what we were dealing with was something like this, where there wasn't an actual mass, but rather fine extensions going out, and it was hiding in the breast. You simply couldn't put your hand or put your fingers around a mass. The reason for this was that the patient was unable to keep the cancer controlled, and cancers that can't be controlled often avoid detection until they are very large.

Q: Doctor, just one moment. The type of drawing on the top there, the mass, now that's composed of cells, is that correct?

A: That's correct.

Q: And the surrounding breast tissue is composed of cells, is that correct?

A: Yes.

Q: Why is it that the feel of the cancer cells is different from the normal breast tissue cells?

A: What we have in the tumor is a mixture of the cancer and scar tissue, to varying degrees. Some patients may have mainly cancer and a little scar tissue or the opposite—a lot of scar tissue and a little cancer, and this represents the patient's attempt to keep it localized. Out here, however, it's fat, because there is a lot of fat in the breast—in between the milk glands, where the milk is made, and the ducts is a lot of fat—and the fatty area simply has a different feel from the cancerous area. One is firm and hard, and the other is soft and generally smooth.

Q: Doctor, why is it that you cannot feel the scar tissue with the hard cancer cells in the bottom drawing that you have there?

A: Because we don't have this mass. We simply have insinuation of the cancer cells, what is called "Indian filing."

Q: Doctor, could you print your name at the bottom there? Could you turn back to the first page, please?

Mr. Brown: Your Honor, could we have Ms. Smith's exhibit marked, please? I believe it would be Exhibit I, and the next one marked, too, please. Thank you.

Q: Doctor, I would like to ask you a couple of questions about Ms. Smith's chart.

With respect to Stage I cancers, if I understood your testimony, it could be Stage I for many, many years; would Stage I be anything from one cell to two centimeters? Is that the definition?

A: The Stage I only applies when the diagnosis is made.

Q: Okay.

A: You can't say it changes later to Stage II or Stage IV.

Q: So before it's diagnosed, there is no stage, correct?

A: That's correct.

Q: Are you familiar with the concept of lead-time bias?

A: Yes.

Q: Could you explain to the jury what that is?

A: The time between the appearance of the first cancer cell and the patient's death can be one year, or it can be 50 years; it depends on the particular patient and the particular cancer.

If we use a mammogram, and pick up the cancer when it's .5 centimeters, it looks as though we have gained this length of time referring to graph. We would be comparing this length of time, picking up the cancer by a mammogram, with this length of time, picking up the cancer by feeling it.

So, it looks as though all the women who get their breast cancers detected early, so to speak, by a mammogram, live longer than those who detect it themselves or have it detected by a doctor. In fact, we have done nothing to alter this length of time, and the difference between this and this is called the lead-time bias. You have biased your statistics by gaining this lead time, but in fact you gain nothing.

Q: Now, Doctor, I would like you to assume that a mammogram might have detected Ms. Garcia's cancer in July of 1982. You have already testified that in your opinion when it was detected would have made no difference in her outcome. We have heard a number of statistics here. Do you believe those statistics to be affected by that lead-time bias?

A: I do not understand your question.

Q: Well, let me rephrase the question. Between July 1982 and March 31, 1983, is approximately nine months. What would be the lead-time bias in Ms. Garcia's case?

A: Nine months.

Q: And it is your opinion, Doctor, that regardless of whether it had been detected in March 1983 or July 1982 there would have been no difference in her outcome?

A: No, I don't think we would have affected this interval.

Q: Doctor, could you write "lead-time bias" at the top of the chart? Your Honor, at this time, we offer Defendants' Exhibit II.

Cross-Examination

By Mr. Trine (plaintiff's counsel):

Comment: Counsel establishes that the witness has been relying on erroneous information and that if he relies on accurate information, the lump felt at Lovelace was probably the same lump detected in New Mexico.

Q: Doctor, in arriving at your opinions in this case, one of the basic assumptions that you have made is that the nodule palpated by Dr. F was in fact in the subcutaneous fatty tissue of the breast and not in the ductal glandular breast tissue itself, is that correct?

A: It was described as being subcutaneous, that's correct.

Q: And you define subcutaneous as a nodule in that layer of fat rather than in the duct or glandular tissue of the breast, is that correct?

A: That's correct.

Q: Now, you have the Lovelace records before you, don't you?

A: Yes.

Q: And you will note that Dr. F indicated that he was sending the patient to the surgical department to rule out a small adenoma in the duct, near the left breast nipple. Do you recall that?

A: I would like to look at his statement again.

Q: Do you have Dr. F's charting for July 27, 1982, before you?

A: I do.

Q: At the bottom of that page, do you see that he is sending the patient to the surgical department, to rule out a small adenoma in the duct, near the left breast nipple?

A: Yes, I do.

Q: And, Doctor, assume further that Dr. F testified before this jury that his definition of an adenoma is a benign growth, usually involving glandular tissue of the breast. Now, if he palpated a nodule that he believed might be in the duct and glandular tissue, and that was the reason for the referral, would you have any reason to dispute his clinical observation of what he believed he felt and where it was located?

A: It seems like there is a discrepancy in what he is saying. He is saying it's in subcutaneous tissue, which means not in breast tissue, and yet he is calling it a duct, and there is no duct in the subcutaneous tissue.

Q: I understand that. Now, let's see if maybe you could answer my question.

Could I have that last question repeated back, please?

(Reporter reads question aloud.)

A: Yes, I do.

Q: Okay. Don't you believe that Dr. F is in a better position to describe what he believed he felt than you are in here today?

A: If he describes subcutaneous tissue, and then says that there is a duct in the subcutaneous tissue, then I am not sure he is in a better position to describe it. What he says isn't making sense. We don't have ducts in subcutaneous tissue.

Q: Right, and so wouldn't you conclude that by subcutaneous he was using that generically, just to mean anything down below the skin, including glandular tissue of the breast?

A: It could just as easily be that what he felt was in fact in subcutaneous tissue, and not in the breast tissue.

Q: Okay, assume hypothetically that Dr. F was correct in concluding that he was perhaps feeling something in the duct, near the left nipple. Didn't they in fact discover in New Mexico that the cancer was ductal cancer?

A: That's correct.

Q: And so that would be consistent with his having felt a lump in the duct, isn't that correct?

A: No.

Q: It wouldn't be consistent with his feeling a lump in the duct?

A: It wouldn't necessarily be consistent.

Q: But it might be consistent?

A: It might be.

Q: And the infiltrating ductal cancer that was found in New Mexico you said is the most common type of breast cancer; 75 percent of the women who have breast cancer have that type of cancer?

A: That's correct.

Comment: Counsel next establishes that Dr. F, who diagnosed the lump as an adenoma, should have performed a mammogram and a biopsy.

Q: Now, an adenoma in the duct would be in breast tissue, wouldn't it, if it's in the duct?

A: That's correct.

Q: And, Doctor, don't you generally make a diagnosis of adenoma by removing it and performing a biopsy?

A: That's correct.

Q: And would most physicians first get a mammogram of a suspected adenoma, before removing it and performing a biopsy?

A: If I felt a lump in the breast, I would both biopsy it and get a mammogram.

Q: But if the mammogram was negative and didn't show anything, and you felt an adenoma in the breast, you would still have to see what it is, if you are suspicious, wouldn't you?

A: You wouldn't feel an adenoma in the breast. You would feel a lump in the breast, and if the mammogram were negative and you felt the lump, you would be obliged to biopsy the lump, no matter what the mammogram showed.

Q: Okay, and that's because you can be mistaken in what you believe that lump might represent, because all you are doing is using your hands and the ultimate answer is under the microscope, right?

A: That's correct.

Comment: Counsel next establishes that one of the defendants could not palpate the lump, because a cancerous lump can be camouflaged during the menstrual cycle. However, if the lump was in fatty tissue, as described by Dr. F, other examiners should have been able to palpate it during their examinations.

Q: Now, if Dr. F's nodule were in fact in the fatty tissue, as you defined subcutaneous, and not in the breast glandular tissue itself, then you would not expect that nodule to wax and wane with the menstrual cycle, would you?

A: That's correct.

Q: When a small lump is in the glandular tissue of the breast, sometimes that lump seems to wax and wane with the menstrual cycle, correct?

A: That's correct.

Q: And, so, if in fact this nodule of Dr. F's were in the fatty tissue, subcutaneously, and not in a duct, or in the breast glandular tissue, you would expect that to be equally palpable, so long as a nodule remains, during menstrual cycles and after menstrual cycles, wouldn't you?

A: Yes.

Q: But if it were in the breast itself, you might not be able to palpate it during a menstrual cycle, particularly if it were very close to one centimeter in size, isn't that right?

A: That's correct.

Q: And yet, if it were very close to one centimeter in size, you might be able to palpate it, after a menstrual cycle, say a week afterward?

A: That's correct.

Q: So that one explanation for an experienced examiner perhaps not being able to palpate in the breast tissue a lump that is very near one centimeter in size would be that the examiner happened to be examining the breast during the menstrual cycle, is that right?

A: That's correct.

Q: But if it were in the fatty tissue, and an experienced examiner were feeling for the nodule that Dr. F describes, even during the menstrual cycle, no matter when the examination took place, you would expect him to feel the nodule?

A: That's correct.

Q: If in fact what Dr. F described was an adenoma, rather than a cancerous lesion, you would not expect the adenoma to change in size, would you?

A: Adenomas can change in size related to the menses, to the period. They are under the same hormonal influence. They are glandular tissue.

Q: Okay, the adenoma doesn't change in size, but the breast glandular tissue can change in size with the menstrual period, making it more difficult to feel the adenoma, isn't that right?

A: That's correct.

Q: But the adenoma itself doesn't change in size?

A: It may change in size, because it's breast tissue and is under the influence of the hormones as well.

Q: Generally, you don't have pain associated with an adenoma, do you?

A: If it's blocking a duct, the duct gets distended, with milk and secretions, and that can cause pain.

Q: Is that a very rare occasion with an adenoma?

A: I don't think I can answer that.

Comment: Counsel next establishes that Dr. F was in error in diagnosing the nodule (lump) as an adenoma. The witness concedes that the breast pain could have been related to cancer, rather than an adenoma.

Q: Doctor, you did not list adenoma as one of the four or five things that can cause pain with breast problems, did you?

A: It's down toward the end of my list. I don't think I gave a complete list. I gave the most frequent causes of pain in the breast.

Q: Okay, you listed mastitis, menses, fibrocystic disease, and occasionally cancer as the four items, is that right?

A: Yes.

Q: And you listed cancer, even though you said that pain only occurs with cancer 5 to 10 percent of the time?

A: Yes.

Q: Adenoma would be even lower down on your list than that?

A: Yes.

Q: So you don't really believe that what Dr. F felt was an adenoma, since there was pain associated with it?

A: It's unclear to me exactly what Dr. F felt.

Q: Well, if you look again at his record, do you note that he described a tender, palpable nodule?

A: Slightly tender.

Q: Well, is it clear enough that there apparently was some tenderness or pain associated with his palpation of the nodule?

A: That's correct.

Q: And in all probability, what he was feeling was not an adenoma, since pain is rarely associated with an adenoma, is that right?

A: Correct.

Q: If you are looking just at the symptom of pain, it would be more likely that that would be cancer than an adenoma in terms of the pain statistics relative to cancer, as opposed to adenoma?

A: That's correct.

Q: And, Doctor, based on everything you know, Theresa Garcia's complaint of pain in the left breast could have been related to her cancerous process, is that correct?

A: It could have, yes.

Q: In addition to an adenoma in the breast tissue being more easily palpated at some times than others, depending on menstrual cycle, a cancerous lump can sometimes be more easily palpated than others?

A: That's correct. The tumors that are dependent upon hormones may wax and wane according to the menstrual cycle.

Q: Do the changes that can take place within a breast during the menstrual cycle also have some influence on whether you can actually feel a cancerous lump in the breast during a menstrual cycle?

A: I think it would make a cancerous lump feel larger or smaller, but I don't think I have ever heard of or experienced a cancer that became palpable and then impalpable, from month to month, or cycle to cycle.

Q: Can a cancerous lesion get smaller and larger and vary in size?

A: Yes, those that have hormonal influence.

Comment: The witness testifies that if the lump felt by Dr. F was not a nodule, it could have been a cyst. The witness is then forced to concede that it was not a cyst, and the patient did not have fibrocystic disease.

Q: Doctor, you told the jury during direct examination that in your opinion what Dr. F had palpated was not the cancer later discovered in New Mexico, is that right?

A: That's correct.

Q: In your opinion, what was Dr. F's nodule, if not the cancer later discovered in New Mexico?

A: It may have been a cyst. It may have been the normal lumpiness that all premenopausal females have in their breasts. It's conceivable that he misread the depth and that it was an adenoma. It could have been a distended duct. It could have simply been normal breast tissue.

Q: Doctor, in your opinion, was it any one of those?

A: The description is so conflicting I have no idea what it was.

Q: Okay, but you can rule out fibrocystic disease, can't you?

A: No, I really can't.

Q: Doctor, fibrocystic disease is usually bilateral and located in both breasts, isn't it?

A: That's correct.

Q: If Dr. F had believed that this was just a cyst, couldn't he have used a needle to aspirate, and if fluid had come out he would have known it was a cyst, and not cancer?

A: That's correct.

Q: Was there any evidence at all in the pathology report of the breast in New Mexico that there was any fibrocystic disease?

A: No.

Q: And you would expect there to be some evidence of fibrocystic disease in the Pap report if in fact this woman had fibrocystic disease, am I right?

A: That's correct.

Q: So can't you rule out fibrocystic disease?

A: I think so.

Q: And, of course, no one who examined the breast at Lovelace gave an impression or diagnosis of fibrocystic disease that you could find in the records, is that right?

A: That's correct.

Comment: Having ruled out adenoma and fibrocystic disease, the witness is now forced to concede that the lump felt in July 1982 could have been the cancer later detected. Further, a mammogram should have been used in July 1982, and it would have shown evidence of cancer.

Q: Now, Doctor, would you concede that there could have been clinical evidence of cancer in the left breast in July of 1982?

A: There could have been.

Q: Doctor, in your opinion, would a mammogram have been a preferred test to take in July of 1982 if there had been any clinical evidence of cancer?

A: That's correct.

Q: If there was in fact clinical evidence of cancer in July of 1982, is it more probable than not that a mammogram would have been positive or suspicious for that cancer?

A: I think a mammogram could have just as easily been normal at that time as abnormal.

Q: In order for there to have been clinical evidence of cancer in July of 1982, would there have to have been a lump of at least close to one centimeter that you could palpate?

A: You would need a lump of at least a centimeter to be able to palpate.

Q: And if you have clinical evidence of cancer, meaning a lump of at least one centimeter to palpate, isn't it more probable than not that a mammogram would pick up that size lump?

A: That's correct.

Q: Mammograms will pick up lumps one-half that size, won't they?

A: That's correct.

Comment: Next, the witness's testimony that this was a rapidly growing cancer is impeached by reference to his written report.

Q: Now, Doctor, in giving the jury your opinion that the cancer that Theresa Garcia had was a very rapidly growing cancer, am I correct that you are relying heavily on the information you have from three different examiners, one in July of 1982, one in September of 1982, and one in December of 1982, who all found nothing to suggest a breast cancer, and yet three-and-a-half months later, a breast cancer was discovered?

A: I think "heavily" is not the right word.

Q: Okay, are you relying on that?

A: That's part of what I consider to be the equation. The other parts of the equation are what it looked like under the microscope and the hormone receptors.

Q: Doctor, do you have the report that you rendered under your signature in this case, to Ingrid Smith, on January 7, 1986?

A: I don't have it in front of me, no.

Q: Let me give you a copy of that to refresh your recollection. I will hand you your report of January 7, 1986, and you can use my marked-up copy. I don't think anything is obliterated there.

Doctor, first, this is a report that you rendered containing your opinions in this case, after having reviewed the records, is that right?

A: That's correct.

Q: And in the bottom paragraph, on that first page, did you in fact state, "Subsequent to Dr. F's feeling a tender subcutaneous nodule in July 1982, examiners, one in July, one in September, and one in December, all found nothing to suggest a breast cancer. Three-and-a-half months later, a breast cancer was discovered. It would therefore appear that this was a rapidly growing breast cancer."

Is that what you stated?

A: That's correct.

Q: Doctor, you gave no other reasons in that opinion letter for its being rapidly growing, other than that, did you?

A: That's correct.

Q: Take a look at it.

A: That's correct.

Q: So, at least on January 7, 1986, the basis of your opinion that it was rapidly growing was solely that three different examiners didn't see it, and yet three-and-a-half months later it was there; therefore, it must be rapidly growing?

A: In my report, that's correct.

Q: Since then, though, you have decided it was rapidly growing for some additional reasons, I gather?

A: If I did not put in the histologic findings along with hormone receptors, it was an oversight.

Q: Didn't you also assume that it was rapidly growing because at the time you wrote your report you assumed that what Dr. F felt was not the cancerous lump later felt in New Mexico?

A: That's correct.

Q: Now, Doctor, would you agree that you cannot determine whether a cancer is growing rapidly or slowly simply by looking under a microscope?

A: That's correct.

Q: And you cannot look at cancer at a particular stage and determine the rate of growth of that cancer by just looking at the stage it's in when it is detected?

A: That's correct.

Q: And I think you even gave the example that that would be like trying to determine how fast a train is traveling by just looking at a photograph of the train, is that right?

A: That's correct.

Q: And you can't do that?

A: That's correct.

Q: But statistically between three and 15 years is the usual range of growth, isn't it?

A: That's the usual range of growth.

Q: And that's what you indicated in your deposition, a three- to 15-year range?

A: That's the usual.

Q: With a seven-year average?

A: That's probably about correct.

Comment: The witness next concedes that his opinions on the stage of cancer that existed in July 1982 are based on pure speculation.

Q: In arriving at the opinions that you gave the jury, you were assuming that this cancer had in fact spread to her lymph nodes by July of 1982. Is that right?

A: That's correct.

Q: Doctor, isn't that pure speculation on your part?

A: That's correct.

Q: When you said that the cancer had spread into the lymph nodes, you did not base that on a reasonable degree of medical probability, is that right?

A: My speculation was based on a reasonable degree of medical probability.

Q: Well, Doctor, do you define reasonable medical probability to be more than a 50 percent chance?

A: Yes.

Q: And do you believe that pure speculation is more than a 50 percent chance of something happening?

A: Whatever happened in July, whatever was going on in July of 1982, is speculation.

Q: In other words, it's just as likely that she did not have cancer cells in the lymph nodes in July of 1982 as it was that she did have cancer cells in the lymph nodes, isn't that right?

A: No, I don't believe that.

Q: All right, I misunderstood you. I thought you said whatever her condition was at that time would be speculative.

A: That's correct.

Q: And you define speculative as being more than a 50 percent chance?

A: Speculative is what you care to speculate.

Q: Well, would you consider something as being probable if it's more than a 50 percent chance? It's more probable it's going to happen than not if it's more than 50 percent?

A: Yes.

Q: And if it's just pure speculation, wouldn't it be less than 50 percent, or is that the way you are using the term?

A: I think this is semantics.

Q: I know, but I'm trying to figure out what your opinion is. So we have got to get our semantics straight.

A: My opinion is that there were probably cancer cells in her lymph nodes in July of 1982.

Q: What is that opinion based on?

A: It is based on the fact that nine short months later, she had at least three lymph nodes involved, and that when we looked at the material from 1983, it looked to be the fast-spreading, rapidly growing type. If you look back in time, in the life of a breast cancer, nine months is not very long. So there probably was not too much difference in what was going on in March of 1983 than in July of 1982. That is, the lymph nodes were probably involved at that time.

Q: That's the basis of your opinion?

A: Yes.

Q: Now, Doctor, is there any way of determining whether Theresa Garcia's cancer cells got into the lymphatic system and deposited themselves in the axilla nodes in July of 1982, other than by taking a sample of the tissue and looking at it under a microscope?

A: There is no other way.

Q: Have there been studies indicating that sometimes the nodes tend to get involved at some later point in the cancerous process, as opposed to some earlier point?

A: We have no idea when nodes become involved.

Q: And you also have no idea as to when nodes became involved with Theresa Garcia, do you?

A: That's correct.

Q: And not knowing that, Doctor, you would have no way of knowing at what point an earlier diagnosis might have made a difference with regard to her survival rate?

A: That's correct.

Comment: The following section illustrates effective impeachment with medical literature and also illustrates the technique of forcing an evasive witness to answer the questions asked.

Q: And, Doctor, there is no way that you can project when distant metastases is going to occur in the cancerous process, is that right?

A: That's correct.

Q: But, Doctor, there have been studies indicating that once a primary cancer in the breast reaches a certain size, it's more likely to involve the lymphatic system, so that the cancer can get to the nodes, isn't that right?

A: There are too many exceptions to that to use the word "likely." Very small cancers can involve the nodes, and very large cancers can involve no nodes.

Q: Doctor, have studies been done to determine to what size the primary tumor grows before it is more probable than not that the cells will get into the lymphatic system?

A: That's impossible to ascertain.

Q: I am asking if there are any studies, Doctor. That's my question. Do you know of any studies that have been done in that area?

A: You can say that the larger the tumor, the more apt the tumors are to spread to the lymph nodes. However, once again, there are too many exceptions to use the word "likely."

Q: Are you saying there have been studies done in that area?

A: That's correct.

Q: And what have those studies revealed?

A: The larger the tumor, the more apt there are to be lymph nodes involved.

Q: Would you use the term "more apt" rather than "more likely"?

A: That's correct.

Comment: The witness concedes that his opinions are contrary to the position taken by the American Cancer Society and that his opinions do not represent the prevailing view.

Q: And you would agree, wouldn't you, that the earlier the detection, the better the prognosis?

A: I think that's open to question.

Q: Doctor, haven't you been teaching this to groups of women for years, that the earlier the detection, the better the prognosis?

A: No.

Q: You indicate you have been associated with and worked with the American Cancer Society as a volunteer?

A: That's correct.

Q: And are you aware of the American Cancer Society's position on the earlier the detection, the better the prognosis?

A: I am.

Q: And have you ever recommended that they change that position in the advertising and information that they give to women?

A: I have stood up at conferences that were sponsored by the American Cancer Society and have said as a minority opinion that screening mammography helping is open to significant question. So the answer to your question is yes, I have publicly disagreed with that.

Q: Are you in fact of that school of thought, and have you lectured at times, that you don't believe early detection is going to make any difference?

A: What I have said publicly is that the question remains to be answered.

Comment: The witness is forced to concede that diagnosis and treatment nine months earlier would have given Ms. Garcia an 80 to 90 percent chance of survival, whether the cancer was slow or fast growing. This section also illustrates how medical literature can be used for impeachment.

Q: Now, Doctor, do you agree that Theresa Garcia had Stage I clinical cancer in July of 1982?

A: I don't know what she had in July of 1982 because I don't know what the size of the primary tumor was at that time.

Q: Doctor, if in fact she had a primary tumor of .8 to .9 of a centimeter at that time, would you classify that as Stage I clinical cancer?

A: That would be Stage I clinical cancer, because no nodes were palpable.

Q: And, Doctor, if Theresa Garcia's primary cancer in July of 1982 was under two centimeters and not in the lymph nodes, and had been detected and removed at that time, would she have the same survival rate whether that was slow- or fast-growing?

A: No.

Q: What would her statistical survival rate be under those circumstances if it was a slow-growing cancer?

A: It would be higher than 65 percent.

Q: What would it be?

A: Purely speculative, but it might be 80 or 85 percent.

Q: And there have been lots of statistical studies to support the 80 to 85 percent, haven't there?

A: Yes. May I make a correction? It might even be 90 percent.

Q: Okay, statistics will vary anywhere from 80 to 90 percent?

A: Yes.

Q: Depending on what study you look at?

A: That's correct.

Q: If it was a fast-growing cancer, the survival rate would be 65 percent?

A: Well, the fast-growing cancers are the ones that make up the 10 or 20 percent that eventually die. If it was fast-growing cancer, I suspect we would drop below that 65 percent.

Q: Now, do you know of any studies that support you on that? Have any studies been done that indicate that a fast-growing cancer falls below your 65 percent?

A: Many. All of the tritiated thymidine studies bear that out.

Q: Are you familiar with a study that defense counsel showed Dr. R, "Acute Carcinoma of the Breast," by Spratt and others?

A: I am familiar with that, yes.

Q: Am I correct that that is probably the most recent study on the difference between slow- and fast-growing cancers of this garden-variety type?

A: I think that article was 1983?

Q: Yes.

A: There have been articles subsequent to that.

Q: Do you consider the statistical study done by Spratt and his group on fast- versus slow-growing as being consistent with the rest of the studies?

A: Yes.

Q: Doctor, if you would turn to Exhibit R and refer to page 221, Table III, am I correct that in this study they divided the cancers into two groups of Fast-1 and Fast-2, and also into slow-growing cancers?

A: Yes.

Q: And did they in fact determine that the five-year survival rate for Fast-1 was a 74 percent survival rate, give or take 9?

A: Yes.

Q: And did they also determine that the fast-growing second class survival rate, which they labeled Fast-2, was an 84 percent survival rate, plus or minus 10?

A: Yes.

Q: And did they indicate that the slow-growing carcinomas had an 87.5 survival rate, plus or minus 5?

A: That's correct.

Q: And this study would indicate that the difference between the Fast-2 and the slow is a difference of 84 percent survival and 87.5 survival, plus or minus some points?

A: That's correct.

Q: And those statistics are consistent with other studies that have been done with fast- and slow-growing cancerous tumors of the breast, isn't that right?

A: That's correct.

Q: In fact, those studied that have indicated an 80 to 90 percent survival rate, in clinical Grade 1, involved cancers of all types, didn't they, both slow- and fast-growing?

A: Yes.

Q: Assuming that Theresa Garcia was at clinical Stage 1 and the lymph nodes were not yet involved in July of 1982, wouldn't you agree that statistically she had a survival rate between 80 and 90 percent?

A: Yes.

Comment: The witness is forced to concede that even if Ms. Garcia was at Stage II in July 1982, she would have had a 50 percent chance of survival with treatment at that time. The following also illustrates the use of deposition testimony for impeachment purposes.

Q: Doctor, am I correct that even assuming some node involvement, you are of the opinion it would have been microscopic in July of 1982, and that would have placed her at Stage II?

A: I don't think I ever said that they would be microscopic. I don't think I ever commented as to whether they would be microscopic or macroscopic.

Q: Doctor, do you have your deposition before you there?

A: No.

Mr. Trine: Would you please give the doctor his deposition.

Q: Doctor, do you recall your deposition being taken by Mari Bush on February 28, 1986?

A: Yes.

Q: When she asked you questions about this case?

A: Yes.

Q: Doctor, if you will, please, refer to page 66 of your deposition. You will recall that you were asked about the opinions that Dr. R had given on various staging as it related to Theresa Garcia?

A: Yes.

Q: And starting at line 16, on page 66, do you recall giving this testimony, when asked about Dr. R?

Question: "And do you have any disagreement with the staging that he has done of the carcinoma?"

"I don't— "

"He is saying she would have had a Stage I carcinoma."

"Well, I do and I don't. She would have had a Stage I carcinoma in July, which meant she had a very small lesion and negative axillary nodes. However, clinical staging, as we have talked about, is only part of the data. You would want the pathologic staging, and I would submit that she would have probably had axillary nodes, although microscopically, she would have been considered Stage II at that point."

Do you recall that?

A: I recall that.

Q: Was it your opinion at that time that she probably would have been at Stage II because you believed that microscopically they would have been able to detect cancer in the nodes?

A: Yes.

Q: Is that still your opinion?

A: Yes.

Q: Am I correct, Doctor, that at Stage II, with lymph node involvement, statistical studies indicate that she would have had a survival rate that would vary anywhere from 40 to 50 percent, depending on which studies you looked at?

A: Yes.

Q: And again, those statistical studies include both fast- and slow-growing cancers, isn't that right?

A: Takes all comers, as they say. All the patients are grouped together.

Q: Fast- and slow-growing?

A: That's correct.

Q: But, Doctor, you are of the opinion that she was at Stage III when the cancer was discovered in New Mexico, is that right?

A: That's correct.

Comment: The witness concedes that it is highly unlikely that the last examination at Lovelace was normal, as claimed, based on the patient's condition when cancer was discovered three months later.

Q: Doctor, would it be unusual to have dimpling and a downward nipple displacement and orange peel appearance with cancer of the breast, just three months after a normal examination of the breast?

A: It would be unusual.

Q: And you wouldn't expect that to happen, would you?

A: That's correct.

Q: If an examination had occurred three months prior to that, you would expect that examination to show some abnormality clinically, wouldn't you?

A: That's correct.

Q: Doctor, can the type of cancer that Theresa Garcia had grow slowly, and then acutely become aggressive? Does that happen from time to time?

A: That would be unusual. But that does happen from time to time.

Q: More often that not, the cancer grows at a fairly progressive rate?

A: That's correct.

Comment: Next, the witness is led to testify against defendants, without realizing that he is doing so.

Q: Doctor, is mammography the most effective technique in detecting nonpalpable breast cancer?

A: Yes, it is.

Q: In fact, are most minimal breast cancers detected by mammography rather than palpation?

A: That's correct.

Q: And can a thickening area of breast as described in New Mexico be seen on mammography?

A: Yes.

Q: Doctor, when women are referred to you, have they almost invariably had mammograms performed by the referring physician?

A: Yes.

Q: Do you have patients who have had negative mammograms referred to you by other physicians? In other words, they have had a mammogram performed, but the results were negative as opposed to positive.

A: Then why would they be referred to me?

Q: Well, let me ask that. Are you saying that every patient referred to you has not only had a mammogram, but it's been a negative mammogram, as opposed to the cancer being detected in some other way?

A: Are you referring to a situation where a woman has had breast cancer, and I am seeing her?

Q: Doctor, let me straighten this out.

A: Give me the scenario.

Q: Are most of your patients referred to you either because cancer has been diagnosed, or there is a strong suspicion of cancer?

A: Yes.

Q: And when cancer has been diagnosed, in almost every case a mammogram has been taken?

A: That's correct.

Q: Now, when there is a strong suspicion of cancer, but it hasn't yet been diagnosed, in those cases, the referring physician has usually had a mammogram performed, right?

A: That's correct.

Q: And in some of those cases, there still is a suspicion of cancer, even when the mammogram didn't show anything?

A: That's correct.

Q: In other words, there was some other thing that caused the referring physician to be suspicious?

A: Yes.

Q: Have you at times diagnosed cancer in those cases, when the mammogram was negative?

A: Yes.

Q: What other diagnostic tools did you use to diagnose cancer when the mammogram was negative?

A: I felt a lump, or a thickening. Or there was an inversion of the nipple. Or some change in the skin.

Q: So you have performed breast exams in order to make the diagnosis?

A: That's correct.

Comment: Next the witness is asked a series of questions to establish that he is biased and that his opinions are therefore not valid and are contrary to the majority view that early detection is important.

Q: Now, Doctor, you are apparently of the school of thought that once breast cancer is discovered, it is already in the system, it's systemic, and late in its course, is that right?

A: That's correct.

Q: And you believe that generally you cannot detect breast cancer clinically until the primary tumor is at least one centimeter in size?

A: That's correct.

Q: You believe that by the time the cancer is one centimeter in size, it's in the system, and late in its course, is that right?

A: That's correct.

Q: And you believe that generally you cannot detect breast cancer clinically until the primary tumor is at least one centimeter in size?

A: That's correct.

Q: So you believe that by the time the cancer is one centimeter in size, it's in the system, and late in its course? It's systemic at that point?

A: That's invariably the situation.

Q: Doctor, is that why on Exhibit KK you indicated that it wouldn't make any difference whether you detected the cancer at one-half centimeter with a mammogram, or at one centimeter by feeling the lump; in either event, the women involved were going to die at this point?

A: That's correct.

Q: So there is really no reason to be involved in the early detection of cancer, because the woman is going to die whether it's detected at .5 centimeter, or at one centimeter, or at five centimeters, is that right?

A: What we are hoping is that by detecting a cancer early, when there are few cells in the system, that the chemotherapy that we then give will effectively kill some, most, or perhaps all of the cancer cells that are in the system. That is why we continue to use adjuvant chemotherapy in these patients.

Q: But you don't personally believe that you can do that, and save lives, is that right?

A: I am not sure. I think that in certain circumstances, we may. But the only other alternative is to throw up your hands and walk away, and I don't think that's acceptable.

Q: Doctor, isn't there a prevailing view within your profession in the United States that one can surgically cure breast cancer, if it is detected in time?

A: I don't think I would call it a prevailing view. I would call it a substantial view.

Q: There is a substantial view that one can surgically cure breast cancer if you detect it in time?

A: That's correct.

Comment: Through the use of hypothetical fact situations that are supported by the evidence, the witness concedes that the cancer should have been detected and treated nine months earlier.

Q: Now, Doctor, I want you to assume hypothetically that the nodule that was palpated by Dr. F was an earlier stage of the same cancer later detected in New Mexico. Okay?

A: Yes.

Q: Assuming that, Doctor, would you have expected a diagnosis to be made during the time she was under the care of physicians and nurses at Lovelace?

A: Yes.

Q: Assuming that physicians and nurses were exercising reasonable care in trying to detect that cancer, you would expect them to have detected it, is that right?

A: Yes.

Q: And would you agree that based on the records at Lovelace, there were many opportunities to detect the cancer if it was there?

A: Four opportunities.

Q: Four different opportunities?

A: Yes.

Comment: The jury is next given an explanation for why the witness has rendered biased opinions.

Q: Doctor, did you state earlier on direct examination that you are an acquaintance of Dr. S?

A: I am.

Q: Did you go to school with him, or was that sometime later?

A: I went to school sometime later.

Q: You see him now and then at various meetings?

A: Yes.

Q: And at St. Joe's Hospital?

A: Yes.

Q: And, Doctor, did you testify one year ago in another breast cancer case that a misdiagnosis was not negligent?

A: That's correct.

Q: And you are presently working on another case involving misdiagnosis of pancreatic cancer, for Irving J's and Ingrid Smith's law firm, is that right, in addition to this one?

A: Yes. I think that has finished, if I am not mistaken.

Q: You are no longer working on it?

A: I don't think so.

Q: Doctor, have you given opinions in other breast cancer cases, favorable to the doctors involved, who are being sued, even though you may not have testified?

A: One or two others, but I cannot recall them.

Q: Doctor, you have never testified for a patient and against a physician in a breast cancer case, have you?

A: Not in a breast cancer case.

Mr. Trine: That's all I have. Thank you, Doctor.

Redirect Examination

By Ms. Smith:

Q: Doctor, Mr. Trine had you refer to your deposition on page 66. I wonder if you could look at page 67 for a moment and tell me if you could explain why you gave the answer that you gave on that date, regarding the fact that it was a Stage I carcinoma.

A: What line is that?

Q: Page 67, line 3.

A: I said, "If you go by stages, let's call her a Stage I, she would have been the 35 percent that did not survive for 10 years."

Q: Doctor, why did you say that?

A: The reason that we go through all these exercises to see what kind of breast cancer it is, and to see what the estrogen binding is, and to see if there is tumor necrosis, or vessel invasion, and all these things, rather than just say, "You have breast cancer," is to try to determine who is going to do well and who is going to do poorly. Obviously, if you have a 90 percent chance of survival with a primary tumor less than one centimeter and negative nodes, what can you tell about why the other 10 percent recurred, why those patients died?

All these studies try to figure out who it is who has the bad prognosis—who are that 10 percent, or 35 percent. Then we give them what we hope is our best treatment to try to improve their survival, their prognosis, and get them to live longer, because we have killed all the cancer cells with our chemotherapy.

Otherwise, we would just say, "You have breast cancer," and leave it at that.

Q: Do you have an opinion regarding the effect of the chemotherapy on Theresa Garcia in New Mexico, whether it extended her prognosis or not?

A: I think at that time she had so much cancer in her system, unbeknownst to the doctors, probably in her lungs and probably other places, too, that there were too many cancer cells in her body for the chemotherapy to kill enough of them so that she would live longer than she actually did.

Q: Doctor, can you say that it slowed her death or not? Is that again an issue that the literature and the physicians are divided upon?

A: It's hard to imagine that it did slow her cancer, because she didn't live much longer after that.

Q: Doctor, you were questioned about the unusual fact that dimpling was seen on March 31, 1983, in New Mexico, and that there was a downward displacement of the nipple, and you indicated you wouldn't expect to see such an abnormality in so short a time. I want you to assume that the visual examinations of Dr. S, Nurse D, Dr. F, and also Dr. J, did not show any physical or skin changes, or displacement of the nipple. Does the information that that occurred so rapidly support or give you any information regarding the fast-growing versus slow-growing aspects of Theresa Garcia's cancer?

A: In no way could this suggest that this was slow-growing or even intermediate-growing. This was a fast growing cancer.

Q: You were asked earlier regarding Stage I survival statistics, and the issue of estrogen-receptor negativity was not included in any of the questions you were asked.

Now, Dr. R conceded that estrogen-receptor negativity was more probably than not present in July of 1982. Does the fact of estrogen-progesterone receptor negativity change the statistical survival rates for Stage I and Stage II in terms of the prognosis?

A: All patients who are estrogen-receptor negative, no matter what the stage, do less well than those who are estrogen-receptor positive.

Q: When you add axillary involvement, is that a cumulative bit of information?

A: Yes, that's another sign that we are dealing with a very aggressive cancer.

Q: Now, Doctor, you were asked some questions about your previous testimony on behalf of physicians. Are you aware that the case that you reviewed on behalf of a physician involving cancer of the pancreas was dismissed?

A: Yes, I am.

Q: And the case in which you testified in court, a year ago, what was the result of that case?

A: It was decided in favor of the defendant.

Q: Doctor, I asked you earlier whether it was your opinion to a reasonable degree of medical probability whether Theresa Garcia's cancer was not clinically detectable in July of 1982, and you indicated that the fact that Dr. S did not palpate anything but a normal breast and normal axilla supported you. Would that also be consistent with the subsequent examinations by Nurse D and Dr. J?

A: Yes.

Ms. Smith: Thank you, Doctor. I have no further questions.

Re-Cross-Examination

By Mr. Brown:

Q: Doctor, I would like you to look at Dr. F's note of July 27, 1982, and could you tell me, Doctor, whether the term "adenoma" is the correct term clinically or medically speaking?

A: Adenoma is one of numerous possibilities of what he could have been feeling.

Q: Okay, does the chart there say that there was an adenoma?

A: No.

Q: What does it say specifically?

A: It says that there is a small, slightly tender, movable, subcutaneous nodule.

Q: What does it say about the adenoma?

A: That apparently was his first choice, because he said, "Rule out adenoma."

Q: He says, "Rule out adenoma"?

A: That's correct.

Q: So he thought it might be?

A: Yes.

Q: Now, Doctor, I would like you to assume that Ms. Garcia's menses had ended two to four days before she saw Dr. S on July 30, 1982. Could you tell us, Doctor, would that be an optimum time or an inopportune time for Dr. S to feel a lump, if a lump existed?

A: If she had finished her period a few days before, then her normal breast tissue would have been shrinking, and any abnormality would have been more easily felt.

Q: Now, let me ask you this. Is a nodule, with pain, in and of itself clinical evidence of cancer?

A: No.

Q: Now, I would like you to stand by Exhibit JJ, again, if you will, please. Based on your description there, and your review of the histological and pathological reports of the type of cancer that Ms. Garcia in fact had, was there any evidence of the type of lump you have described that you have drawn at the top of the chart in her breast?

A: No, there was not.

Q: What type of cancerous tissue was found in that breast?

A: We call it diffusely infiltrating.

Q: Have you described that on that chart?

A: That's more apt to be this here.

Q: You are pointing to the bottom?

A: To the bottom.

Q: Now, Mr. Trine asked you a number of questions regarding the term "speculative," "more likely than not," and "reasonable degree of medical probability." Do you recall that line of questioning?

A: Yes.

Q: What do you mean by the term "speculative"?

A: Everything that we are looking at backwards to July of 1982 is speculative, because we have no idea what the situation was, so we can only speculate as to what was going on at that time.

Q: Based on the histological and pathological microscopic evidence that you have seen of Theresa Garcia's actual cancer, do you have an opinion within a reasonable degree of medical probability as to the type of cancer or whether a lump existed in July of 1982?

A: I do.

Q: And what is that opinion?

A: My opinion is that there was no lump or mass palpable and if you looked at the breast microscopically, you would have seen the insinuation of the cancer into the breast tissue, as I described, and you would probably have seen cancer in lymph channels, and blood vessel channels, and also tumor in lymph nodes.

Q: Now, Doctor, Mr. Trine asked you whether it was usual to find dimpling and a disorientation of the nipple, three or three-and-a-half months after a thorough clinical examination. Do you recall that question?

A: Yes.

Q: Was Ms. Garcia's cancer a usual type of infiltrating ductal carcinoma?

A: Her cancer was most unusual in numerous ways that we have discussed already.

Q: Now, Doctor, I would like you to examine Exhibit R, a document entitled, "Acute Carcinoma of the Breast." Do you have that article?

A: Yes.

Q: Now, that's by Drs. Spratt, Pulchank, Houser, and others, is that correct?

A: Yes.

Q: Is that a famous, prominent article in the medical literature on breast cancer? Is it one you are familiar with?

A: Yes.

Q: And you have been familiar with it for a number of years?

A: No, it just recently came to my attention, but it corroborates what I have seen in my own experience.

Q: You are familiar generally with the contents of this article?

A: Yes.

Q: In Table III, which has been referred to by Mr. Trine, different types of carcinomas are described, Fast-I and Fast-II. What generically does "fast" mean?

A: I would have to review the article.

Q: Okay, let's go on. With respect to Fast-I, it says, "Cumulative five year survival rate, 74 percent, plus or minus...." Is that correct, Table III?

A: Yes.

Q: And for Fast-II, it's 84 percent, plus or minus 10 percent, is that correct?

A: Yes.

Q: Now, Doctor, that's for aggressive cancers, as a whole?

A: Yes.

Q: Below that, on the same chart, Table III, it says, "Carcinoma with lymph node metastasis." What does that mean?

A: That means cancers that have been found that already have spread to lymph nodes.

Q: And what is the percentage of the cumulative five-year survival rate for that classification?

A: About 66 percent.

Q: Now, do any of those figures on Table III have distinct classifications for fast cancers, which are with nodal involvement, hormone-receptor negative, and diffuse?

A: No, they do not.

Q: Would it be fair to say that the type of cancer that the pathology reports show Ms. Garcia had is not distinctly exhibited on these statistics?

A: Yes.

Q: Do you have an opinion within a reasonable degree of medical probability whether the distinct type of cancer Ms. Garcia had, hormone-receptor negative, nodal involvement, diffuse, and fast-growing, would show a higher or lower percentage if it were included on Table III?

A: It would fall lower.

Q: How much?

A: I would guess at least 25 percent.

Q: I would like you to look at the conclusion of that article, on page 222, in the very right-hand column under "Summary." Could you read the conclusion to the jury, first?

A: The timely discovery of curable carcinoma through screening and early treatment is compromised by the existence of acute carcinoma with adverse properties. The existence of an acute carcinoma must be considered in planning and promoting any public health program, for the control of carcinoma of a breast.

These carcinomas will surface under any contemporary available screening or detection program through no physician or patient error. These carcinomas have identifiable properties and their occurrence should not be the basis of a malpractice suit, since their evolution is not presently preventable.

The available data on actual doubling times obviously provides truncated distributions, since they contain no data on the faster subsets of carcinomas that surface in the interval between screenings too quickly to permit measurement of size and calculation of doubling time.

Q: Doctor, how many women were involved in this study on which the particular research project or this article is based?

A: Over 10,000.

Q: Over how many years did the study progress?

A: I would have to look in the body of this.

Q: Well, let's go on. Doctor, do you agree with the conclusion set forth in this article?

A: Yes, I do.

Q: Now, Doctor, Mr. Trine or maybe it was Ms. Smith, asked you some questions about metastasis of the lung. How long would it take for one cell in the lungs, which traveled from the main cancer to the lungs, to develop to such a state where it was detectable on X ray?

A: I suppose if you had a very fast-growing cancer, it could take between one and two years.

Q: Do you know when X rays showed that Ms. Garcia had metastasis in the lung?

A: I think it was 1984.

Q: Do you recall what month?

A: April or May.

Q: Could it have been June?

A: June.

Mr. Brown: Thank you, Doctor, I have no other questions.

Re-Cross-Examination

By Mr. Trine:

Q: Doctor, you indicated that one of the reasons that you felt this was a very fast-growing cancer was the condition of the patient when the cancer was discovered in New Mexico, and how quickly death occurred after that, is that right?

A: And how quickly she went from a normal exam three months before, in December, to what was seen in March.

Q: Okay, let's cover those both then.

Doctor, first, with regard to the condition of the cancer when discovered in New Mexico, I thought you said earlier that because the doctors there did not recover the entire tumor and left part of the cancer in the breast, that in your opinion that was not treatable by the X ray treatment that was being rendered, is that correct?

A: I felt that that was not optimal treatment.

Q: You felt there should have been a mastectomy?

A: That's correct.

Q: Doctor, isn't that why the cancer probably progressed so rapidly, for the next two years after that?

A: No. The reason I would recommend a mastectomy is because if you leave a lot of cancer in the remaining breast, and then you radiate it, what happens all too frequently is it recurs in the radiated area, and then you have a terrible situation, because you can't operate. You can't radiate. That area grows, ulcerates, bleeds, and is never controlled. It's a question of what we call optimizing local control.

Q: Doctor, assume hypothetically there were only three nodes involved, as they found in New Mexico, and all the cancer had been removed from the breast, and appropriate treatment rendered, this patient could very well have survived for a period longer than she did, isn't that right?

A: If you assume that the only cancer in her system was the three lymph nodes involved plus the primary in her breast?

Q: Yes.

A: Then she would have been cured.

Q: Oh, she would have been? Okay.

A: If that's the supposition.

Q: Okay. So the fact that she wasn't cured doesn't have anything to do with how fast the cancer was growing at that time, isn't that right?

A: I don't think you can jump to that conclusion at all. What I am saying is that cancer was already long since in her system.

Q: Doctor, do you know where those three nodes were located that they removed?

A: Where in the axilla?

Q: Yes.

A: You mean whether they were low, intermediate, or high?

Q: Right.

A: I don't know.

Q: Now, Doctor, if they were high and intermediate and there was no tissue that was removed that was low, wouldn't those nodes be the nodes nearest the primary cancer?

A: No, it's the other way around.

Q: Okay, where was the primary cancer?

A: Mainly in the middle and throughout much of the breast.

Q: I see. Now, Doctor, you indicated again on examination that on Exhibit JJ, the lower part of your diagram is the most probable condition that she was in New Mexico, is that right? As opposed to the upper part?

A: In New Mexico and in Denver.

Q: New Mexico and in Denver?

A: Yes.

Q: And this is the one you earlier told the jury you wouldn't be able to palpate?

A: That's correct.

Q: Doctor, would it surprise you then that the doctors in New Mexico did palpate what they felt to be a firm substance of 1.5 To 2 centimeters at a specific location under the breast?

A: Yes.

Q: That would surprise you?

A: No, I knew that that was the case.

Q: Oh, I see.

A: But they didn't feel a mass. They felt what you described.

Q: You said, I believe, that a doctor feeling this would feel what felt like normal breast, isn't that right?

A: No, I said the doctor would have difficulty feeling a mass there, because in fact there is no mass. There is simply a diffuse thickening. The mass is on the upper drawing.

Q: But if a doctor felt he was feeling something he could measure in size, like 1.5 and 2 centimeters, he would be feeling a mass rather than just a firmness, wouldn't he?

A: Well, as I recall, there was even a difference of opinion in New Mexico, before the biopsy was taken, as to whether that was cancer or not.

Q: One last question, Doctor, with regard to this study that you were asked to listen to, when the summary was read to you, on Exhibit R, I believe it is. Doctor, isn't it correct that that summary is in fact describing those cancers that had been undetected in a screening one year and then the following year detected, indicating that if in fact you can't detect cancer a year before it is detected, the doctor is not at fault?

A: That's correct.

Q: Isn't that what it's saying?

A: Yes.

Q: Okay, and you agree with that?

A: Yes.

Mr. Trine: We all agree with that. Fine. Nothing further. Thank you.

Mr. Brown: I have no questions.

THE COURT: Understand, Ms. Smith, that usually we do not permit re-re.

Ms. Smith: I appreciate your indulgence, Your Honor.

Further Redirect Examination

By Ms. Smith:

Q: Doctor, the study that you have been asked to look at concerns 10,128 women screened over a period of five years, is that correct?

A: Correct.

Q: And of these women who were screened over a period of five years, 115 carcinomas were found. Is that also consistent with that article and your recollection of it?

A: One hundred and fifteen? No. Where do we have 115? If I add the bottom negative family history, 115, and the positive, 48—I would tend to add those two up. Unless I have missed something.

Q: So the total is 163 cancers that were found in that population of 10,128, a very small portion of the 10,000?

A: Yes.

Q: And of the 163 cancers found over the five years, we have been discussing a subset of fast-growing cancers?

A: Correct.

Q: And those are cancers that didn't show up on a mammogram taken a year earlier?

A: That's correct.

Q: And so they surfaced during that interval?

A: Yes, they were called integral cancers.

Q: And you understand that Theresa Garcia was seen by Dr. S eight months prior to the detection of cancer in New Mexico?

A: That's correct.

Q: And when she was in fact diagnosed, she had skin changes as we have discussed?

A: That's right.

Q: Doctor, that information regarding the skin changes, does that help you determine whether this is in fact an acute cancer or not?

A: This would be equal with being an integral cancer.

Q: That doesn't mean it wasn't present?

A: That's correct. That means it showed itself clinically, within one year of two examinations.

Q: The fact that it doesn't show itself clinically has to do not just with size, but also with diffuseness and other characteristics of cancer which are discussed by the radiologist? It doesn't deal only with size, does it, whether a cancer is detectable or not on mammography?

A: That's right.

Q: One final question, Doctor. Do you recall in the records noting that Theresa Garcia was seen by Dr. J two days after she began onset of her menses?

A: I don't recall when it was in relation to her menses.

Q: Would you look very briefly at Dr. J's notes on December 14? Do you see the information that she gave about menses December 12?

A: I don't see it, but it's not a good presentation.

Q: All right, Doctor, let me ask you to assume that.

A: Okay, I will assume that.

Q: Let me ask you further to assume that when Theresa Garcia was seen by Nurse D on September 29, she gave a history of having completed her last menses on September 18.

A: Yes.

Q: Is that historically how that is charted?

A: Yes.

Q: I would like to hand you a calendar of 1982, and without reference to any of the markings on it, ask you to calculate backwards, from September to July, and tell me when Ms. Garcia would have had her menses, knowing that she had regular periods every 28 days, lasting for three days?

A: September 18—so 28 days before that would have been August 21. Four weeks before that would have been July 24, and four weeks before that—

Q: That's far back enough, the 24th of July. If she had periods of three days' duration, you would expect that she would have terminated her period somewhere between July 24 and 26, give or take a day or two?

A: Yes.

Q: And based on that information, Doctor, can you tell me whether Theresa Garcia had her menses when she was seen by Dr. S on July 29, a week later?

A: She probably had finished her menses, so that her breasts at that point should have been as small as they were going to be.

APPENDIX G

SUMMATION

Below is William Trine's summation in a medical negligence case brought against two obstetrician-gynecologists in Cheyenne, Wyoming, and a local hospital. The doctors and the hospital were charged with the negligent failure to timely diagnose and properly treat a pregnant woman who had symptoms of both a placenta abruptio (separation of the placenta) and a possible placenta previa (low-lying placenta partially covering the cervix). In depositions and during trial the ob-gyns attempted to shift the blame, faulting the hospital for not having an ultrasound technician available at night to perform ultrasounds. They also attempted to shift the blame to the hospital's department of anesthesiology, claiming that the department was at fault because it did not have an anesthesiologist available to perform an emergency cesarean section once the proper diagnosis was made. There was evidence in the case that records had been altered to shift the blame from the ob-gyns to the hospital and the hospital's anesthesia department.

The chief defense arguments were that the defendants were not negligent in failing to timely diagnose the need for a c-section and in failing to observe signs of fetal distress; that the failure to perform an earlier c-section was not the cause of the baby's brain damage, but the brain damage was the result of a premature birth; that there was no ultrasound technician available during the night to conduct tests that would have shown the placenta previa; and that once the need for a c-section became apparent, there were no anesthesiologists available, which delayed the procedure. Further, it was defendants' position that the brain-damaged baby would not survive more than a few years and damages should be reduced accordingly, and that if the infant survived, it should be placed in the state institution because those facilities are adequate and much cheaper than residential care.

SUMMATION

Ladies and gentlemen, the awesome responsibility for this case and Matthew's future will soon be in your hands. Most of you are serving for the first time as jurors, and you might well ask how you go about arriving at a verdict.

Well, you've got the court's instructions, which give you the law, and the law is not complicated. You are the fact finders, and you apply the facts as you find them to the law. Instruction 4 tells you that if Dr. B's care and treatment momentarily fell below the accepted standard of practice as it is defined by law, he was negligent. If the nurses' care fell below the accepted standard of practice, they were negligent, and the hospital is liable for that negligence.

The court's instructions tell you that the burden of proof is on the plaintiffs, on the Green family, to establish their case by a preponderance of the evidence. The instructions don't say "beyond a reasonable doubt." They don't require 100 percent scientific proof. They don't require the plaintiffs to be three-fourths right, just 51 percent right. And the instructions tell you that we must show that the conduct of each of the defendants, either alone or in combination, caused Matthew's injuries.

You will note from the instructions that the defendants are charged with negligence, not intentional conduct. It can be negligence caused by simple forgetfulness. Professional people are liable for their negligence; they are not immune from suit, and that is as it should be. Doctors have something to sell that we need—expertise—and we must rely on them blindly, for a fee. If a doctor runs a medical red light, he is legally responsible, just as you or I would be if we negligently injured someone.

So, was Dr. B negligent? You bet! There were two separate acts of negligence, and we only had to prove one of them to receive a favorable verdict. Dr. B failed to perform a timely c-section when he had two separate reasons for performing one.

I want to simplify two weeks of medical testimony for you, and I hope I've done so in the charts that I've placed before you. If you'll look at the first chart, you'll see that Ann Green was in her third trimester of pregnancy when she came to the hospital and immediately started bright red bleeding. We now know from all the medical evidence that if you have bright red bleeding in your third trimester of pregnancy, it's going to be caused by one of two conditions—a placenta previa or a placenta abruptio. If there's no pain with the bright red bleeding, it's generally a previa. If it's accompanied by pain, then it's an abruptio--and she came to the hospital in pain and with bright red bleeding. With an abruptio there's only one treatment that can be rendered, as I've indicated on the bottom of the chart: An emergency c-section. If you've got a placenta previa in the third trimester, you don't have to do an immediate c-section—unless the woman is in labor. If she starts labor, you must immediately perform a c-section because you are jeopardizing the lives of both the mother and the infant if you don't.

Dr. B was presented with the symptoms of a placenta abruptio and with the symptoms of placenta previa. Either set of symptoms would call for an emergency c-section. Both conditions went undiagnosed and untreated while Dr. B was on duty at the hospital that night.

The labor pattern is indicated on this chart by the name of each witness, every time there was labor charted in the hospital records: what that labor was; when it occurred; and how many minutes apart contractions were. The evidence of bright red bleeding and when that bleeding occurred is also charted for you from the testimony of the nurses who observed the bleeding and from the testimony of Mr. and Mrs. Green who also observed it.

The doctors have denied that they were aware of bright red bleeding, or that Mrs. Green was in pain during this period of time. But there's evidence, charted for you according to the observer's name and the observation time, as noted in hospital records and from testimony in this case.

In addition to the evidence of symptoms that support an abruptio—bright red bleeding and pain—we had in this case evidence of an irritable uterus, which all the doctors indicate is a further symptom of abruptio. We also have evidence of abnormal fetal-monitor tapes showing decelerations and an irritable uterus. That evidence was available to both of the defendant-doctors and would have allowed them to diagnose an abruptio. I've also charted for you a very simple diagram showing you when fetal-monitor tapes are normal, when fetal-monitor tapes are abnormal, when those tapes show no fetal distress, and when they show fetal distress. I've simplified it because you've heard hours of testimony about fetal-monitor tapes. You probably are now as expert in reading these tapes as the nurses and doctors who have testified.

Dr. B was fortunate to have a patient with all the symptoms of abruptio, but he didn't make that diagnosis. He admits in his testimony that if there had been active labor, he would have had to have performed an immediate, emergency c-section. But he claims there was no labor, and that's why he didn't perform the c-section. We now know Mrs. Green was in active labor.

Dr. B's second excuse for not performing a c-section is that he asked for an ultrasound during the night. However, there was no ultrasound technician available, and hence the hospital is to blame, because if he had had the results of an ultrasound, he would have diagnosed a previa.

His third excuse is that the infant was born prematurely at only 34 weeks of gestation, and even with a previa you do not perform a c-section if the fetus is only 34 weeks old and there is no labor. Again, that excuse applies only to the previa; he never once addressed the question of abruptio. He has no excuse for not diagnosing the abruptio. In failing to diagnose it, he is negligent, and he is liable. Of course, we now know that Matthew was not premature. From all the evidence, Matthew was at 38 weeks' gestation. Since 38 to 42 weeks' gestation is full term, Matthew was full term.

Dr. H replaced Dr. B at 7:00 a.m. during Mrs. Green's labor. Prematurity of the baby is not Dr. H's excuse for negligence, because he admits that when he came on duty at 7:00, he knew that the mother was in active labor. With the mother in active labor, it doesn't make any difference whether the baby is premature. You've got to do an immediate c-section.

The lack of an ultrasound cannot be Dr. H's excuse either, because the ultrasound technician came on duty at 7:00 and the ultrasound showed a placenta previa. Dr. H informed the family that Ann Green should have an immediate c-section. But, he stated, there was no anesthesiologist available. He had checked, and all four of them had started procedures at 7:30 that would continue for three hours. In fact, we know that one of the anesthesiologists had offered to do a back-to-back, covering two patients at once, but that Dr. H felt that was too dangerous for the mother and would wait for an anesthesiologist to break free.

Now, ladies and gentlemen, I'm not going to try to rehash facts with you. What I do want to do is talk to you about this case in a way that I think will help to explain Dr. B's and Dr. H's conduct. What did they do when they discovered that Matthew was potentially brain injured? They retraced their steps and attempted to cover up the facts, because they realized they had been negligent. And how do we know this? Look at the facts, and look at the records.

Dr. B said that ultrasound was not available that night. We produced the ultrasound technician, who explained that she was called by Dr. B to the hospital at 12:30 that morning—before Ann Green was admitted at 1:30—because Dr. B had had another patient with placenta abruptio. But Dr. B had diagnosed his other patient's placenta abruptio from the bright red bleeding plus pain. So after calling the ultrasound technician out of bed, he cancelled the ultrasound and sent her home. I assume that Dr. B believed that we would never discover that, and that's why he said that there was no ultrasound available. He forgot about that first c-section, or he simply didn't want to tell us about it.

It's not that Dr. B was attempting in any way to harm Ann Green. What happened was that he was embarrassed about the fact that he had called the technician out of bed, then cancelled and made her go home. He wasn't about to do it a second time that night. So he simply didn't call her, even though Mrs. Green should have had an ultrasound.

Dr. B's second excuse was that the baby was premature. Ladies and gentlemen, I saw that startled look on most of your faces when I circulated the blown-up copy of the hospital record, because it showed that the pediatrician's statement that the baby was at 38 weeks' gestation had been altered. That altered hospital record was the only evidence that Dr. B and Dr. H used to show 34 weeks' gestation; their own office records and all the records from the Children's Hospital in Denver indicated that the baby was full term.

So, what did Dr. H do then to try to protect himself? He said that the anesthesiologists were all tied up and unavailable. Well, we all know now that was not true. I called all four anesthesiologists to the stand and they all said: "No, we didn't start until 8:30." One of them had said "Dr. H, I don't like to do this, but I'll bump my scheduled surgery in order to accommodate you," and Dr. H had said, "Well, I think we can wait." Why did he do that? Well, I would suggest to you that in a small community like Cheyenne, Wyoming, where everyone has to get along well together, Dr. H didn't want to offend another surgeon by bumping scheduled surgery.

Then Dr. H did some things that were contraindicated, based on all the medical testimony. He told the family there was no anesthesia available; he started an alcohol drip; and he put Mrs. Green on narcotics to try to stop the labor because he knew that with a placenta previa he had to do an immediate c-section if labor continued. He further depressed an infant who was in fetal distress by getting the child drunk.

There's an interesting question that was never answered. I asked Dr. H: "Doctor, why is it that the discharge summary shows a dictation and typing date one month after Ann Green and Matthew were discharged from the hospital, in violation of hospital rules and regulations?" I also asked him: "Doctor, why is it that the admission diagnosis and history record was dictated and typed two weeks after Ann Green and Matthew were discharged from the hospital, in violation of the 48-hour rule at the hospital?" And you remember his answer. He said, "I don't know what happened, but probably they lost the original dictation and I had to redictate it." So I had to put on evidence that the dictating equipment was all working properly during that time.

Why would it be redictated? What was in the original dictation that Dr. H didn't like? And why did he wait four weeks? Because, ladies and gentlemen, it was two to four weeks after this birth that the doctors at Children's Hospital in Denver discovered that the infant might be cortically blind and severely brain injured. So it was two to four weeks after the birth that Ann and John Green came back to Cheyenne.

You will recall that nine months after this birth, John Green, who then knew he had a cortically blind and brain-injured child, asked for a meeting with Doctors H and B, and said: "What happened? Why do we have a brain-injured child?" And Dr. H and Dr. B told the father: "John, there was no ultrasound available that night. Had we had ultrasound available, we now know we would have discovered this was a placenta previa." They told him there was no anesthesiologist available that morning. Had there been an anesthesiologist, they would have done an immediate c-section. They told him the fetal-monitor tapes were normal, and therefore the disaster must have occurred in those last few minutes before the c-section was performed. They told him all of this damage to the infant must have occurred after the fetal-monitor tapes were removed. They also told him, "We think we were wrong on our estimate of gestational age. Matthew was really premature and was only 34 weeks, and you frequently see unexplained brain damage with premature babies."

Now you can understand why I introduced as evidence the doctors' answers to the first set of interrogatories, questions that they had to answer under oath: because they said in those answers the same thing they told John Green in their meeting nine months after the birth. After receiving those answers, we took the depositions of the anesthesiologists, we looked all over this nation for the nurses, who were no longer in Cheyenne, we searched for an ultrasound technician, and we found every one of them.

And what did we discover? We discovered that ultrasound was in fact available that night. That anesthesia was available that morning. That Ann Green did in fact bleed in the hospital as she had been telling us with tears in her eyes, although the doctors denied that. And we discovered that the fetal-monitor tapes were abnormal.

So what did Doctors B and H do after we discovered all that? They asked their fellow doctors and former teachers to come to Cheyenne, Wyoming, and testify before you good people. Dr. C from Texas and Dr. D from Denver both testified that the delay was justified if the baby was premature. They both testified that, who knows, the baby might have sustained this brain injury before Ann Green ever came to the hospital. They so testified to try to excuse their former students' negligent conduct.

But wasn't it interesting that Dr. C, who is supposed to be an expert on brain injury in children, was not even provided with Matthew's records from Children's Hospital in Denver? He tried to slip his opinion in, you'll remember, and the judge ordered it stricken because it was improper without those records. And Dr. D said, "Well, the fetal-monitor tapes all look ominous to me, and if they all look ominous to me, then that means there was probably brain injury before Ann Green ever came to the hospital." Isn't it interesting that their own expert testified, "Gee, these tapes are ominous" after Dr. B and Dr. H said, "No, they're normal tapes."

And not one witness was called to refute Dr. E, the neonatologist from Denver, who testified in precise detail from the Children's Hospital records that this brain injury occurred in the last three hours before Matthew was born. No one said he was wrong. No one.

So we have established conclusively that the fetal-monitor tapes were abnormal and the abnormalities were consistent with an abruptio; that bright red bleeding did occur; that there was ultrasound available; that there was anesthesia available; that Matthew was a 38-week full-term baby; and that Ann had both a previa and an abruptio that should have been timely diagnosed.

What about the hospital's liability? The question is, did the nurses' failure to chart symptoms and did their failure to report fetal distress to these doctors contribute to these injuries in any way? You must decide that. Would either doctor have acted differently if the fetal-monitor tapes and the nurses' charts were full of red flags? If the late decelerations had been noted? If the bright red bleeding had been charted, would either of these doctors have acted differently? You must decide whether or not the nurses were so busy between 2:30 and 5:30 a.m. that they didn't have time to chart. And if they were, why didn't they ask for help that night?

In summary, then, if Dr. B could have prevented this disaster by reasonable care, he is liable. If Dr. H could have prevented this disaster by reasonable care, he is liable. If the hospital could have prevented this disaster by reasonable care, it is liable. You can find against any one, or all three.

Now what about damages? The law tries to restore people to the position they would have been in had there been no negligent conduct. Well, that's easy with property damage: If someone negligently burns your house down, you have the house appraised. You can collect for the value of the house and build, perhaps, an identical house. But you can't give Matthew back his brain; it's gone. You can't give Ann and John Green a normal and healthy son. So, although it's crass and it's no substitute, you assess money damages to compensate them for these losses in all the years ahead. The court has given you an instruction that lists each of the items of damage to which Matthew is entitled, and you are to place a specific amount opposite each of these items of damage: first, for the physical and mental pain and suffering for Matthew; second, for his disability; third, for his loss of earning capacity after he is 20 years old; and fourth, for his future medical and attendant care. I don't know what it would be like to be Matthew, to be a child in a boy's body, and then forever a child in a man's body. We know that Matthew feels hunger, cold, heat, pain; he hears his mother's voice and relies totally on his mother for infant care, a helpless child in a growing body.

But how do you assess damages for permanent injury and disability? There's no amount of money to compensate him for being deprived of the opportunity to see, to love, to create—so you can only use your collective best judgment.

And permanent disability? The brain is unique, irreplaceable. No value can be placed on it, because you can't buy one anywhere. So again you must use your collective best judgment in deciding what damages to assess for his loss of the use of the brain and for his cortical blindness.

With respect to loss of earning capacity, we have heard testimony by all the doctors that Matthew probably will not live out the life expectancy of a normal child who's now three-and-a-half years old. So the instructions tell you that you have to decide what his probable life expectancy is, but only for the purpose of deciding his future medical expenses and attendant care. That's only fair, because he shouldn't be awarded damages for medical expenses or attendant care he's not going to receive.

But, ladies and gentlemen, look at the instruction on loss of earning capacity. The court specifically tells you that you shall assess damages for loss of earning capacity based on the life expectancy of a normal healthy child who is now three-and-a-half years old. That is also fair, because the defendants deprived him of the chance to live a full life, and he's entitled by law to compensation for the loss of the earnings he would have received had he been permitted to live a full and healthy life.

You heard the testimony of Dr. F the economist. He gave you an absolute minimum figure, which was $843,113, and then he gave you some figures above that based on the cost of a college education and technical training, and the compensation for various occupations that Matthew could have pursued as a normal, healthy individual.

Dr. F also projected the figures of attendant care for the future, and he gave you a variety of figures. Interestingly, Dr. F's testimony on future loss of earning capacity is uncontroverted. The defendant chose not to call an economist, or any expert witness, to contravene what Dr. F said. I've placed those charts before you again so that you can glance at them, and you'll have them in the jury room to study carefully.

So, ladies and gentlemen, with regard to the variety of figures involved, I suggest that you give Matthew the benefit of the doubt. It's his only day in court. His legal guardians, John and Ann Green, can't come back in 40 years if your assessment of his damages is inadequate.

Now there is another point I want to address, and it is a very emotional issue as far as I'm concerned. What about all this testimony about the state institution at Lander, Wyoming? Apparently its an excellent institution, perhaps one of the finest in the United States. But it's still a state institution. It's operated by the taxpayers, and subject to the whims of the government and the legislature. That state institution may not even be here in 20 years, because we all know there is a plan nationwide to close down state institutions and provide community care. The defendants would have you limit Matthew's damages to force John and Ann to place Matthew in the state institution.

Apparently, the defendants would have you deprive the Green family of economic freedom of choice. You know that elderly people can look about and select the best available care facility or nursing home. they have some freedom of choice and are not condemned to a life in the state institution. Well, the defendants are asking for a meager damages assessment and are asking you to condemn Matthew to a life in the state institution. The defendants, and not the state of Wyoming, are responsible for Matthew's condition. The defendants tried to shift the blame to the anesthesiologists, then to the Green family, then to the ultrasound, and, having failed all that, to the taxpayers of the state of Wyoming. Now John and Ann Green have a claim in their own right; they are entitled to the freedom to live and work where they choose; the right to be near their son if they so desire; the right to provide the best possible care for Matthew, if that care is reasonable and will help Matthew and will ease their burdens. Ladies and gentlemen, you should give Ann Green and John Green peace of mind.

That brings to mind another topic that I have difficulty discussing without becoming emotional. Perhaps everyone on the jury is aware of the intuitive way parents care for their young. Ann and John Green will be saddled forever with that gift from Mother Nature, because they will have an infant as long as they live. They will forever have a child who is two to three months old, eventually in a man's body. How will they be able to devote any time, care, and attention to their other children and to each other when they are saddled with this instinctive psychological phenomenon for the rest of their lives?

Matthew should be placed in a residential care facility that gives Ann and John Green peace of mind, so that they don't worry about whether Matthew is in pain, whether he is being held during his seizures, or whether he is being fed properly. Ann and John have to be able to devote their thoughts and energy to their other children, while at the same time being assured that Matthew is not in pain and discomfort.

Ladies and gentlemen, this case involves damages in the millions of dollars, damages that are difficult to assess and evaluate: total blindness, the destruction of a brain, Matthew's loss of the right to the happiness of childhood and to growing old with dignity and pride. The 12 of you come from all walks of life, and you bring to the courtroom your combined wisdom and knowledge. You come from different geographic areas and have different educational backgrounds. Yet your verdict must be unanimous. So the verdict you finally render in this case is the melting pot of your combined wisdom, knowledge, experience, and feelings, and together you speak as the conscience of the community—a community with the reputation of doing justice. Your verdict should be in an amount that satisfies you so that 20 years from now, when you think of it, you won't worry about the Green family, and you won't ask yourself, "I wonder if it was enough? Is the family doing well now?"

It would be presumptuous of me, or of defense counsel, to tell you what your verdict should be. The damages that you should assess are dictated by the evidence that shows damages ranging from $2.5 million to $5 million. We ask only that you fairly and reasonably assess each and every element of damage to which each member of the family is entitled.

The Green family has struggled for three-and-a-half years. I've shouldered the responsibility for this case for two years and, believe me, it weighs heavily on my mind. I've had many sleepless nights seeking justice for this family, and now I turn them over to you. My job has ended, and yours has just begun. May God help you in your deliberations.

ABOUT THE AUTHORS

William A. Trine is a senior partner in the Boulder, Colorado, firm of Williams & Trine. He received his undergraduate degree from Colorado State University and his law degree from the University of Colorado. A former president of the Colorado Trial Lawyers Association and of Trial Lawyers for Public Justice, Trine has authored and lectured extensively. He has been featured in all editions of *The Best Lawyers of America* and is a member of the Inner Circle of Advocates, the International Society of Barristers, and the American Board of Trial Advocates. Articles authored by Trine were selected for publication in *The Best of TRIAL* and *The Best of TRIAL: Products Liability*.

Paul N. Luvera of Mt. Vernon, Washington, practices law with his wife Lita and is a member of the American Board of Trial Advocates, the American College of Trial Lawyers, the International Academy of Trial Lawyers, and the International Society of Barristers. He is the President Elect of the Inner Circle of Advocates. Luvera received his undergraduate degree from the University of Washington, St. Martin's College, and his law degree from Gonzaga University. He has written four law books, contributed chapters to six law books, and published more than fifty articles in legal journals.